D0911888

THE QUACK'S DAUGHTER

THE QUACK'S DAUGHTER

A True Story
about the Private Life
of a
Victorian College Girl

REVISED EDITION

GRETA NETTLETON

To Jane
Lucky winner

UNIVERSITY OF IOWA PRESS
Iowa City

University of Iowa Press, Iowa City 52242
Revised edition copyright © 2014 by Greta Nettleton
www.uiowapress.org
Printed in the United States of America

INTERIOR DESIGN BY TERESA W. WINGFIELD

No part of this book may be reproduced or used in any form or by any means without permission in writing from the publisher. All reasonable steps have been taken to contact copyright holders of material used in this book. The publisher would be pleased to make suitable arrangements with any whom it has not been possible to reach.

The University of Iowa Press is a member of Green Press Initiative and is committed to preserving natural resources.

Printed on acid-free paper

LIBRARY OF CONGRESS CATALOGING-IN-PUBLICATION DATA

Nettleton, Greta, 1957–
  The quack's daughter: a true story about the private life of a victorian college girl / by Greta Nettleton.—Revised Edition.
    pages   cm
  Includes bibliographical references and index.
  ISBN 978-1-60938-242-1, 1-60938-242-0 (pbk)
  ISBN 978-1-60938-243-8, 1-60938-243-9 (ebk)
    1. Keck, Cora, 1865–1921. 2. Vassar College—Alumni and alumnae—Biography. 3. Women—Education (Higher)—United States—History—19th century. 4. Women musicians—United States—Biography. 5. Women physicians—United States—Biography. 6. Davenport (Iowa)—Biography. I. Title.
LD7182.9.N47 2014
378.0082—dc23
[B]   2013044159

The core of the project is the diary. Thank you, Cora—

you reached out to me across the emptiness of time when

I needed it most, with warmth and love.

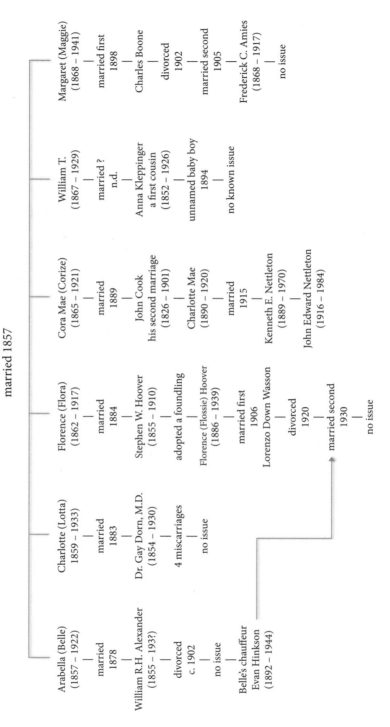

Rebecca J. Ilginfritz (1838 – 1904) | John Conrad Keck (1827 – 1911)

married 1857

Arabella (Belle)
(1857 – 1922)
—
married 1878
—
William R.H. Alexander
(1855 – 1933)
—
divorced c. 1902
—
no issue

Belle's chauffeur
Evan Hinkson
(1892 – 1944)

Charlotte (Lotta)
1859 – 1933
—
married 1883
—
Dr. Gay Dorn, M.D.
(1854 – 1930)
—
4 miscarriages
—
no issue

Florence (Flora)
(1862 – 1917)
—
married 1884
—
Stephen W. Hoover
(1855 – 1910)
—
adopted a foundling
—
Florence (Flossie) Hoover
(1886 – 1939)
—
married first 1906
Lorenzo Down Wasson
—
divorced 1920
—
married second 1930
—
no issue

Cora Mae (Corize)
(1865 – 1921)
—
married 1889
—
John Cook
his second marriage
(1826 – 1901)
—
Charlotte Mae
(1890 – 1920)
—
married 1915
—
Kenneth E. Nettleton
(1889 – 1970)
—
John Edward Nettleton
(1916 – 1984)

William T.
(1867 – 1929)
—
married ?
n.d.
—
Anna Kleppinger
a first cousin
(1852 – 1926)
—
unnamed baby boy
1894
—
no known issue

Margaret (Maggie)
(1868 – 1941)
—
married first
1898
—
Charles Boone
—
divorced
1902
—
married second
1905
—
Frederick C. Amies
(1868 – 1917)
—
no issue

Contents

Vassar College . . . shaped itself in her mind into an innumerable number of records that form the raw material from which all history is written.

—LUCY SALMON, VASSAR PROFESSOR OF HISTORY, 1915

254 & 256 Main Street,   Vail Brothers,   Poughkeepsie, N. Y.

Cora "Corize" Keck, graduate of Vassar's School of Music in 1886.

PROLOGUE

At seven o'clock sharp on Sunday evening, December 8, 1889, a young lady recently graduated from Vassar College stepped down onto the platform of Chicago's La Salle Street Station, gripping a small valise in one hand. Taller than most, she scanned the crowd of arriving passengers. The freezing platform was jammed with bowler-hatted businessmen, and ladies in silk jostled with exhausted immigrant parents clutching infants and children. A scout from the Dakota plains in buckskins, escorting two Indians dressed in robes and feathers who had a large yellow dog, gestured to a porter. Jets of steam hissed impatiently from the waiting train behind. Cold weather and a stiff eastern breeze barely blunted the odors seeping into the concourse from the nearby Chicago River, fouled by carrion from the Union Stockyards. The strangers pushed past, pouring through the exits out onto the streets of America's second largest city, famous for its toughness and its brazen appetites. Buffeted by the mob, the young woman stood alone, watching anxiously as the platform emptied.

Cora Keck was the daughter of Mrs. Dr. Rebecca J. Keck, the self-described Greatest Lady Physician of the West and proprietress of Mrs. Dr. Keck's Palatial Infirmary for All Chronic Diseases (Established Permanently since 1865) at the corner of Sixth and Brady streets in Davenport, Iowa, and she was eloping with a man she had decided was the love of her life. This headstrong young adventurer was my great-grandmother, and the sixty-three-year-old coconspirator for whom she was waiting, John Cook, would eventually become my great-grandfather. The driving motive for the adventure was that Cora's mother was against the match. Cora's mother called all the shots for the Keck family. In her opinion, although rich and socially prominent, the man was just too old.

For a bride, Cora Keck was no ingénue, either. She was already twenty-four, dangerously close to being an old maid by the social standards of her day. Age made Miss Keck experienced and independent; she staged her decisive escape via the Davenport train depot with practiced precision, using technical skills she had developed at Vassar College in Poughkeepsie, New York, where she was accustomed to entertaining herself off campus without permission and getting back undetected by college authorities on a regular basis. This was a feat that she repeated over and over, alone and with friends, sometimes returning to campus and climbing in through her dormitory window after drinking champagne and playing roller-skate polo with townie boys as late as three in the morning. Cora was a romantic, a girl of action and a compulsive flirt whose young life was shaped by her struggle to become a serious, independent person free of the crushing influence of her formidable and highly controlling mother. She was also a passionate and talented musician, stifled in her ambitions by the customs of her era. She flung herself into love with courage and charisma as beautifully as she had in performing virtuoso piano solos on the concert stage at college.

I first met Cora Keck in the pages of a diary that she started in late March 1885 and kept during most of that year while she was studying piano at Vassar's School of Music. The diary was a "philopena," which in Victorian times was a gift of friendship, usually given as a forfeit in a memory game. Cora received her diary on March 22, 1885, from one of her closest friends, Marian Austin, a fellow Vassar student from Honolulu, Hawaii; Marian may have forgotten to shout out "Philopena!" after the two shared two halves of a nut and would then have had to fork over the penalty gift. How lucky for me that she did. For months, Cora wrote daily and with enthusiasm.

I grew up knowing almost nothing about Cora or her family until 121 years after she set her pen to paper. In the spring of 2006, at the age of forty-nine, besieged by a sense of personal disconnection, I decided to look into my family genealogy via the diary to see whether I could locate any long-lost cousins in the Midwest. On the second page, dated Sunday, January 4, 1885 (the diary began retroactively, with the new year), Cora caught my attention when she described a party she attended with her friend Kitty Rogers during her first outing in New York City: "Arrived home at 4 A.M. on a Sun, as bad as some of the western girls hour, but this was owing to the distance from Laurence Mansion. I had a most delightful evening simply grand. First time out from College and I tell u I made the best of it as the Faculty had no ears nor eyes on one girl astray from home."

I immediately wanted to read more about this wild girl from Iowa. What was she up to in Gilded Age New York City society? Unlike most people's idea of a great-grandmother, she sounded like a pistol. Because Cora wrote in spidery, old-fashioned script that was extremely hard to read, I decided to type out a few pages of her diary to get a feel for what was in it. In enticing increments, Cora's feelings and goals, her unusual family background, and the daily activities of a student of music in Victorian America began to emerge. Her writing captured a time of high hope and excitement in her life, a time when she was developing self-awareness as a young adult. Cora was easy to like; she was full of talent, life, and humor. I was startled to discover that she was not very different from many young women I know today, and I began to connect with her as a person. She began to occupy a gray area, halfway between a real great-grandmother and a living fictional character in a romance of my own making.

Having once started transcribing the diary, I could not stop; it was a therapeutic prop during a difficult time in my own life, and I kept typing until the whole thing had become a document fifty-four pages long. The handwriting, as I have said, was extremely hard to read. There were tantalizing gaps and many abbreviated references to people and places that were unclear. As quickly as one uncertainty was solved, another would emerge. Where was the Laurence mansion? What did New York City look like in 1885? Who were these people she mentioned so often and so cryptically—Gus E, Mame R, "dear Charlie," and Mary S? Even her slang was hard to understand. What did it mean to "go back on" someone? To "get mashed"? To be a "gone girl"? Just for sport, I began searching the Internet for a few items to see what would come up and was thrilled to discover that many of the places Cora visited, the people she met, and the events she mentioned were easily found, both as contemporary images and in historical sources. (See the glossary for definitions of obsolete words and phrases.)

I started to let myself slip into 1885 America as a kind of mental escape. Although I had been a history major in college, I had focused on other parts of the world and generally avoided U.S. history as much as possible (hadn't we learned all those dull factoids about the presidents in high school already?), so the feeling of discovering something new as I plowed through dusty old information almost made me laugh. It wasn't new at all, except to me. It was like learning about an exotic foreign country that was also strangely familiar. As my data multiplied—on topics ranging from the top tourist sites in old New York to the origins of college education for women (the United States was far ahead of Europe) to the birth pangs of modern medicine (the United States lagged way behind Europe)—I began to see the possibility of re-creating this lost world, brick by brick, through the eyes of my personal guide, Cora Keck, and to thrill to the hunt of tracking down the traces that Cora and her family left behind them. The realness of each detail I found clicked into place, one after the other. Although I didn't know it when I started, a fantastic story was lying in wait for me, one that would swell into a five-year research project.

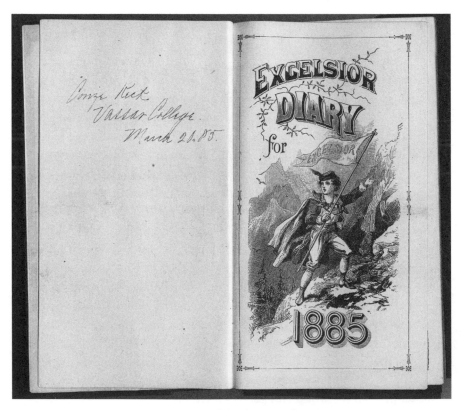

Frontispiece of Cora's Vassar diary.

∞

VASSAR WAS THE BEST THING that ever happened to Cora. Although she was born into a struggling working-class family, the Kecks became wealthy very suddenly, and during her teenage years, Cora was raised as an indolent rich girl. She entered Vassar as an indifferent student with poor work habits and a sloppy, laissez-faire attitude toward her precocious musical talents. Her mother and two of her older sisters, Belle and Charlotte (who often went by the nickname of Lotta), all razor-sharp businesswomen, alternately dominated and neglected her while spending long months on the road earning tens of thousands of dollars for Mrs. Dr. Keck's controversial patent medicine business and reinvesting much of the profits in Chicago real estate. All the while, they stayed one step ahead of the law, keeping track of a series of circuit court trials in various counties across central Illinois in order to answer repeated charges brought against Mrs. Dr. Keck for practicing medicine without a license. (At the time, women doctors used both "Mrs." and "Dr." so that clients immediately understood their status, both professionally and as married women.)

These three powerful women had long before judged and dismissed Cora's business abilities as negligible, so she was pushed aside and left to grow up, wild and mostly unsupervised, under the kindly and unsuspicious care of her father, who looked after the household. Mr. Keck was an unworldly inventor of farm machinery who seems to have been somewhat dumbfounded by his wife's success. He also may have suffered from serious depression; his emotions probably never recovered from the battering they got in the brutal public failure and buyout of his foundry in Fairfield, Iowa, a result of the national banking Panic of 1873.

That financial crisis catapulted Rebecca Keck from her role as housewife into that of financial savior of her family and set all the elements of Cora's story in motion. Unfortunately, the Keck family paid a severe price for their newfound wealth: Mrs. Dr. Keck's business success turned them into social pariahs. Her strong ego alienated potential colleagues; she claimed that her treatments were based on "an entirely new principle, and though discovered by a woman and never thought of or applied by professional men . . . yet has the most essential principles and scientific truths underlying it," and she was not shy in describing a case she took in Peoria as "One of the Greatest Cures in the Annals of Medicine."[1] Her rivals in the medical establishment, particularly in the Scott County, Iowa, Medical Society and on the Illinois State Board of Health, could not forgive her ability to succeed in their private professional arena and responded by dragging her reputation through the mud. The accusations that she was a medical fraud tarnished her name sufficiently that her existence has been almost completely erased from the historical record, by modern scholars as well as by her contemporaries.

Any newspaper advertising for physicians was taboo in that era, and flashy medical announcements served as a benchmark divider between the "regulars" and the quacks. Mrs. Dr. Keck traveled a regular circuit, boldly advertising her arrivals and departures from rented rooms and treating hundreds of new and returning patients with herbal remedies during each visit. She was openly derided by the regular M.D.s and outraged public health officials, who took great satisfaction in lumping her together with the malicious swindlers and traveling medicine showmen who plagued the medical landscape of the time—the Kickapoo Joy Juice sellers, the mutilating "cancer specialists," the Diamond Jim medicine show barkers and Wild West tooth-pullers, and the mail-order merchandizers of invigorating electrical belts for stimulating men's virility.

Cora's mother became a public figure subject to persecution and controversy. She was singled out and publicly maligned in the *Chicago Daily Tribune* in February 1880 by the secretary of the newly created Illinois State Board of Health, John H. Rauch, M.D. Summing up the results of his crackdown on unqualified practitioners during 1878 and 1879, he declared, "There are now only two itinerants in the State as far as known—G. C. Dunn and Mrs. Keck, the latter of Bloomington and Peoria," and added, with vitriolic intensity, "action should be taken against them . . . no time should be lost to get rid of these 'blots' and 'stains': they were foul and DAMNABLE IN EVERY WAY."[2] The Peoria Medical Society jumped in to support Dr. Rauch and declared that Mrs. Dr. Keck had to be stopped from practicing in the city, referring to her in its society minutes as "that itinerant charlatan, the so-called Mrs. Dr. Keck."[3] But neither Dr. Rauch nor his colleagues could put her out of business, and she just kept getting richer as time went on, in spite of one economic crash after another.

These problems cast a long shadow over Cora's social life and that of her two younger siblings, who all lacked the business skills necessary to become important contributors to the family business. It was hard for them to emerge as self-reliant adults from behind the protective brick walls of Mrs. Dr. Keck's luxurious mansion and infirmary at 611 Brady Street. They became isolated, withering on the vine, living at home as adults and supported by their powerful mother and older sisters. This made for a claustrophobic family atmosphere.

Cora went to Vassar almost by accident. She was sent off to college not because Mrs. Dr. Keck wanted her daughter to be educated to develop a career of her own, but because Vassar's prestige offered a way for the Keck family to hold up their pride in the face of public ridicule. It was a way for Cora to escape the small-town snobbery that locked her older sisters out of the social pages of the Davenport papers and to aspire to a good marriage with someone far from the frosty drawing rooms of Davenport's social elite, who had closed ranks against her entire family after her mother's well-publicized arrests and court cases became the subject of gossip. Ironically, Vassar's greatest gifts to Cora—self-esteem, independence of spirit, and higher aspirations for her musical talent—don't seem to have been an important part of her family's cost-benefit calculations.

To make this story work, I have deliberately pushed Mrs. Dr. Keck into a supporting role (a move she no doubt would have found intolerable) and put Cora at center stage, where she longed to be. It's an excellent metaphor for Cora's own life—she must have known at some level, consciously or unconsciously, that she would never amount to anything until she took charge of her future, left home, and moved ahead on her own. Her younger siblings might shrivel in her mother's shadow; not Cora. She had gone to Vassar. She was determined to live her life differently.

SEVERAL MONTHS AFTER I got involved with Cora's diary, my mother's move to assisted living sent four antique trunks filled with more of her personal belongings my way. Inside were three large scrapbooks bulging with mementos from Cora's two years at Vassar in the 1880s; four elegant, leather-bound, gilt-edged photo albums filled with unnamed portraits and tintypes; a bound book of Cora's sheet music; two more diaries; and many other bits of miscellaneous family debris. The photo albums and the Vassar diary had just undergone a first dramatic escape from destruction; one of my sisters, who was living in New Orleans at the time, had them at her house when Hurricane Katrina hit the Gulf Coast in 2005. With great effort, she managed to ship the precious artifacts north to safety ahead of the storm, while simultaneously packing to evacuate her house. Following that trauma, as soon as it was feasible, she and her husband moved to California to a tiny apartment with no attic or basement. The photo albums ended up back in the trunks, but as I mentioned before, I started to look through the diary. My other sister was only mildly interested in the trunks, which are large enough to cause a storage problem in most houses, even ones that have attics and basements. As the three of us worked together to help my mother downsize her life, we emptied the trunks and sorted the material to get rid of some of the bulk inside of them. The problem we faced was to find a way of saving the best of the family's historical artifacts that

was practical and manageable during a single weekend. The idea of sending some or most of the ancient contents of these boxes to the landfill, unexamined, haunted me. I lived nearby and had a basement. I volunteered to take the trunks "as is," with most of the contents repacked and still intact.

At one level, my sisters had a point. The week after the move, I looked at the trunks piled up on one side of my garage and tried to wrap my mind around the massive amount of work that would be necessary to go through them and understand their contents. I realized I had to make a major commitment to the project or

The pile of trunks that preserved Cora's family artifacts.

I might as well give it all up to the landfill anyway. Who else would ever be interested? No museum or professional historian could be persuaded to accept the trunks—they barely have the time or funding to pursue their own research commitments these days, let alone other people's. So I decided to put aside all my other work and take a professional risk. I would open the trunks. I would examine what was in them. Then I would write about what I found.

I brushed the dust off the first lid and lifted it open.

I quickly discovered that the older ordinary things get, the more interesting they become—it was almost a miracle that this cluster of related artifacts had been preserved. Decade after decade, the dusty, beaten-up trunks quietly protected a fragile corner of the nineteenth century in so much detail that, like a time machine, they vaulted me over a chasm of forgetfulness into my family's past. Cora filled her three large scrapbooks with every kind of souvenir imaginable, from college catalogs and rulebooks to laundry receipts, to wishbones from two Thanksgiving dinners at Vassar, to concert programs, newspaper clippings, marriage announcements, and telegrams. She kept a scuffed-up "memoryabil" that was an informal photo album of tintypes of all her friends and flirts (so homely and falling apart that I had almost discarded it during the move) and three albums of formal, but unidentified, studio portraits, called "cabinets," taken on special occasions. Cabinets were the formal photographs mounted on cardboard that everyone put in their photograph

Page from Cora's memoryabil.

albums. Tintypes were cheap and quick and could even be made outdoors to record spontaneous moments. Fortunately, Cora wrote down, in illegible penciled scrawls, the names of many of the people, dates, and events for the images in her tintype album. The memoryabil thus turned out to be a kind of Rosetta Stone, because in it she identified many of the people she wrote about in her diary. Nevertheless, the puzzle of matching the anonymous faces in the photograph albums to real people proved one of the project's most difficult and exciting mysteries.

Cora's photo albums, filled with unidentified portraits.

It is a rare treat for a researcher to be able to work with such old materials with no limitations as to time or access. It would have been impossible to do quickly. It's taken me years to absorb all the disorganized personal information and figure out how to pull a coherent story out of it. I have had to live the material to be able to understand it. There was no one to ask when I got stuck. The emotional link I felt with my family's history made the process feasible.

WHY HAD WE NEVER, as a family, really looked at these trunks and their contents before? Growing up, I was only vaguely aware of a blur of unknown relatives who would have been important to my father's mother, Charlotte, who was Cora Keck's only child. As it happened, all these mementos were saved as a direct response to flu-borne tragedy. In early February 1920, my twenty-nine-year-old grandmother returned from a dentist's appointment to her room in the Taft Hotel on Chapel Street in New Haven, Connecticut, complaining to my grandfather that she didn't feel quite right. She died of the flu fewer than two weeks later, on a bitter Sunday at 1:35 in the morning. My father, aged three, was parted from his mother forever. Out in Chicago, when Cora received the news that she had lost her only child, she fell to pieces emotionally, stopped eating, and followed Charlotte to the grave a year later, in 1921, when she was only fifty-six. Mother and daughter died almost forty years before I was born. This double blow obscured Cora's story and cast a long shadow over the lives of her descendants. Charlotte's family memories and point of view disappeared along with her love. Her death cast a profound shadow of grief across three generations.

My grandfather found it almost impossible to talk about the beloved bride he lost so young. He remarried and life moved on, although I know he carried the pain of his loss buried in his heart all his life. He was especially indifferent to his dead wife's family past because of Mrs. Dr. Keck's "embarrassing" business career, which everyone understood to have been ridiculous or absurd in some major way. The pain inflicted on my father by his mother's early death was another big part of the family silence. "Don't ask him about it," I was told. "It's too painful." A dutiful child, I kept my curiosity to myself, and although I had ventured into our attic and opened the trunks several times, I hardly dared to even touch those little boxes tied up with string, tucked in among envelopes, rolled up pieces of canvas (my grandmother Charlotte had been a talented portrait painter who studied at the Art Institute of Chicago), and framed photographs, in case it would hurt my father's feelings. Now it's too late to ask him any questions; he has been dead for nearly thirty years. In this book I have finally dredged up the stories my father should have heard as a child. Perhaps, somewhere and somehow, he is able to share what I am doing and appreciate his grandmother's and great-grandmother's extraordinary achievements.

∞

THE HISTORIAN LYTTON STRACHEY once declared with the confidence typical of his era, "The history of the Victorian Age will never be written; we know too much about it." In fact, we know much less about that era today than he did in 1918 when his book *Eminent Victorians* was published, because modern-minded people all over the world are energetically throwing Victorian books and artifacts away every day of the week. Any amount of ostensibly worthless, old, outdated information can be eventually forgotten if enough people put their minds to it.

Even with this helpful winnowing of basic research sources by the whirlwind duet of time and entropy, the problem remains: industrious Victorians wrote about themselves to excess, modern scholars have added piles more, and Google Books is jammed full of publications from that era that anyone can read for free. So a disclaimer: this book is a bit like looking through the wrong end of binoculars at an overwhelmingly large western landscape stretching out toward the horizon and then attempting to describe the scene by using tweezers to select a few facts here and there. I have compensated for my narrow scope by staying acutely focused on details, connecting the dots in Cora's personal life and going as deeply and accurately into my personal area of interest as possible. I have tried not to put anything in this book that I wasn't absolutely sure of—even in assigning names to photographs of friends and family members about whose identity no one left alive in the world could contradict me.

During this process, I have had to discard a number of presumptions I had about how women were treated by American society in the nineteenth century. Generalizations can show plenty of cracks if you adjust your focus to close-up. I discovered that no matter how few legal rights females might have been given in the past, like any other biological entity engaged in the struggle for survival, women have always had opportunities. Smart and energetic Victorian women moved ahead with their lives, rights or no rights; when they saw their opportunities, they took them.

Compared with the preceding centuries of U.S. and European history, the Victorian era was one of tremendous progress for women. Ironically (in view of the many modern negative stereotypes), it was the Victorians who were the first to take practical steps to increase female freedom and independence, legally, intellectually, and socially, and the United States was far ahead of Britain and the rest of Europe in this process. Women's property and inheritance rights, their ability to conduct business, to get a college education, to divorce, and even to limit family size—these are all phenomena of the nineteenth century in our country and were brought about well before women gained the right to vote.

Vassar College was at the front of the pack in this process. It is important to remember that the college was started and later run by men who respected women's native abilities and were consciously trying to give young women more options in their lives. However, a dire reality facing Vassar graduates in the 1880s was that after they graduated from the capsule of professional excellence that had been created inside the college, they were turned loose into the indifferent outside world, dressed up with no place to go. They were prepared to enter a life of professional equality that in many cases did not yet exist outside Vassar's walls.

This was particularly true for young women who completed the rigorous conservatory-level musical training offered at Vassar's School of Music. Until well into the twentieth century, professional classical music institutions and organizations strenuously resisted women's entry longer than many other fields. The New York Philharmonic only reluctantly accepted its first female musician as a member in 1966 under severe outside pressure. Yet in April 1886 Cora Keck was already performing at a professional level onstage at Vassar in a piano quartet with three string players from the New York Philharmonic. It would be another eighty years before a talented young woman such as Cora could dream of earning a living as a performer on an equal basis with New York City's professional musicians without suffering automatic ridicule as a pretentious amateur. One only has to think of Groucho Marx and his jokes about Margaret Dumont's quavering mezzo-soprano vocal solos to get the whole picture.

∞

I HAVE WRITTEN THIS BOOK at a personal level because it is about my own great-grandmother. Therefore, for better or for worse, my working analytical model is that people in her era must have had to solve the same kinds of problems in their lives that I have had to. As a visitor to a foreign land inhabited by my close relatives, I have traveled through our shared past with respect for the natives I found there and for their exotic culture. I have assumed that they had the same longings for love and material success, for esteem from their peers and family members, and for the health and well-being of their children as we do today. They struggled against loss and disappointment; they made mistakes and were struck by illness and misfortune from time to time, just as people of our own times are. They believed and acted sincerely on some principles yet failed to do so on others—can't all of us say that about ourselves?

Getting Cora's diary was an accidental opportunity in my life comparable to Cora's accidental enrollment at Vassar, and it has turned out to be one of the best things that ever happened to me. As I set out on a purely personal journey to discover the lost stories of the women in my family back in the "old country" of nineteenth-century Iowa, I realized that my great-grandmother's story touches many themes that are crucial to the wider study of nineteenth-century women's history in the United States; the fundamental similarities between Cora's life and our own times were so striking that I have begun to see the 1880s as a departure point for understanding modern American life. We need to own these stories in order to understand ourselves. Cora's imagined emotional support has given me the courage and the means to strike out toward a fully creative life

A tintype from Cora's memoryabil, Davenport, May 1887.

during a difficult period of disillusion in middle age. She and I have certain things in common—a lifelong appetite for adventure and independence that has always conflicted with a yearning for love and family connection. I believe that we really understand each other.

THE QUACK'S DAUGHTER

DR. MRS. KECK'S

FOUNDED by Dr. Mrs. KECK, for the purpose of perfecting and developing her NEW AND ORIGINAL METHODS OF TREATMENT for the *alleviation* and *cure* of the many forms of *Chronic Diseases*, which constitute the great bulk of human suffering.

The *success* with which this INSTITUTION has met from its *commencement* is the *greatest evidence* of the INCALCULABLE VALUE of its *Special Feature*, DR. MRS. KECK'S ORIGINAL TREATMENT.

Beautifully situated and *centrally located* in one of the *healthiest cities* in the *Mississippi Valley, finished* and *furnished* in the finest possible manner, both for *elegance* and *comfort*, conducted under the auspices and *personal supervision* of the *Greatest Physician* to *Chronic Diseases*, in the *West*, DR. MRS. KECK; this establishment is to the *invalid* a *favored health resort*, a *haven* of as *great promise* as most approved and successful medication and most careful management can make it.

ESTABLISHED
PERMANENTLY
SINCE
1865

THE following system of *Branch Offices* has been established to meet the Constantly Widening Demand for DR. MRS. KECK'S services, and at the solicitation of thousands of the afflicted people who were not able to make the pilgrimage to her Infirmary at DAVENPORT. Some of them have been maintained for nearly 20 years:

Branch Offices:

PEORIA, ILL.
BLOOMINGTON, ILL.
CEDAR RAPIDS, IA.
WEBSTER CITY, IA.

DR. MRS. KECK visits these offices, personally, every 2 months. Patients also treated through correspondence. Medicines sent by express to any part of the United States and Canada for treatment under *the New Method.*

ADDRESS, enclosing stamp,

DR. MRS. KECK
MEDICAL INFIRMARY
611 Brady St.
DAVENPORT, IOWA

MEDICAL INFIRMARY

Sixth and Brady Streets, DAVENPORT, IOWA

THE CELEBRATED

Remedial Treatments and Prophylactic Measures

As originally proposed and developed by DR. MRS. KECK, to prevent the advancement and promote the eradication of certain diseases, are applicable to

|| ALL CHRONIC DISEASES ||

AFFECTING THE

Lungs, Stomach, Liver, Bowels, Kidneys, Head, Throat, Ears, Eyes, Rectum, Skin, Blood and General System,

TO NERVOUS DISEASES AND THE COMPLICATED COMPLAINTS OF FEMALES.

Also the best of success of all diseases following La Grippe.

☞ Consultation, Personally or by Letter, Free of Charge

Four-page flyer for Mrs. Dr. Keck's infirmary ca. 1894.

CHAPTER ONE

The Wickedest City in America

I have always understood that money made in the patent medi-cine business is a practical bar to social success.
—GEORGE ROWELL, THE "FATHER OF MODERN ADVERTISING"
(*Forty Years an Advertising Agent, 1865–1905*)

When I was a small child growing up in Cheshire, Connecticut, my father used to mention Davenport, Iowa, in connection with his mother's relatives in a detached and bemused tone that hinted at some important, undisclosed information. My father, who was Cora Keck's grandson, was the great-grandson of the notorious Mrs. Dr. Keck, which makes us both the direct descendants of a famous quack. This is a surprising thing to discover for anyone who ever knew my father, a deeply private man whose entire life was shaped by his careful integrity and devotion to family responsibilities. He was respected by hundreds of friends and colleagues accumulated during a career that included five years as a volunteer ambulance driver for the American Field Service during World War II, during which he received a medal for bravery under fire, and decades of service to the well-known inter-national student exchange program.

When families have skeletons like this hidden in the closet, they usu-ally try to keep the door firmly shut. But no one can resist dropping some tantalizing hints about the possible scandal here and there in con-versation. In the case of Mrs. Dr. Keck, her name was so tarnished that her story has been ignored not just by my relatives, but by historians all across the United States. The stigma of the patent medicine busi-ness and the shame attached to the slanderous term "quack" are still so strong in our culture that few people are willing to boast about, or even to admit to, that kind of family tie—it's apparently as bad as, or even worse than, prostitution, stock-market swindling, and street crime.

My father never filled us in on any further information about the Keck relatives or the place where they were from, so instead of a town, I imagined Davenport to be a large mahogany dining room sideboard floating in the middle of a golden field of ripe wheat under a vast, clear, and empty sky (at least, that's what I thought a "davenport" looked like). When I was thirteen, my paternal grandfather died, and an ornate silver creamer and sugar bowl engraved with "Mrs. Dr. Keck" suddenly appeared in our kitchen. My mother and sisters joked about the awkward pair of honorifics that decorated their sides, and offhand remarks were made at the breakfast table that there were no women doctors back then. Again, my father said little about these people who were his direct ancestors because most of the Kecks had died before he reached the age of five, so he couldn't have known much. Nevertheless, on the basis of this slimmest bit of historical evidence, I promoted my great-great-grandmother, Mrs. Dr. Keck, to the status of first lady doctor west of the Mississippi. This is how family myths get started—because children love to repeat striking stories and grand claims so much that they quickly turn fact into fiction as time fogs up the facts and details. I was wrong, of course, but as it turns out, not as wrong as one might think. The story of Cora's mother and the family business turned out to be much more complicated than that.

When my long-widowed mother moved to a small apartment in a retirement community, the sugar bowl and creamer came my way again, along with the four trunks filled with Keck papers, diaries, and

The silver sugar bowl and creamer from Mrs. Dr. Keck's dining room.

photographs. By now, everyone who knew anything about the back-story behind these items had been dead for decades. I read and reread Cora's Vassar diary after typing it out, and while I learned much less than I had hoped I would from its pages, it stoked my hunger for more information.

So, 125 years after Cora left Davenport on a train for Vassar College in Poughkeepsie, New York, I left Rockland County, where I live in a small town near New York City, and flew out to Davenport in July 2009 to explore my personal unknown territory. I booked the short flight to Chicago, rented a car, and headed west on Interstate 80 in a wobbly little Hyundai. As I clutched the steering wheel to avoid being overturned by passing trucks, I thought about that dreamscape of the lonely mahogany sideboard floating in the fields. A yawning gulf of personal disconnection stretched across time in front of me; a rip that reached almost to the edge of the family fabric. Our sparse population of lineal offspring probably shouldn't even be compared to a piece of fabric; my family's history is more like a few dangling threads. My two sisters and our three children are Cora and Mrs. Dr. Keck's only living descendants. I felt as if my drive could last for nine decades; I felt as if I were chasing some kind of mirage. Death had swept all my connections off the table.

In fact, less than two hours later, I crossed the Mississippi River and exited the interstate onto the western shore. The un-mysterious city of Davenport, Iowa, materialized as the highway signs assured me it would, surrounded by rolling hills covered with green corn, and no surreal, abandoned furniture appeared anywhere among the endless rows of well-tended stalks. I was surprised to discover that, for a formerly Western town, Davenport is actually very close to the East where I grew up.

During my peripatetic youth, I lived in the Northeast, the Deep South, Texas, Brazil, and California, but I had never crossed the heart of the United States except by plane. For me, it was like taking a trip back to "the old country" to discover my family's Iowa roots. Everything I saw in the Midwest was new to me—careless remarks to the effect that "there's nothing out there in fly-over territory" fell by the wayside as I drove across northern Illinois; the productivity of the farms I saw was overwhelming. Every acre of dirt was devoted to making our daily bread in one form or another. I thought about the Hudson River Valley landscape that I am most familiar with: once the pride of nineteenth-century American agriculture, the still-fertile region is now littered with broken-down barns and vine-choked, abandoned farmhouses. This was not true in Illinois and Iowa. The ancient word that sprang into my head as I gazed left and right through the windshield was "abundance," and the emotional reaction that stayed with me afterward is how fragile that abundance is. Large families filled with children, fields filled with crops, barns bursting with stock—people seem to expect these things will always be there, strong and alive, but I can see from my own family's past and the landscape I've come to know well in the depressed rural areas of upstate New York that it all might be better understood as a temporary illusion.

Davenport was built on bluffs that rise gently from the Mississippi River bottomlands to a height of about one hundred feet above the flow of water, the only stretch between Minneapolis and New Orleans where the river runs from east to west. The boulevards leading up to the crest of the hillside are still lined with large, handsome houses built during the late nineteenth century. Gallant survivors that escaped the wrecking ball or the arsonist's torch now sport freshly painted turrets, cornices, and gingerbread and continue to look out to the south across the river toward Davenport's slightly rusty sister cities of Moline and Rock Island, Illinois.

I checked into a bed and breakfast in the restored mansion of jazz trumpeter Bix Beiderbecke's German grandparents, who once ran a prosperous wholesale grocery business selling food to the army, the Mississippi riverboats, and wagon trains heading west. I already knew that Cora's house at 611 Brady Street had been torn down, but the location was only a few blocks away, and I wanted to get a feel for how she might have lived her daily life by walking the same streets she had walked.

Few of the buildings left on Cora's block of Brady Street are ones she would have recognized—the town hall, the Episcopal church, the Davenport Academy of Sciences, and the bankers' mansions have all disappeared, leaving vacant lots and some boarded-up structures that are available for lease or sale. A large three-story medical arts building of 1960s vintage occupies the lot where Mrs. Dr. Keck's Infirmary for All Chronic Diseases used to stand at the corner of Brady and Sixth streets, and the sprawling Palmer College of Chiropractic, the mother school for the entire field of chiropractic medicine, founded by Mrs. Dr. Keck's business competitor and neighbor Daniel David Palmer in 1897, begins one block farther north at Brady and Seventh. It is the only visibly prosperous business entity in the neighborhood.

A note taped to the front door of the ground-floor office of Upper Cervical Care of Iowa at 602 Brady Street advised me that Dr. Sharon H. Hesse, the alternative medical practitioner whose office it was, would be "back soon." I felt a frisson of uncanny connection. It was as if the ghost of Mrs. Dr. Keck were still handling the business side of things from her distant place in the spirit world; she had even managed to find a new tenant for her property who was a female physician, more or less aligned with her alternative naturopathic medical philosophies. Several wind chimes hung from the ceiling, and piles of advertising fliers covered the reception desk, which was decorated with red, white, and blue candles and a candelabra draped with silver Mardi Gras beads. Dr. Hesse's pamphlets advertised treatments for ADD/ADHD, chronic fatigue syndrome, fibromyalgia, arthritis, trigeminal neuralgia, seizures, sleep problems, digestive problems, back pain, migraines, high blood pressure, and learning disorders—all the modern, typical, chronic health complaints that regular doctors "are glad to be rid of," not unlike the list of chronic complaints that Cora's mother specialized in treating, which, according to her advertising brochure, "constitute the great bulk of human suffering."

One hundred and twenty-four years earlier, in 1884, when Mrs. Dr. Keck was still directly in charge of the treatments offered at the infirmary at 611 Brady Street, Davenport was living its golden age, and all the luxurious buildings along the prestigious avenue were new. The city had grown quickly during its first fifty years. Close on the heels of the initial wave of "original settlers" of English ancestry from Ohio and New York came thousands of new arrivals from Germany, and by 1870, more than three-quarters of Davenport's urban population had German last names. The Germans brought to the shores of the Mississippi their love for Mendelssohn and Beethoven, along with a fondness for summer beer gardens, shooting clubs, and zither playing. They even organized a German-language theater, a place where respectable women were welcomed onstage as performers and musicians, unlike at the English-language venues.[1]

Cora's family background bridged these two cultures. Both of her parents were Pennsylvania Dutch, descended from eighteenth-century Swiss and German religious refugees called Anabaptists, whose descendants we know today as Mennonites and Amish. Many Pennsylvania Dutch continued to speak German within their communities well into the nineteenth century. John Keck's traditional chin whiskers hint at a sober, religious background. After leaving Pennsylvania for Iowa, both of Cora's parents became stalwart members of the Methodist church, which was known in those days for its support of progressive moral reform issues, including a woman's right to pursue gainful employment, and for temperance, the nineteenth-century morals movement that aimed to outlaw all manufacture and consumption of alcohol. Temperance was closely linked to other reforms, including the abolition of slavery. The Methodist church was emphatically not known for supporting any kind of theatricals; strict and dour behavior was the expected norm for respectable Methodists of both genders.

As a transportation hub, Davenport naturally had its wild side. The goings-on in Scott County made the powerful advocates for temperance who dominated politics in the rest of the state of Iowa fume. Travelers who stepped out of the Chicago, Rock Island & Pacific Railway depot at the corner of Fourth and Perry streets in 1884 would have found it hard to believe that Iowa had introduced compulsory statewide prohibition that year. A busy saloon stood right across the street from the station and was open at all hours, while four large brothels beckoned customers within a short stroll in both directions.

The Perry Street station was located at the western edge of Bucktown, the city's thriving red-light district. In the 1880s, Bucktown boasted somewhere in the vicinity of 130 saloons, along with a number of other racy entertainment establishments for sporting men (and for ordinary men who were acting that way), including twenty or thirty assignation houses, short-stay hotels, and brothels, while five breweries and seven wholesale wine and liquor dealers operated unmolested by law enforcement of any kind.[2] Bucktown was said to be at least as bad as Chicago's notorious Levee district, and some stiff-backed reformers claimed it was worse, leading William Randolph Hearst's Chicago papers to label Davenport as "the Wickedest City in America" in 1903.

Despite the action down in Bucktown, the rest of Davenport was pretty respectable in character, especially as one gained altitude up the side of the bluff. Placement on the hillside measured social status as clearly as a yardstick. Davenport's town hall and two well-built, mainline Protestant churches stood right across the street from the Keck mansion, and the Catholic bishop's residence commanded the summit of Brady Street hill. While Cora Keck's house was only a kitty-cornered block away from three brothels, which she would have walked past every time she came from the railroad station, that block and the railroad tracks along Fifth Street formed an invisible dividing line separating the river flats of Bucktown from respectable Davenport.[3]

CORA WAS NEW TO WEALTH, having lived through a dramatic family financial reversal as a child. Her earliest memories were of a dusty little farmhouse on the outskirts of Fairfield, Iowa, where she was born on May 3, 1865, two weeks after President Lincoln's assassination. Her father, John C. Keck, a trained mechanic, had moved west to Iowa from Pennsylvania to seek his fortune. While her mother kept busy as an efficient housewife and mother of five daughters and one son, Cora's father opened a small workshop and foundry and began inventing and manufacturing farm machinery, including timothy riddles and sorghum cane mills. The Kecks did not stand out from the crowd of young families in town except that Cora's mother was a little more organized and energetic than most, a perfectionist in her kitchen and devoted to nursing her sick friends and relatives. At the Eighteenth Annual Fair of the Jefferson County Agricultural Society in September 1869, Rebecca showed her skill at the stove when she swept the jam and jelly division with five first-place winners. This was at the same time that she was nursing her younger brother George and his wife Sarah, both of whom died of tuberculosis fewer than two months later.

Cora was eight when the national banking panic overwhelmed Iowa's farming economy in September 1873. In 1874, annual earnings for John

[Left] Rebecca J. Keck at about age thirty-six, in a portrait taken in Chicago ca. 1873. [Center] Cora Mae Keck, age six, in a portrait taken in Fairfield, Iowa, in 1871. [Right] John C. Keck, about thirty-five years old, in a portrait taken in Bloomington, Illinois, ca. 1862.

Keck's foundry fell from more than $6,200 to $35, and a competitor named A. Demarce bought him out.[4] The following fall, the ruined ex-foundry owner was observed bent over in the roadside weeds side by side with his wife and older daughters, hurrying to pick as many ingredients as they could before the first frost killed the medicinal plants she needed to brew her home remedies on the family's woodstove. Rebecca's skill, efficiency, and perfectionism in the kitchen were their only hope for survival. The family was reduced to living in a series of shabby rented accommodations. Enduring her family's public financial humiliation with spirited resolve, Rebecca began selling her catarrh tonic door to door. Three years later, in 1876, the Kecks moved to Davenport and continued to rent rooms, which they shared with a constant stream of Mrs. Dr. Keck's patients in a cramped, soot-covered former Methodist Episcopal parsonage, squatting next to the railroad tracks at Brady and Fifth streets.

Now, with her husband's full support, it was Rebecca's turn to see her business take off. Three years later, when Cora was fourteen, the Kecks' difficult circumstances were magically transformed by her mother's "unbounded business success." On June 2, 1879, Rebecca Keck paid $12,000 in cash for one of Davenport's biggest real-estate trophies, the John P. Cook mansion at 611 Brady, one block north of the parsonage.[5] Mr. Cook (the grandfather of dramatist George Cram Cook) had lost most of his property to creditors following the collapse of his wildcat bank in Florence, Nebraska, during the national banking Panic of 1857. The Cook family then suffered ultimate humiliation as Iowa's most notorious itinerant quack transformed his former family dream home into "Mrs. Dr. Keck's Palatial Infirmary for All Chronic Diseases." She must have been eyeing the property enviously for several years; a regular doctor had been leasing the premises and running an eye and ear infirmary there since 1874.

Triumphantly, Rebecca moved her family in and two weeks later reopened the building to the public. The sale was described in detail in a two-column article in the *Davenport Gazette* and was the subject of gossip for months afterward. The redecoration, painting, and graining inside the entire building were created by "the masterly hand" of Mrs. Dr. Keck's brother-in-law, Thomas S. Hamilton, of Wooster, Ohio, who traveled to Davenport expressly to execute the work. Hamilton had very advanced taste and used decorative motifs on the walls and ceilings of the public rooms downstairs that are recognizably influenced by such leading British designers of the late nineteenth century as William Morris and the architect Owen Jones.

Cora's mother scored a resounding double victory with her takeover of the Cook mansion; the displaced tenant at 611 Brady, Dr. Edward F. Hazen, M.D., was not only a professional competitor who energetically advertised his own dubious cures for catarrh, he was also the secretary of the Scott County Medical Society, an organization actively engaged in trying to put Mrs. Dr. Keck out of business. To the leading families of Davenport—the Cooks, Pecks, LeClaires, Griggses, and Lanes—Mrs. Dr. Keck's nouveau riche real-estate deal was a social calamity. They were so deeply uncomfortable about her business activities that they pretended she simply didn't exist.

Living well was the best revenge. Most of Cora's extended family came to live in the grand house, including her grandmother, her parents, her younger brother, and one or more brothers-in-law (depending on the year), and three of her four sisters. Family and guests arrived through a low wrought-iron gate that faced Brady Street and climbed a long, steep flight of marble steps to enter the main door of the mansion, framed by white marble Ionic columns. A separate entrance into the basement led to Mrs. Dr. Keck's consulting office.

According to the 1880 census, three teenage live-in maidservants, Amelia, Ida, and Lulu, and a young man named Robert Shepard who looked after the Keck's horses and carriage lived under the eaves in the attic. Mrs. Dr. Keck's patients checked in and out of bedrooms built for their accommodation in a new back addition. The original mansion had already featured wash sinks and water closets (that is, toilets). Most people still considered those to be luxuries when Mrs. Dr. Keck undertook her renovations and really impressed everyone by installing steam heat and covering the now-redundant fireplace hearths with colorful silk draperies. On the south exterior wall, a graceful, New Orleans–style wrought-iron balcony allowed family and visitors to step outside and admire the Mississippi River passing majestically by at the foot of the Brady Street hill.

BEFORE I LEFT FOR IOWA, I spent hours examining the mostly un-identified faces in Cora's four photo albums, trying to figure out the names and identities of her family. One by one, I carefully slid each cabinet portrait out of its paper page and turned it over, only to find a blank back in almost every case. All I could learn was the name of the photography studio and the city where the picture was taken. Why didn't anyone write down any names? My heart sank when I realized how little information I had to go on.

Things began to improve as I started to collect basic information about Cora's parents and five siblings from the U.S. censuses of 1860, 1870, and 1880. (The 1890 census was largely destroyed in a fire in 1921.) I created a detailed spreadsheet with information about Cora's immediate family and began working on matching names to faces. I met a genealogical collaborator online: Marge Hetzel, a superb information sleuth and long lost e-mail "relative." Marge is descended from Cora's sister Lotta's husband's uncle (through another branch of the Dorn family) and was my go-to for the many thorny genealogical problems that came up while I was working to reconstruct the home lives and relations of all of Cora's friends and classmates.

Cora's Vassar College senior portrait was signed, so I had that as a reference point. I had names and ages and genders from the census. As I got to know the faces, some obvious patterns emerged, family resemblances helped, and I eventually discovered the main characters. Cora's parents, John Conrad Keck and Rebecca Ilginfritz Keck (sometimes spelled Ilgenfritz), were clearly featured in two of the albums in the same place of honor, in a pair of portraits on the first page, and it became obvious that two of Cora's older married sisters were featured on subsequent pages along with their husbands. Lotta's handsome husband, Dr. Gay Dorn, M.D., signed two of his portraits with a flourishing signature—one of the few people to do so. Cora's younger brother, Willie, appeared next, and her youngest sister, Maggie, who was described by a disgruntled in-law of Cora's as "mentally deficient," was photographed frequently with Cora and her friends. Her pictures are all identified, and she must have been much loved by her family despite her handicap. However, at this early stage, many people were still missing from my lineup.

I discovered seven different images of Cora's mother in the albums. Over the decades, Mrs. Dr. Keck gazed at the camera calmly and pleasantly. She always wore her fiercely curly hair pulled straight back in a tight bun and used the same simple drop earrings, with a bit of lace tucked in at her neck above her solid-looking shoulders. She presented herself as a woman without vanity, consistent in her personal appearance even as she grew wealthy. One of her portraits, taken in Peoria around 1880, looks so much like the portrait of Lydia Pinkham engraved on millions of boxes of Lydia Pinkham's Vegetable Compound that I believe the resemblance is deliberate and that Rebecca consciously copied the look to strengthen her brand image. It's easy to imagine from her expression that she showed a warm and confident bedside manner with her many patients, meanwhile standing ready to respond to business problems with unswerving determination. She was, according to memoirs written by my grandfather (who never met her but who knew all her six children and married her granddaughter), "by all accounts, extremely practical and realistic in all her affairs."

It is likely that practical medical and business matters held little interest for my great-grandmother Cora Keck, who was Mrs. Dr. Keck's fourth daughter. In fact, Cora worried that her beloved Mama thought her "quite frivolous." Tall and athletic, Cora had blue eyes that made a fine contrast with her deep brown hair, and her dark, arched eyebrows

Cora, about fifteen years old, ca. 1880,
wearing a beaver fur coat and western hat.

Mrs. Dr. Keck, about forty-two years old, ca. 1880.

were elegant and expressive. At nineteen years of age, she wore her long hair pulled straight back in a knot, with her curly bangs pouffed on top of her forehead in the latest fashion. Everyone agreed that while she was not beautiful, her energy and charm made her extremely attractive. People also commented that she was somewhat impetuous and that her set of wild teenage friends, who came mostly from blue-collar families, were even more so. Cora was a naturally gifted musician, undisciplined but, in the eyes of her new piano teacher, Professor Hugo Braunlich, full of immense potential.

ORIGINALLY CONSTRUCTED as a show-off McMansion by a socially prominent but unlucky financial speculator in 1857 and later fallen into disrepair in the hands of negligent creditors, Cora's home at 611 Brady Street was, in the spring of 1883, once again lovingly restored as the flagship and social showpiece of Mrs. Dr. Keck's unbounded business success. Cora's daily life revolved around enjoyment of her mother's prize. In the summer, she went riding in the family carriage with her younger brother and sisters and sat outside in the grassy yard under the shade of several large trees to read books; she flirted with her visitors in the elegant great room, known then as the main parlor; she filled her bedroom upstairs with small treasures and an ever-expanding collection of new clothes and accessories; and she received holiday visitors with her extended family in the imposing two-story front hallway with its sweeping staircase while they waited in anticipation for the moment when the sliding doors would be opened to reveal a glittering Christmas tree in the music room behind.

As one of the younger children in the large family, Cora carried on her pleasant, vivacious social agenda under the radar, so to speak, because there were many important irons in the fire in the Keck household at 611 Brady Street that didn't concern her. The three powerful and capable women who ran the family business, Cora's mother and her two oldest sisters, Belle and Lotta, also dominated the household, and they were usually rushing around, skillful at keeping many plates spinning in the daily press of business. The home atmosphere combined equal measures of hustle, diligent industry, and agitated commotion, stew, and botheration, particularly in the spring of 1883, when a catastrophe hit that threatened to put an end to everything that they had achieved during the decade since Mr. Keck's foundry had collapsed in 1874.

In the first week of April, Mrs. Dr. Keck "contracted, from exposure, a pleuro-pneumonia, which became gravely typhoidal in character" while seeing her patients in Quincy, Illinois.[6] She had worn down her health through overwork, although the trickles of sewage running down side-street ditches toward the nearest river that were a common site in most towns she visited certainly would have played a role in her infection. She had four or five branch offices in eastern Iowa and central Illinois that she visited once every two months, and while she was on the road she typically worked twelve hours at a stretch, consulting with sixty or seventy patients each day. The Quincy *Whig* wrote, "and so goes the rounds of Mrs. Dr. Keck's life truly a life of labor, and without the seventh or even the seventieth day for rest, for someone is constantly seeking her aid."[7]

While Mrs. Dr. Keck's life hung by a thread in a room at the Tremont House hotel in Quincy, dismay and fearful consternation prevailed at 611 Brady Street in Davenport. Cora and her family were distraught at the prospect that their beloved wife and mother might die. Her energy and drive, her ability to project a forceful response to all problems, not to mention the steady stream of income she produced, might suddenly vanish out from under all of them. What would they do without her? Who would carry on?

Because Mrs. Dr. Keck traveled so much, during her absence, a lot of her authority rubbed off on her oldest daughter Belle, who was eight years older than Cora and who ran her own and her mother's fast-growing portfolio of real-estate investments as smoothly as she managed her mother's advertising schedules and the manufacturing of all the bottled medications. However, Belle had no interest in or feel for medical care; she entirely lacked the knack for empathizing with the suffering of strangers, so it was Lotta, six years older and Cora's favorite sister, who apparently responded the most forcefully to the potential downfall of the family business. Lotta had been managing Mrs. Dr. Keck's Peoria branch office at 515 Fulton Street for several years. The key to their survival might be to try to affiliate with a credentialed medical professional, and she was in a position to do something about this problem immediately.

Mrs. Dr. Keck did not die in a room at the Tremont House, however, and as soon as she was well enough to travel back to Davenport to be there for the ceremony, on April 11 Lotta married a young man with impeccable social and medical credentials she was dating in Peoria named Dr. Gay Dorn, two weeks after his graduation from Chicago Medical College.[8] No wedding announcements were published in the Peoria newspapers, probably because publicity about his new family link with the famous quack might have sabotaged his application for state credentials. A week later, the Illinois State Board of Health issued Dr. Dorn's license to practice medicine, and he filed his certificate with the county clerk to open a practice in Peoria at 515 Fulton Street at the same address as Mrs. Dr. Keck's branch office.

EARLY IN MAY, shortly after Cora's eighteenth birthday, she sat down with most of her family to the main meal of the day, their moods badly dampened by the ongoing crisis. Mrs. Dr. Keck lay in bed upstairs, still too weak to resume her grueling schedule. Served at noon in the high-ceilinged dining room, the Kecks' family dinner amounted to a ceremonial ritual. Light poured in through two tall windows flanking a sideboard with three tiers of shelves that displayed an array of expensive, ornamental eating equipment. In a photograph of the dining room taken by a professional, probably in the late 1890s, my silver sugar bowl and creamer can just be discerned in the front row of items on a middle

The dining room at 611 Brady Street, Davenport, Iowa.

shelf, part of a large and expensive tea and coffee service to be polished and rolled out for important visitors on important occasions. (These are the only household items from the entire mansion that have survived to come down to a descendant.)

Cora's father began the meal by bowing his head to say a familiar old-fashioned grace in German, mentioning his wife's illness in particular, and they all picked up their heavy silver spoons to start on the broth, thickened with cabbage and rice.

Cora's youngest sister Margaret might have improved the gloomy atmosphere by announcing that everyone in her sixth-grade class had to write a grammar exercise that would be exhibited at the Iowa State Fair. Here was a problem that could be solved easily. Everyone loved Maggie. It was typical of her that she could make things feel almost back to normal for a moment, even in the worst circumstances. The usual conversational bedlam broke out as Maggie's older sisters all began to voice their strong and diverse opinions about what should be done to help her with her task. At age sixteen, she could still barely read and write because of her severe learning disabilities—in fact she misspelled her own name and that of her late husband on his gravestone in 1917. Her ten diagrammed sentences, on the other hand, were written correctly with suspiciously perfect penmanship. (Maggie's little relic is still on exhibit today, bound into a handsome Moroccan leather album with a gilded title on its spine and carefully filed in a long row next to many others just like it on a shelf in the Davenport School District's small basement museum.)

Maybe Belle suggested that someone else in the family, such as her flighty sister Cora, write those sentences for her. Perhaps Cora immediately turned and passed the chore off onto her lonely sister Flora. Flora wouldn't argue with that logic because she was usually without any plans whatever for the rest of the day.

Flora, who was three years older than Cora, probably sat at the table staring morosely at the Egyptian-style clock decorated with sphinxes and obelisks ticking on the mantelpiece. I can't describe her face or her husband's face because Cora did not save a photograph of her as a bride, nor did Cora give Flora and her husband a separate page in her photo album, and I think that this gap also says something important about Flora's role in the family dynamics. Her mouth doubtless had the pinched, sour expression of someone dogged by disappointment all her life. Mrs. Dr. Keck's will mentioned Flora last of all her six children; she received only the leftover furniture. Mrs. Dr. Keck dragged Flora along on her business trips only if Belle and Lotta weren't available. Flora wasn't an executive like Belle and Lotta, and maybe she didn't have good people skills and found it hard to care about the disgusting health problems of the broken-down farmers, quarry workers, railroad laborers, and housewives who lined up in front of her in the crowded hotel rooms that Mrs. Dr. Keck used as consulting parlors.

Belle's lawyer husband, William R. H. Alexander, also sat at the table. On this particular day, I imagine that he was suffering from some kind of internal turmoil, and Cora might have noticed him frown sharply and begin to drum his fingers on the tablecloth. Cora did not like him, although they had lived together in the same house for five years since he married Belle in 1878. He was striving to establish himself as a mover and shaker in the Davenport business community with mixed success. One of his portraits shows a man gazing at the camera with an earnest expression, completely unaware of the fact that the left side of his bowtie has sprung open. His current anxieties began on April 11, the same day that Gay and Lotta were married, when he signed a $300 note (worth about $30,000 in today's money) for a fictitious grain purchase with a Davenport grain broker, R. M. Dixon of Dixon, Reed & Co.[9] Now, William worried about how quickly he had been persuaded to go along. He was fast losing confidence that he had made a sharp insider's deal; instead, the realization was dawning that Dixon was a powerful conniver habitually used to manipulating small players. A cold voice in the back of his head suggested that the whole business was probably

[Left] Cora (left), Flora (?), and Maggie, ca. 1887. [Center] Belle Keck Alexander, about twenty-one years old, ca. 1878. [Right] Belle's husband, William R. H. Alexander, ca. 1878.

unlikely to come out in his favor. In order to derail this nerve-racking train of thought, he lifted his stemmed water glass in a mock toast to Maggie for possibly representing the family so well at the state capital of Des Moines. He then dabbed his mustache with his linen napkin.

"I have an announcement to make," he said. "I have received an appointment at the Veterans' Bureau as a Special Examiner of Pensions. My uncle, Congressman Moses McCoid, has finally secured the post on my behalf. Belle and I are going to move to Washington, D.C."[10]

This bombshell was probably met by stunned silence. Cora's brother-in-law was hoping to find himself a safe and profitable sinecure by joining the ranks of bureaucrats who evaluated applications submitted by Civil War veterans for their pensions. The Pension Bureau had been in the news a lot in 1883, and agency officials were on the defensive. (Modern historians point to it as the single largest swamp of U.S. government corruption in the nineteenth century.) Twenty years after Civil War hostilities had ended, the rate of payouts was actually increasing because entrepreneurial law firms advertised widely in newspapers across the country to drum up the volume of claims, not unlike ads soliciting plaintiffs for asbestos suits one hundred years in the future. Unruffled by these problems, he was eager to live in the East in a more fashionable city, and Washington suited his aspirations nicely.

"Washington?" Belle must have exploded with outrage. "We can't move to Washington. I can't run Mama's business from there."

This would have been a good moment for Mrs. Dr. Keck to rise from her sickbed and make a dramatic appearance at the entrance to the dining room, dressed in her sacque and slippers. She would have had to set the record straight right then.

"You don't run my business, Belle. You *help* me run my business. There is a difference in that, I think."

Forget the risk of dying of typhoid fever and the unexplored need to groom a successor physician capable of carrying on her treatments for the next generation. Mrs. Dr. Keck claimed the first and only completely new medical theory thought of by a woman; there was clearly no one alive who was going to fill the shoes of the celebrated catarrh specialist and greatest female physician in the West. None of her six children could do it, certainly not Cora—not even Belle.

CHAPTER TWO

These Leap Year Girls Are Getting Awfully Bold

. . . a rebellious girl is the spirit of that bewildered empire called the American Middlewest.

—SINCLAIR LEWIS, *Main Street*

With so many dramas churning up the daily lives of her mother and older sisters, Cora doubtless found it hard to attract attention of any kind, positive or negative, from her family. Neglect has its advantages for boisterous teenagers—she had a lot of freedom to pursue her own activities. The year 1884 was a leap year, which in those days meant that gender etiquette could be reversed on February 29. Girls could openly take charge and ask boys out, while paying for the evening's entertainment. Cora immediately took advantage of her opportunity to organize a trip to the Collins Brothers roller rink across the river in Rock Island with all her friends. The *Davenport Democrat*'s "Leap Year notes" noted "a sleighing party in D. went over to the Rock Island roller skating rink last evening. The ladies did the thing up in the latest approved style, bearing all the expenses. The following ladies and gents participated: Lill Reid, Grace Barlow, Cora Keck, Frank Anderson, Will Mossman, and several others." Taking advantage of opportunities was a Keck family strong suit.

Midwestern papers used to publish a long column of gossipy news squibs down the middle of the front page of each issue that listed everyone, male or female, of any wealth or stature, who might be coming or going, and for any purpose, business or social. It was like a local version of Facebook. Cora clipped and saved every notice that mentioned her name. No such comprehensive aid to the nosy historian was allowed to appear in the more repressed and proper Eastern papers. It's clear that Cora, unlike her sisters, was not being excluded completely from social notice in the press, although her friends mentioned above were

Tintype "On Exhibition only for Three Days." Cora (right, wearing spectacles) posing with a friend inside a frame held by two dudes, in 1886.

telegraph boys, bricklayers' apprentices and printers' helpers, not Harvard students, and they were not being invited to an exclusive party by anyone from an original settler family, merely going out together to a public roller rink.

Roller-skating was not just done for the exercise, of course. Cora noted down her personal rules for what she liked to do with her friends at the rink:

SUNDAY AFTERNOON 4 P.M. JUNE 3, '83

Thirteen ways to flirt at the roller rink:

1. Eye Flirt—casting the eyes up then down winking a little = I love you.
2. Winking the right eye = you're at liberty to try to flirt.
3. Closing the right eye = you use too much slang.
4. Looking down = I am sorry.
5. Holding one eye firm, gradually winking the other = you are lovely.
6. Half wink = We'll flirt.
7. Shutting one eye and then the other = I love another.
8. Looking cross-eyed = I am engaged.
9. Giving a grim wink to the company = I hate you.
10. Looking right at the person to whom you are talking = no more at present.
11. Roll your eyes to the ceiling = you're just lovely.
12. Make a tear in right eye = I am lost.
13. Closing both eyes = Don't tell.
The End. The little flirt.

Cora also enjoyed outings with her pals to Black Hawk's Tower. This new public picnic ground and amusement park overlooked the Rock River on a tall bluff at the far terminus of the equally new Rock Island trolley line and featured a terrifying toboggan slide called Shoot the Shoots. Like Rock Island's rows of brilliant electric streetlights, which had just been installed along the town's main street, less than a year after the great white way on Broadway had gone electric in New York City, the slide was a local sensation. At the top, passengers climbed into flat-bottomed boats made of logs; the chocks were pulled free, and the boats rocketed one hundred feet down the steep bluff on a greased incline and shot out at the bottom one hundred yards across the water.[1] An electric cable powered by the streetcar line pulled the boats back to the top afterward. It cost a dime to ride, which was a lot of money to spend on a couple of minutes of fun, but everyone agreed that even if you had to scrounge up the money, the thrill was worth it. Cora practically shivered in anticipation at the violent thrill of hurtling downhill at fifty miles an hour with the wind tearing off her hat and water spraying up on all sides as they hit the Rock River at the bottom.

Toboggan Slide at Black Hawk's Tower.
Courtesy of the Richardson-Sloane Special
Collections Center, Davenport Public Library.

In the middle of all this socializing, Cora got a mash letter from an unemployed, undereducated, and seriously depressed traveling salesman named H. B. Johnson, who was staying at Baugh's European Hotel in St. Paul, Minnesota. ("Mashing" was the Victorian term for boldly propositioning someone of the opposite sex for sexual purposes. Flirting was a lighter, more romantic version of the same activity.) Unfortunately, the first page of the letter has been lost, but the second reveals enough details about Cora's candid correspondent for any concerned and responsible parent to find it worrisome, even today:

> . . . as I have no news of working and having nothing to keep my mind steady. I have been traveling for some time.
>
> Candidly speaking I do not believe I shall ever be happy till you and I become acquainted, to have seen you in your carriage, sitting there

with such grace and ease, your sparkling beauty has completely demolished me.

I find since leaving your city that I have an acquaintance their or
used to have at any rate, she is now married to whom I cannot say, her
name used to be Miss Wakefield if you know of any person by that
name you will confer a great favor on me by letting me know to whom
she is married.

I will now close hoping that you won't throw this letter aside but
will kindly answer it and help to make the life of your unknown
admirer happy—
Yours ferverently—
H. B. Johnson
S. Paul, Minn c/o Gruebel

It's hard to imagine less promising potential boyfriend material than
Mr. H. B. Johnson. "You're nice-looking," he wrote her, in effect, "but
I'm out of work, I'm emotionally unstable, I'm a transient with no fixed
address, and by the way, I'm still interested in another girl you might
know whom I *really* liked." Most of the sentences look like stock phrases, probably cribbed from a reference book on how to write a love letter,
a resource that young men resorted to frequently in that era. It's a mystery to me why he was so obtuse with his phony sentiments, and how
he could have found out an address to write to Cora, but presumably
he did so through a third party who knew her. He was obviously troll-
ing for a rich girl to solve his personal cash-flow problems. I can easily
imagine Cora sharing this letter with her friends Edith Ross and Hattie
Wakefield (but never with her parents) in an extremely insensitive way
and then gluing it into her scrapbook because H. B. Johnson made
them all laugh out loud.

Cora's friend Hattie Wakefield was from Bloomington, Illinois. Her
father, Dr. Cyrenius Wakefield, was one of the most successful patent medicine manufacturers in the country. During the 1880s, he was
enjoying all the luxuries and benefits of a prosperous retirement after
having handed over control of most of his business affairs to his oldest son, Oscar, in 1870. Dr. Wakefield was a mentor for Mrs. Dr. Keck
in her early years, and the families were close friends for decades. It
is likely that the large Wakefield laboratory and printing facility in

Cora's sketchbook with Wakefield's Blackberry Balsam label.

Bloomington produced, bottled, and shipped most of Mrs. Dr. Keck's medications to her thousands of mail-order customers, since it is hard to imagine these tasks being carried out efficiently from the back of a private home.

Although 150 miles of poor roads separated Davenport and Bloomington, the towns were well connected by rail, and the families socialized together frequently. In 1883, Hattie's brother, Homer, came to visit the Kecks in Davenport. Cora then visited the Wakefields and their neighbors, the Eddys, in Bloomington several times in 1884. The Eddys were Oscar Wakefield's in-laws, and Gussy (Augusta) Eddy was another close friend of Cora's. There was perhaps some loose talk from time to time that Cora and Homer might eventually be married, since it seemed like a natural match-up, but Cora never took this possibility particularly seriously—she thought Homer was too youthful and silly.

IN THE MIDST of her active social life, Cora continued to show aptitude at the piano. Since this talent would become the key to her future in many ways, it is worth imagining what it would have been like to listen to her play. From the very beginning of this project, I have spent a lot of time considering the larger issue of whether she deserved a shot at higher musical education. Was she just a dilettante, or was she the real thing? And how should I define "the real thing"? Should musical status be based entirely on one's ability to be hired as a professional and earn money? Today that definition includes tone-deaf, lip-synching pop stars but leaves out most of the world's struggling violin prodigies. Is all amateur music by definition inferior? Cora agonized at length about this issue at college, as did those around her, particularly her piano teachers and her oldest sister Belle.

As an adult, Cora had all the sheet music she liked to play bound into a book that I still have. This book has been the key to my understanding of her musical abilities. All her teachers' names, markings, and fingerings are there, along with the dates that the pieces were assigned, written at the top of the title pages. Cora learned the basics of her piano technique from a teacher named Mrs. Smith, whose name appeared written at the top of a simple song by Adolfe Henselt called "If I Were a Bird . . ."

By the time she was seventeen, Cora was studying with one of Davenport's most prominent musicians, Professor Hugo G. Braunlich, who was a very distinguished person. Even after living in the United States for more than thirty years, Professor Braunlich still radiated an aura of European glamour. His father was a German physician who had started a hospital in the 1830s named Lindenhoff, near Dresden, that served mental patients from royal families (of which there seemed to be a copious supply in those days) and who used to wear court dress to work to avoid offending his patients' sense of etiquette. Hugo played piano for his father's patients so beautifully that one of the moonstruck grand dukes once gave him a ring set with two diamonds. Hugo never sold it, even after he arrived in the United States as an impoverished political exile in 1851. Father and son were politically very liberal and shared strong democratic sympathies. According to a handwritten Braunlich family history, at the age of seventeen, Hugo had served as an officer's adjutant during the Revolution of 1848 in Dresden. Captured and sentenced to death by the royal government, the young man was pardoned on the condition that he and his whole family would "remove to America and never return." Composer Richard Wagner had also manned the same barricades in 1848, being thrown out of Dresden into political exile at the same time as the Braunlich family.

Hugo was a handsome man of erect carriage, with aristocratic manners; his granddaughter Alice recalled that during her piano lessons she "stood a little in awe of him." He had learned to play cello and piano in the 1840s in Germany, a time and place saturated with musical genius. The composer and famed concert pianist Franz Liszt frequently toured eastern Germany during Hugo's youth, so it is extremely likely that he was mesmerized by the brilliant, mystical ecstasy of Liszt's concert performances at the height of his powers, perhaps more than once.

On March 12, 1883, Professor Braunlich assigned Cora a piano "paraphrase" composition by Franz Liszt based on a theme by Rossini called La Charité. If Cora was able to play this piece at age seventeen, she would have had to have been exceptionally talented. Liszt's music has been described by the music critic Charles Rosen as being of "conspicuous technical difficulty"; performing it, he says, is "something like an athletic feat," requiring not only bravura skill but large hands and considerable strength and stamina. Liszt's opera paraphrases, of which Cora learned at least four, contain difficult finger exercises expressly designed to create musical "showpieces" of "stupefying public effect."[2]

I discovered that Henry Braunlich, Hugo's great-grandson, still lived in Davenport, and I called him up out of the blue in the summer of 2009. He was enchanted to hear an update about one of his great-grandfather's piano students and kindly took me out to a sumptuous dinner on my birthday at one of Davenport's social fixtures, the Outing Club, during which he provided me with a detailed family history written by his Aunt Alice (a summa cum laude graduate of the University of Chicago in Latin and Greek). From this document and from papers provided by other members of the Braunlich family, I was able to reconstruct many details of Cora's musical education.

Each week after school, Cora walked downhill on Brady Street and several blocks west along the railroad line through the middle of town to get to the Braunlichs' humble redbrick house at the corner of Fifth and Brown streets for her lessons. Professor Braunlich played piano and cello with equal skill and was a founding member of Davenport's De

Bériot string quartet, named in honor of a now-forgotten composer and violin teacher in Brussels, Belgium. When the famed New York conductor Theodore Thomas and his orchestra toured through Davenport in 1877, Professor Braunlich was apparently invited to play a solo with them that, according to critic Charles Edward Russell, was so extraordinary that it introduced classical music "outside of the bounds of 'Dutchtown' where before it had maintained an almost exclusive habitat."[3] This commentary reveals how ignorant English-speaking people were of the glories of fine classical music during the 1870s, which they apparently viewed as some kind of obscure, German folk activity.

Cora's teacher reviewed her practice routines in his small, sunny parlor facing Fifth Street, while long trains filled with hopeful settlers in search of cheap farmland chuffed along the tracks just a few yards away on their journey west to Leavenworth, Kansas, and Omaha, Nebraska, shaking the dainty blue teacups in the china cabinets each time they passed. While Cora probably had a tendency to skimp on the drills and scales by Czerny that the professor assigned to develop her technique, he was patient. He was always precisely focused on the matter at hand and had such a soft voice that she sometimes missed what he was saying when a train was going by. This encouraged her to listen to him more carefully. "Push

Prof. Hugo G. Braunlich, Cora's piano teacher in Davenport.

zee dynamics more, more, *more*," he would tell Cora, "I must tell you, Rossini's nickname vas *Mr. Crescendo*." Cora giggled when he shared these bits of musical gossip, which he knew delighted her. She loved and respected her teacher so much that she placed his cabinet portrait next to her grandmother's on the fourth page of her family photo album, ahead of her sisters, a startling discovery I made when Henry Braunlich mailed me a photograph of his great-grandfather Hugo.

After her lessons during the spring and summer, Frau Elise Braunlich might have offered Cora delicious wine jelly or invited her out into the backyard, which her husband had landscaped into a beautiful garden. He had studied to be a forester during his youth and continued to earn part of his living as a landscaper and garden designer. Protected from the uproar of the traffic out front by the mass of the house, the back lawn was an island of peace. Pigeons cooed in their cote in the small barn nestled against the base of the bluff at the back of the lot. A winding path led across the grass past a large bed of roses in the center to a small honeysuckle arbor. A compact kitchen garden included a gooseberry bush and a white asparagus bed filled with little hills of dirt to cover the shoots of *spargel*. Cora couldn't have known it, but this peaceful, respectable home had had a tumultuous beginning; handsome young Hugo had been a penniless left-wing political exile; Elise's wealthy parents had forbidden their marriage, and they had eloped.

Wild as she was, I think that even during high school Cora often practiced hard because she truly loved to play the piano. She would sit down on the adjustable stool in front of her family's upright in the large hall next to the living room and lift the lid. Because it was springtime, everyone was out for a change, and the house was empty except for Lulu, one of the maids, rolling a carpet sweeper back and forth under the dining room table in the next room. Cora liked the feel of outdoor air while she practiced. The high windows in the main parlor were open, the sashes pushed up, and the lower tier of inside shutters folded back against the wall to let the mild breeze blow in off the Mississippi River, which sparkled in the hazy sunlight as it flowed by in the distance.

Pulling the folio for La Charité from the large stack of music piled on the top of the piano and setting it on the rack in front of her, she spread her fingers across the smooth ivory keys to strike the first chord. After several weeks of work, she already had a good command of the notes; in some parts it seemed as if you needed twelve fingers to hit all the keys, but Cora had large hands, with slim fingers as long as her father's, and she knew how to roll the chords. She leaned forward to check her teacher's markings for fingering and dynamics. Then, with a shake of her head, she began to play. Even though no one in the family was there to hear, cascades of notes filled the Keck mansion and poured outside.

Somewhere in the midst of the shimmering foliage of runs and arpeggios, a melody began to emerge as Cora worked out the musical ideas. Without words, the balanced intervals in the little phrase seemed to urge people laboring uphill on the sidewalk to treat each other with generosity, just as the composer had intended. Cora tried to make it more impressive by speeding it up. Over and over, the little phrase came back, faster and faster, and as the speed and urgency increased, so did the volume and so did the mistakes. Right in the middle of a chaotic run of notes, the music stopped abruptly.

Cora was also a party girl. Slamming the lid of the piano loudly, she decided to finish practicing for the day and change her clothes. Edith Ross, Bert Brockett, and Will Mossman had invited her on an outing to go over to Rock Island to Black Hawk's Tower. They were coming by to pick her up later that afternoon. Cora practiced hard when she felt like it, but no one except her mother could make her sit down and do it if she wasn't in the mood. Since her mother was always out of town on business, Cora's schedule was not highly regulated.

BY NOW, CORA was going around as "Corize." She thought that this self-invented version of her name sounded much more elegant and sophisticated, particularly since she now lived in a mansion, and she wanted to impress the young people she hung out with at Davenport High School. The school's elegance and modern grandeur matched her aspirations. Back when she was thirteen, Davenport's city fathers had invested $65,000 (about $6.5 million in today's money) in a new building; the school was three stories high, and, sporting a bell tower topped by a fancy modern cupola, it was the most imposing building in the Tri-Cities area. It offered a comprehensive selection of courses that included higher mathematics, philosophy, political economy, Latin, chemistry, astronomy, physiology, history, drawing, and bookkeeping, for girls as well as boys.[4]

As a girl studying at Davenport's high school, Cora had some impressive female role models to follow. It wasn't just her mother's example. Respect for equal access to education for women was widespread in Iowa. Phebe Sudlow, the nation's first female school superintendent, had been appointed to her post in Davenport almost ten years before, in 1875. Coeducation was the norm in the state at every level—even the medical department of Iowa State University had been accepting women applicants, albeit somewhat reluctantly, since the first class entered in 1871. Davenport's business directory for 1884 listed five female physicians besides her mother, and several of them were members of the Scott County Medical Society.

However, professional ambition wasn't Cora's style; she generally avoided the straight academic subjects, preferring art and music. She saved six sketchbooks filled with drawings that show her steady progress as a talented artist. In one of her notebooks, she solved geometry problems with a pencil and compass, and in another she drew a beautiful still life in pencil showing accurate shadows and botanical details. The

Davenport High School, circa 1885. Courtesy of the Richardson-Sloane Special Collections Center, Davenport Public Library.

Wakefield's Blackberry Balsam label pasted to the back cover of a third drawing book could have come from Hattie, or maybe from Cora's lukewarm flirtation with Hattie's brother Homer.

In 1878, when Cora was thirteen, she jotted down the following incident: "Yesterday noon, L Mitchell, B. Benson, M. Peck, Georgia Le Clair, Fanny Morrison (Do you like her??) N. Lillibridge, Bertha Glaspell and I all went downstairs and stood on the steps outside and yelled like so many Indians. Of course we got reported and got into the dickens of a scrape." Bertha Glaspell would certainly have needed to blow off steam at school; her single mother, Martha, was president of the Davenport branch of the Woman's Christian Temperance Union— an occupation that in Davenport demanded delusional persistence— and no doubt she ran a tight ship at home to compensate for the quixotic futility of bringing her temperance message to America's Wickedest City. (The playwright Susan Glaspell was a first cousin once removed of Bertha's and went through the same Davenport schools as Cora, eleven years later.⁵) At this point, Cora's group of friends included several "top-drawer" girls from Davenport's most exclusive social stratum, including the nationally known surgeon Dr. Washington F. Peck's daughter, Mary, and Georgia LeClaire, a granddaughter of one of Davenport's founding patriarchs, Antoine LeClaire. The moment was spontaneous, informal, at school, and a single incident, but it appears to me that Cora was comfortable with all these rowdy ninth-graders and was included in their gang of friends. Mrs. Dr. Keck's scandalous legal problems and her real-estate battle with Dr. Hazen were still in the future when Cora recorded this incident. Three years later, Cora became separated from her former friends by an unbridgeable social gulf.

I'm struck by how much this slice of life at Davenport High School resembles the classic 1950s American high school experience of stage and film. Sex and courtship were clearly the focus of much of life's meaning for Cora's generation, not work or religion, as would have been the case for their pioneer parents. It was all about "He likes me," and no one was rushing to the altar, either. These young people were not focused on starting a family; they were interested in having fun. Cora and her friends spent most of their time flirting with each other while roaming around Davenport in unchaperoned packs to get ice cream and lemonade and go to the roller rink; they drank beer and champagne and smoked on the sly; they went to school in a large, centrally heated, well-lit building with hallways, lockers, a gymnasium, and spacious classrooms. They were divided into today's familiar-sounding social cliques—academic grinds and popular party kids. They used a lot of slang, they wanted to rebel against authority, and girls wanted to have as much freedom as the boys did. The mythological era of American teen culture seems to have been already falling into place—these Midwestern teenagers of 1882 sound less like clichéd Victorians and more like "bobby-soxers" from *Grease.*

Cora's friend Edith Ross, the daughter of an architect, had a rebellious teen attitude that would not look out of place in the film *Rebel without a Cause*: "She told me then that she couldn't do anything with me," Edith wrote to Cora about a teacher at the high school they had nicknamed the Dragon, who was concerned that Edith's slipping grades might prevent her from applying to Smith College. "I had become too hardened (Let us smile)." How cynical is that?

Cora's lifestyle is sounding rather limited, but I am afraid that I am also limited in what I can say about her at this point in her life, based on a few items a teenager chose to save in a box for her own posterity. It's probably random, and clues about more substantial topics, such as Cora's relationship with her mother, her musical ambitions and her family responsibilities, churchgoing, and so on, have disappeared. But it does tend to support my theory that Cora was an unlikely candidate for higher education, particularly at the nation's first and most prestigious women's college. Though outwardly happy, Cora was drifting badly without much direction in her life. A talented musician who played piano with considerable technical skill, she had not finished high school. She obviously cared little for most of her academic subjects. All she could think of to do was make house calls on her friends; set up plans for entertainments, dances, and musicales; and go on sleighing and roller-skating outings at a mind-boggling pace with the many young men and women she knew in the upper Mississippi valley.

On second thought, she could think of quite a few things to do— they just weren't serious things. She was not joining the family business, as had Belle and Lotta. She was not yet planning to get married. She was not going off to college. She was not settling down to anything. She was drifting.

Poor old Davenport—"Dear old D," as Cora always called it. Though prosperous, technologically advanced and even officially anointed as outstandingly wicked, it had totally lost its place in the vanguard of national mythmaking, along with much of the rest of the region we now know as the Midwest. For her parents' generation, it had been part of a thrilling open Western frontier that inspired tens of thousands of adventurers to drop their humdrum lives and go west to seek their fortunes. Davenport was now the kind of place that inclined a young woman like Cora to look for equal and opposite inspiration in the idea of setting out *eastward* in search of adventure and opportunity. Perhaps it was during a music lesson at the Braunlich house that Cora began to dream about a world beyond her comfortable life in her small city on the banks of the Mississippi. Professor Braunlich might have suggested the idea to Cora of studying piano at a conservatory in the East, such as the one at Vassar College.

But it was her mother's brilliant response to chronic wounding social insults that gave Cora her chance.

CHAPTER THREE

Vassar's Crisis and Cora's Humiliation

B y a strange coincidence, in 1884 Vassar College was drifting too.[1] "Drifting" actually understates the problem; in that year, Vassar was in the grip of a serious crisis. Poor management and declining enrollments were dragging the nation's premier educational institution for women closer and closer to the edge of bankruptcy; by the spring of 1884, the administration and trustees were afraid they would not be able to fill enough beds in the large Main Building to keep the college open past the fall semester. News coverage was intense, and after she arrived in Poughkeepsie, Cora clipped at least a dozen articles about the crisis, saving them in her scrapbooks. (Unfortunately, all of the clippings she saved were trimmed so closely that the exact dates and names of the newspapers are unknown.)

> Women are now admitted to 120 of the colleges in the United States, and that is the reason Vassar college has of late years suffered somewhat financially. It used to have almost a monopoly of the women students.

Most of these 120 colleges were single-sex, particularly on the East Coast, while others, including the new land-grant colleges in the Midwest and Cornell University in Ithaca, New York, were coeducational. The most aggressive competition was coming from new women's colleges, particularly Smith, in Northampton, Massachusetts, and Wellesley, outside Boston. Cora's own state of Iowa offered excellent college-level education for women at the University of Iowa in Iowa City, while the already-famous University of Michigan at Ann Arbor was also coed. (As if that weren't enough, many finishing schools for young ladies called themselves colleges but allowed for easier admittance, and offered less rigorous programs of studies.)

[35]

The Keck's mansion and infirmary at 611 Brady Street, in 1901.
Courtesy of St. John's Methodist Church, Davenport, Iowa.

In a panic, Vassar's president, the Reverend Samuel L. Caldwell, placed a blizzard of classified recruiting advertisements in sixty newspapers and magazines across the Northeast and Midwest in May and June 1884 to try to fill the many empty dormitory rooms in Vassar's Main Building and cover the bills for running the huge operation, which included its own steam heating and gas lighting system.[2] Founded in 1861 by the wealthy Poughkeepsie brewer Matthew Vassar, it was the first college in the country (and as far as I know, in the world) to provide a top-flight Ivy League education to academically gifted young women. By the 1880s, Vassar had evolved over the twenty years of its existence into an internationally famous brand concept known to newspaper readers as "the first great educational institution for womankind" and "the pioneer institution for the higher education of women." When Cora referred to "glorious Vassar" in her diary, she spoke from the bottom of her heart along with thousands, maybe even tens of thousands, of ambitious young women in cities, small towns, and rural backwaters across the United States.

Vassar inspired the creation of England's first college for women, Royal Holloway College, which opened its doors in 1886.[3] Thomas Holloway, the college's founder and main benefactor, was heavily influenced by a Vassar trustee, the Reverend William Hague, in the design of his new female educational institution. Mr. Holloway had made his fortune in the patent medicine business as the manufacturer of Holloway's Ointment and Holloway's Pills and was, of course, looking to overcome that barrier to his family's social advancement with his gift. I just can't seem to get away from the patent medicine angle in this story—it was a fundamental part of nineteenth-century life.

The public eye was always focused on Vassar. Its fame spawned a genre of insulting antiwoman humor in America's newspapers that imitated the popular jokes being made about naive and unattractive bluestocking Boston girls; any scandal connected to it was guaranteed to sell newspapers like hotcakes. On a more positive note, several best-selling series of books were written about life at Vassar to inspire the aspirations of young women readers, one called *Two College Girls*, by Helen Dawes (class of '78), and another *The Three Vassar Girls*, by Lizzie Champney (class of '69). These were similar to the popular books written for the general public about the mischievous doings of young men studying at Yale and Harvard.

Despite this prominent public reputation, by the fall of 1884 Vassar had reached a dangerous tipping point—it was almost not a college anymore, as defined by its own enrollment categories. Only 144 students were actually enrolled in the four-year academic program; the remaining 129 young women at the school were divided between the Preparatory Section (51), Painting (25), Music (32), and Special Courses (21). (The last category is hard to pin down exactly—it looks as if it were designed to give extra subject-matter expertise to older students who were interested in teaching.) Vassar was rapidly losing its identity as a female version of Yale or Harvard and was being swamped by nonacademic and underqualified paying customers, flirting with the dangerous possibility that it might be reduced to prepping students for Smith and Wellesley.

VASSAR ALREADY HAD ONE conspicuous alumna from Davenport. Mary Schuyler Lane went there after graduating from Davenport High School in 1880. A member of a distinguished original settler family, she was the daughter of one lawyer, James T. Lane, and the sister of another, Davenport's future U.S. district attorney Joe T. Lane. Mary (whose nickname was Mattie) was three years older than Cora and pursued a double major in Vassar's schools of music and art. She graduated from college in the first week of June 1884 and returned home to Davenport.

The entire town had read the reports of Mary's glorious graduation. According to the *Davenport Democrat*, Miss Lane was awarded her diploma with high honors, which can't be true—women who completed their studies in Vassar's schools of art and music were given only certificates, not diplomas, and no category of high honors is mentioned anywhere in the college catalog. On the basis of other clippings Cora saved, it would appear that all small-town newspapers in Iowa and Illinois arbitrarily awarded highest honors to every young lady who went off to college and was mentioned in their pages, whether she graduated or not. As a cultivated young lady of taste who moved in the city's top social circles, Mary Lane and her experience in Poughkeepsie would have been the subject of all kinds of talk, envy, and admiration. Mattie's Vassar credentials influenced her own friends, and even people who didn't socialize with her family. It looks as if she started a small fad in the early 1880s in Davenport, to Send Your Daughter to Vassar.

Later that June, it's not hard to imagine this scene: Cora might have been returning home down the Brady Street hill from some event at the First Methodist Church at Ninth Street, and she might have passed by a small group of young women she recognized from high school, standing on the sidewalk in front of Dr. Washington F. Peck's mansion with its mansard roof and fanciful tower at 723 Brady Street, one block uphill from the Keck Infirmary.[4] Mary Peck might have been standing there talking with her neighbor, Elizabeth Griggs, who lived at number 741, and Dr. Hazen's two daughters, Auzella and Laura, might have come up to join them from their father's office at the corner of Fourth Street, where one of them had a small art studio. Mattie Lane, just back from Vassar, stood in the middle, the center of attention. The informality of Cora's ninth-grade social groupings was now a thing of the past, and as young ladies of eighteen and nineteen, Mary Peck and Cora Keck were no longer yelling like wild Indians off the back porch of the high school together. In fact, they didn't do anything together anymore. Their social lives were rigidly separated.

Mattie didn't notice Cora's approach at first, because she was excited to have finally attracted the attention of Elizabeth Griggs. Elizabeth was surely the most self-possessed young person in Davenport, and she enjoyed her ability to intimidate people, even older girls who were already college graduates. Miss Griggs was also the smartest person in her high school class. Extremely attractive and just as chilly, she had selected a couple of friends from the crowd of classmates who aspired to that honor, on the basis of their academic prowess, elegance of clothing, and cool demeanor. The best, most eligible young men in town saw in her an irresistible challenge, since it was so incredibly hard to attract any kind of warm notice from her.

Elizabeth had very high standards in everything she did. Rather than risk being unprepared and failing Vassar's tough entrance exams, she was skipping her senior year at Davenport High School to go straight to Vassar in September as a preparatory student, and she and Mattie Lane were exchanging important information about what a girl needed to know about picking the right roommate at college. The other girls listened enviously.

As Cora approached, the entire group fell silent. The whispering began just before she passed out of earshot. All those girls had heard their parents dish the dirt about Mrs. Dr. Keck and her patent medicine business. Seeing that "appalling" woman's lively daughter walk past, they could not restrain their urgent need to review some well-known facts and innuendo, and add several new ones to the rotation, knowing full well that Cora was perfectly aware of the nature of their conversation.

Everything was out there in the newspapers for anyone to read. "Anyone" includes generations of historians and academics and even Mrs. Dr. Keck's great-great-granddaughter, who happened to start skimming through the digitized pages of the *Davenport Gazette*, the *Chicago Tribune*, and the *Peoria Journal* 125 years later on the Internet. With the confident tone of a legal insider, Mary Lane would have informed her friends that Cora's mother had been put on trial in circuit court in Peoria *four times* for practicing medicine without a license and once spent a night in jail in Paris, Illinois, when she couldn't make bail.[5]

The surgeon's daughter, Mary Peck, contributed the rumor going around the Scott County Medical Society that Mrs. Dr. Keck was still publishing a health cure testimonial letter in her ads from a dead man named Rudolphus Hoffmann who had succumbed to consumption four years ago.[6] On the sun porch at the Griggses' house at number 741, Elizabeth had overheard her parents suggest that their neighbor Mr. Keck, who looked like a Dunker with his strange, old-fashioned chin whiskers, was a failure as a man and as a husband because he let his wife earn all the money while he sat on his back porch playing the accordion.[7] Just before Cora disappeared from view, Auzella Hazen acquainted everyone with the tidbit that back in the '70s, Mrs. Keck had been arrested for selling liquor without a license because her Kidney Tonic had so much alcohol in it. "And she's a Methodist and a temperance lady too."[8] They giggled.

Most mothers in Davenport were not getting front-page news coverage of this type. Cora would have been hurt to the quick as talk about these incidents spread through the community and trickled down among her classmates at the high school. Knowing Cora, I am sure she handled confrontations such as this one without letting her tormentors see that her feelings had been hurt. Acting as if she had heard nothing, she would have turned through the low wrought-iron gate at number 611 and hurried up the steep flight of steps into the Keck mansion. Once inside, she leaned hard against the solid, beautifully carved front door, pushing it shut to lock all the nasty chatter out. Those girls used to be her friends when she lived in the little house on Perry Street, before her mother became so controversial, so successful, and so talked about.

She would have called to her papa. Perhaps they sat together at the dining room table while he tried to soothe her anger. He probably pointed out that getting into an open row would not accomplish much other than giving the girls more to gossip about. He was descended from generations of Mennonite pacifists, and this was how his parents and grandparents before them had always approached conflict. His gentle kindness made those girls' contempt for her father and her family hurt even more, making Cora feel slightly sick.

Shortly after this bruising encounter, Mrs. Dr. Keck returned from one of her regular visits to her branch office in Peoria. Members of the press publicly praised her "plucky and indomitable disposition." The *Bloomington Leader* went so far as to say that she was "the terror of all who attack her." Described in an editorial endorsement as "more than a match for her enemies," her immense authority and will stood unmoved, like a bulwark, against the combined attacks of all the regular medical authorities in four states. Although her mother undoubtedly had some comforting things to say to Cora about her hurt feelings, she would immediately have moved on to start shaping a forceful strategy of response.

Mrs. Dr. Keck always handled her thorny public relations problems by fighting back from a position of strength. Stung by the false gossip about the testimonial, she immediately contacted one of her oldest allies in town, Edwin W. Brady, a wealthy factory owner and publisher of the temperance paper the *Northwestern News*, to ask him to help her publicize the fact that Mr. Rudolphus Hoffmann was actually alive and well and working every day at his job in a stone quarry. (Brady's public endorsement actually ran several months before my imagined scene, on February 1, 1884.) It appeared on page two of the *Davenport Democrat* alongside a letter written by Mr. Hoffmann, of 134 West Second Street, who, in words that could have inspired a later witticism of Mark Twain's, declared, "There is a report in the city that I was dead and buried. This surprised me greatly."

Mrs. Dr. Keck began to quietly seethe with frustration because she did not immediately see a good way to help her daughter. She must have wrestled with twinges of guilt. She was keenly aware of the social liabilities that dogged her children, particularly the girls, because of the ostracism and stigma attached to her professional life.

The parlor at 611 Brady Street with portraits of John and Rebecca Keck displayed on easels against the back wall.

After Sunday dinner, most of the Kecks gathered in their main parlor, which was a cool, dark refuge in late June. It was the finest room in their fine house. The sixteen-foot ceiling was papered with intricate Islamic geometrical patterns copied from a ceiling in the Alhambra palace in Spain, and the walls were covered with William Morris–style flowered paper from England. The enormous windows were half shaded by folding shutters at the top, and delicate Madras lace panels overlapped below to let fresh air in and keep prying eyes out. Cora, still in a low mood, entertained her family by playing appropriate selections on the piano in the music room across the hall: Beethoven's *Pathétique* Sonata, followed by Chopin's Funeral March.

As energetic and capable as she was, Mrs. Dr. Keck still had not figured out what to do about Cora's humiliation outside the Peck house, and she loathed inaction. She tapped her foot impatiently while she read the paper. Done with her piano playing, Cora sat gloomily on her favorite piece of furniture in the center of the parlor: a three-way back-to-back spiral stool called a tête-à-tête, with dark velvet cushions and a fringe that trailed down to the boldly patterned Brussels carpet. It was perfect for flirting, since you could turn around and look over your shoulder and then quickly turn your back again in case you wanted to unnerve anyone sitting next to you. But Cora didn't feel like flirting with anyone right now. Her face burned with anger as she reviewed the cruel comments she had heard on the sidewalk. The heat made sweat trickle down her back into her undergarments in places where she could not scratch because of her stiff corset.

Matthew Vassar with fund-raising cashbox.
Courtesy of Vassar College Archives.

Turning the crinkling pages of the *Chicago Inter Ocean*, Mrs. Dr. Keck noticed one of the Vassar ads. She stopped tapping her foot. It read: "Vassar College, for the liberal education of women . . ."

Here was the answer.

The ad touted the creature comforts and modern conveniences of the college facilities (including an elevator and an on-campus telephone and telegraph office) and solicited applicants for every program the college offered, particularly the college preparatory classes and the two-year programs offered by the painting and music schools. Mrs. Dr. Keck began to smile for the first time in two days. In a brilliant stroke of the genius that characterized her business success, she framed a dramatic response to the cold-blooded small-town society snobbery that had hurt her daughter's feelings so badly. She would send her slightly wild, immensely talented, headstrong daughter to college. And not just any college. She would go to Vassar, where Mary Lane had gone.

GETTING CORA INTO VASSAR was supposed to be difficult. From its opening day in 1861, the academic program aimed for high standards equivalent to what would be expected of students at Yale and Harvard. Matthew Vassar wanted the college he founded to "accomplish for young women what our colleges are accomplishing for young men."[9] Vassar's gatekeepers meant to keep the finishing-school types out and to let in only serious, academically ambitious young women. So, in an era before SATs existed, Vassar administered its own tough entrance exams in English grammar and literature, Latin, Greek, German or French, rhetoric, the history of the United States, geography, arithmetic, algebra, and geometry. These tests were given at the college in June, before graduation, and for three grueling days in September, before the college opened for the fall. Because of deficiencies in the way young women were educated at the high school level in that era, these entrance exams created a substantial supply-side problem for the college.

To give more women a chance to gain entrance, Vassar allowed applicants who were at least fifteen years old and who could pass the basics (arithmetic, English grammar, geography, and U.S. history) to get up

VASSAR COLLEGE,

No. *37*   *Sept. 17,* 1884.

EXAMINATION CARD.

Miss *Corize Mae Keck,*

Residence, *Davenport, Ia.*

Age, *18*   Testimonials, *Satisfactory).*

I. Preliminary Examination.

STUDY.	MARK.	REMARKS.	EXAMINER.
Eng. Grammar..			
Arithmetic........			
Geography.........			
U. S. History....			

Certificate Supt. Schools,
Davenport, Ia.
Admitted
S. L. Caldwell, President.

*Cora Keck's Vassar
entrance application.
Courtesy of Vassar
College Archives.*

to speed in the other required subjects by enrolling at Vassar as "pre-paratory students," in effect making Vassar its own prep school.[10] This was the program that Elizabeth Griggs was about to enter—she had gone to Chicago in June to take entrance exams in those four subjects. Candidates with sufficient money and self-discipline could even hire recent Vassar graduates to tutor them until they could pass the entrance exams; the president kept a list of tutors' names in his office to hand out in response to inquiries.

Another roundabout route was to try for Vassar's schools of art and music. Applicants merely had to present testimonials of good character; "give evidence of sufficient natural talent for the art in which instruction was to be given"; pass the basic exams in English grammar, arithmetic, geography, and U.S. history; and pony up a minimum of $500 a year for tuition and room and board. The college catalog hints at the average technical level of most applicants to the School of Music: "Before entering upon the regular course of piano-forte training, the student should be able to perform the moderately difficult sonatas of Haydn and Mozart." Cora was far beyond that point already with her music, but she was below the stated minimum level in her academic qualifications.[11]

By chance, Mrs. Dr. Keck's inquiry to enroll Cora at Vassar came at just the right time. By the summer of 1884, with its budget shortfall swelling to crisis dimensions, Vassar loosened its requirements for the art and music schools even further. All you had to do was present a certificate from your high school saying you had already passed the required basic courses. At that moment, any applicant with a purse and a pulse received an eager response—even someone whose mother was in the patent medicine business. Sending Cora to Vassar College was not only possible, it was a slam dunk.

THE RESPONSE FROM POUGHKEEPSIE arrived in late August, delivered through the brass mail slot of the huge front door of 611 Brady Street and addressed to Mrs. Dr. Keck. The thin envelope was mixed in with a steep pile of letters on the rug from strangers pleading for assistance with their many health problems, but it carried the news everyone was waiting in breathless expectation to hear. Cora could go to Vassar.

Aug 20, 1884
Dear Madame,
    The certificate of your daughter's work has been received and will be of use when she presents herself at College for admission. It seems to be satisfactory.
    Settlements of the account with the Treasurer will be made after the admission, + it will be well for her to bring a check for the purpose.
    We shall be glad to see her + promote her happiness in any way we can.
Very Truly Yours,
S. L. Caldwell

The personal acceptance letter was handwritten by the president of the college. The Reverend Caldwell's tone was welcoming, but quickly got to the point: "Don't forget to send your check."

What certificate had been sent to Poughkeepsie? Incredibly, Cora's college application form has survived (on microfilm) to the present day. Vassar's college historian, Elizabeth Daniels, rescued several cartons containing early student application packets from a Vassar basement in the 1980s, and the microfilm of these documents provides a fabulously detailed look at the inner workings of Vassar's admissions department one hundred years earlier.

Although Cora is not on record as having graduated from Davenport High School, in mid-August, the superintendent of schools for Davenport, Mr. J. B. Young, filled out a Certificate of Examination for Admission to Vassar College on behalf of Miss Cora M. Keck showing that Cora had performed satisfactory work in the four required courses. This certificate was far below what the college required for a girl to be admitted as a freshman to Vassar's academic program, but it was sufficient to get her into the School of Music. Mr. Young also attached a very standard-sounding letter of recommendation noting that she was "an industrious, capable young lady and I feel sure you will have no occasion to regret any favor you may show her or any confidence you may place in her."

On the heels of President Caldwell's letter, Professor Priscilla Braislin sent a separate message to Cora outlining when she should plan to arrive at college, how her room assignment would be made, and how she should go about setting up her academic schedule. The news was delivered less than a month before the college year began. Cora was expected in Poughkeepsie on Wednesday, September 17, and she had to prepare and pack enough clothing for ten months away from home. She had to arrange her train trip, and relatives all along the route had to be alerted that she was coming.

Hattie Wakefield decided to throw a big party for Cora at her house in Bloomington as a farewell send-off. She invited thirty guests who danced to live music until very late at the Wakefields' mansion at 301 East Grove Street, and the Bloomington newspaper reported that Cora impressed everyone with some magnificent piano playing, most likely including the Liszt piece she had been working on since March: "Miss Keck is a very fine pianist, and she delighted the guests by rendering several difficult selections in a very artistic manner."

Back home in Davenport, as the moment of final departure approached, bedlam broke out in the Keck household. Just when some system was beginning to emerge from the chaos, Lotta blew in from some business she was attending to in Peoria with the remark, "Now let's get things organized around here." Reigning over all was Mrs. Dr. Keck. The doctor had hurried back to Davenport from a circuit visit in Quincy, Illinois, correctly anticipating that in case of Vassar's acceptance, she would have to give Cora's departure her full attention if her fairly disorganized daughter were to get to Poughkeepsie on time. Cora's golden brown embossed leather Saratoga trunk was carried upstairs and put down in the middle of her bedroom, where it sat with its lid flung back and the top tray set askew, waiting to be filled with linens, dresses, hats, gloves, shoes, corsets, and maybe even an extra bustle, collapsed flat for storage. As an experienced train traveler who had visited Bloomington, Peoria, and Chicago on her own during the previous year, Cora already knew what she would want to pack and how to get her clothes to fit into her luggage. At the bottom of the trunk, where the pages would not be damaged, she carefully placed the sheet music that Professor Braunlich had assigned to her, including La Charité and Beethoven's *Pathétique* and Moonlight sonatas. Cora had a blank scrapbook with three owls on the cover, and she put that in too; maybe Hattie Wakefield or another close friend had given it to her.

I CAN IMAGINE the dramatic scene of Cora's departure a few weeks after President Caldwell's letter had arrived. She could be gone for several years if she didn't return for summer vacation. The family group clustered around her on the platform of the Perry Street Depot, and emotions ran high. Belle gave her handkerchief to Maggie, who was crying, then handed Cora her basket of food for the journey, since the dining car was too expensive, and furthermore, a young lady traveling by herself would not have felt comfortable dining alone. Willie hung back from the action, looking lost, while Lotta made sure that Cora's trunk and other baggage were loaded on board; she would ride with her as far as Chicago. Mrs. Dr. Keck touched her tallest daughter on the shoulder, smiled at her, and reminded Cora to work hard and be careful with her money at college. Cora hugged her father, who was even taller than she, and as he folded her into his lanky arms, he patted the back of her head carefully so as not to dislodge her hat.

The train came into the station in a cloud of smoke, steam, and flying cinders. Everyone watched Cora and Lotta disappear up the steps into the carriage. Flora forlornly waved goodbye as the coaches jerked one after the other and began to move, and worried about how she had so few other friends with which to fill her time now that her lively younger sister was going away. With her heart pounding in her chest, Cora pressed her face to the glass to watch her beloved family rapidly vanish into the curve of the tracks behind.

Her melancholy evaporated quickly. As the train crossed the Mississippi and slowly rounded another bend in the tracks beneath the six-story clock tower of the Rock Island Arsenal, Cora leaned back into her seat and closed her eyes, smiling like a crazy person and pointing her toes, poking them into the side of the carpet bag jammed under the seat in front. She was on her way to New York.

CHAPTER FOUR

Memorable Date of Entrance

*Miss Corize Keck, who has been visiting in the east the past
month, entered Vassar college the 17th. Miss Keck, who is quite
a musician, intends finishing her musical education at Vassar.*

—FROM THE *Davenport Gazette*

Although Cora did not yet have her diary and didn't record the
details of her arrival at college, she glued the engraving of Vassar's Main Building into her scrapbook, and the few words she wrote
underneath convey everything about how she felt: "Wednesday, September 17, 1884. Memorable Date of Entrance."

The experience of arriving at Vassar for the first time invariably had
a great impact on young women of the era. In a description of her
own first arrival, Lizzie Champney, the author of the *Three Vassar Girls*
books and a graduate of the class of '69, captured the sense of unreal
opportunity that quickened women's souls—they could hardly believe
that an experience such as Vassar actually existed and they would be
part of it:

> Tired by my long journey, I drove out from Poughkeepsie between
> green hedge-rows to the opening of the college at dusk on a Septem-
> ber evening. Built in the French style of Mansard, the Main Build-
> ing's façade recalls vividly the Tuilleries palace . . . silhouetted against
> the reflected afterglow of the sunset, the mass loomed mysteriously
> through the dim twilight and a procession of lights twinkling down
> the long corridors gave it all the appearance of some scene of enchant-
> ment, which might vanish at the wave of the conjurer's wand.[1]

Leaving Poughkeepsie's train station in the college horse car, Cora
followed the same route out of town on Raymond Avenue that Lizzie

Vassar College, Main Building entrance, circa 1880.
Courtesy of Vassar College Archives.

Champney had taken. An elaborate two-story gatehouse appeared in the middle of the farm fields, and the horse car pulled up in front of the arched entryway of the Lodge, which faced a small lake circled by willows. Cora entered the gravel drive through the Lodge archway and stared up in awe at the huge, dark redbrick edifice of Vassar's Main Building before crossing the college lawn to climb the double-sided grand staircase to the main floor.

A loud hubbub of voices filled the hallway. The decor in the public parlors immediately struck her as far plainer than she had imagined; the windows had no draperies, and the inadequate number of mismatched pieces of furniture in the public reception rooms were carefully arranged in small groups in an obvious attempt to fill up the large empty rooms.[2] There were no palms or plants, and one of the settees was just a piece of rattan porch furniture. They had put in a nice flowered carpet, though. She felt very nervous for a moment, then collected her feelings, squared her shoulders, and moved forward to join the crowd. As a new student, she had many administrative details to take care of.

She presented her mother's check for $500 at the treasurer's office, which had a huge iron safe in it taller than a man. Mrs. Dr. Keck's check covered Vassar's regular tuition of $400 per year plus the $100 fee for music study. Beyond this, she had to pay for many extras, for weekend spending money, for transportation, and for clothing appropriate for Cora's activities; I estimate that she spent close to $800 each year to send her daughter to Vassar, equivalent to about $80,000 in modern money. It was the most expensive college in the country at the time.

Paid up, Cora received a certificate to show that all her bills were taken care of. She mounted the stairs to the third story and waited to meet with Vassar's president, the Reverend Caldwell, chatting excitedly with other young women in line for the same purpose. The college president was a handsome older man with gray mutton-chop whiskers and a natural gift for interacting with young people, and he made an effort to help each new student feel comfortable as he examined and approved each academic schedule.

For the fall semester, she would take private piano lessons with Miss Jessie Chapin at the seventh period on Tuesdays and Fridays in room 5 in the music hall. At her mother's request, Cora was placed in freshman-level German class, taught by Miss Minna Hinkel, from 9:15 to 9:55 A.M., in room 11. She also took harmony (part of the wider music theory curriculum), embracing various forms of composition and instrumentation, taught by the director of the School of Music, Professor Frederick Louis Ritter, at the sixth period on Mondays and Thursdays. Finally, she arranged a schedule for her regular piano practice times.

On the other side of the main stairwell immediately to the right of the library, was the Lady Principal's office. Cora was directed to wait in line there to see Miss Abby Goodsell, the college administrator who would assign her roommates. This was just one of Miss Goodsell's thousands of responsibilities, which involved running almost every detail of all Vassar's students' lives, with the assistance of another, younger Vassar graduate, Alice W. Harlow. Miss Goodsell's office was surprisingly small, although her private apartment and parlor were second in size only to those of the college president, and her little desk seemed hardly big enough to manage a nursery school, let alone a college population of 275 students. The preparatory students gave her the most headaches; they were often as young as fifteen and were in need of constant supervision compared with the older students enrolled in the four-year college program, usually serious scholars who were much more focused on their academic goals. She must have kept a lot of things in her head, and she was known for never neglecting a single detail.

"Miss Keck, I should like to speak to you a moment," Miss Goodsell said, coming out to summon the next girl in line. Inside the office, she handed Cora a

Miss Abby Goodsell seated at her desk. She left a position at Wilson College in 1881 to serve as Vassar's Lady Principal for ten years, retiring in 1891. Courtesy of Vassar College Archives.

copy of the Students' Manual, which explained the sequences of bells that signaled the daily class schedule and laid out the rules for behavior at college. Miss Goodsell tended to be brief and efficient, even relentless in striving to carry out every detail of Vassar's rules and regulations correctly, but she was always courteous. (Vassar's Special Collections has preserved a folder of mementos of Miss Goodsell, including fifty actual phrases students remembered her as having said, preserved in a booklet auctioned off by the senior class in 1886 called "Chips from Life." Quotations from Miss Goodsell are from this booklet.) Cora saved two copies of the dark green rule booklet, remarking dryly in a pencil notation next to one of them, "Something to consult daily."

CO

CORA'S FIRST ROOMMATES were Marian Austin and Eveline Wood-mansee, and her calling card from the fall indicates that parlor 54 was "My first parlor," located two doors down the hall from the Lady Principal's office. Eveline was starting at Vassar on the lowest rung of the ladder, as a Prep Level III student (equivalent to being a sophomore in high school), while Marian was enrolling as a Prep Level I (equivalent to a high school senior), because she needed only a year more of preparation before she could take Vassar's entrance exams and be admitted as a freshman. Cora was, of course, enrolled as a first-year student in the School of Music.

Entrance examinations for the incoming freshman class were going on downstairs in the classrooms on the ground floor, and the three girls could feel tension and anxiety thick in the air as they arranged the few belongings they had with them. Their trunks were coming later, and for the moment, they had very little to do. Cora opened the window in their suite parlor to let the September breeze blow in to lighten the atmosphere, and the distant sound of whistles from trains and steamboats two miles away on the Hudson River naturally led to the topic of traveling to Vassar. Cora's nine-hundred-mile solo trip from Iowa had been long and adventurous, but Marian's six-thousand-mile odyssey from her home in Honolulu was even more exhausting. I doubt that Eveline had ever been farther than fifty miles away from her home in Morrisania, an elegant new suburban housing development recently sprouted from the rich farmland in the Bronx, near New York City. She was the daughter of a wealthy shoe manufacturer, Luman S. Woodmansee, and like Cora, she was the middle child in a large brood of siblings. Her family's house had extensive grounds kept in shape by an elderly gardener, and many of her neighbors were nouveau riche families with foreign-born parents from Ireland, England, or Germany enjoying their first taste of the material abundance of the American dream.

Cora described her train trip through Chicago, across Ohio to Pittsburgh, then across the entire length of Pennsylvania until she reached Philadelphia, where she was excited to meet her first cousin, Warren

Kleckner, a shy young man whom she had immediately developed a big crush on.[3] Cora's cousin was twenty-one and still living with his parents. He had been born in the California goldfields, where his father and uncle had earned a small fortune running a bank for miners in a town named Port Wine. The Kleckners had lost most of their money in the Panic of 1873 and were forced to return east to start over again in another trade.

Leaving all traces of his boyhood in the mining camps of the Sierra Nevada far behind, Warren had become a city boy and wore pince-nez glasses perched on the bridge of his nose. He worked diligently at his entry-level job at the Central National Bank in downtown Philadelphia, but he worked hard only because he was intelligent, naturally efficient, and precise, not because he liked the job. In retrospect, it's easy to see that he had no intention of living out his life as a docile cubicle clerk in a bank (photographs from the era show that U.S. managers started using office cubicles shortly after the end of the Civil War). According to my grandfather, who knew Warren well, he carried himself erect, and always walked briskly, as you might expect from a young man with ambitious plans on his mind.

Cora reported to her roommates that she began to flirt with him mercilessly. He was a cool customer,

Warren Kleckner at about age seventeen.

though, and so far from sentimental that you could say his judgments sometimes verged on explosive contempt. The more solemn and perplexed he became, the more affection she lavished on him, making silly jokes about "spooney guys" and leaving one of her gloves behind at his house. I mention Warren in particular, because, in spite of this teasing, or maybe because of it, Warren and Cora remained close friends all their lives. Based on Cora's comments and observations, it is clear that Warren had no interest in girls per se, and never would in the future, either. However, he seems to have appreciated the fact that his cousin, who acted so silly, also had backbone and spirit; she left home to go to Vassar and might even be the kind of person who could make something remarkable out of herself, which was one of the few points he cared about in other people. Warren was also a music lover who knew real talent when he saw it. Like my grandfather, Warren had no patience for people he considered fools, a category that for him included a large fraction of the population.

In New Jersey, at the end of the western line, Cora disembarked with her Saratoga trunk in tow, and took the ferry across New York Harbor to Manhattan, where she changed to the Hudson River Line at the old Grand Central Station. Passing through the city so quickly gave her a tantalizing taste and the desire to visit again as soon as possible; but within an hour or two, she was back out in the countryside, traveling north along the eastern shore of the Hudson River past huge estates and bucolic farmland in Westchester County, her view punctuated by the grim shape of Sing Sing prison stepping down to the water's edge on the Tappan Zee in Ossining, and the dramatic scenery of the Hudson Highlands, where Bear Mountain, West Point, and Storm King loom above the narrowed river like the sides of a fjord and the rail line squeezes past their feet at the bottom of steep cliffs.

For many students coming from the far West and Midwest, it was typical to arrive unchaperoned, as Cora had, but Marian had traveled such a distance that she came to college accompanied by her mother. It took six days for them to cross the Pacific to San Francisco by steamboat and then four more days to cross the continent by train. Marian's route led right through Davenport. "Did you see me waving at you?" Cora joked. The August heat was stifling on board the un–air-conditioned trains, but when passengers opened the windows for relief, clouds of smoke and cinders came in with the breeze; train travelers always arrived at their destinations caked with dirt.

In researching this book, I was surprised to discover how self-sufficient these young women from the former frontier regions were as travelers and incoming freshmen college students. I imagined that Vassar would be populated with helpless Victorian maidens guarded by ferocious chaperones, but that concept turns out to be mostly incorrect for typical

American young women in the Gilded Age. Cora traveled alone for nine hundred miles and established her life at college entirely by herself. In 1892 a Vassar student from Michigan named Harriet Wood advised a friend coming as a freshman the following year not to bring her mother along for the start of school because her mother would just get in the way.[4]

There were some exceptions; the Southern girls Mary and Louisa Poppenheim, who enrolled at Vassar in September of 1882 and 1884, respectively, came from an extremely protective and conservative family in South Carolina and had much less freedom than Cora.[5] The sisters always traveled back and forth to college from Charleston accompanied by their father or another relative, because they were afraid that if they were seen traveling alone, someone outside of their social set would look down on them for losing tone. Needing a chaperone at all times was the ultimate signal of privilege and social status. Even so, none of the four Poppenheim sisters (who all graduated from Vassar) could be described as helpless, simpering maidens—they were ambitious academic overachievers who rose to the top of Vassar's campus hierarchy and commanded the respect of the entire Vassar community.

Restless and keyed up, Cora and her roommates might have decided to take a walk around the outside of the Main Building to explore their surroundings. A hundred yards beyond the south end, they admired the Calisthenium, the ornate brick edifice where the School of Music and the Art Gallery were located. They strolled past the nationally famous observatory where advanced students studied astronomy with the famous Professor Maria (pronounced Mur-EYE-uh) Mitchell and continued onward to check out the tennis courts set up in the Athletic Circle at the north end of the building, ringed by large yew bushes. Cora and Marian were both dying to learn to play. Always the sophisticated city girl, Eveline Woodmansee would have known all about this fad that had recently taken the fashionable socialites at Newport by storm. She had learned to play with her brothers over the summer in her family's backyard and could show them how. The college provided all the necessary items through the new tennis club, although players often carelessly left the wooden rackets and balls out overnight in the rain.

At 5:15 P.M. the three roommates went down for their first dinner at college. As they descended the central staircase at the center of the Main

Building, they heard a commotion. Several weeping girls who had failed their entrance exams were leaving the campus. The main doors swung shut after their departure and there was silence. They slowed down and looked at each other for a moment before proceeding into the dining room. The realization started to sink in that Vassar was a place where you had to make your mark or leave. It was a sobering thought.

ON ONE OF MY EARLIEST TRIPS to the Vassar Library Special Collections, I scanned down the list of students who had entered college at the same time as Cora and was startled to find that a second girl from Davenport, Iowa, was also matriculating at Vassar in September 1884. That was when I discovered Cora's coldly remote relationship with her Brady Street neighbor Elizabeth Griggs. Hers was only a single name on a list, but its presence spoke volumes. Unfortunately for me, Elizabeth Griggs left no descendants, and no photographs of her have survived. I dug up a few details about her life with great difficulty because she exists in Cora's story only in a reflected way—I can detect her presence only through her absolute absence.

On the surface, the girls had a lot in common. Elizabeth lived in another mansion on Brady Street one block uphill from the Keck infirmary. She was one year younger than Cora, and the two girls had gone through the same schools growing up. Like Cora, Elizabeth didn't graduate from Davenport High School, but unlike Cora, she was a very good student. Elizabeth entered Vassar in the same preparatory class as Cora's roommate and close friend Marian Austin. There were only six girls in the Prep Level I class; nevertheless, Cora does not mention Elizabeth Griggs anywhere in her Vassar diary or in her scrapbooks.

Elizabeth was the only daughter of Francis H. Griggs, the busy, brilliant, and socially reserved president of the Citizens National Bank of Davenport and his wife, Candace. According to his biography in a Scott County history published in 1895, Elizabeth's father came from a distinguished Boston Brahmin family in Brookline, Massachusetts, and graduated from Harvard in 1854. He went west soon afterward and made a fortune in commerce and banking in Iowa, being "a man of indefatigable industry."[6] He was a freethinker who did not attend any church, nor did he set aside time to join any civic groups or involve himself with social and cultural pursuits. Famously brilliant and cool, even cold, under pressure, he singlehandedly put the entire Minneapolis & St. Louis Railroad out of business in 1892 during the nation's largest receivership (bankruptcy) case using just $30,000 worth of bonds and coupons, by demanding that several mortgages be closed at once and that the road be sold to the highest bidder to satisfy his debt.

As far as I know, most of the Ilginfritzes and Kecks and their numerous cousins never finished elementary school, let alone went to Harvard. Mrs. Dr. Keck's patent medicine business flourished like a patch of vigorous and unsightly weeds outside the pale of Davenport's respectable medical establishment. Unlike a proper doctor, who relied on word of mouth and discreet professional referrals to build a practice, Mrs. Dr. Keck was not ashamed to run flamboyant ads that claimed miraculous cures on the front page of the *Davenport Gazette* several times a month. No one seemed to be able to stop her. In 1881, when the Scott County Medical Society finally succeeded in ousting her from the *Davenport Business Directory* physicians' listings, she promptly emblazoned the entire back cover of the next year's issue with a gaudy ad for her infirmary.

Rebecca Keck undoubtedly enjoyed the satisfaction of sending her daughter off to the same school as the daughter of these people who were not interested in socializing with her family. Better than that, if her daughter was successful in her piano studies and made many friends there, the snobbery that dogged her in Iowa might fall away in Poughkeepsie. What more could a mother ask?

CHAPTER FIVE

The Green Girls

If it weren't for beer, we wouldn't be here!
—GRAFFITI ADDED TO A POSTER ANNOUNCING
A TEMPERANCE MEETING AT VASSAR

Vassar's Main Building was designed by the famous American high-society architect James Renwick in 1861 and has been the subject of intense analysis ever since, as much for its quirks and problems as for its grandeur.[1] In 1884, all Vassar's students still lived in this one building. So did the faculty, including the men (all married with families) in private apartments and the women (all single) in rooms next to those of the students. For twenty-five years, the building shaped the life inside its walls almost as forcefully as the ideals of the founders and of the people still teaching and studying there.

The college was self-contained, like a spaceship or an ark. A large ell housing the two-story chapel on the second and third floors and the dining hall on the first floor projected out the back. The college fed approximately 350 people three times a day, seven days a week from kitchens and storerooms in the ground-level basement. The nine wide hallways in the Main Building also served as a promenade when bad weather prevented the students from walking outdoors; each was two hundred feet long. Following completion of construction in the fall of 1865, it was said to be the largest building in the United States. Thirty or forty servants employed by the college lived in attic rooms clustered at the top of the two front towers and in the basement near the kitchen, and they provided cooking, cleaning, and laundry service to all the building's residents. A gas plant supplied lighting and a steam boiler heat. Matthew Vassar's main goal had been to make the building he was paying for "magnificent." The rest had to follow that consideration. I could accuse him of vanity, but being a worldly man, he also

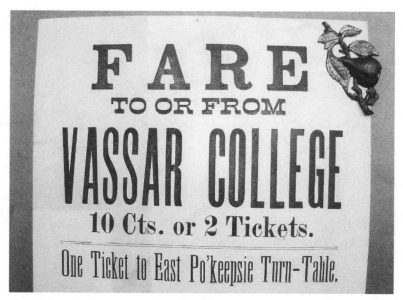

Page from Cora's scrapbook.

understood a fundamental political principle: if the college wanted to become an important institution, it had to assert its place in society by occupying an important building.

To Lizzie Champney, Vassar's Main Building looked like a palace, glowing with magical lights in the middle of a big field outside of the town of Poughkeepsie. For some, the massive community embodied the idealism of early-nineteenth-century utopian visionaries such as Robert Owen, who hoped that living arrangements in self-contained, arklike buildings such as those he proposed for New Harmony, Indiana, might miraculously solve many social problems. To some modern eyes, the original concept of Vassar's Main Building leans a little too closely for comfort toward the standard Victorian approach for planning an insane asylum, designed expressly for restricting people's freedom by keeping female students in and intruders out. Later in our story we'll see how effective that plan was in practice.

Cora never complained very much about the building or her living arrangements, except as regards her laundry. In the first week of October, Cora was charged for extra washing she sent to the laundry. On

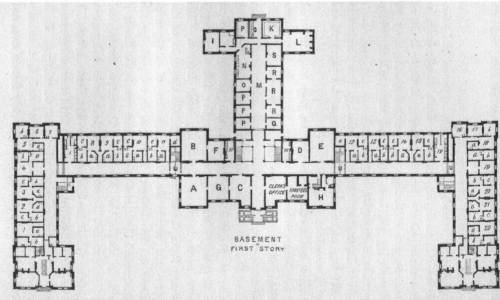

*Vassar College Main Building with floor plan showing dormitory rooms in the
basement level, where Cora lived during most of her two years at college.*

the same page of her scrapbook, next to the envelope with the bill for this overcharge, we find a note she sent to Miss Goodwin, the laundry lady, marked "strictly *private*. Miss Keck did not receive a pair of drawers she sent to the laundry Thursday." Four more laundry overcharge notes were glued to this page alone. This issue became a running joke for her—she saved scores of these notices throughout all three of her scrapbooks.

The sleeping arrangements had their own profound influence over Vassar's all-female culture. Each suite included three small bedrooms arranged around a small parlor, and each was originally intended to house five students. When enrollment was high in the early 1870s, this required many students to share the tiny rooms, which meant they had to share a bed, since two pieces of furniture could not fit into the narrow space. Fortunately for Cora, by 1884, with enrollment way down, President Caldwell had unwittingly ensured that most students got their own private bedrooms. The parlors are all closed off from the corridors, and this gave the girls a great deal of privacy out of sight of the hall teachers and Lady Principal, a freedom certainly unintended by the college's founders.

I made my first visit to Vassar in 2008 already so well acquainted with the details of its layout in 1884 that I was absurdly shocked to see the many changes that had taken place on campus since then. I felt like a time traveler. The gatehouse, a greatly loved structure, had nevertheless been torn down to make way for a palatial Gothic-style library. The bucolic dirt carriageway of Raymond Avenue has been upgraded into a multilane city street with high curbs and a busy traffic circle, and two dozen other buildings, including dormitories, a chapel, classroom buildings, athletic facilities, and science buildings, now overshadow the old Main Building, which looks much smaller than I had imagined it. The upper floors of the Main Building are still used as a dormitory, although some renovations have changed the public and office spaces, and a modern cafeteria and student center have replaced the old ell in back.

"The freshman enters Vassar in great fear and trembling," wrote one Vassar alumna for a New York newspaper article that Cora saved in her scrapbook. "The green [inexperienced] girl has to learn the corridors and class-rooms, and there are many, many of both." Even so, the open courtesy extended to all new students was remarkable. Several alumnae of the time remarked in print on how democratic Vassar's social life seemed to them when compared with life out in the real world. For instance, etiquette required all the upper-class students to visit all the newcomers. Older girls in the college went out during the early days of the term, card case in hand, to call on each of the freshmen on their corridors and introduce themselves. After this, calls and visits were more informal, and parties were given.

This structured approach to making newcomers feel welcome folded Cora into college life right away. Her talent as a pianist had already put her in demand. A week and a half after her arrival, she received an invitation from May Livezay, a new student in Prep Level III, to play piano on the evening of September 26 for an "Exoteric" performance; "they are to have a vocal piece and would like to have an instrumental one from you," May wrote. Exoteric was an extracurricular group for the preparatory students that put on informal entertainments about twice a month. On Sunday, October 12, someone named "M" sent Cora a note written in a messy scrawl on torn paper: "a model note—eh?" asking her to "Come down to the Lake." It was probably from Marian Austin, her roommate. At Vassar, Cora was no longer the quack's daughter. She was Corize Keck, the girl who could play the piano so well.

THE MAIL WAS DELIVERED to Vassar students twice a day during the week, in the early morning and at noontime, and Cora and her family and friends wrote to each other frequently. Cora's close ties to this network of far-flung relationships were a strong part of her emotional support structure. She often refers to members of her family as "My beloved ones." None of these letters that were delivered to Cora at Vassar has been saved, except when she glued a few into her scrapbooks. I often wonder who decided to throw them out. Did Cora toss them right away? Did she save them as carefully as her scrapbooks, only for them to be discarded later by an executor or my grandfather? Either way, it is a tremendous loss. I no longer have the voice of Cora's mother or her other family members, so I have had to fall back on my imagination to flesh these people out instead.

Cora noted in her diary details about the frequency of this correspondence, so at least I know how close she was to various members of her family. Her mother dominated, of course, sending her telegrams with instructions on what she was to do and short news bulletins (this was when telegrams were an expensive form of communication usually reserved for urgent matters), weekly letters, and frequent fancy boxes filled with food or gifts, as was the case at Christmas and Easter, and on Cora's birthday on May 3. Besides her mother, Cora wrote most frequently to her sisters Lotta and Maggie and often to her little brother Willie, who thoughtfully sent her birthday cards, and to Lotta's husband Dr. Gay Dorn, M.D., whom she nicknamed "Doctor." She regularly corresponded with her Davenport piano teachers, Professor Braunlich and Mrs. Smith. She seldom wrote to her sister Flora, and never to her bossy oldest sister, Belle. Cora was always eager to open gift boxes from Belle—they contained items from the most expensive stores in Chicago, in the best taste—but Belle was extremely critical of her musical talents, and Cora had little use for Belle's husband, William H. F. Alexander. Curiously, Cora never corresponded with her father, either, and he is always mentioned in her diary as a component of the parental team, as in "Mama + Papa believe . . ." or "Mama + Papa expect . . ."

Money was also sent by mail; Cora's mother would send her as much as $35 every month at college, and at the end of the year she sent her $65 in two separate letters (the equivalent of almost $1,000 in today's money). "Mama thinks I do not keep up to the standard for frugality. she thinks I am not frugal enough. better call me a spend schrift + be done with it," Cora wrote. She was extremely sensitive to her mother's criticism of her spending habits and felt ashamed to be called a spendthrift. The Pennsylvania Dutch were often caricatured in the nineteenth century for being tight with money, and true to this stereotype, the Kecks attempted to set strict limits for their daughter's spending while she was at college. Wealthy as she was, Mrs. Dr. Keck's fortune was only a fraction of the nearly infinite assets controlled by the famous plutocrats who dominated the Gilded Age economy of the United States in New York, Pittsburgh, Chicago, and other major cities. Scanning through the senior portraits of Cora's classmates in the Vassar archives, I soon learned to spot the differences between wealthy girls' really elegant and well-made clothes and Cora's simpler and sometimes ill-fitting dresses, clearly highlighting the gaping difference between "small-town rich" and "real" money. Cora would have seen the contrast too, and shortly after her arrival, she set about trying to get her mother to pay for new dresses that would not look so out of place in the sophisticated Eastern atmosphere.

AT VASSAR, CORA'S GLAMORIZED NAME of Corize was often shortened to Co or Coz. Most of her friends and siblings also used several versions of their names. One day early in the semester, Cora brought out her blank scrapbook with three owls on the cover. On the first page, her new friends at Vassar all made sealing wax impressions and signed their names—Dunning, Corbutt, Rogers, Austin, L. Harris, Donohue, G. Perine, J. Edwards, and Clark. Next to this colorful lineup of red, blue, gold, and green blobs, an extra, bright red wax impression bears the seal of the "Central National Bank, Phila." Cora probably nicked a company stamp from her cousin Warren during her visit in September and then sheepishly had to mail it back to him when he protested.

She also seems to have left something of her own at his house, most likely the glove I mentioned in the last chapter. Later in October, Warren sent an urgent telegram to Cora at college: "If article is missed, tell her to write me immediately." On another page, Cora saved this cryptic note: "Send article immediately, don't disappoint me. C.M. Keck Spooney, Spooner." According to my 1859 edition of *Webster's American Dictionary*, the first meaning of "spooney" is to be silly, foolish, or unduly sentimental. It can also mean being sentimentally in love.

Vassar College gatehouse (the Lodge) and horse car to Poughkeepsie.
Courtesy of Vassar College Archives.

Warren must have stiffened up immediately upon receiving this note. She really gave him a hard time.

Cora put a lot of interesting objects into her scrapbook besides traditional paper items. One of her roommates had luxuriant long hair, and Cora stole a hairpin from her. A slightly cracked nut got taped to page 17 labeled as "C.O.D. Specimen of Vassar Chest-nuts." Cora glued a match into the book on page 3, remarking, "a last match. One of few things bestowed by the college—go to grocery for the rest." These matches were needed to light the gas lamps at night.

For "the rest," she went into Poughkeepsie with gangs of new friends. Most students rode on the college horse car that went into and back from town on a regular schedule, but the distance was short enough that girls sometimes walked if the weather was nice. All Vassar students were allowed to sign out and go to Poughkeepsie on Saturdays, and on that first errand they would also have paid their first visit to Smiths Confectionery, an ice cream store, restaurant, and luxury caterer.

These beloved ritual visits to Smiths recur throughout Cora's diary, and in the papers of almost every Vassar student of that era, almost every weekend. Next to one of their advertising cards Cora wrote, "The favorite retreat of the city of Po'K." Smiths was an unofficial Vassar institution. (The Smith brothers later achieved national prominence with their famous cherry-flavored cough drops, which were popular as candies during my childhood.) The students also shopped at a Japanese imports store called Farringtons for colorful napkins, fans, and other exotic Asian goods. Van Kleeck's dry goods offered beautiful, gaily decorated advertising cards.

Best of all, Poughkeepsie offered the same unfettered opportunities for meeting boys and wild behavior that Cora had enjoyed back home while roller-skating in Rock Island on Leap Year Day. Her scrapbook features this fatuous news item from the *New York World* about the new roller-skating rink and its effects on Vassar College:

"THE RUINOUS RINK" FEB 15

The deadly Skating Rink has eaten its corroding way into Vassar College . . .

They will skate.

The Faculty are powerless against the new enemy. The sound of the gliding wheels is heard in the corridors at night. The class in transcendental philosophy carry the deadly instruments in their reticules [bookbags] side by side with Kant and Schlegel. The staidest damsels have been caught buckling on the winged boot while on their way to the village.

Mashing in a collective way now threatens to become general where flirting hitherto has been unknown. The school whose members could not be lured outside of the college grounds except on Commencement day at West Point now insists upon going down to the village every night.

In this dilemma, the Faculty appealed to the parents, and it is said that the deadly influence of the roller-skate has so demoralized the American home that the mothers wrote back: "Let the girls slide; <u>we</u>

all skate too." [Cora added in ink: "latest"] At this, the solemn professors have thrown up their hands and there is serious thought of converting the Vassar Art Gallery itself into a Rink to keep the girls indoors.

So, of course, on another Saturday that fall, Cora and several friends immediately went downtown to try it out. On the way, she collected four Van Kleeck cards, "Presented by that 'cheeky' clerk who wanted to go to the rink too, so sorry he couldn't."

CHAPTER SIX

Mugwumps and Oysters

I really got serious about turning my research into a book in the fall of 2009. By chance, the calendar for that year exactly matches the calendar days of the week for 1885, and this coincidence became a source of inspiration for me; it put me on Cora's schedule. Each morning before sitting down to write, I would take my dog for his walk in a park near my house that overlooks the Hudson River and, undisturbed by phone calls and obligations, ponder what Cora might have been feeling or seeing on that same day 124 years before. (Of course her scrapbooks started in the fall of 1884 when she entered college, before she got the diary, so not all the dates in this story exactly matched my own writer's time.)

One crisp October day, I saw a small flock of late birds make a brave charge together out of a treetop in a swoop of dark silhouettes—or maybe they were just leaves blown high in circles against the cloudless blue sky. Cora might have paused to watch exactly the same beautiful sight as she was coming back to college from the cider mill on a Sunday. She was walking alone on October 19, 1884, through the deep ravine that cuts behind Vassar's Main Building below Sunset Hill. All Vassar students were required to take an hour of outdoor exercise every day. Cora often walked with her friends, and these regular outings were a source of great pleasure to her, for the conversation as much as for the fresh air and exercise. On this particular outing, sad nostalgia replaced her usual high spirits, and Cora preferred to walk by herself, alone with her thoughts, which she recorded in her scrapbook: "My pleasant walk of 40 minutes. Leaves from my favorite walk, the glen Oct 19, '84. Nothing but leaves on a Sunday in Autumn—nothing but leaves—nothing but leaves. The melancholy days have come, the saddest of the year. Plucked from my Sunday promenade, Oct. 19, Sunset Hill."

She bent down to pick up three golden beech leaves and at the next turn of the path, five or six red sugar-maple leaves. Cora's faded, flat

Page from Cora's scrapbook: "Leaves, leaves, leaves, nothing but leaves."

leaves crumbled in my hands as I opened her scrapbook the first few times. I missed them immediately. Small chips of nineteenth-century leaf still cling to the patches of glue she used, and stains on the page left by their veins and outlines show exactly what they used to look like, so I know what kind of trees they came from—beech, sassafras, and maple. Feeling guilty for my carelessness, I picked eight twenty-first-century leaves of the proper species on October 19, 2009, and pressed them flat, intending to replace them in Cora's scrapbook.

They did not strike me as a real substitute, so they faded in a little pile on the front hall table in my house until they became pale brown and wrinkled and, thinking of her long-lost melancholy, I threw them back outdoors. I have had to accept entropy in this project—things that Cora created will fall apart, no matter how hard I try to protect them.

THROUGHOUT THE FALL, Cora began to settle in to her studies in Vassar's School of Music. "The object of the school is to give complete courses of musical education in singing, piano-forte and organ playing, to those who have the requisite gifts and are prepared to submit to the necessary discipline."[1] Run by the nationally prominent composer and conductor Frederick Ritter, the music school had its own, independent sphere of influence in the Calisthenium. This fanciful redbrick pavilion with an arched roof flanked by two decorative towers is still standing next to Vassar's Main Building, although the interior has been completely altered and replaced by a modern arts and performance center. In 1884, a picture gallery and the painting studios occupied the upper floor, and on the lower floor of the building, the students had access to two dozen pianos in separate practice rooms, along with a library of fifteen hundred musical scores.

Art and music students did not have to live at the college, and several local women musicians from Poughkeepsie, Highland, and other nearby Hudson River Valley towns enrolled as day students alongside Cora for only $100 per year. Music students were supposed to stay in the program for three years, but most graduated with their music certificate (not a full Vassar diploma) after two.

Professor Ritter maintained important musical connections outside of Vassar's campus
that raised the quality of his conservatory program to a near-professional level for students
who could make the grade. In New York City,
he had close ties with the New York Philharmonic (known then as the Philharmonic Society), and he hired a steady stream of Philharmonic musicians to travel up the Hudson
by train to play at Vassar. Once a year in the
spring, a few of the top students in the music
program earned the honor of joining some
of these Philharmonic musicians onstage in a
chamber music recital in Vassar's chapel.

*Prof. Frederick L. Ritter, director of
Vassar's School of Music. Courtesy
of Vassar College Archives.*

In addition to his responsibilities on cam-
pus, Professor Ritter was the music director for the large and magnifi-
cently decorated Collingwood Opera House (now known as the Bar-
davon) in the city of Poughkeepsie. He organized and conducted a full
season of concerts there featuring a roster of internationally known
guest soloists accompanied by New York Philharmonic musicians and
the Poughkeepsie Vocal Union, a semiprofessional chorus composed
of almost one hundred men and women. All the music students were
expected to attend these events, joining an audience of wealthy local
luminaries and Vassar faculty. Professor Ritter also worked closely with
Richard Hayman, a voice teacher in Poughkeepsie and the choir director for the Vocal Union. Hayman's daughter Georgina, a student in the
School of Music for the year 1884–1885, was one of Professor Ritter's
favorites, equally talented as a singer and at the piano. Miss Hayman
would subsequently become Cora's great rival for the honor of being the
most talented pianist in Vassar's School of Music.

Cora had two lessons per week with her instructor, Miss Chapin,
and spent several hours in the Calisthenium each day practicing the
piano and attending her other music classes. She also began to attend
meetings of a student organization called Thekla, the extracurricular
club associated with the School of Music, held in a hall on the second
floor above the old riding ring. Thekla committee members organized

a schedule of small informal performance workshops that allowed the students to gain confidence and prepare for major recitals by playing for each other. Student recitals were performed in front of the college community in the chapel on the second floor above the dining hall in the Main Building. This gave the young women the illusion of professional achievement without exposing them to the glare of public scrutiny outside of the protective confines of the college walls. Unfortunately, even the best Vassar students were not permitted to play for the general public at the concerts at the Collingwood Opera House. Allowing college girls to appear on the public stage would have been seen as immoral by most of the girls' parents.

Cora's piano instructor, Jessie Chapin, was the daughter of a wealthy commissioner for the Erie Canal. (Despite her last name, she had no connection with the Chapin School in Manhattan.) Miss Chapin had graduated with great promise from Vassar's music program in 1872 at the age of twenty-three; her family encouraged her talent by sending

Jessie Chapin, instructor of piano. Courtesy of Vassar College Archives.

The Calisthenium housed the School of Music, the Art Gallery, and the gymnasium.

her for further musical training to Germany, where cultural norms permitted women to perform onstage, and I presume that she must have had a taste of what it was like to be a musician with a public career. She stayed in Europe for several years, returning home from Hamburg on the German liner *Pomerania* in September 1875. After this brief fling with freedom, she returned to Vassar. Except for Professor Ritter, all six of the instructors in Vassar's School of Music were women, and none had the academic rank of professor. At the time that Cora became her student, Jessie Chapin was thirty-six years old, single, and living in an apartment on the second floor of the south end of the college's Main Building. After almost fifteen years of diligent effort, the long hours she had to spend working with the less than talented students whose tuition money was keeping the college afloat must have begun to weigh on her heavily.

Professor Ritter reserved all the important teaching responsibilities and the small number of really talented students for himself. Instructors lower down in the hierarchy, such as Miss Chapin, took charge of students with less obvious potential and sometimes even found themselves teaching beginners, who were allowed into the School of Music if they were enrolled elsewhere in the college as academics, preps, or special students.

I imagine that Miss Chapin harbored dreams of advancing herself in Professor Ritter's eyes by training a girl who would become a star performer in the Vassar music program. However, most of the new students assigned to her that fall were dabblers and dilettantes, like the Southerner Louisa Poppenheim, who knew nothing at all about music or the piano.[2] Miss Chapin was also sometimes assigned miscellaneous students of unknown potential, like Cora Keck, whom she might have sized up as a raw-looking girl from a disreputable family somewhere out in the Midwest with ambitious pretensions but no work ethic or solidity to her playing. Miss Chapin would have politely masked her disappointment as she listened to each new student play a first piece for her, and her thin lips must have assumed their characteristic tight expression of disappointment and disapproval with increasing frequency as she grew older. Cora was startled and disappointed to find that her new teacher was not instantly filled with admiration for her ability to pound out thousands of notes at top speed in the Liszt piece. At home, it never failed to impress everyone.

ON OCTOBER 18, three weeks after her arrival at college, Cora made an expedition into Poughkeepsie (she often abbreviated it as "Pokey" or "P.") to the tintype shop, where she and a classmate named Mary Donohue, whose scrapbook has also survived to the present day in the Special Collections at Vassar, went to get a quick snapshot made of themselves, and incidentally to meet attractive young men who might be there on the same errand. As they mingled at the photography studio, the Vassarians and their admirers joked about the city of Philadelphia, spouted Shakespearian quotes, spun outrageous puns, and riffed about Vassar's long-ago discarded and embarrassing original name of "Vassar Female College." Someone made racy references to ladies' underwear . . . twice. Three young men in bowler hats posed for the Vassarians, like three young peacocks, looking very vain. In her memoryabil, Cora penciled next to the tintype: "how do u know a

Northern <u>dude?</u> Oh. my they are cute (the girls all say)." "Dudes" were young men who dressed well, attended a good school, and had "expectations" for a successful future. Cora didn't always learn their names. The best ones came all the way to Poughkeepsie from Harvard, Yale, or Andover—they were "à la dudes."

> "Now Mary + Cooke were dude and dudette
> they walked up the hill to see the sun set."
> "My first two callers—a spoon"
> "They say he was spoony but I think he was not.
> When he but took the spoon to contrive a plot"
> —Shakespeare

The <u>Dude</u> "corsets" [2x . . .]

The two groups exchanged images that they would carry back to their respective colleges to show their friends as trophies and parted with a flourish of nearly French farewells. (See image on p. xix.)

In addition to the daily walks outdoors, Vassar students also took physical education classes (calisthenics and light gymnastics) several times a week in the cramped, inadequate gymnasium, which had to share space in the Calisthenium with the Art Gallery and the School of Music. The Calisthenium had originally been built as a horse-riding academy, but that program was discontinued by Vassar's trustees early on, "because of the excessive expense," after the handsome riding instructor, who was a retired Austrian hussar, supposedly fell in love with one of his students and abandoned his family to run off with her.

Despite outcries from his critics, Matthew Vassar insisted on having a program of regular exercise for all Vassar students when he was creating the college. A large majority of authorities at the time were afraid that exercise might damage young women's health and femininity (reading between the lines, I believe they really meant fertility). One of the wonderful strengths of Mr. Vassar's approach was how much intellectual capital he drew from his native common sense. He and his team of college planners shrugged off many bad ideas suggested by crackpot outside experts. Cora clipped an interesting article on this topic:

"Study and Health"

Mlle. Lucie Hall, doctor at Vassar College, is going into the question of the hygienic influence of hard study on women, with regard to the remarkable diminution of large families in America . . . she found that young ladies at Vassar College are generally in far better condition, as far as her health is concerned, than the majority of her sex.

Apparently the patriarchs were worried that the educational process might wear down American women's physical ability to bear children. With her simple study, Mrs. Dr. Hall pointed out quite correctly that the lack of large families was more a matter of the young ladies' choosing not to have children than of any physical feebleness brought on by the stress of college life.

It should be mentioned that Mr. Vassar, who rose from a family financial crisis to become the owner of the nation's largest brewery in just fifteen years, did not create Vassar College by himself.[3] He did, however, set the goal, collect a group of highly qualified educators and architects, and provide all the money that they needed to do the job well, which is a good recipe for success. He also stamped the place with his intangible spirit. He was known for his warmth, generosity, quirky humor, and tenacity, and he visited his new college frequently during its first four years in the early 1860s, attending to its needs and problems with care. The old businessman's blithe self-confidence showered down on his young ladies; he wanted to inspire them to be successful despite barriers, because he had had to overcome so many obstacles in his own life. Matthew Vassar's boyhood difficulties included several near-drownings, three bouts of typhus, narrow escapes from a mad bull and a poisonous snake, expulsion from school at a young age, and finally, a disastrous factory fire that caused his father's nervous breakdown and his older brother's early death and that left him in charge of the family's beer business at the tender age of twenty.

Matthew Vassar obviously enjoyed navigating through stormy waters. Having faced down death, built up his brewing business from nothing, and then beaten back the threat of New York's short flirtation with strict temperance laws in the 1850s, he felt ready for any new challenge, no

Raymond Avenue in front of Vassar College in 1885. Courtesy of Vassar College Archives.

matter how impossible and controversial: why not start a true college for women that would offer a full liberal arts curriculum equivalent to that offered to young men at Ivy League schools? A devoted son and brother of two powerful and capable women, he probably rubbed his hands together with glee as he contemplated how his new college would irritate and confound America's grouchy professional misogynists.

Members of the earliest classes spontaneously organized a surprise birthday party for Mr. Vassar in April 1866, the spring of the first academic year. They wanted to thank him in person for making their educational opportunity possible. This created the college's oldest ongoing tradition, Founder's Day. As later events would show, Mr. Vassar endowed his college with a spirit of loyalty and institutional affection that was almost more valuable, in the long run, than his money.

THIS LOYALTY WAS RECEIVING its most severe test during the budget crisis of 1884, in front of Cora's eyes. The clippings that Cora read and saved tell the story plainly: Vassar was rescued from collapse in

1885 by its own alumnae, who went to the mat to save their adored institution. According to the *New York Herald*, "Vassar's loyal daughters . . . have upheld the Vassar standard unflinchingly against a flood of discouragement which no outsider can appreciate or comprehend. Had it not been for them, the institution would certainly have gone to the wall years ago." No one cared as much as they did about the college's future. Not accidentally, they knew how to take effective action, thanks to their education.

At Vassar, girls learned how to have opinions of their own; this was even more important than what the opinions actually consisted of. For instance, politics was not an official course in the curriculum, and American women could not vote, but Vassar's inmates took a keen interest in the topic, with the full support of the faculty and president. Cora clipped this article written for a New York newspaper by one of her Vassar classmates, Mary Sheldon, sometime in the late 1880s: "Almost as soon as a freshman arrives at college, she is classified according to her political complexion as a republican, democrat or mugwump, and begins to hold heated arguments on politics with those of other beliefs. Many of the girls have no opinions of their own at first, but it doesn't take long to develop them or absorb them from others. As election approaches, the excitement rises to fever heat."

The year 1884 was a presidential election year, and the popular Maine senator and two-time secretary of state James G. Blaine (Republican) was running against the governor of New York, Grover Cleveland (Democrat). At the time, many Republicans were former abolitionists who supported Reconstruction in the South and more rights for African Americans. Today they would be considered liberals, and their ranks included a large percentage who were members of the progressive, well-educated, and wealthy Protestant establishment. Republicans also favored temperance (prohibition). The Democrats, on the other hand, were unforgettably and embarrassingly summed up by one of Blaine's supporters as favoring Rum (anti-temperance), Romanism (pro-Catholic), and Rebellion (pro-Southerners, anti-Reconstruction).

Vassar College was decorated with flags and bunting in red, white, and blue, and raucous partisan campaigning broke out on every corridor. New York newspapers took a lively interest in the goings-on at Vassar:

"Among all the places that have been excited over the election, few have felt the agitation more strongly than Vassar College," wrote one contemporary reporter. "On Monday night they determined to have an election among themselves and nearly all took part. We were unable to learn the result except that the majority for Blaine was very large, and included almost every one of the professors and teachers, who also voted."

The first results from the national election started to come in late Tuesday via regular bulletins and were posted on sheets of brown paper tacked up in a conspicuous place in the hallway near the telegraph office. When the bells struck for the end of classes on Wednesday, there was a rush downstairs to see if any more definite news had been telephoned in about the final outcome of the neck-and-neck race. On Wednesday evening, everyone at college heard results that seemed to proclaim Blaine to be the next president of the United States. The 1884 election was one of the closest in U.S. history; only the Bush/Gore election of 2000 hinged on fewer individual voter choices. Just 1,067 votes (out of more than 1 million) cast for Grover Cleveland in New York gave that state's thirty-six electoral votes and national victory to Cleveland, and the final counts took several days to come in.

Vassar College didn't wait for the recounts, to its long-lasting chagrin. So, at 8 P.M. on the freezing Wednesday evening of November 6, tar barrels were set on fire in the courtyard outside the college to light up the building façade. A display of brilliant fireworks followed. The Blaine party whipped up a torchlight victory procession using candles from their rooms and marched through the corridors cheering for their candidate's victory. Mary Sheldon, who would go on to a career in journalism and write for New York newspapers under the pen name "Mary F.X." after she graduated, wrote in detail about the spectacular and famously premature celebration in a letter home to her parents: "There were four girls who carried a bier with the effigy of Cleveland in it, and the marchers all wore white skirts, black waistes with large bows of red, white and blue ribbon on their left shoulders, and fancy caps on their heads, and each carried a Chinese lantern or a broom in her hand. They had cromo [chromo] pictures of Blaine for banners."[4]

Cora was an enthusiastic Republican. She wrote: "Blaine, October 5, 1884" on a scrap of muslin in her scrapbook (wrong month? what was

Politics at Vassar College.

Among all the places that have been excited over the election few have felt the agitation more strongly than Vassar College. The students there seem to be all politicians, and during the whole campaign before election were greatly interested. On Monday night last they determined to have an election among themselves and nearly all took part. We were unable to learn the result except that the majority for Blaine was very large, and included almost every one of the professors and teachers, who also voted. After the vote the Blaine party determined to have a parade so they brought out their candles from their rooms, and formed a "torchlight" procession, which marched through the corridors, cheering for Blaine and Logan. The Cleveland party, some of them, imitated the tactics of their friends among the sterner sex by throwing water on the paraders, and several were pretty thoroughly wet.

Next day, being election day, Blaine and Logan badges, red, white and blue neckties and ribbons and miniature flags were plenty, and in the evening there was as much eagerness to learn the result at Vassar as here in the city. During the evenings the Seniors got up another parade, only, as the Lady Principal had forbidden any more carrying of candles, they took umbrellas, and with them outspread and with each bearing the name BLAINE in large white letters, they marched through the college and shouted and cheered to their hearts content.

Wednesday the feeling was too feverish to allow of much studying. In class it is reported that an unusual number "flunked," but the teachers were indulgent. When the hours for dismissing and changing classes were reached, every girl sat ready to start at the tap of the gong and when the bell struck there was a rush pell mell for the bulletin boards to see if any late or more definite news had been telephoned out. No bulletins in this or any other city have been scanned more eagerly than those at Vassar, for the Vassar girl is no dainty, delicate creature who fears to speak above a lady-like simper. She shouts and cheers, and we think we shall have to say, yells, with as lusty a vigor as the youth at Harvard, or Yale, or Columbia. The College halls fairly rang again as the dispatches favorable to Blaine were made known, and it is reported that if Blaine is really elected there is to be a celebration of the event that will be memorable in the annals of Vassar.

More Politics at Vassar.

The good-na tion We was so tion. pathy the na for a study sion a corrid weath mane superintendent grounds, and they were very brilliant. When the marching was over the procession by some manœuvre was brought to a halt before the closed doors of the dining room, where stood the President and Lady Principal, who had provided oysters and crackers for them, and had invited the officers and other students to join. The happy part of the arrangement was that the Democrats, in black with Cleveland badges, waited on their opponents, singing two original songs with great applause. The President and Superintendent made some remarks adapted to promote good humor and pleasant feeling. The President very distinctly gave them to understand that while everybody could think, and if she had the chance, vote for either candidate, the College was on no side, only entirely and loyally American, and the country was first, whether to-morrow B or C or C or B was President.

ACATION.

ughkeepsie, is one of ning in the country enchanting maidens. d the Holidays is a 700 pupils, and Hans ticket seller of the ad, is sent up from e pasteboard for the jewled darlings of his last visit Hans hind the treasurer's op" in the college. the college corridors was the college office awaiting customers, when the maidens left their rooms, and, joining each other, skipped along the corridors in threes and fours and fives, romping, laughing, joking and chatting on one of the pleasantest indoor excursions of the year. In a jiffy, almost, the treasurer's office was filled with beauties from New Orleans, Indianapolis, Chicago, St. Louis, San Francisco, Troy, Cleveland, Boston, Bangor, Hartford, etc. "Tickets!" exclaimed Agent Miller, who had faced just such a battery of flashing eyes year after year.

"I want a ticket for St. Louis." said a modest little maiden. "How much?"

"Thirteen dollars."

"Why, that's cheaper than a year ago, isn't it."

"Yes; cut rates now; the price was $23.75 last year."

Turning to another miss, the agent said, pleasantly: "Where do you want to go to?"

"I want three tickets for San Francisco."

"Three hundred and thirty-seven dollars and fifty cents."

"My! That's quite a reduction. We paid $369.05 last year."

"Yes ma'am; cut rates now, you know. Next!"

"Ticket for Chicago, please."

"Ten dollars, miss."

"Well, now, ain't that good? I paid $19.50 last year."

"Yes; next!"

"Nashville, please."

"Eighteen dollars and fifty cents."

"That's considerably cheaper than before."

"Well, I should say so."

And so the pretty little creatures came and went for an hour or more. The holiday rush from the college this year was greater than ever before, solely because of the low rates. There were not 15 students left be-

Page from Cora's scrapbook: "A piece of the broken chandelier from the night of our Blaine procession."

she thinking?) and also saved a scrap of red velvet ribbon, "worn by V-? the night of our skirt + jersey procession." A piece of broken glass is glued to the page next to it: "A piece of the broken chandelier from the night of our Blaine procession." Mary Sheldon did not mention the breaking glass. The procession obviously teetered on the edge of total anarchy—according to one newspaper account, "the Cleveland party, some of them, imitated the tactics of their friends among the sterner sex by throwing water on the paraders and several were pretty thoroughly wet."

The victory procession wound its way through the corridors, cheering and shouting, and came to a halt at the entry to the dining room. President Caldwell and Miss Goodsell, the Lady Principal, swung the doors open for the marchers and invited the faculty, officers, and other students to enter for a feast of oysters and crackers. A sheepish pro-Cleveland celebration was organized to tidy things up later in the week after the news arrived that Grover Cleveland had actually won the election.

BACK HOME IN DAVENPORT, the election took a back seat to Keck family celebrations. Cora's sister Flora married a railroad engineer, Stephen W. Hoover, on Wednesday, November 5. Cora wrote "Happy Miss Keck. Nov. 5 '84" in pencil next to the announcement, to describe her impression of her sister's feelings as a bride. As was typical at the time, Flora and her fiancé were married at home by the pastor of her family's church, the First Methodist Episcopal Church. A beautiful wedding announcement was sent to Cora at college. The thick white envelope contains several tiered layers of creamy matte board tied together with a white silk tassel and edged in gold, with hand-lettered calligraphy that reads, "Mr. & Mrs. Stephen W. Hoover will live at 611 Brady Street."

One of Davenport's tireless social reporters provided a short if overbaked description of the wedding service that appeared in the *Davenport Gazette*: "It was a quiet and private affair . . . there were present only the immediate relatives of the high contracting parties . . . but they enjoyed an elaborate wedding supper, numerous and costly wedding presents, and they will take a 10-day trip to Omaha and the west." Apparently neither Flora nor her husband had any friends that they wanted to invite to their wedding. Notices were bravely sent out and printed up in newspapers in Fairfield, Iowa, the Kecks' former hometown, and in Quincy, Illinois, where Mrs. Dr. Keck did a lot of business, but the social cachet of having your daughter marry a common laborer was zero.

Flora's new husband had started his career as a fireman for the Chicago, Rock Island & Pacific line, which had its hub in Davenport, and around the time of his marriage, had been promoted to engineer. The job was physically demanding and dangerous. A fireman singlehandedly shoveled as much as a ton of coal into the firebox during each thirty-six-hour shift, and train crews fought exhaustion while maintaining a precise schedule to arrive at sidings in time to avoid head-on collisions with oncoming trains that shared the single line of track. In Cora's diaries, he comes across as a taciturn and aloof man; in the beginning, she did not call him Steven—he was Mr. Hoover. It was a different story at work; his friends and co-workers on the Rock Island road called him "the Knocker." He would have been proud of his position because he was the best-paid man on the train crew;[5] small boys of the era envied railroad engineers the way today's kids admire airplane pilots and astronauts. In 1887, the Rock Island *Union Weekly* announced a new speed record set by S. W. Hoover, driving Engine No. 70, who "brought a stock train 104 miles in four hours."[6] (That's an average speed of about twenty-five miles per hour!) Steven Hoover was almost certainly a member of the Brotherhood of Locomotive Engineers, the nation's oldest rail labor union, but it is unlikely that he would have been involved in left-wing labor activism, since the BLE had a reputation for being far less militant than other brotherhoods during the savage railroad strikes that swept the country during the 1870s and 1880s. "Best-paid" was a relative term—Mr. Hoover earned $3.50 a day, a dollar more than his fireman or the brakemen hopping across the gaps between the moving boxcars back on the rest of the train. Cora spent that much on ice cream at Smiths for one of her dorm-room parties.

After the excitement of the presidential election died down, it was back to the regular academic routine at Vassar. On November 7, Cora was summoned by the superintendent of laundry to the laundry office between 3 and 4 P.M. to claim a lost article.

CHAPTER SEVEN

College Pie with Tomatoes—Entirely New

A s the cold wet weather of November closed in, Cora and her room-mates changed rooms and moved down two floors to the base-ment level to parlor 6 on the north corridor. The basement level was set aside to house the younger prep level students, and everyone under-stood that they had to earn their way upwards through the ranks, liter-ally and academically. So it is likely that during her first year, Elizabeth Griggs lived nearby in another basement room, although Cora does not mention her presence. Cora's small window was often darkened with cold rain, and she and her roommates had to light the gas lamps in their suite earlier and earlier each afternoon. A long pipe snaked down from the fixture on the ceiling to feed gas into the table lamp in the center of the room. The bright flames put out as much heat as light. On one of these evenings, Marian sat in the straight chair, Cora relaxed in the small rocker, and Eveline draped herself on the folding wooden chaise longue for some conversation. These odd pieces of furniture were the only three seats in the room.

They discussed the advantages and disadvantages of their new loca-tion; students universally disliked the basement rooms because they were dingy, close to the laundry and kitchen, and had no view of the surrounding landscape. However, they were two floors removed from the eagle-eyed supervision of Miss Goodsell and nearer to the south corridor where most of the other preps were housed. Cora also noted how easy it was to climb outside through the windows and leave the col-lege or reenter other rooms whenever necessary—a maneuver that they might have found too nerve-wracking to execute on the upper stories.

They spoke about home and their far-away families with longing. Marian's blood had thinned out living in Hawaii, although she knew all about cold weather. Her family was originally from the snow-choked city of Buffalo, New York. Her father, a lawyer named Benjamin Hale

Austin, suffered from ill health, and his doctors recommended a change of climate, sending him to live in the Sandwich Islands (as they were still sometimes known) in 1876 when Marian was twelve.

Marian had attended the Punahou School, a secondary school started in 1841 by Presbyterian missionaries in Honolulu. The school is still in existence and serves Hawaii's best students today—in fact, President Barack Obama is a graduate. In those days, however, the education that Punahou provided was not so good; Marian's tutor in Honolulu wrote to Miss Goodsell in July 1884 that Marian had not been given "proper schooling or discipline," her school had been "lax," and "standards of scholarship here are very low." Nevertheless, he found Marian to be an exceptionally apt scholar, who only needed method and neatness in order to excel, and added poignantly, "I am sorry to lose her."[1]

In an era when families did not usually send their sons to college, let alone their daughters, Marian's parents showed a remarkable commitment to her education. Because of this, Marian was feeling the pressure of the stiff entrance exams looming in her future. She planned to take them in June in order to enter Vassar as a freshman the next September, in 1885. Many evenings, Marian must have continued to work on preparing for her Latin and mathematics recitations long after the evening study hour ended with three peals of the bell at 8 P.M.

Eveline, who was in Prep Level III, was less concerned about the three years of work she faced before she could apply to join Vassar's freshman class. She would do what she could, but if she didn't get in, she maintained that she was perfectly capable of making other satisfactory plans for her life. After prepping at Vassar, she was willing to go to college somewhere else, or skip it altogether and get married right away.

THE NEXT WEDNESDAY, Cora attended her first Soirée Musicale. These formal concerts took place in the college chapel and featured small ensembles of well-known professional musicians from New York City conducted by Professor Ritter. The performances were fundamentally important to Cora's musical training in a way we cannot imagine. Classical music was neither popular nor widely played in the United

States during most of the nineteenth century. Most Americans, including some of Vassar's music students, had never heard serious classical music before. They lived without radio, without records, without film and television, and the only way to become an educated listener was to attend live performances. Touring superstars such as Jenny Lind might sing an aria or two out in the hinterlands at the large theaters in the South and Midwest known as "opera houses," but audiences usually went to those venues to hear famous speakers on tour, such as Mark Twain, Oscar Wilde, Frederick Douglass, and Henry Ward Beecher; to see actors such Sarah Bernhardt and Edwin Booth or vaudeville and minstrel shows, not to hear the European grand opera of Verdi and Wagner. Musically, Americans were more inclined to the wildly popular national fad for banjo playing, and they liked songs with words, such as those composed by Stephen Foster.

"Longhair" or intellectually demanding instrumental music from Europe was a slow-growing import. This situation was gradually starting to change in the 1880s, as a growing audience of Americans heard works by composers such as Beethoven, Brahms, and Weber for the first time, performed by new symphony orchestras just being started in Boston and St. Louis. New York City was unique in North America (and probably in the Western Hemisphere) in having not just one, but two orchestras in the 1880s—the Philharmonic Society of New York, founded in 1842; and its break-away progeny, the Symphony Society of New York, which was founded by Franz Liszt's former concertmaster, Leopold Damrosch, in 1878. New York's huge immigrant German population (as numerous as the Irish) formed a large part of both the talent and the enthusiastic audience for these two organizations. There was also famously a row at the front of the orchestra section filled with devoted opera-loving "regulars" who were all gay men. The small number of Anglo socialites who decorated the Diamond Horseshoe balcony at the opera house had the annoying habit of talking to each other between the famous arias and leaving for social engagements at the second intermission.[2]

Cora's academic schedule was not demanding, and after she had struggled to memorize her daily recitation for German, and completed her work for harmony class, she was always tempted to slack off. She

liked to call on her many new friends up and down the corridors of the
Main Building and did not darken the door of the library during her
first months at college.

Although music students were expected to perform for each other in
the Thekla room above the Art Gallery on a regular basis, Cora, new to
the school, was not yet much involved. During her first year, both the
president and treasurer of Thekla were friends of Mary Poppenheim, a
four-year-program student well known on campus as a respected stu-
dent-body leader, who was also studying piano on the side. Mary (or
May) comes into Cora's story not only because she was involved with
the School of Music, but also because she and her younger sister, Louisa, whose nickname was Loulu, left behind a complete set of detailed
letters home to their mother in Charleston, South Carolina, that have
been published in book form. This invaluable resource has allowed me
to explore the private social life of some of Cora's classmates outside her
immediate circle.

Despite Vassar's consciously democratic social structure, in practice,
Cora and her friends would seldom have crossed paths socially with

Mary Poppenheim, Vassar class of '88.   *Louisa Poppenheim, Vassar class of '89.*
Courtesy of Vassar College Archives.   *Courtesy of Vassar College Archives.*

the two Poppenheim sisters and their circle at college. May and Loulu's friends all came from "nice families" and were members of a far higher social stratum than the Kecks, despite the fact that the Poppenheims were not particularly wealthy. An invisible line wound through time and space, through the hallways, vacations, leisure activities, and extra-curricular organizations, keeping the girls who defined themselves as "nice" safely away from the ones who weren't—and, it also almost goes without saying, from a third group of girls—the ones who were so dull or unattractive or poor that they didn't matter.[3]

Loulu mapped out the Thekla power structure during the fall semester of 1884: her sister Mary's close friend Gus (Augusta Harvey) was the president, and Gus nominated herself to be vice president during the spring; another friend, Minnie (Mary W. Shaw), was treasurer during the fall.[4] Minnie Shaw was only marginally acceptable to the socially discriminating sisters; Loulu described her as "conceited" later that winter. Cora quickly discovered that these girls were very choosy about whom they included in their activities. Cora attended Thekla performances four times throughout the fall but was not invited to serve on the organizing committee—nor did she perform. She was apparently something of an outsider in the music department at the start, and she was not practicing piano terribly hard. She played a lot of tennis with Marian instead.

EVERY NIGHT, WHEN THEY HEARD the ten strokes of the college bell at 10 P.M., the gas had to be extinguished and all students had to be in bed before the last bell had finished striking. Although the corridor teachers patrolled the hallways to check that lights were out, this rule was not enforceable. The parlors were hidden from the hallway by a row of dorm rooms, and it was easy to block the light escaping over the transom of the entry door by covering the glass with a heavy blanket or raincoat.[5]

In the mornings, ten more strokes of the bell jarred everyone awake at 7 A.M. The students had forty-five minutes to use the bathroom and get dressed. Louisa Poppenheim liked to get up every morning before

The Lady Principal, Miss Abby Goodsell, Vassar class of '69.
Courtesy of Vassar College Archives.

seven and take a plunge bath before breakfast. At a quarter to eight, eight strokes sounded the signal for breakfast, and everyone was supposed to go downstairs to the dining hall promptly, in advance of the tardy bell that rang four minutes later, "to avoid crowding and confusion at the doors."[6] Then the dining room doors were officially shut. To get in, latecomers had to crack open the door to enter in full view of the entire college and explain themselves to the Lady Principal.

Miss Goodsell ran a tight ship. "Tardiness at meals has been increasing of late," she would announce with obvious displeasure to the rows of guilty backs bent over their plates. For good measure, she sometimes added, "Just look around and see the noise in the dining room," which would be quite a trick, if you think about it.

Luncheon went from 12:15 to 1:15 in two shifts. Ten girls sat at each table in a regular assigned seat and dined with a faculty member presiding. College maids served and cleared the food, making the half hour allowed for eating quick and efficient. Cora referred to the German-language table as the "German halle" and seems to have eaten every meal with her German instructor, Miss Minna Hinkel, which is how she came to be friendly with her teacher despite her abysmal language skills. Although the tables were covered with tablecloths and cloth napkins (paper napkins and plastic trays had not yet been invented), the floors were bare boards and the chairs were inexpensive "saloon" style chairs we would recognize from cheap hotels in Wild West movies, the "fifty-cent chair" from Sears & Roebuck Co.[7] The surroundings were practical and clean, but not particularly luxurious. There was nothing on the bare white walls to absorb the sounds made by a hundred diners, so keeping the noise level down was probably important.

Afternoon study hours ended at five o'clock, and following a short break, eight strokes of the bell announced dinner, which was the main meal of the day, at 5:15 P.M. Cora had a vigorous appetite and really looked forward to every meal: "On arising thought of nothing else save

Vassar College dining hall, decorated for a holiday.
Courtesy of Vassar College Archives.

for the delicious lunch for-with-coming the meat 'coquetts' etc. and the ice cream on a Wednesday Dinner. Most everyone is acquainted with the weekly menu at Vassar; in fact me knows whats coming on the table before it appears. What was it? was it cream or ? 'delicious pie' College pie wth tomatoes entirely new." Maybe Cora was describing an early form of pizza.

Most of the food served in the Vassar dining room was produced locally at a large farm owned by the college, and all of it was "organic," since chemical fertilizers were not introduced into U.S. agriculture until the early twentieth century. In Cora's day, it was easy to be a "locavore"; you could look out of your dormitory room window every April and watch plows at work in fields right next to the Main Building, each pulled by a pair of horses. The food must have been extremely healthy and well prepared. In nineteenth-century photographs of Vassar students and faculty, very few people pictured appear overweight. In fact, in the fall of 1885, Mary Poppenheim eagerly reported to her mother that she had gained eight pounds at college, in order to reassure her of its healthy regime. Unlike our own times, the old newspapers did not contain advertisements for weight-loss products. I suspect that Vassar's regular regimen, offering locally produced, organic food served at three balanced meals each day and requiring plenty of sleep and moderate, daily exercise, may have been a good way to stay fit and healthy. The tightly laced corsets that women had to wear were certainly not healthy, but if nothing else, they probably limited overeating. The original college program (with schedule, but minus the controlling supervision of the Lady Principal) could probably reopen today as a health spa in the Berkshires, if only the intended patrons could carve out several years to commit to attend.

The tone of life on Sundays at Vassar was relaxed and pleasant, in contrast to the relentless academic pressures of the weekdays. Cora carried out most of her letter writing on Sundays and noted in her diary how many she wrote every week: "At 12:10 Laura, Mae Carbutt and I took our ½ hrs constitutional came back in time for Dinner and after entertaining Miss Edwards in an agreeable manner wrote all afternoon. Wrote 6 letters one to Prof. Braunlich, Gus E., Maggie Keck, Aunt Kate, Mame R., Mary S. made a few calls [visits to other dorm rooms] and retired after taking my Sunday evening bath. So retired at 9:30 P.M. 10 I mean."

Throughout the week, daily nondenominational prayers were conducted in the chapel above the dining hall for a half hour after dinner, but this obligation was apparently easy to cut, and Cora often failed to go. On Sundays, all students were required to attend an unpopular Bible study class at 9 A.M. as well as regular Sunday church services at 11. Cora seemed disconnected from her spiritual life. She was accustomed to cutting daily chapel and even the Sunday church services and seldom expressed any opinion about Vassar's religious offerings. "I was very busy writing letters this A.M. after preparing my Bible class lesson. We all went up to the classroom but Miss Leach [the Bible instructor] failed to make her appearance, much to the delight of all the girls present," Cora wrote, with irreverent enthusiasm. On another weekday she noted sarcastically, "Took my regular hour constitutional walk, then after dinner went to Chapel for a change."

Students easily obtained permission to go off campus and attend church in Poughkeepsie. Cora's mother was a Methodist, so Cora occasionally went into Poughkeepsie to attend services at the Methodist church. She paid little attention to the celebrity preachers who came through Vassar, failing even to note down their names, and she found the Reverend Caldwell's preaching exceedingly dull, as did many of the other students. "At 11 A.M. we heard a very interesting sermon by the Rev. so and so, nothing like the Rev. Caldwell"—here's one thing that Cora and Mary Poppenheim agreed on. Earlier in the year, Mary had written home, "I am determined not to be bored by Dr. Caldwell's sermons."

In general, Cora did not express deep thoughts about abstract ideas anywhere in her diary. Most Sundays, she woke up complaining about the ill effects of some kind of exhausting dissipation from the night before, either flirting with boys till a late hour at parties in New York or eating too much with her female friends on campus. She cut chapel or was off campus in New York City eight times out of the eighteen Sundays at Vassar during the time she kept the diary. It's safe to say that she was not devout. This was probably a big point of friction between Mrs. Dr. Keck and her impetuous daughter.

CORA KECK AND ELIZABETH GRIGGS were not the only new arrivals from Iowa at Vassar that fall. On October 15, Miss Keck climbed the grand staircase to the fourth floor of the college to chat with Cora Louise Scofield, age fourteen, of Washington, Iowa, who shared a tiny room on the south corridor with her sixteen-year-old sister Clara Jane. The Scofields had just enrolled together at the lowest level of the academic hierarchy in Prep Level III. My great-grandmother took a friendly interest in her junior namesake, making an immediate impression by lighting a stick of letter wax to make a red seal next to the childish script in Miss Scofield's diary. The University of Iowa Libraries recently made this relic available online, and late in my research process, I found a new angle on my great-grandmother's first few weeks at Vassar.[8] The two Coras, Keck and Scofield, were preparing for a dramatic farce called "How the Colonel Proposed" for Exoteric on November 1. Everyone in the cast was a newbie from the Midwest. Tall and older than most, Miss Keck took the male lead, as Colonel Titbottom Forsyth, while little Miss Scofield had to play the part of the old maid auntie. I detect the hidden hand of Miss Goodsell behind this encounter; she would have carefully gathered up the artless Midwestern fledglings into a troupe to help them assimilate into the Vassar community. A week later during a stroll around the college grounds, Corize gave her younger friend a "relic" keepsake, which I presume was a social card she didn't want from a Davenport type named Max Robinson.

On the second Saturday in November Cora went off campus to Poughkeepsie to do some errands. As she climbed onto the omnibus on Raymond Avenue to go into town, she met Mr. Horace Eugene Corwin, a student at the Eastman National Business College in Poughkeepsie, who lived at 24 Washington Street. After an interval of conversation, he gave her a cigarette, "one of the kind an Eastman dude uses," a sweet caporal wrapped in Kinney rice paper.

What do you do when you land a big fish? Eat it right away? Or firmly resist the delights of the table and display it up on the wall as a trophy? Cora decided to save this prize and glued the cigarette into her

Cigarette advertisement, ca. 1900. Courtesy of the Library of Congress.

scrapbook, along with a "shinplaster fiver" from the Eastman College Bank of Poughkeepsie. Shinplasters were private IOUs that were used in the cash-starved nineteenth century as a substitute for real money. Eastman students presumably used the Eastman dollars at local businesses for some of their college expenses or to learn about business and banking. Since shinplasters were often worth less than the paper they were printed on, their name suggested a general perception that they could be better put to use lining boots for warmth in the wintertime.

Cigarettes from dudes were common currency for Cora. Later in the year she wrote: "I had a few 'cigarettes' given as a 'philopena' by Mr. Vedder of Columbia College New York so took advantage and smoked them immediately after the 10 o'clock bell. They made me so sleepy + probably accounts for my feeling so badly today." Ivy League à la dudes seemed to make a practice of offering cigarettes to young ladies when they wanted to "make a mash." "Came home oh so giddy—youths who flirted with their cigarettes," she wrote on another occasion.

The girls were flying under the radar with this particular rebellion. Vassar's college rulebook of 1882 did not even bother to forbid the consumption of alcohol or cigarettes. I think that these activities were so out of the question for young ladies that their parents would have been seriously disturbed and even insulted if the college so much as implied that this kind of misbehavior might occur. In contrast, the rules for their brothers down at Columbia College in New York City (now known as Columbia University) explicitly forbade the use of pipe tobacco, cigars, snuff, and chewing tobacco on the college premises.

In the 1880s and throughout the following decades, cigarettes were associated with a racy lifestyle. When a college girl like Cora lit up, she was reaching outside the boundaries of a safe and proper life. Cigarette smoking went on to become a morally charged issue at women's educational institutions in the early twentieth century. At Vassar, it was seen as "contrary to the spirit and traditions of the College" for decades, until 1929, when the college finally caved in and set up a senior smoking room for students in the Main Building with card tables for playing bridge and tall standing ashtrays. One wise and aged Vassar alumna, an expert in the study of anthropology, summed it up this way in the early twentieth century: a Victorian girl who smoked was making "a gesture of the brothel."[9]

CHAPTER EIGHT

Abandoned at Christmas

Winter came early that year, and it snowed before Thanksgiving. Cora's teeth started to give her trouble, and she made a dentist's appointment with Dr. Miller in Poughkeepsie on Saturday, November 22. Dr. M was a favorite Vassar dentist, known to be polite, gentlemanly, and very expensive. Cora's new friend Kitty (Kate Bonnibel) Rogers went with her. The slush wasn't deep enough for sled runners, and the horses struggled to pull the horse car into town through the awful mess. The appointment turned into a two-hour ordeal. Beforehand, Kitty had suggested a visit to the tintype shop to help distract Cora from her unpleasant errand, and they met two handsome dudes there. Perhaps preoccupied by her aching jaw, Cora did not record either of the dudes' names or colleges, merely noting "a terrible time at the Dentist" under the image in her memoryabil.

Kitty was from New York City and had enrolled in Vassar's School of Art halfway through the semester on October 17. Her entrance examination grades were among the highest of any of the girls whom Cora knew, and she easily could have entered the preparatory program and gone for an academic degree.[1] However, she did not have professional ambitions and chose to spend her time in the art studio sketching and painting from live models with Professor Henry Van Ingen. Among Cora's New York acquaintances at Vassar, Eveline was a good tennis opponent, but there was something superficial about her, and she and Cora drifted apart as soon as they stopped rooming together. Kitty Rogers was different; she, along with most of her family, became Cora's close friend for life. As Thanksgiving vacation approached, Cora telegraphed to her mother to ask for permission to go to New York for the holiday with Miss Rogers. Cora received her answer via telegram late on Wednesday the 26th: "Yes go, but don't miss School too long—Be careful. Mrs. Dr. Keck."

"First Year + type at Vassar. the time @ the dentist. Bonabel Rogers, Nov. '84." A tintype of Cora (in grey dress) posing with Kitty Rogers (in white) and two dudes.

Unfortunately, the permission must have arrived too late for her to catch the train on Wednesday afternoon. Cora was left behind. She accepted her disappointment without comment and soon consoled herself with the magnificent Thanksgiving dinner that was served at college from three to five o'clock in the afternoon on Thursday. The menu featured two soups, then roast turkey and young pig, followed by chicken pie and baked macaroni. Garnishes of gherkin pickles, celery stalks, and Spanish olives were arranged artistically in a line of cut glass dishes down the middle of the tables, forming a special decoration for the occasion. On the side, the students chose from serving bowls mounded with baked sweet potatoes, creamed onions, mashed potatoes, and baked tomatoes. Then came mince pie, cream puffs, oranges, apples, bananas, almonds, and raisins. Just in case they weren't full yet, platters of ice cream, macaroons, fancy cakes, and candies appeared at the finish. Cora saved a nut in her scrapbook, "One of the ten courses of our ThanksG' Dinner." In the evening, the students in Exoteric put on a performance of "The Decorative Sisters."

The week after Thanksgiving, Cora's dental situation worsened. She spent two hours at Dr. Miller's on Saturday and returned a third time for another hour and a half of painful attentions on December 5. She was so sick from her toothache that she spent part of the week in the infirmary, and her friend Jane Perine, a Special Courses student from Tennessee, sent her a note: "Dear Corize, Mary tells me how you suffered all night. I am so sorry and to night, if you will let me I will stay with you in order to try to release you or to keep you company. Your friend, J. A. Perine." Neither aspirin nor antibiotics existed in the 1880s, so patients had to literally "be patient" and fight off fevers and infections by suffering through them and waiting for their immune response to overcome the illness.

On December 17, Cora went out walking on Vassar's grounds and brought back a piece of birch bark, writing the day and date on it in plainly etched letters. It was the same day that funeral services were held in Philadelphia for Warren's uncle, Amandes Kleckner, who died earlier that week. The younger brother of Abraham, former president of the Bank of La Porte (near the mining camp of Port Wine) in the Sierra

Nevada goldfields, and lately wholesale grocer of 1816 N. Twenty-first Street in Philadelphia, had passed on.[2] Cora could not go to the funeral because of her college schedule, and she paid her quiet respects in her own way to that unseen but ever-present and haunting Victorian companion, unexpected early death.

The next day, a ticket agent from the Hudson River Railroad was sent up from New York City to sell tickets to all the Vassar students who wanted to travel home for vacation. He set up shop at the treasurer's desk. Fares in 1884 were dramatically reduced for most destinations compared with the year before: for a trip to St. Louis, the rate had dropped from $23.75 to $13, and for a one-way ticket to Chicago, it fell by almost 50 percent, from $19.50 to just $10.

Marian Austin left for Buffalo, New York, two days later, leaving an address where Cora could write to her over the next few weeks, while Cora submitted the required permission form to Miss Goodsell so she could spend the Christmas recess with Kitty in New York City. She wanted to take the 1:45 train from Poughkeepsie to New York via the Hudson River Railroad, and she planned to take one trunk. But it didn't happen. She needed permission from home to leave the

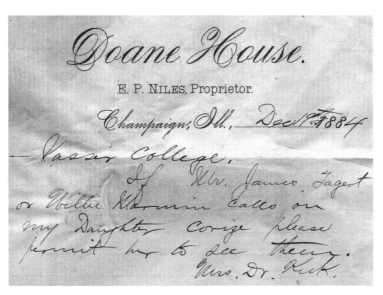

Only surviving example of Mrs. Dr. Keck's signature.

campus for the winter break, and Mrs. Dr. Keck did not send it. Nearly all of Vassar's students took advantage of the low train fares to travel, leaving Cora and fourteen other girls at the college building over the holidays. Cora must have felt stranded, left dangling for the second time that fall by a mother who was apparently too busy to attend to her daughter's needs but unwilling to delegate the responsibility elsewhere. This looks like a real blunder, as in "Oops. I forgot about my daughter at college." Cora could have written to her father for permission just as well, but apparently that wasn't the way things were done in the Keck family.

On the same day Cora was hoping to leave Vassar for her Christmas vacation, Mrs. Dr. Keck was seeing her regular patients at a hotel called the Doane House in Champaign, Illinois. Instead of answering Cora's telegram and giving her permission to visit Kitty, she wrote a letter to Vassar filled with misspellings: "If Mr. James Tagert or Willie Marmin calls on my Daughter Corize please permit her to see them. Mrs. Dr. Keck." (The

"The step ladder Edition" Top to bottom: Minnie Keiter '87, Fannie Clark '90, Cora Keck '86, and Laura Harris '90.

names should have been spelled *Taggart* and *Marmon*.) It must have been maddening for Cora to get this message instead of the one she actually wanted. I have no evidence that either youth ever visited Cora; Will Marmon was much younger and boring, and she did not mention James Taggart anywhere in her diary or scrapbooks. Marmon, the Wakefields' young friend from Bloomington, Illinois, was studying at Andover Academy, but the only thing he ever did was to send Cora a book of Easter hymns a year later. This probably explains why she said

Page from Cora's scrapbook with Homer Wakefield's cigarette tied to a string.

so little about Will—he was not only too young, he was a little too dutiful and religious for her taste.

Meanwhile, Miss Goodsell wrote, "Miss Keck may go to room 20 for the vacation," and Cora changed rooms to the other end of the building on the south corridor to be near the other girls stuck at college during the holidays. On December 21, she and three of her fellow holiday outcasts, Minnie Keiter, Laura Harris, and Fannie Clark, went into Poughkeepsie to the tintype shop. They called themselves "the college quartette" and cemented their sense of solidarity by staging some creative poses for tintypes that Cora put into her memoryabil. Wearing silly hats, they stood in a row and held up a piece of canvas under their chins, crouched behind a ladder and put their heads through the steps in a vertical stack, and finally put on ice skates and posed in front of an outdoor scene painted on canvas.

Homer Wakefield had not forgotten about her; he sent her an invitation to a reception put on by the Company G Fourth Infantry, Illinois National Guard, at the Ashley House on December 24, 1884 (tickets cost $1). He enclosed a dance card and tied the tasseled string around a cigarette. Thinking about those festivities taking place six hundred miles away in Bloomington must have made Cora feel even more desolate and abandoned. Was Homer Wakefield still her only romantic option? Her family expected that she would be able to marry an Eastern fellow at Vassar, but how was she supposed to meet such a person?

On Christmas Eve, the girls exchanged some small joke presents. Someone gave Cora a shiny new horseshoe nail tied with a bright red ribbon, which she put into the scrapbook, noting that it was from "Xmas evening Room J." On Christmas Day, Cora's mother finally went to the telegraph office in Davenport and sent permission to the college for her to leave campus: "You can spend Holidays in New York or Philadelphia all well. Mrs. Dr. Keck." Cora telegraphed Kitty on December 29: "Leaving on the 1.05 train meet me at Harlem. Coz"

CHAPTER NINE

First Time Out from College

THURSDAY, JANUARY 1, 1885

My first morning in New York ate breakfast at 10½ A.M. Came home from the party at Dr. Rodenstein's at 4 AM.—had a grand time watching the old year out and the new in . . .

These are the first sentences in Cora's diary, written in her vigorous and distinctive spidery handwriting. It was actually March when she recorded these events, but even two and a half months later, her recollections were clear: "In the morning, we went out of doors to see Kitty's place. The 'Laurence [Lawrence] Mansion on the Hudson' is a lovely, large white house on a beautiful hill bordering the river."

Standing between the huge Doric pillars on the back veranda of Kitty Rogers's house at the top of the high bluff at 134th Street on New Year's Day, Cora took in the magnificent panorama visible for several miles in both directions. The North River (as this part of the Hudson used to be called) was even busier than the Mississippi in Davenport. Steamships, ferries, and tall-masted schooners jammed the wide channel from one side to the other in the cold morning as busy packets threaded their way through the crowd with blasts from their deafening calliope steam whistles. Ice floes tinged with pink scattered light across the water's surface. Clouds of dust and smoke hid the Palisades cliffs lining the opposite shore, and constant muffled thumps of explosions rolled across the water. The huge quarries stretching from Weehawken up to Edgewater and Fort Lee were detonating hundreds of pounds of dynamite per day, around the clock, seven days a week, chewing into the rock face at a furious pace to supply fill for thousands of active building lots in the city.[1]

The Rogerses lived in Manhattanville, still practically a rural suburb in the 1880s and now the part of New York City called West Harlem.

*The Lawrence mansion at 134th Street in New York City overlooking the
Hudson River, residence of Kitty Rogers and her family during the 1880s.
Courtesy of Manhattanville College Library Archives, Jenner Collection.*

Although it is hard to imagine today, the Hudson shoreline of Manhattan Island above Fifty-ninth Street was widely admired for its rustic
beauty before the Civil War. John B. Lawrence, a member of a family
that numbered at least one New York City mayor in its ranks, built
Kitty's house as a summer residence in about 1810.[2] In 1885, parklike
grounds covering five city blocks, from 133rd to 138th streets, still surrounded the Rogers home.

While strolling around the frozen lawns of the mansion, Kitty, her
younger sister Mame (short for Mary Louise), and Cora rehashed Cora's
debut the night before in the New York social whirl at Dr. Rodenstein's

New Year's Eve party. Their host, a close family friend and neighbor in Manhattanville, was the director of the Manhattan Dispensary, the first public hospital to serve low-income residents of upper Manhattan. He was a brilliant physician and philanthropist who built his career advocating for the welfare of the poor people who were crowding into unhealthy tenement buildings being thrown together in "the Hollow" down below the bluff along 126th Street. With the assistance of her husband and friends in the hospital's Ladies' Auxiliary, Mrs. Rogers had just raised $14,000 to construct a large new building for the dispensary at 131st Street and Tenth Avenue that was set to start construction in three months, on April 1. The Rodensteins were celebrating this gift, and Kitty's parents were the guests of honor at the evening's celebrations. Cora then marveled how, at three in the afternoon on New Year's Day, "the callers commenced coming and continued till a late hour. We had quite a party, dancing and singing. Corbett called, but to my dissatisfaction only stayed a few minutes. I thought of a year past when I received callers in Peoria, Illinois with Min Lindsay and what a nice time I had, and how I had to hurry back to high school. But now I am a Vassar student at last, and I enjoy Vassar life immensely and New York City even better."

The bright lights of the big city were shining in Cora's eyes; her high school friend Min Lindsay was only a grocer's daughter, and now here she was staying in a house built by the family of one ex-mayor of New York City and rubbing elbows with another, Dr. Rodenstein's father-in-law, Daniel F. Tiemann. Cora still thought fondly of her friend Minnie, but the comparison was stark, and the action in New York was really thrilling.

Over the course of the weekend, Kitty's personable neighbor Edgar M. Corbett gave Cora three copies of his calling card that she glued into her scrapbooks, some marked up with illegible, inked annotations. Cora and Ed stayed lifelong friends, although each married someone else. My grandfather, who met Ed thirty years later, described him as "a mild-mannered and kindly man, who dressed like a sport and wore a brown derby hat." When Cora first met him, his family owned several very successful silk mills in Paterson, New Jersey, and along with his brother, he was just getting involved with running the family business.

The next day, Friday, January 2, 1885, Cora, Mame, and Kitty slept till after noon, since "after my dissipation of Thurs. evening we were extremely tired and I thought we would rest, so we remained in retirement till 12:10." Friday was Ladies' Reception day. After lunch the three friends ventured out into the frigid winter weather to call on several family friends: "We called on Mrs. Teaman [*sic*] off the Boulevard, and Shultz. Then we went further down in Harlem. But it was extremely cold so we returned home to prepare for our evening engagements."

Daniel F. Tiemann was the genial owner of a large paint factory called the Tiemann Color Works and had served as mayor of New York City from 1857 to 1860.[3] He lived next door to his grown son, Peter Cooper Tiemann, so I am not sure whether Cora and Kitty called on Daniel's wife or Peter's wife; it is likely that she met both of them during the round of parties that weekend. While serving as mayor, Daniel Tiemann forged political links with William Marcy Tweed, otherwise famous to the world as Boss Tweed of Tammany Hall, and the ex-mayor was now enjoying a benevolent and prosperous retirement in his rambling farmhouse surrounded by gardens on a side street off the avenue now known as upper Broadway. Kitty's family and the Tiemanns were closely tied by friendship across several generations.[4]

That evening, "Mrs. and Mr. Rogers accompanied us to the theater to hear Fanny Davenport in the play Fedora," a popular French drama about lovelorn Russian aristocrats by Victorien Sardou. "We went to the Metropolitan Hotel theater at Thirty-ninth Street—no, it's called the Metropolitan Opera House, not the hotel theater." Cora sometimes misremembered details in her diary; as the program she saved from this evening's performance in her scrapbook confirms, it really was the theater, not the opera house. "As many times as Fanny Davenport has been to Davenport [Iowa], I failed to hear her. I enjoyed this performance very much." In 1887, Sarah Bernhardt took over the role and played it for a year at the Star Theater.

On one of the days she spent in New York, Cora ate lunch with Kitty, Mame, and Mrs. Rogers at the noisy, bustling Central Café at 46 West Fourteenth Street, between Fifth and Sixth avenues, which offered a female-friendly atmosphere, a pressed tin ceiling, and white tile walls. The huge two-page menu offered thirty daily specials, including deviled

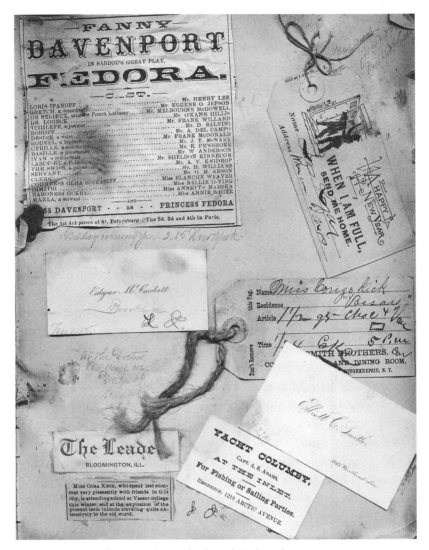

Page from Cora's scrapbook with Fedora theater program.

crab and quail on toast for 45 cents each and veal cutlets picquets à la Chalon for 50 cents. During the meal, Cora shared inside jokes with Mame and Kitty that she recorded in her diary—it seems that they were extremely amused by the city horse-car drivers, who manned the small wooden omnibuses that ran on iron rails.

A contemporary guidebook to New York described horse-car dray-men as the coarsest and rudest characters that visitors were likely to encounter on the streets of the city. On the way home from their first daytime expedition together the day before, Cora and Kitty had gotten into a wrangle with one of these snarling louts when they tried to board a car at 126th Street at the bottom of the steep hill and ride up the Grand Boulevard (now called upper Broadway) to the Lawrence mansion at 134th Street. For some reason, they didn't have enough money to pay the full fare, and the driver yelled at them and forced them off the omnibus back into the snow: "Hey there! Stay there if u haven't any car fare! Walk there!" No doubt he shouted a string of other, riper Anglo Saxon insults at them, as he lashed up his tired team of horses and drove off, that Cora chose to omit from her diary. She and Kitty ended up trudging in the cold the nine blocks up the steep hill from 125th Street to Kitty's house.

The incident delighted Cora so much that she wrote "Hey there! Stay there!" down a second time in her scrapbook, illustrated with a small drawing to show the action, and then referred to it a third time when noting down an "Ah! There" 30-cent expenditure in her biweekly accounts. For weeks afterward, Cora's circle of friends needed only to throw out the first few words of the driver's insult to make one another crack up with laughter.

On Saturday, January 3, Cora wrote: "Had our breakfast of a late hour as usual we soon prepared for the elevated where we went flying down to 32 Street + then over to 5 Avenue to Dr. Bulkeley's to fulfill my engagement Mrs. Rogers accompanied me hence. Took lunch at the St. Dennies." Mrs. Rogers apparently arranged the medical appointment for Cora. After the doctor's visit, Cora lunched with Kitty and her mother at an equally fashionable hotel restaurant in the ladies' shopping district at the Saint Denis Hotel, whose French name Cora was unable ever to spell right. Everyone agreed that the Saint Denis restaurant was one of the nicest in the city, especially because it was less pricey than the exquisite Brevoort and the glittering Astor. Ed Corbett took the rest of the day off from work at his office on Grand Street in Soho to show Cora and Kitty the sights in New York.

*Eighth Avenue elevated crossing open farmland on its way
to 155th Street, ca. 1885.*

*View of the Brooklyn Bridge in 1885, Currier & Ives engraving.
Courtesy of the Library of Congress.*

Wall Street in 1883.

At 73 Grand St. we were to meet Corbett who was to show me some of New York. He was acting as chaperone as Mrs. Rogers left us in his care. We went to the grand Post Office, the Inauguration Building and then down Wall Street. We then went over the grand Brooklyn Bridge and went to Beecher's church. Then thought we would have our tin-types taken but broke the cameo (naturally speaking) and returned to New York tintypeless.

We came home at a late hour for Dinner and had to make our toilet in 40 minutes as it was then 8 P.M. and we were going to a party. We arrived at Mr. Deerings at 9:10, which was very late. Met Mr. Nick Rogers, Speere and Morrison. Corbett, my escort, was very attentive.

The hosts at the second party Cora attended were Mr. Rogers's sister, Mary May, and her husband, Mr. James Deering, a property lawyer, who introduced Cora to a large group of Columbia students. At that time, Columbia College (later Columbia University) was a small, elite institution for about three hundred students, located on a pleasant, tree-lined Gothic Revival campus at Forty-ninth Street and Madison Avenue, a site now lost under towering office buildings and the Helmsley Palace Hotel. Most of the Deerings' student guests were studying medicine, since everyone at the party was closely linked by family and social ties to Dr. Rodenstein's Manhattan Dispensary. One whom Cora mentioned in her diary was Caldwell Morrison, a nineteen-year-old senior at Columbia's College of Physicians and Surgeons who would receive an A.B. degree in medicine a year later, in 1886.

I can't imagine how Cora's conversations went with these young medical students when she told them about her mother's business as a self-taught eclectic itinerant physician and owner of Mrs. Dr. Keck's Palatial Infirmary for All Chronic Diseases, out in the wilds of Iowa. Columbia's course catalog for 1884 expressly disqualified any eclectic, homeopathic, or other so-called irregular practitioner from taking on medical students as apprentices to receive their degrees. These Columbia dudes were also dead set against women's rights; only twelve of the sixty-three graduates of the class of 1887 favored the idea of coeducation, and a misogynistic "science-fiction" satire in their yearbook about what life would be like with women on campus would certainly have offended a Vassar student at the time as much as today. Cora did not develop a romantic relationship with any of these young men. They would have been polite to her because of her status as a guest of the Rogers family but quietly horrified by the girl's mother's tainted professional life. Cora remained unruffled by the problem and played tag and hide-and-seek with Ed Corbett among the curtains.

In contrast to these callow college boys, Kitty's attractive young uncle Nick Rogers was thirty-one, almost ten years older than the rest of the crowd. Nick was a grain and horse-feed dealer and devilishly charming. If he resembled his much older brother James, Kitty's father, he would have had curly, reddish hair, and his small, muscular frame would have been charged with energy and testosterone. I'm guessing that he was a good specimen of the nineteenth-century bachelor "sporting man" à la Rhett Butler. The typical sporting gent was considered "bad company" by straight arrows of the era, such as the author of *Hills Business Manual of 1884*. According to

Satirical drawing of a "girl graduate" from the 1887 Columbiad yearbook. Courtesy of Columbia University Archives.

Mr. Hill, the sporting gent might be without respectable employment, and he certainly would drive fast horses, wear "flash jewelry," frequent gambling houses, use intoxicating drink, chew tobacco, and speak with profane language. In spite of this, or rather because of it, Cora was instantly smitten with Nick.

In Nick's rakish approach to life, I can see that the Rogers family rose from humble roots. Twenty-five years earlier, during the Civil War, Nick's widowed grandmother, Mrs. Parker, owned and ran a roadhouse that was a way station for coaches going to Boston. The tavern and post house was located down by the docks at Twelfth Avenue and 131st Street and served a rough, all-male clientele. Tough as nails, old Mrs. Parker had recently died at the advanced age of eighty-five, two years before

Cora's visit. Her grandson carried the traces of his colorful background with elegant nonchalance. He owned a fast horse and did as he pleased.

Through the family's political connections and astute business deals, Nick's oldest brother, James, had become the wealthy patriarch of the family, and by age thirty-nine, the tavern-keeper's grandson had acquired one of the biggest trophy houses in the neighborhood. It's a story of very probable improbability—no less a man than Cornelius Vanderbilt had gotten his own start in similar circumstances, fifty years before, as a bare-fisted jack tar on the New York waterfront. In fact, the Commodore's first, tiny office was on the rail line just north of Manhattanville.

James Rogers began as a brick and lime dealer who also owned a fleet of heavy horse-drawn wagons, or "teams," that delivered lumber and other building materials to New York City construction sites from the barge docks and railroad depot at Manhattanville. The era offered a clever businessman with political connections many opportunities. Freight vessels crowded Manhattanville's busy wharf at the river's edge in 1886 so closely that boats sometimes had to wait in line for several days to unload their cargoes of building materials to supply the 778 buildings under construction between Fifty-ninth and 110th streets.[5] New York City was growing at an exponential rate. While still in his twenties, in the fall of 1872, James Rogers was called to City Hall to testify in front of state senate commissioners in a Tweed ring corruption case known as the "Harlem Swindle." Everyone on the senate panel was very interested to know what had happened to 59,000 feet of clear pine boards, 28,500 feet of black walnut, and 3,750 feet of common pine that had been purchased by the city of New York and shipped to Manhattanville by barge.[6]

The lumber was intended to be used to build the Ninth Circuit courthouse across town in Harlem at Sixth Avenue and 128th Street. Mysteriously, most of it was accidentally delivered to the building site of ex-senator H. W. Genet's new mansion, a block away at the corner of Fifth Avenue and 127th Street. The commissioners peppered Mr. Rogers with questions about his role in the process. "I could not tell you," he replied monotonously to every one of the twenty or thirty questions, "and I don't know who can." No delivery invoices seem to have been kept, nor could anyone involved remember anything about how many draymen were involved or where they had been instructed to leave their loads. These impenetrable record-keeping problems are a perennial feature of big government revenue "shrinkage" during any massive public works project. James Rogers was friendly with many influential people in the city government. Based on the evidence I have uncovered, I think that it's safe to say that he was a card-carrying member of the Tweed ring. It was an ideal time and an ideal location for him to make a lot of money; like Tammany Hall's George Washington Plunkitt, Kitty's father practiced "honest graft"; he "seen his opportunities and he took 'em."

I ACTUALLY BEGAN RESEARCHING this book in New York, not Iowa, because Cora started off writing about New York and because I live nearby. Every time I drive into Manhattan from my home in Rockland County, I drive down the West Side Highway and cross over the hollow that was once Manhattanville at 126th Street. Today, sooty brick warehouses and massive subsidized public housing projects crowd together up the steep sides of the bluff where Kitty's white-columned mansion once stood. I look at the empty river and imagine a busy waterfront crowded with ferries, freight barges, small steamers and tugs; I think of the tall hillsides rising sharply on each side of the glen where 126th Street meets the shoreline as still covered with trees; I try to subtract the massive billboards advertising TV shows and fashion brands and superimpose long vanished steeples, Catholic colleges, and even a fanciful Moorish pavilion decorated with blue paint and gilt ornamentation that used to perch on the cliff above the railroad tracks at 138th Street.

What Cora and Kitty knew as Grand Boulevard was originally an old colonial postal route called the Bloomingdale Road. The boulevard remained unpaved throughout the 1880s in most of its uptown sections, in order to provide soft footing for carriage horses, and presented passersby with a regular rotation of mud, ruts, and dust, depending on the season. Spindly elm saplings marched uphill next to the sidewalks on each side of the broad carriageway, which was lined by long, high walls that surrounded the wooded grounds of private estates. Grand

Boulevard was renamed Broadway when the new subway line (the No. 1 train) was installed in 1901, and a large viaduct was built across the chasm where the village used to be.

The Lawrence mansion was one of the most prominent of a series of fading, outdated trophy properties situated on the bluffs above the Hudson River that had been constructed during the fifty years before the Civil War by such renowned men as Alexander Hamilton and Joseph Bonaparte (Napoleon's brother and the former king of Spain), who were looking for a fashionable address, a beautiful view, and clean fresh air far away from the contagious diseases that menaced the crowded, pig-infested streets downtown.[7] By the 1880s, the winds of change were blowing through the neighborhood, and its days of fashionable residential cachet were numbered. Demolition and development threatened. Across the avenue from Kitty's house stood the impressive new Hebrew Orphan Asylum, finished the previous October on the site where the old Devlin mansion had been torn down. The biggest change was still to come: in the early 1890s a "full-fledged and utterly vile" gasworks covering twenty-five city lots was built near the boulevard at 131st Street, a source of odors so horrible that, according to the *New York Times*, they caused nausea and vomiting, which instantly made the neighborhood unlivable for anyone who could possibly afford to live anywhere else. Dr. Rodenstein's hospital went into immediate decline, and Kitty's parents chose this moment to move down to 120th Street in late 1894.

St. Mary's Episcopal Church, the oldest church in Manhattanville, still serves parishioners in West Harlem on 126th Street, and carefully kept church records provided me with a detailed insider's look at the network of warm personal relationships that held New York's political machinery together in the second half of the nineteenth century. Everybody in Manhattanville, rich or poor, attended St. Mary's. Kitty's mother, Anna, who was raised a Catholic, had originally come to Manhattanville from Ireland and boarded with the Cowen family, who were church members, while she worked as a schoolteacher. Anna joined St. Mary's in 1859 and was married there four years later, during the height of the Civil War, to James Rogers, another descendant of Irish forebears.

St. Mary's has held its ground, steadfast, in the midst of the almost inconceivable physical changes that have occurred all around it, the latest upheaval being a tidal wave of expansion by Columbia University, which is now in the process of a northward building spree destined to swallow up every trace of the old village—except, perhaps, the church and its humble wooden rectory next door. I contacted the minister of St. Mary's, the Reverend Kooperkamp, in 2008. He took an immediate interest in my research project, meeting me on a steaming day in June and welcoming me in through the side door, past several courteous, sleepy-looking older African American men waiting in line to participate in one of the church's drug rehab programs. It was the first time in the course of writing this book that I had reached out beyond my own family's artifacts, and the addictive bug of researching New York City history bit me hard that day. Opening a small closet filled with items stored in a haphazard manner, the church secretary reached up to the top shelf and pulled down a plain banker's box containing several old ledgers. I spent hours that afternoon sitting on a plastic chair, searching through these nineteenth-century records for names I recognized. I hit pay dirt within a few minutes.

The lives of the entire Rogers family, going back four generations, were recorded there in neatly inked line entries of christenings, marriages, church membership, funerals, and other notations that even revealed how people died and who was a godparent to whom. Names I knew from Cora's diary descriptions of party hosts and guests leaped out at me from the pages. I collected enough information to construct a detailed family tree for Kitty Rogers. I found out how the Tiemann family and the Rogers family were linked for generations. Most tellingly, one of Kitty's younger uncles, Daniel Tiemann Rogers, was named at his christening in 1857 after the newly elected mayor Daniel Tiemann, who became his godfather. Kitty's father, James, later served for decades as a vestryman for St. Mary's, side by side with the ex-mayor's son, Peter.

ON SUNDAY, JANUARY 4, 1885, Cora wrote: "Arrived home at 4 A.M. on a Sun as bad as some of the western girls hour but this was owing to the distance from Laurence Mansion I had a most delightful evening simply grand first time out from College and I tell u I made the best of it as the Faculty had no ears nor eyes on one girl astray from home." Cora clearly admired those wild Western girls for their willingness to ignore the limitations of Eastern propriety. One can only wonder who escorted Cora and Kitty home, and how? Their poor coachman must have nearly frozen while he waited outside in the dark. I doubt that anyone was able to wake up in time to make it to morning church services at St. Mary's that Sunday. Ed Corbett was supposed to call and take Cora to Brooklyn to hear the Reverend Henry Ward Beecher preach his Sunday sermon, "but the atmospheric currents were otherwise than pleasant so we remained home." Cora probably overslept, but she claims that cold winds prevented this outing;

Cabinet portrait of Kitty's neighbor, Ed Corbett.

Beecher died just two years later, and Cora missed her chance to hear an orator who was nothing less than a national monument.

Cora and Ed Corbett were not particularly religious. Why would they travel all the way to Brooklyn in the middle of winter to go to church? Henry Ward Beecher, brother of Harriet Beecher Stowe and the minister of the Plymouth Congregational Church in Brooklyn Heights, was once "the most famous man in America" because of his fiery support for abolition before the Civil War and his charismatic talent as an orator and preacher. Plymouth Church accommodated six thousand listeners and was often filled to overflowing. Tourists waited as long as an hour outside on Sunday mornings to get a seat.

Even though it was Sunday, Cora and her hosts went out again after six o'clock tea: "Took the elevated to the Parkers', where we spent a very pleasant evening. I met several young gentlemen and ladies. A gent named Mr. Justice Ward seemed quite toney, but was not up to my ideal of a New Yorker." Mr. Ward was the son of the architect of Manhattan College's magnificent new building facing the Grand Boulevard at 131st Street, but that wasn't enough to please Cora's taste. She seems to have already become extremely discriminating after three days in the city. The Parkers who hosted the get-together were surely related to the old innkeeper, Mrs. Parker, who was Kitty's great-grandmother. It being Sunday, Cora and Kitty returned home earlier, at 10:40 P.M. and "had a fine lunch etc."

On Monday, Cora wrote that her next to last day in New York "was giddier than ever. We went downtown at 12 to meet Corbett and then over to Brooklyn again. We received a tintype that has a prominent place in my 'Memoryabil.' We took several turns on the Elevated and finally reached the 63rd Street skating rink. It was a lovely Rink and we had a rich time rolling around. This I enjoyed."

After reading about Cora's two tries at photographing her New York outing, I searched through all her scrapbooks and albums for weeks for this Brooklyn tintype, which she had removed from the memoryabil. I finally found it a month later in the back of the last of her scrapbooks; miraculously, it survived the ages and now has a prominent place in this book. Although not mentioned in most published histories of Central Park, a wooden roller-skating rink must have been erected at Sixty-third Street, nine blocks south of the popular ice skating pond in front of the Dakota at Seventy-second Street. If Davenport and Poughkeepsie had roller rinks, New York certainly had to have one too.

Cora returned to the Lawrence mansion with her friends for dinner and then left for another party at the Kehoes' nearby: "I met so many nice gentlemen; Mr. H. Coehoe [sic] (better known as Harry) was very entertaining at the luncheon and had to know all about the Vassarians by heart. I met Mr. Cooke, a lovely blond, just rich, and had a giddy time with Nick Rogers too. We had a lovely waltz—in fact I enjoyed myself better that night than any." Nick Rogers had really caught Cora's eye and reappears several times later in the diary. He did not give Cora his card. In fact, I wouldn't be surprised if he had never bothered to get

"The Brooklyn Tintype, January 2, 1885." Ed Corbett flanked by Kitty Rogers (left) and her sister Mame, with Cora (seated).

any printed. I see him as the kind of man who would not have wasted time or money on social niceties.

On Tuesday, January 6, Cora wrote: "The last day left for shopping. We went all around, and took lunch at the St. Dennies. We went to all the large establishments." In those days, women did not usually buy finished dresses—they were designed and fitted individually by a dressmaker, who worked from pattern books and by consulting fashion magazines such as *Godey's Lady's Book* or *Harper's Bazaar*. However, hats, feathers, purses, shoes, jewelry, buttons, decorations, fabric, lace for collars, and many other dry goods were sold at enormous "emporiums" such as A. T. Stewart, Lord & Taylor, B. Altman, and Macy's.

At the end of the afternoon, Cora and Kitty began to pack to return to college, and Cora bid her hosts farewell. "Harlem is a superb place," she wrote, "as my friend lives there, but I made so many pleasant acquaintances, too, that thrilled me. I think New York is simply grand but I like Philadelphia better, and Chicago the best of all, probably because I am used to it . . . and New York is so large and noisy. But there were dozens of Vassarians in the steam car going back to Poughkeepsie, which made it not so lonesome."

CHAPTER TEN

Vassar Girl on a String

Arrived at Vassar at 8:30 P.M. Ate supper and went to my parlor. In
a short time, Laura Harris entered and we decided to be roommates.
This was gladly seconded and we resolved to move out of our separate
rooms, P.6L and P.22½ and share the room P. 12½ F. W.

Laura Harris was one of "the college quartette" who had been
stranded with Cora at Vassar over the Christmas holidays. Like
Cora, Laura was a Midwesterner (from Chicago) and in her first year at
Vassar.

WEDNESDAY, JANUARY 7, 1885

Being much fatigued with my journey to New York, including all
the dissipation I endured, I thought I would not take breakfast but
remain quiet, so I did. At 9 A.M. I arose and went to Gibsons for milk,
and having purchased a box of cake at the St. Dennies in New York, I
breakfasted on the named delicacies . . .

   Had my regular recitations, and after lunch I went to bed and wept
for a change. This is probably because I had such a giddy time in the
City. I unpacked and looked forward to the time I could move and get
out of the horrid North corridor, out of Miss Davis's way so she would
not reprimand me so often.

It's tough to return to dull routines after a fantastic vacation ends.
While thinking about her own future, Cora seems to have become overwhelmed by Kitty's fast and glamorous New York society lifestyle, and
she dissolved into tears in the privacy of her bedroom. She could not
seem to explain this outburst to herself. She had visited a social milieu

*"Three little maids from College." Cora (at left) pretending to sneak out of Vassar
with a friend named Sue and Mame Rogers (right).*

that was her heart's desire, but could she ever make that kind of life
happen for herself? At the end of her life, Cora suffered from severe
depression, and this is one of several hints I picked up from her diary
that alerted me to what might be in store for her—the subtle indication
of a flaw buried deeply beneath her jaunty public persona. "Laura Harris brought me 8 letters from the morning mail which revived my failing
spirits more."

It helped reanimate Cora's spirits to aim a jab at a convenient, annoying authority figure. In this case it was her nemesis, the "horrid" corridor teacher Miss Davis (Vassar College class of '78, majored in math and physics), who was a Southerner from Hampton, Virginia. Corridor teachers lived unenviable lives; they were often overqualified, underemployed recent college graduates without the credentials to become full professors, and they patrolled the college community's front lines daily, trying to keep some level of order among the hundreds of high-spirited young ladies whose welfare they were responsible for. Every Monday evening, Miss Davis met with her charges. Each student was expected to report honestly about her behavior during the previous week and confess if she had breached any college rules. The meetings were supposed to be compulsory, but you could cut: "Was absent from corridor meeting but was excused," Cora wrote later that spring.

If Miss Davis showed a sour face to her charges, I will forgive her for it in retrospect. She was educated for a career in math and physics but was unable to break free from Vassar's gilded confines into a real job on the outside world. Today, a Vassar graduate with that kind of training would be headed for engineering school or a Wall Street career. Instead, Miss Davis found herself marooned on a college hallway in a low-paying job involving no more intellectual stimulus than being a camp counselor would. There were in fact many gilded cages filled with frustrated, intelligent, ambitious women in 1885, and Vassar was one

Drawing by Mary Donohue of their corridor teacher, Miss Davis, as the devil. "Young ladies, I'm surprised—What's the meaning of this?" Courtesy of Vassar College Archives.

of them. Worse, Miss Davis was no doubt well aware that many of the young girls whose lives she controlled would soon be sailing out of college to marry wealthy men, at which point they would instantly far surpass her limited station in life. It's no wonder she was touchy.

Laura was starting at the bottom of the heap in Prep Level III, along with Cora's roommate from the fall, Eveline Woodmansee, and twenty-six other young women. They were presumably hoping to be admitted to the regular four-year academic program as freshmen. In practice, many would fall by the wayside before reaching that goal. Based on some rough calculations using the number of former preps who succeeded in enrolling as freshmen in September 1884, I estimate that the throughput of this program was a dismal one in twenty.

Someone wrote the following ditty about Laura, and Cora put it into the scrapbook later in the winter at the end of February:

"The college quartette, December '84. Minnie tickled, Laura sympathetic, Co determined." Cora (tallest) with Laura Harris (left), Fannie Clark, and Minnie Keiter (in skates, sneezing).

Miss Laura Harris is now a "Prep"
+ if she isn't "dropped"
she'll be a senior yet.—u bet?

Laura was the only one of Cora's friends to score a perfect 5 on the English grammar section of the college entrance exams, and the principal of the Moseley School in Chicago who wrote her recommendation declared that she "exhibited marked traits of excellence as a pupil" and had "superior promise." His confidence was not misplaced. Unlike many of the other preps who started in 1884, Miss Harris proved to be both smart and persistent, graduating with a B.A. from Vassar's four-year program in 1890. She enrolled at the University of Chicago in 1891, went on to a career as manager and executive for Allies Inn in Washington, D.C., and eventually sent three of her four sons to the U.S. Military Academy at West Point.

DURING THE PREVIOUS YEAR, Vassar's management crisis had deepened. The old "fossils" serving on Vassar's board of trustees closed ranks as alumnae criticism mounted. A dynamic and competent group, the national Vassar Alumnae Association had about six hundred members; local chapters in Boston, New York, St. Louis, and Chicago were particularly active and effective. In April of 1884, the Boston chapter had sent a letter to the trustees signed by ten of its leading members outlining their criticisms of President Caldwell. He was a failure, they said, because of his lack of executive ability, his lack of energy in promoting the college's growth, and his failure to maintain Vassar's former prestige.

According to an article in a New York newspaper, which Cora clipped and saved in her scrapbook, the Boston letter "was tabled on the grounds that it was informally addressed, and no notice whatever was taken of it . . . no answer was returned to the senders, although they are described as being among the most prominent of the graduates of the college and ladies whose opinions are entitled to great weight." Word of this snub spread quickly. The New York chapter of the Alumnae Association held a meeting at Delmonico's restaurant in January and sent its own stinging letter to the trustees up in Poughkeepsie. To ensure that they would not be ignored as their sisters in Boston had been, they leaked a copy to the *New York Herald Tribune*. Cora clipped and saved the *Tribune* article and several others about the fierce management struggles, as did many of her classmates. The letter openly attacked the men on the board and called on President Caldwell to resign: "the management of the college should be entrusted to energetic men of business, not old fogies and elderly clergymen, who have succeeded in running it down to its present low condition."

The Boston alumnae backed up their criticisms with specific examples of President Caldwell's negligent management style: "One teacher at a large school, it is charged, who was anxious to prepare students for Vassar wrote to the President and asked him for information. The answer was, 'We have no time to give information. You can look at the catalogue.' The college at this time was $7,000 in debt, and the college had lost 100 students since 1874 (over the previous 10 years)." They also pleaded that the three new trustees slated to be elected at the annual meeting in June 1885 should be men of business, not clergymen, and called for a woman to be elected to serve on the board for the first time. This January letter was ignored as coldly as the one from Boston had been. Even the newspaper leak was not enough to get the trustees to pay attention.

Rumors swirled through the dormitory corridors—Loulu Poppenheim heard that tuition would go down by $100 the next year, because the college might get more students and decrease its debt that way; she also heard that the main meal of the day, dinner, was to be switched to noontime from 6 P.M. to save money. Everyone knew that the alumnae were calling for the resignation of Dr. Caldwell as president of Vassar. A confrontation was building. In June, when trustees, alumnae, students, graduates, and parents converged on the campus for commencement, all hell was going to break loose.

MORE RUMORS ABOUT VASSAR erupted in the news in the second week of January.[1] A Westchester County love affair that turned into a sensational elopement featured a phony link to the college. Over and over, Vassar's prominent name popped up in the Victorian newspapers as a "go-to" brand concept to elevate the drama of ordinary romantic adventure.

An article in the *New York Times* headlined "Gone to Join Her Lover" alerted readers to tantalizing details about "one of the belles of the village of White Plains," a seventeen-year-old-girl named Minnie Newman. As she departed for the train station on January 18th with her two trunks, Minnie told her mother that she had enrolled at Vassar College and was on her way to Poughkeepsie. However, Vassar and Miss Goodsell had never heard of her. Instead, she boarded a train for New York City to meet her lover, John D. Fiske, Esq., who claimed to be from a prominent family in Philadelphia. In her wake, Minnie left a string of unpaid bills for shoes, cologne, and scented soaps.

During their impassioned courtship, Mr. Fiske had convinced Minnie and her mother, Adeliza, that he was a respectable Philadelphia lawyer, the author of "Fiske's Law Register and Court Record," published at No.

403 Market Street. Appearances weighed heavily in that era before Internet background searches; according to a reporter, he was "quite dudish in his toilet, wearing fashionable clothes," and sported fur trimming on the collar of his overcoat. Adeliza was a divorced woman without any real resources, but she also appears to have kept up a convincing pretense of wealth, hoping that her pretty daughter would marry well and rescue the household from their reduced station in life. It was the perfect setup for an O. Henry story—Minnie's mother puffing herself up with social pretense versus the wily junkyard lawyer, handy with his dirty tricks, both trying to reel in what they believed was "a big fish."

Everyone "understood Miss Newman and Mr. Fiske to be engaged," but he evaded setting a definite marriage date by suggesting that two years of education at a boarding school or college would be useful to Minnie, because he "moved in the highest circles in Philadelphia" and "wanted a wife who was well educated and could support her position creditably."

He soon had two Saratoga trunks delivered to Minnie's home for her to pack her trousseau in preparation for her schooling, which he emphasized had to happen before the wedding. Minnie's mother and her grandfather, who seem to have belatedly realized that the suitor might not be all the man that he seemed to be, rapidly lost control of the situation.

A letter addressed to Minnie arrived from Brockton, Massachusetts, on the 13th that revealed that Fiske had been disbarred by the Plymouth County Bar Association on ten charges and had two ex-wives in two states, who had both divorced him for abusive treatment. "I think you must have some property, as that is all he seemed to want from his other wives," the writer declared. Furious to learn that Fiske was playing a con game on her, Adeliza kicked him out of the house and sought legal counsel for "breach of promise." Twenty minutes later, Minnie's paramour pressed a diamond ring into her hand and rushed to the train station for Philadelphia.

Instead of obeying her mother's plea to break off the relationship, the headstrong Minnie stuck to her man, viewing him as "a greatly persecuted person." Five days later, she left home to join her lover. "Her departure has created no surprise in White Plains, as it was expected."

Instead of a glamorous finishing school or a Main Line lawyer's mansion, Minnie's new home in Philadelphia turned out to be a common boardinghouse. Whatever the pleasures of his passionate embraces, Fiske had little else to offer Minnie in material comforts. Because she was underage, her mother was legally entitled to break up the relationship, and the Society for the Prevention of Cruelty to Children took up the case. Fiske sued to get her back, but by April, his lawyer learned from Minnie that "she wished to have no more to do with" her former lover.

Cora read the *New York Times* regularly and easily could have noticed this story, although she did not clip it for her scrapbook. But she would have known the whole narrative arc by heart: if a girl from a prominent family eloped, it was news, notorious news, and she was risking everything for the word of a man who could turn his back on her and destroy her future without a second thought. It was a dandy way to be publicly humiliated. Eloping could lead as easily to irreversible disaster as it could to true love and happiness.

As a coda to the story, in the summer of 1890 the *Times* noted that out in California, Mr. John D. Fiske, lawyer and manager of the Fresno opera house, had been shot in the back three times in front of the Grand Central Hotel and died on the floor of a nearby drugstore "with the blood streaming from his lips." He was blackmailing an inventor in a patent deal, and the angry victim hunted him down and killed him. Going west was a standard nineteenth-century escape route for men evading unwanted responsibilities; I don't see that Minnie had much of a future with that fellow in the long run.

ON SATURDAY, JANUARY 21, Cora attended her first public concert of the season at the Collingwood Opera House in Poughkeepsie with a fellow music student, Lotta Wix, from Hoboken, New Jersey. They caught the earliest horse car, which started off from the college at seven on a bitterly cold, windless night lit by a full moon. From the outside, the Main Building was beautiful in the brilliant light. Every windowsill was filled with snow, and long dark shadows leaped out from the base of every tree and wall in stark black-and-white relief. The passengers pressed their boots onto the hot bricks laid in straw on the floor to keep their feet warm. At the opera house, Cora settled into her seat number C73, Parquet, next to Lotta, and listened to the orchestra of forty musicians from New York City's Philharmonic Society tune up. A dramatic soprano from Germany, Madame Eugenie Pappenheim, was going to sing Mendelssohn's 42nd Psalm with the chorus and orchestra in a stirring, emotional finale.

The Poppenheim sisters, who felt that the famous Miss Pappenheim must practically be a relative, decided to attend the concert at the last minute despite their worry about the high cost of the tickets. They ended up sitting right across the aisle from Dr. and Mrs. Caldwell, surrounded by other Vassar faculty. They didn't mind this at all, although they felt constrained to act "straight." May was naturally conservative and came by this ability easily; she later wrote to her mother that Mme. Pappenheim's dress "left her arms and neck bare, but her dress was so high that even prudent prudish *me*, I did not disapprove of it." She wrote three full paragraphs about every detail of Mme. Pappenheim's appearance and clothing, noting that "she had lines about her mouth which showed she was old" and as an afterthought threw in a remark at the end praising the quality of her singing.[2]

In the crowded lobby after the concert, Cora and Lotta Wix recognized the faces of several young men. These were guys she had seen around Poughkeepsie, riding horseback on Raymond Avenue by the college, or headed out to the Hudson Valley Driving Park on Hooker Avenue to watch the trotting races, or coming into Smiths for ice cream. The girls pretended to take no notice of them. Cora especially sought to avoid eye contact with the Eastman dude, Mr. Corwin, who seemed to be trying to force his way through the throng in their direction. She worried that she might have to send him a squelcher, as Cora Scofield had had to do twice to get rid of Will Bishop, an undesirable "type" from Muscatine, Iowa, she had met at the Poughkeepsie roller-skating rink.[3]

On January 29, Vassar declared a college holiday to observe the national Day of Prayer for Colleges. The girls were required to attend three prayer meetings and three lectures in the chapel lasting from half past nine in the morning until nine at night. Cora took no notice of it; I learned about the event only by reading the Poppenheims' letters. She also failed to mention a reception that Dr. Caldwell and his wife gave for the entire college on February 3. Apparently fifty other girls chose that same weekend to leave college for more exciting social commitments in New York City.

That same day, a young lady living in Kitty's household in Manhattanville, maybe one of Kitty's cousins, wrote Cora to inquire about Ed Corbett, who seemed to be the center of everyone's attention.

> My Dear Miss K,
> We are indeed lonesome since you + Kitty left here. Ed, do you know any thing of him? Is he attending school or has he gone west? . . . I continue to have an interest in him I will ask how does he appear Mentally. His, I think, is a rather serious case + needs treatment—either the faith cure or Homeopathy is the only thing that will reach him. I will prescribe: Encouragement 40 drops etc. etc. . . . Pour the above in a barrel filled with dignity; stir with a staff of independence in the hands of some other fellow.

Although he was handsome, considerate, kindly, well dressed, and wealthy, everyone agreed that Ed Corbett lacked self-confidence and force of personality. This was a problem. At the other extreme, Cora had met two "Harvard's" at the tintype shop the week before, on January 23, who were "completely 'off'" with anger about something. The two arrogant "swells" posed together, with one sitting in a chair wearing a bowler hat and the other sitting in his friend's lap and holding an expensive walking stick. They left behind not one, but two images of themselves, then stormed out of the photog-

"2 Harvards, completely off. The dudes (angry)." Tintype from Cora's memory-abil, taken on January 23, 1885.

raphy studio without even giving their names. Excessive male forcefulness could be a problem, too.

BECAUSE CORA FIRST RECEIVED the diary as a gift on March 22, she reconstructed only the most important winter events from memory. She felt very guilty about certain activities that she could not resist, and they comprise the bulk of her entries. Her next diary entry comes a month later.

THURSDAY, FEBRUARY 5, 1885

"My Fatal Day" that of telling a falsehood to Miss Goodsell. I had my engagement for an appointment with Doctor Bulkley and want to keep it, and at the same time, I am deceiving my Parents. But I know they will forgive me when I explain it all to them as I certainly was suffering greatly and I mean to repent just as soon as I see the beloved objects.

Miss Goodsell wanted to know if my parents were aware of my expected visit and engagement [the doctor's appointment]. It was oh! so hard to succumb to the inevitable—I smiled and answered in the affirmative, but they don't know at all.

When I first read this section, my imagination ran wild. What on earth was going on? Secret doctor's visits? Cora's own mother was a doctor. Why didn't she just write home about her problem? And what *was* her problem? Nothing else in the diary gives any hint of ill health or sickness, but Cora visited Dr. Lucius D. Bulkley's office on East Thirty-seventh Street just off Fifth Avenue at least six times throughout the academic year 1884–1885. She also visited Vassar's in-house Quaker physician Dr. Eliza M. Mosher several times. But on this outing, she doesn't sound very sick at all.

Well, I had permission to go to New York, for the first time without
a telegram from home. Here I was really going on my own accord.
I had to rush around that morning to take my Music lesson and to finish packing, as I was going to take my Reception Dress for the
evening party at the Rogers'. Frauleine Hinkel excused me a few minutes earlier from German class, and Kitty and I ate our lunch at the
depot.

We arrived in New York at 3:30 P.M. We went up to the Rogers and
got dressed for the evening. I had a grand time. So many gentlemen
were there. I never could have been more attractive. I received more
engagements than I wanted. Mr. Haskins was lovely—so was Morrison, Nick, Corbett, Harry Coehoe and Mr. Quinn succeeded too.

The latest was "A Vassar girl on a string." This was because I was
twined around and around my neck with tinsel to perfection.

We had a terrible time trying to go to sleep. Kitty did not sleep any
as we retired at 3½ A.M.

On Sunday Cora added only one more sentence: "The day I had
so much fun Flirting in New York with the college boys." She saved
many souvenirs on several pages in the scrapbook from this weekend.
A small paintbrush is fastened to one page with a blob of black sealing wax—"(taken prior to my visit to New York Feb.6.85. Taken from
the Studio-)"—a card from the Central Café on Fourteenth Street and
some pressed leaves from a bouquet decorate another page, which also
has five two-line rhymes cut from the newspaper. Cora highlighted two
of them in particular as being relevant to "Nick":

Oh! That I had been ten thousand miles away,
Ere I saw you on that fatal day.

Dearest, don't make me feel so jealous,
But do stop talking with those fellows.

The other three Valentine's Day couplets compared her heart to a

Page from Cora's scrapbook: "Vassar Girl on a string, Feb. 6, '85."

burning coal and wished that someone would turn two into one and consent to marry her in the future. She didn't put Nick's name next to those.

Cora also saved a piece of the golden tinsel that one of the good-looking young men had playfully wound around her neck during the party. "'A Vassar girl on a string' Feb 6, '85," she wrote next to it. Attached to the yellowed page with a bit of lavender silk ribbon, after 125 years the small tangle of glittering threads still carries the freight of that shining moment of excitement and expectation in Cora's heart—the world was her oyster right then, and she was loving it. Her future was still in front of her, and it looked so good.

During this same weekend, Cora went with Kitty and Mrs. Rogers to her appointment with Dr. Bulkley. Here is Cora's brief summary of what a typical visit to the doctor in 1885 was like:

> We had to wait at Dr. B. about an hour as there was so many Patients. He saw me at last and pronounced me much better. It certainly was

50% better than in January. My pulse had come down from 90 to 88 beats. He gave me a new prescription and I had it filled at Dr. Speers. At dinner I had my glass of milk the Doctor said I must drink milk instead of eating when I am hungry so every lunch I expect to march out of the Dining room with a glass of milk.

With the exception of her dressmaker's bill, Cora's medical consultations were by far the most expensive items in her accounts; she spent more than $30 on these visits—the equivalent of two train tickets back to Davenport. Dr. Bulkley's office was in the heart of the most fashionable part of Manhattan, and in June 1885 he traveled to Europe for a week as the private physician to a wealthy client. He was clearly a top medical specialist. But in what?

The reference department at the New York Academy of Medicine provided me with an easy answer to this mystery. Dr. Bulkley was a specialist in diseases of the skin; he had treated more than eight thousand cases of eczema and fifteen hundred cases of acne by 1885. Cora probably had eczema. She mentions that she "was suffering greatly." Eczema is usually more painful than acne, and the complexion of her face never showed any trace of pimply outbreaks in any of her pictures. Dr. Bulkley believed that diet and menstruation both had important effects on the disease. He prescribed a special diet and medications that she obtained from a druggist named Haas and drew a little map of how to get to Haas's drugstore on the back of the first prescription he gave her.

Mrs. Dr. Keck openly boasted that she could cure eczema in an 1894 advertising flyer for her Catarrh Infirmary. A farmer in Webster City, Iowa, wrote a testimonial letter thanking her for curing his case after five years of treatment with her blood purifiers. Nevertheless, Cora must have found that her mother's eclectic herbal medications weren't effective for her skin problems. Simply by making a doctor's appointment, Cora was taking a stand with all the enemies who had ever accused her mother of being an ignorant pretender and a crooked charlatan. She was turning her back on her mother's alternative medical philosophy and crossing over the "charmed line" to consult with a member of the same antagonistic brotherhood of M.D.s who had blacklisted her family and refused to treat a severe burn she had had when she was thirteen years old. Perhaps she was influenced in her doubts by the criticism and contempt she had heard from the doctors and young medical students she had met while visiting Kitty's family. Maybe she was getting tired of hearing her mother's high-pitched medical pronouncements. "Nearly thirty years of active practice have brought my METHODS AND MY PREPARATIONS to a high degree of perfection," Mrs. Dr. Keck declared in her medical manifesto, while boasting of "the INCALCULABLE VALUE" of her "ORIGINAL TREATMENT."

Cora was now establishing herself as a doubter; her visits to Dr. Bulkley not only would have offended her mother's pride, they would have been an open rebuke to the honesty of her advertising. For Cora, going to that doctor was practically the same as calling her mother a quack to her face.

"At about this time," Cora wrote, "I had heard of Mama's terrible dream; she dreamed that I was very ill and that the Faculty telegraphed for Papa and Mama to come if they wanted to see me alive. This worried me awfully as Mama wrote that it was a caution for her to warn me against things." Cora was feeling pretty guilty, but not enough to change her program of secretive activities. Cora's mother certainly had good instincts—from her standpoint, her daughter really would have been in need of some sort of warning, since Cora was cheerfully lying to the college administrators and sneaking off campus for lengthy weekend visits in New York without her permission. Not only was Cora rejecting her mother's medical expertise, she was also finagling her way into an active off-campus social life that her parents knew nothing about, with people they had never met, under circumstances they knew nothing about. She sounds very modern.

Right after the premonition of her mother's terrible dream, Cora received a letter from her friend Hattie Wakefield in Illinois; Hattie's father, Dr. Cyrenius Wakefield, died suddenly of pneumonia after catching a bad cold. Hattie was distraught. "Every day seems darker to me," she wrote. "I do not think I can ever be happy again, as I have lost the dearest one on earth . . . Cora you ought to be a happy girl because you have both a father and mother . . . Pa and I had been together so much and attended so many places of interest. All is over now; I do not take interest in any-thing."

Death and depression, laid out in black and white. All reports to the contrary, I would suggest that our forebears in the nineteenth century suffered the pain of death and losing someone they loved as deeply as we do today. And it is not hard to imagine that the regular doctors of Bloomington who shunned Dr. Wakefield because of his patent medicine business might have snickered with *schadenfreude* at the old man who presumed to call himself a physician but found that he could not cure his own case of the grippe.

∽

IN POUGHKEEPSIE two weekends later, the newspaper reported plenty of snow with a firm surface and moderate temperatures. Everyone hurried outside to take advantage of the perfect sleighing conditions.

SUNDAY, FEBRUARY 22, 1885

Washington's Birthday is a legal Holiday and of course they had to give it to us. So the Faculty gave the day on Monday. Spent my Sunday very piously. "Such is life at Vassar."

I am longing for the morrow to come. The other girls all went home to take advantage of the Holiday. My Friend Kitty went home—how I long to accompany her. Of course she invited me, but I did not dare to accept, as I take advantage a little too often of the short distance from Vassar to New York.

Feeling bereft and left out, Cora leafed back through her scrapbook to the page with the dried leaves on it filled with sad thoughts from October 19. "I never needed a man so bad in all my life, Feb 22, '85," she added in pencil.

—————— CHAPTER ELEVEN ——————

Oh! U Wretch!

⟶⟶⟶

During the winter of 1885, a Vassar insider who preferred to con-
ceal her identity gave a "confidential" gossipy interview to a
young journalist in New York City. Let's call her "Miss V." The reporter
wrote up an "exposé" three columns long of college life at Vassar with
the insulting headline of "Vassar Virgins' Vagaries" and spiked it with as
many wild details as possible, no doubt at the request of the same editor
who chose the silly headline for the article, which Cora clipped and pasted into her second, larger scrapbook. Starting with its disrespectful headline, it is a good example of the thinly veiled contempt that many male
journalists and curmudgeonly men of the 1880s liked to inflict on Vassar's
independent young women in order "to take them down a notch."

> On Saturdays, whenever there is snow, the long hills to the east of
> Poughkeepsie are alive with Vassar girls coasting on their little red
> sleds. You would be astonished by the dash and vigor displayed by
> these elegant young ladies when there is no young man around to look
> at them. Taking headers down rocky hills and screeching with mirth
> when they meet with a mishap is considered having a grand time.
> When they get tired of such sport they "hitch on" behind any farmer's
> sled [large farm wagon on runners, pulled by horses or oxen] which
> chances to pass by.
>   One day an old Dutchess county farmer, who had a string of Vassar
> girls tagging behind, trotted his team five miles into the country with-
> out stopping to give them a chance to untie their sleds. They screamed
> and grew mad and hurled slang and damaged chewing gum at him
> during most of the distance, but he merely chuckled to himself and
> drove on. When he finally turned them adrift they had to trudge back
> through the snow to the college on foot, as no teams came along to
> give them a lift.

Stereoscope image of fashionable East Thirty-fourth Street in New York City, ca. 1885. Courtesy of the Library of Congress.

A different, more friendly article in the *New York Herald* from the winter of 1885 complained about the damage done to the college by the nationally popular genre of "Vassar jokes," favored by cigar-chomping newspaper editors and publishers across the country: "nothing kills like ridicule . . . The deadly paragraph of the alleged newspaper humorist, taking Vassar for its theme because it is the representative female college, has done it more injury than the writers would believe . . . Many a girl has been sent to Smith or Wellesley because these colleges have escaped the time-dishonored jokes about the 'Vassar girl.'"

This same article praised Vassar's Alumnae Association and its powerful money-raising abilities. The headline ran: "Vassar's Loyal Daughters—Raising Funds to Build a $20,000 Gymnasium. Mrs. Thompson's Generous Gift. How the College has Struggled with its Enemies—Alumnae Secure Recognition." The article provided an intelligent, respectful overview of how effective the alumnae were in the struggle to help Vassar out of its financial difficulties.

On the basis of the many news items about Vassar that Cora clipped and saved, it appears that the writers and editors at several different New York papers were engaged in a vigorous public dialogue about the role of educated women in the United States. Cora would certainly have noticed this. The tone of these articles allows me to divide them into two distinct groups: the ones that show respect for the college and its accomplishments, and the others that ooze condescension and contempt for anything a young woman might try to do. For every putdown that was published, whether serious or comic, some ally would publish a sympathetic article in defense of the dignity of Vassar and its students. This public form of debate in print inspired Cora's classmate Mary Sheldon to become a journalist after graduating, and her articles, which Cora also saved, were often written to refute specific insults and criticisms.

ON WEDNESDAY, MARCH 4, 1885, Grover Cleveland was inaugurated as the twenty-second president of the United States. Now it was payback time for the mistaken Blaine victory celebrations, and the *Poughkeepsie Eagle* reported in detail on the "Hilarious Democratic Vassarians" who "got square with the Republican girls who hurrahed for Blaine last November." The magnificent oyster victory dinner of November 5 had been a running joke all winter, and Cora's scrapbook contains a note from a friend reminding her that Cleveland had won and that oysters were being served—most likely a ribald poke from a Democrat.

Vassar's celebration of the presidential inauguration mimicked the grand events in Washington, D.C. Dressed in elegant outfits, the students and faculty circulated in the public rooms on the main floor by the grand staircase and chatted while the musicians tuned up for dancing. The college parlors and reception rooms were decorated with red, white, and blue bunting; portraits of the outgoing and incoming presidents, Chester A. Arthur and Grover Cleveland, flanked the entrance of the dining hall on gilded easels. No young men were invited to this dance; the girls escorted each other, and Cora's dance card listed her current best friends, including Jessie Starkweather, Eveline "Wood" Woodmansee, and May Carbutt (who were all vigorous tennis players); Lilly

Yates, from the School of Music; and the two academic achievers Marion Austin and Minnie Keiter. The Glee Club split into two sections: one sang from the anti-Cleveland perspective, referring to Cleveland as the reviled "little Democrat" who almost "got left again," while the winning side responded briskly by singing "Triumphant are we . . . we've eaten the crackers and stew of humiliation, and now you must too."

Although she clipped articles about politics from New York newspapers and put them into her scrapbooks, Cora paid little heed to national events in her diary and utterly failed to mention the inauguration there. This was no doubt because she was already scheming with Kitty to arrange their next unauthorized trip to New York City. A month after the first illegal evasion, they put their second plan into action.

THURSDAY, MARCH 5, 1885

I requested to go to meet Miss Goodsell in her room at her Office hours to arrange about going to New York. I hardly knew how to commence such a tender and quickening subject, but I braved up and told her that I had an engagement with my New York doctor, which was all O.K.

MISS G.: "Does your Mama know u are going to N.Y.?"

STUDENT: (Somewhat exsighted) "Yes." (She doesn't know)

Kitty was awaiting out side to know the result + when I enformed her I could come back on Sunday was extremely delighted—we both went flying down the stairs. That's the day I drew $15, too. Oh! u wretch!

Cora didn't write any details in the diary about what she did that weekend. I checked her cash accounts pages, which she carried out neatly and dutifully every two weeks with regular, major computation errors. Her accounts for the second two weeks of March show that she spent only $6.21 on regular expenses, not $15 in two days. No clues there either. It's likely that Kitty's family entertained the same group of young men Cora had already met. While the specifics of Cora's and Kitty's weekend are lost, the general picture is not. By 1885, the Rogers family had become socially prominent within their community and mixed with a diverse and ambitious social set from the Upper West Side neighborhoods of

Kitty's parents, Anna Rogers (left) and James Rogers (right), ca. 1890.

Bloomingdale, Manhattanville, and Washington Heights. Cora saved two newspaper articles that Kitty sent her three years after they had both left Vassar. One described a huge charity fund-raiser for Dr. Rodenstein's Manhattan Dispensary and Hospital in Manhattanville, and the other was a notice about the Rogerses' twenty-fifth wedding anniversary; these articles gave me some clues about who was in the Rogers family's social circle. One article was illustrated with a woodcut of Mrs. Rogers's portrait, which allowed me to identify the pair of photographs Cora had of Kitty's parents in one of her photo albums.

The hospital's Ladies Aid Association included the wives of many socially and financially ambitious couples. One friend of Annie Rogers was Mrs. Ida Alice Flagler, the second, much younger wife of the Standard Oil magnate H. M. Flagler. Ida had been the young nurse to the first Mrs. Flagler, who had died of tuberculosis in 1883, and she boldly wed the widower after an indecently short interval. Red-haired and fiery in temperament, she had been married for two years in 1885 and lived most of the year in St. Augustine, Florida, to avoid being snubbed by friends of the first Mrs. Flagler. Others with whom Annie Rogers socialized included Mr. and Mrs. Isidor Straus. Although Straus would take over Macy's department store in 1896, in 1885 he was still running the crockery and glassware department with his brother, Nathan. Several of the Rogerses' other friends were connected to the Philadelphia firm of Drexel & Morgan; in particular, Annie Rogers worked on a charity event with Mary Robinson, another out-of-towner who had recently married J. Hood Wright, a Drexel partner and philanthropist. Louisa Poppenheim and her circle of New York friends did not think much of the Drexel family. In June 1886 she wrote to her mother, "Miss Drexel is our class president for next semester. Most of the nice girls in the class are very much disappointed."

Although wealthy, the Rogerses and their social circle were explicitly and emphatically not included in Victorian New York's famous social elite, the "Four Hundred," a highly restricted subset of New York's ultra-fashionable citizenry that included the author Edith (Jones) Wharton, who achieved lasting fame by portraying the narrow lives of a group small enough in number to be squeezed into Mrs. Astor's Fifth Avenue ballroom and feel socially comfortable in the process.[1] By the 1880s, the once untouchable Vanderbilts had evolved into prominent Astor guests, but the Rogerses and their friends were still grasping at much lower rungs of the city's golden social ladder.

If the West Side was on the wrong side of Manhattan's social map, Manhattanville was off the map entirely, and Annie Rogers's Irish ancestry was a known obstacle to social climbing. Descendants of German immigrants, such as the Rodensteins and Tiemanns, encountered similar problems. Their connections to the notorious Tammany Hall political machinery probably didn't help, either. That kind of snobbery was undoubtedly painful to Annie Rogers. In the 1900 census she decided to redefine her heritage, giving her own and her parents' birthplaces as "New York"; perhaps she had been telling people she was from a native New York family for long enough that she forgot it wasn't true.

ON MARCH 11, CORA WROTE: "After Chapel we girls prepared for the evening Concert in Po'K. Something we look forth to with so much pleasure, really anticipating entirely too much as we are often left." It was very fine, she noted, adding gleefully, "we succeeded in getting 'Reserved' seats." Cora's classmate Georgina Hayman sang the soprano part in a vocal quartet taken from Mozart's Requiem. Vassar students were not generally allowed to perform in these public concerts at the Collingwood in Poughkeepsie. This exceptional departure from the norm shows that Georgina was both extremely talented and a special protégée of Professor Ritter. Georgina's father was also the chorus master for the Vocal Union, so he would have been there on the stage with her. Sitting in her reserved seat, Cora might have felt very inferior to Miss Hayman, but she did not mention this in her diary, noting only that "the great Ovide Muslin and the violinist Mr. J. B. Van Vliet accompanied . . . it was very fine."

Cora lied to Miss Goodsell a third time on Thursday, March 12, for another New York trip with Kitty, a week after the previous outing. Once again, she was given permission to leave the college for an important doctor's appointment. This time Cora was acutely aware that she was taking advantage of Miss Goodsell's kindness and braced herself for more stern, long-distance premonitions from her doting parents.

Miss Goodsell gently told me I could go, and asked who my chaperone was and when I would return to Vassar again. She hoped I would have a pleasant time and asked what train I wanted to take and told me my breakfast would await my coming in the German halle. . . . 'Oh! u wretch!'

Friday A.M. I expected a letter or telegram from home informing me of something that was not going altogether right . . . to say I was worried in mind was an understatement, as I certainly felt wrong and the feeling seemed to increase instead of me becoming used to wrong doings.

It certainly is hard to succumb to the inevitable. I gave way, resolved to go to New York, and braved up and told Bro. Sam to call me at 6½ A.M. Saturday.

SATURDAY, MARCH 14, 1885

At 6½ A.M. I heard two gentle raps on my parlor door. Laura heard them and boisterously informed me that I was going to the City (N.Y.) for a change. I dressed myself and repaired to the Dining Halle, there to meet several others like myself, probably all worried about being caught because our Mamas did not know we were out.

This nervousness stemmed not only from Cora's basic human reluctance to lie to people who cared about her, which is as relevant today as it was in 1885, but also from something more foreign to many of us—the strict social controls that were supposed to govern proper young middle- and upper-class women's lives in premodern America.

After returning from this junket, Cora helpfully provided me with a contemporary quote on the topic of Victorian morals that still sounds thundering, 125 years later: "'If u are once found u are lost.' –Rev. Spaulding P.S.V.C." Literally, this should mean that if it were discovered that a young lady had violated the strict boundaries of decent behavior, there was nothing she could do to redeem her moral reputation, and she would be "lost" to decent society forever. Edith Wharton memorably portrayed a social catastrophe of this kind in *The House of Mirth*, written in 1905, in which the reputation of a New York socialite is ruined after she is seen visiting the private rooms of a male friend and later of a married man, even though she did not have a sexual relationship with either of them. At first reading, I imagined the Reverend Spaulding to have been a fierce, visiting religious speaker, not a regular Vassar faculty member. His moral authority must have been huge and intimidating; Cora reiterated this line many times throughout the diary. He must have made the girls shake in their shoes.

How easily my preconceived ideas about the limits on the lives of Victorian women led me astray with this one. The Reverend Robert Spaulding was, in fact, a fictional character from a farcical 1884 hit Broadway play, *The Private Secretary* by Charles Hawtrey. Vassar's Philalethea Dramatic Society performed it (with the express permission of the Madison Square Theater) on December 13, 1884, and the Reverend Robert Spaulding was played by a Miss Fox.

According to the contemporary novelist, essayist, and critic G. K. Chesterton, the Reverend Spaulding was "the meekest of the meek, whose hair is parted down the center, who is very limp, whose trousers are four inches above his shoes, who wears galoshes and who suffers from a chronic cold."[2] He was so dense and so gullible that he mistook the "if u are found u are lost" phrase, spoken to him several times by the beautiful young Miss Ashford, for a mysterious password. In fact, this misunderstanding provides the comic climax of the play. Cora's

Rev. Spaulding was a wholly ironic cultural reference. The play spoofed the gravity of the moral system, and Cora quoted it not out of fear, but in raucous irony, to make fun of the rules, their enforcers, and her frequent school evasions.

The 1882 Students Manual of Vassar College doesn't say anything about the price Cora could have paid for breaking the rules against leaving campus without the proper permission. However, Miss Goodsell submitted a Lady Principal's Report to the president of the college at the end of each school year, and thanks to these once top secret documents, I found out what really happened with disciplinary matters behind the scenes.[3] At the Vassar Library's Special Collections, I read through all her handwritten reports from the 1880s, including both years that Cora was enrolled, barely suppressing a sharp feeling of anxiety that the Lady Principal might enter the room at any moment and catch me reading her private correspondence with the college president. I was surprised to find that Miss Goodsell used reassuring tones to gloss over specific problems as much as possible. Putting her own management skills in a good light, she would declare that "a cheerful compliance with the decisions of authority even when these come in conflict with strong personal wishes, are almost universal, disobedience, untrustworthiness, are the exception, and by no means frequent." Most years, however, one or two girls had to be expelled and their names mentioned to the president.

During her first year as Lady Principal in 1881, Miss Goodsell underwent a baptism of fire while handling a wild crisis. A girl named Miss Magnus was caught stealing, and Miss Goodsell believed that she was a kleptomaniac. Miss Magnus was so afraid of her father, who had been summoned to come and remove her from college, that she was seized with nervous convulsions and died suddenly of a heart attack in Miss Goodsell's office. That same year, Miss G. G. Williams was expelled for persistent and flagrant disobedience and for continued inattention to study. Nothing as bad occurred again until 1890, when Miss Rector (a freshman from the tiny prairie town of Blue Earth, in southern Minnesota) was expelled in "the most serious case that has occurred for many years," because she had forged a Harvard certificate to gain entrance as a freshman. The college took its honor system seriously, and lying was the worst thing a student could do.

Sneaking off campus with young men from Poughkeepsie was the next worst thing. In June 1887, a year after Cora's graduation, Miss Goodsell reported that "early in the college year, a student met two young men in the grounds in the evening, and persisted in maintaining a false version of the affair, laying the blame upon others, as well as by a past course of untruthfulness, and made herself an undesirable member of our community. Her parents were asked to remove her from the college."

Cora was thus taking a huge risk every time she told a lie, and she must have known what was at stake. "It certainly would be dreadful to be discovered," she noted in her diary, but she reflected with fatalism on why she was ignoring the dangers. "Not so, my Friend—I've been to New York three times, but arrived home all O.K. each time." The fact that she successfully outwitted disaster several times seems to have reinforced her confidence, and the adrenaline thrill she got from each successful deception probably became addictive.

Cora also believed that everyone lied if necessary, especially when they got "called up" to Miss Goodsell's office to answer for an infraction. She shrugged off these worries with fatalistic remarks: "How hard it is to tell a falsehood i.e. a lie and such I did when I had to see Miss Goodsell, but such is life at Vassar. They all do, especially when called up. But I never shall forget that feeling and often reflect on my escapes to the City but dread having to inform my beloved ones at home. I mean to do this myself and will when I have my second year's romance [i.e., adventures]." Cora had the best intentions of making amends by unburdening her conscience and telling her parents everything—but later, *later*—not right now, when she was having so much fun.

At the end of Cora's first year, in June 1885, Miss Goodsell reported to the college president, "We have had no cases of serious discipline this year." Sharp as she was, she did not discover that Cora and Kitty had been lying to her repeatedly and leaving campus under false pretenses throughout the entire winter semester. Vassar's traditional, strict parietal rules apparently begged to be broken by anyone with a bit of spirit—many others were sneaking out just like them. Once again, Cora dismissed the problem with a shrug, remarking, "Such is life at Vassar."

CHAPTER TWELVE

Only 17,000 Minutes till Our Next Vacation

Marian Austin first appears in Cora's diary on a brisk March day in 1885: "A 'Windy' day so I wore my 'sky blue' veil. It was much becoming to me. Marian wore hers also. After drifting with the wind for 20 or so minutes we finally settled on a subject—spreads. I concluded I would have mine after my sojourn in New York City, on the 14th or the 21st of March. This seemed a suitable time, as I could purchase things at Macys, Candi's etc."

Bundled up in warm scarves, the two young women, one tall and one short, walked side by side on the still-frozen campus paths planning and joking about the festive indoor dorm-room picnics that Vassar students were accustomed to put on for each other, called spreads. "We made out a good menu," she wrote. "She is planning to have 'Claret Punch' and I am planning 'Shampaign' or nothing at all—We did not dare mention this for fear of being squelched or, oh. no. entirely left on a spread. Marian decided to have raw oysters, and I plan to serve stewed ones,

Stereoscope image of the skating pond in Central Park, ca. 1885. Courtesy of Library of Congress.

as we could use our culinary articles to a better advantage. After our 30 minutes of constitutional exercise I repaired to my favorite resort and she to her 'Livy.'"

Cora's "favorite resort" was actually the grinding drudgery of her Czerny piano drills in the music building. While first typing up the diary as an uninformed visitor to the Victorian era, I took everything Cora wrote literally. As a result, I completely misunderstood many of her remarks until it dawned on me that her tone was often extremely ironic. While Cora and Marian joked about serving alcohol and cooked oysters to their guests, no one actually drank anything stronger than seltzer water while on Vassar's campus, and most cooking was impossible in the dorm rooms, although Cora and Marian figured out a way to make popcorn from the heat given off by the gas lamp on the tabletop.

Marian projects an aura of calm, sociability, and intelligence whenever she appears on the scene. She was the kind of friend who would not only give Cora a diary as a philopena instead of a less useful gift, but also inspire her to fill it with regular revelations about her private life for the better part of a year. Her expression is controlled and determined,

Marian Austin, Vassar class of '88.

as one would expect from a young woman who had traveled nine thousand miles to attend and graduate from the world's first women's college. For all her academic abilities, Marian was also a fierce competitor on the tennis court and courageous about participating in several off-campus escapades with Cora when the opportunities presented themselves. Strong bones in her face and a startlingly solid neck hint at her physical vigor and athletic strength.

Meanwhile, Cora's relationship with Laura Harris was coming under increasing strain because of her weekend parties in New York with Kitty Rogers. A diligent student, Laura found it difficult to get her work done with Cora's "extra-curricular activities" constantly interrupting her. However, she stood by her roommate in solidarity against the fiendish Miss Davis when Cora woke up late and overtired on Monday morning after her New York expedition on the weekend of March 13 and 14.

New York was too much for me, so I see. Laura and I remained in retirement till 10:30 A.M. much to my discredit. After the college Breakfast, who was want to appear but Miss Davis herself. "Are u ill, Miss Keck and Harris?" "Yes, I am unwell and Laura is keeping me company."

I absented myself from Bible class and ½ hrs German. To my great satisfaction I was excused by President Caldwell without any apologetic style (which is much needed at Vassar on such occasions). Took my regular constitutional with Laura topic "Our loved ones at home"

MONDAY, MARCH 16, 1885

A notice was given out in the Dining room that an eclipse of the sun would be seen at 12½ P.M. and we could view it, providing we'd use the smoked glass supplied by the good Mr. Wheeler. Had a good Harmony lesson—no octaves or fifths this time and an unusually good lesson in German, and at noon I succeeded in getting my glass smoked sufficiently to gape at the "moon in front of the sun" and hence the proclaimed eclipse. It was quite visible to the naked eye.

Cora was lucky to have attended Vassar just in time to meet Maria Mitchell, Vassar's legendary astronomy professor, whose charismatic sup-

Vassar astronomy professor, Maria Mitchell, in her observatory with a group of students in 1886. Courtesy of Vassar College Archives.

port for women's education in the United States is still widely admired today. Professor Mitchell included every student at the college in her passion for the stars by organizing events such as this general viewing of the solar eclipse. She was the opposite of an elitist; she was an idealist with a generous soul who believed that if it were true that even one woman deserved equality with men, then all of them must have it. An unfortunate tendency of some nineteenth-century feminist trailblazers was to jealously reserve the benefits of feminism for the privileged few who were extraordinarily brilliant, ambitious, and accomplished and had therefore "earned" them. Maria Mitchell reached out to all young women at the college, across the board, without patronizing anyone.

Cora was not enrolled in the four-year academic program. She was the epitome of an academic underachiever. Even so, she mentioned Professor Mitchell several times in her diary. She never mentioned any other professors outside her own class schedule. Professor Mitchell was obviously well known deep down into the ranks of the dilettante paint-ers and Level III preps because she did not disdain to share her enthusi-asm for learning with them. Her many student admirers became alum-nae, and over the passing decades, her life's accomplishments assumed the form of inevitable perfection, developing into a myth described in the *Vassar Alumnae Monthly* of June 1911: "Prof. Mitchell's observatory was for many years a vivid center of college life. . . . First on the faculty in reputation, and second to none in power, she stood for her belief in the most absolute in the cause of woman's education . . . stories of her oddities, her kindlinesses, her paradoxes, her unconventional sinceri-ties, were rife in the college during the happy years of her service."

However, while Cora was at Vassar, Professor Mitchell's position was not so secure. In early 1885, Cora clipped an article in which a New York reporter wrote: "For nearly a year there have been rumors that the trust-ees are in favor of retiring Maria Mitchell from the astronomy depart-ment and having astronomy taught by the professor of mathematics." The situation at Vassar had sunk so low that the world-famous Profes-sor Mitchell was on the verge of being fired, probably to save money, and replaced by Professor Priscilla Braislin, while the astronomy depart-ment was to be phased out. While all the infighting was going on, the redoubtable future president of Bryn Mawr College, M. Carey Thomas, visited Professor Mitchell and reported having a "typically paradoxical conversation" with the legendary educator, who spoke "sarcastic, rath-er bitter, wholly loyal things" while lying on the couch at full length.[1] The dire situation would come to a head during tumultuous meetings between the college trustees and the Vassar Alumnae Association held during commencement weekend in June.

On one occasion, acting nicely for a change, Cora's corridor teacher suggested to Cora that she should visit Professor Mitchell's observatory: "At two Miss Davis made her appearance and invited me to gape on the firmament through the telescope up at the Observatory. I did this with much pleasure as it was the first time I ever viewed the firmament through the Vassar telescope at Prof. Mitchell's." Cora's elliptical style makes it sound as if she went to the observatory in the middle of the afternoon, but this was when she received the invitation, not when she went to look through the telescope.

∞

ON MARCH 17, CORA NOTED: "A hard frost last night, which makes things very lovely out this A.M. I wait as usual for my morning mail. In the meantime, I am preparing that horrid German translation." She was in over her head with the freshman German curriculum and constantly struggled with her dreaded German homework. She was supposed to be translating part of *Einer muss heiraten*, a popular, short comedy drama filled with clever dialogue and droll situations written in 1850 by Alexander Wilhelmi (né Zechmeister). The play was frequently used in Ivy League curriculums as a text for German students. The title means "one must marry." The topic uncorked an unpunctuated outburst of anxious frustration in Cora's diary:

> "Einer musz heiraten" + so we will, or at least one of the Vassar girls will and she certainly will not be classed among the ones that are dammed to be old maids for I mean to just as soon as I get mashed (rather meet my fate) woe be unto my Parents—I am a gone girl so far my ideal has not made his appearance and I am dammed to suffer and just one more year at Vassar too and he's to be an Eastern fellow at that.

Cora uses so much slang that a modern reader can hardly understand what she's saying. "Getting mashed" meant getting blatant propositions from a man, while "meet my fate" meant to get engaged. "A gone girl" had several meanings, ranging from "a hopeless case" to "totally infatuated with someone" to "pregnant and ruined"; Cora seems to be saying that her case had become so hopeless that she might throw herself into the marriage game recklessly, without parental approval. She was apparently determined to marry the first suitable man who asked her, as long as he was from the East.

It's hard not to conclude from this day's entry that Cora's primary goal in attending Vassar was to find a suitable husband who lived as far away from Davenport, Iowa, as possible. This is a strangely modern scenario. Aside from a few details relating to Cora's more compressed timetable, it's not so different from the life plan of *Sex and the City*'s

Carrie Bradshaw, who moved to New York City from somewhere "less important" in order to flirt with New York men, have fun first, then find true love and eventually marry Mr. Big. Carrie was not academically inclined either. Cora finished the day's entry on an upbeat note: "I knew enough fellows in New York to quiet me for a while. They are oh. so giddy—just my style u know."

The next day she received a disappointing letter from her cousin Warren. Cora spent most of the spring semester trying to get him to come to Poughkeepsie to be her escort for the Founder's Day cotillion on May 1. Always courteous and dutiful, he was strangely unavailable emotionally. He had written her a very formal letter two weeks before, on March 9, in which he abandoned a previously more affectionate way of writing to her and abruptly addressed her very formally as "Miss Keck." This really made her mad. I'm not clear about how Warren's mother, Aunt Kate, became involved in this quarrel. On March 18 Cora wrote: "So sorry as Warren has gone back on me [disappointed or failed to come through]. I don't know what to do—he certainly is very 'spoony' to do such a thing. I know its a cold day when his Mother goes back on him but we are out for a change. Our friendship only to be renewed when I go to Phila. again, so I hope too: Oh. how angry I was. Words fail me."

Meanwhile, Cora began preparations for her spread, which she planned to hold on Friday, March 20. This was one of the reasons that she was writing to her cousin; Warren's father ran a wholesale grocery business on South Water Street in Philadelphia, Kleckner, Shimer & Co., Wholesale Grocers, Flour and Commission Merchants, and she had ordered a box of delicacies from them to supplement the items she was getting from Smiths Confectionery in Poughkeepsie.

THURSDAY, MARCH 19, 1885

Very calm, received a few letters had a cold breakfast + practiced the same as usual did not "flunk" in German some what "squalched."

Lunch favorable, at 3 P.M. went to Po'keepsie to Mrs. Lewis's [Cora's dressmaker] and Smiths Bro ordered my cream cakes, fruit etc. for my spread Friday evening. Waited a long while for my box but to no avail—left as usual.

Came home in time for Dinner, and in the evening studied at German, prepared my Harmony and repaired to the Music Halle to study my Music.

Then repaired to the gymnasium to the "Gyms" so much enjoyed by all of us Vassarians—I do love to be in my gym suit—I tell u I look swell.

I came home in time to fool Miss Rogers in the bathroom by whistling. oh! the "caloupe" "au revoir"

The gym suits were a universal favorite among Vassar students. Gus Harvey of Roanoke, Missouri, signed up to take "gyms" just to get the suit. One could order the suits with and without an added skirt. No one wanted the skirts—they cost an extra $4 and got in the way during the exercises. "Our teacher has no skirt so it must be better not to have one," wrote Miss Poppenheim, although she dithered in letters home to her mother over the issue of whether going skirtless might be too immodest.

On the morning of her first spread, March 20, Cora wrote: "Very pleasant weather but extremely cold. 'By gum' it's hard writing in a '<u>Diary</u>.' I practiced all morning. There were no dudes in the Music Halle so it was somewhat lonesome. I had my general scolding from Professor Chapin: 'Don't go so fast. you never will acquire the requisite amount of solidity.'" She concluded the entry with "Lunch at 12:15 no soup—Gingerbread."

The spread was that evening in parlor "twelve and a half" on first corridor north. Cora had sent out eight or nine handwritten invitations to selected friends, along with little handwritten menus, earlier in the week. "Menu: Olives, Conserves, Crème a la glace, Gateau, Fruit, Confiserie." The refreshments started to arrive late in the day. As soon as classes were finished, she and Laura rushed to decorate their parlor with paper lanterns and to arrange the orange napkins, printed with a green and purple Japanese Samurai horseman design, that she had bought at Farringtons. Vassar's stewards' department provided dishes for serving the food, and these were laid out on the cot beds, the window sills, the table, and even the floor, since the room was small and did not have much furniture in it.

At 3 P.M., Cora's box came from Philadelphia. "oh! how happy I was on gazing on the delicacies. Received my boxes from Smiths at the same time. At 6 the 'girls' congregated in my parlor for the 'dessert' 'a la glace' etc." The girls dispatched three quarts of ice cream and two cakes (chocolate and angel food), along with apples, bananas, oranges, and assorted candies. They also browsed on a jar or two of imported olives, which seems like a strange item to eat with sweets, but these were imported, expensive, and therefore very fashionable, so everyone served them.

Cora's spread was a success, as was usual with her social activities. She was lively, funny, and emotionally engaged with her friends. She was the one who entered the room, brought in a whirl of energy, and really made the fun happen. When the eating was done, the girls still weren't done with the party: "the colation proved successful and we repared after chapel to Room J where we passed the evening very gaily Dancing. A very few gentlemen, only four, gazed upon the festive 'Vassarians,'" she added with cheerful irony. These young men would have been admitted to the Main Building as guests of other students in the main parlors, and hearing the music, they might have gravitated down the hallway to Room J to watch the action.

The next day, Saturday, Cora noted, "Even pleasanter than yesterday 'by gum' I wished it was Spring."

Only 17,000 minutes till our next vacation, which is in April (college closing April 1st and reopening April 7th) Had a lovely time replacing [cleaning up] our rooms this A.M. after last nights sport. Practiced very little this A.M. and this afternoon too; too busy with a box from Auntie. olives, my favorite. At 3½ P.M. Bonnie Belle [Kitty Rogers, whose middle name was Bonnibel] and I went to the Dress Makers had a lovely walk + chat too. No "a la lads"

While she was in Poughkeepsie with Kitty, Cora went to Van Keuren Brothers jewelers to pick up her new Vassar College monogrammed pin, which was ornamented with tiny seed pearls and cost $3.75. Sadly, it has been lost.

Back on campus, she again complained that there were "No 'a la dudes' to enliven the Music apartments this aft." Vassar's rulebook was explicit in forbidding any male guests from entering the grounds or college buildings without their first having been given written permission from a particular girl's parents, and this letter then had to be "placed in the hands of the Lady Principal." This would seem to exclude any strange young men wandering up hill from Poughkeepsie, but in practice, there seem to have been many "dudes" and other visitors hanging around the college grounds, particularly outside the Calisthenium, where they frequently came at night to listen to Cora and other young women practice the piano and to watch them dance.

The sound of stealthy footsteps in the darkness was covered by the loud chorus of tiny frogs called spring peepers that lived in the brook in the ravine behind the college, whose urgent mating cries defied the skim of melting ice that had silenced them all winter long. The young men only looked through the windows and did not venture inside to talk to the young ladies. Animated by their secret audience, the dancers swirled around with pleasure that was well spiced by the attention they were getting, while one of their group provided the music on a piano. Apparently, the music building was carelessly patrolled by the college guardians.

"My first night writing the actual days enjoyment, as I commenced writing my 'Diary' Saturday evening, having just received it from Marian for a Philopena," Cora wrote on Sunday, March 22. "I think I will enjoy it very much when I get every thing made up [that is, caught up to the current date]. I am writing this between Dinner and chapel so to save time." Cora was busy for several days with this task. Even so, she found time to write six letters, including one to Professor Braunlich, her kindly piano teacher back in Davenport. She was very preoccupied with her music studies and hoping for some advice about how she could improve and satisfy her hard-nosed college instructor, Miss Chapin.

Meanwhile, in that era before childhood vaccinations, an epidemic of mumps swept through the college. The treatment at the time to relieve the pain and swelling of the glands under the neck was to tie a hot towel tightly around the chin. All the sick girls were sent into quarantine in a part of the building called the tower. "Every one is catching the epidemic of 'Mumps,'" Cora recorded. "Four cases in the infirmary (rather up in the Towel). Several girls sent home & Kitty R. went home Thurs.

with them." According to the *Little Giant 'Cyclopedia of Ready Reference*, published in 1893, standard remedies for mumps that a typical regular physician of the time would have prescribed would have included "a decoction of camomiles and poppy heads" (that is, opium), plus James' powder (made of bone shavings and antimony, a toxic element similar to arsenic) and calomel (a mercury compound). To reduce fever, a spirit of nitric ether mixed with diluted nitric acid, sugar syrup, and camphor was used. Luckily, Cora's health was unaffected, and she did not have to take any of this sickening brew of toxic chemicals. Aside from her problems with eczema, she seems to have been robust and carried on with her nonmusical activities without interruption.

CHAPTER THIRTEEN

The Girl of the Period

———◦◦◦———

Although described by one of her students as "frailty personified" and barely five feet tall, Miss Chapin loomed high in Cora's anxieties.[1] During the winter of 1885, Cora was turning out to be a disappointment to her. With students who had no talent, she was sweet-tempered and tolerant, but with students who had potential, Miss Chapin had uncompromising standards and demanded the utmost rigor and thoroughness. Miss Keck continued to rush through her pieces and make the same mistakes over and over, while her instructor stretched her thin lips together under her very long nose and glared in annoyance. Cora wrote in March, "Took my Music lesson, but was squelched perfectly awful as I thought I was 'getting on' beautifully in my piece. But behold, from 112 metronome I was lowered to 88 metronome in time, and I certainly feel as if I was not progressing at all. And as to the concert in May I'm sure I will not be up to time [that is, back to the faster pace of 112] Woe be unto me if I have it not."

While her teacher tried to correct her careless keyboard technique and unresponsive attitude, Cora spun listlessly back and forth on the piano stool in the music studio and stared absently into the half distance. Miss Chapin was fast losing patience with this student, who seemed to have trouble applying herself to routine but important tasks such as drilling on scales and arpeggios in each key to improve her fingering and technique. Cora could not impress her with superficial flash and flurries of fast notes. Miss Chapin was looking for the depth and confidence of piano technique that comes from many hours of disciplined hard work, and she was not getting it. She must have been grinding her teeth with frustration; she had finally been assigned a student who had the makings of a music department star, but she couldn't get the girl to put in the effort required to make it happen. Cora had native talent, but she was wasting it. She apparently did not care if she remained a musical

Frontispiece of Cora's Beethoven sonata, from her book of bound sheet music.

dilettante all her life. Cora herself could not understand why she was not progressing as well as her teacher expected and did not like being reined in. With all her hectic social activities and squelchings in German class, she was sinking deeper and deeper into a well of frustration.

When I first read about Miss Chapin in the diary, I took an instant dislike to her, as her severity tends to conform to everyone's worst image of a grim Victorian disciplinarian spinster. However, the more I learned about the lives of Vassar's earliest alumnae, the more I came to appreciate Miss Chapin's side of the story. She had good reasons for her harsh response to Cora's poor work ethic. She had graduated from Vassar's School of Music in 1872 as part of an earlier generation of women who really understood what a miraculous opportunity it was to get an advanced education. She had gone through the program determined to make a career for herself in music as an independent single woman, and she must have found it difficult to overlook the fact that Cora was clearly at Vassar hoping to find a husband from a higher social stratum, not to work hard at her music. At age thirty-six, Jessie Chapin was probably anxious about and frustrated with her own future. Even though she had found a job in the field for which she was trained, in many ways her situation resembled the "gilded cage problem" that oppressed Cora's corridor teacher, Miss Davis. The only place Miss Chapin could find paid employment was at the place that had created her, not in the real world.

Miss Chapin's tense relationship with her flighty student went right to the heart of Vassar's academic and financial crisis. Cora entered Vassar as part of the threatening tide of underachievers surging in through the front doors to keep the college afloat financially. As an alumna, Miss Chapin might well have shared the sentiments expressed in that 1884 letter sent by the ten distinguished Boston alumnae to Vassar's board of trustees. Those women, all academically gifted graduates of the four-year program, dismissed students such as Cora and her friends as nothing but "a means of increasing her [Vassar's] numbers which has lowered the standard of her class room work," and warned that Vassar was about to lose "that place of honor among Colleges for women which we, as her Alumnae, have justly been so proud." In desperate language, the alumnae advised immediate action to purge the college of as many of the underachievers as possible because "the policy of inactivity is suicidal." Did Jessie secretly wish she could purge Vassar of slackers like Cora?

CORA'S MOOD CONTINUED to be as damp as the weather. She was increasingly worried about not having received any letters from home since the second week of March. She "went exercising with Miss Drake," a sophomore from Englewood, Illinois, a suburb of Chicago. Their walk "was directed toward 'Sunset Hill.'" Mud was everywhere, and the faded purple thorn bushes and wet brambles sagged toward the ground along the edges of the road. The two young women had to pick their way along the dirt road and step on the high parts of the wheel tracks that were still frozen to avoid sinking their leather boots into the puddles. From the top of the hill, Cora surveyed the rotten, gray sky and bare fields lined with stonewalls and leafless trees that stretched down to the edge of the Hudson River. Cora was gifted and prolific in giving love, but the other side of this coin was that she could swiftly fall into despair if people around her did not provide an equal measure of constant care and attention in return. She surveyed the emptiness of the landscape and felt unprotected from its desolation. Her family was so far away—thousands of miles and three days of hard travel. She felt desperately homesick.

"Alas," she wrote on March 24, "this Tuesday one week and one half that I have not heard from home it almost breaks my heart to think of it but I presume they are extremely busy and Dear Mama is not home hence no letter this is the longest time that I have experienced (endured) without hearing from home and I hope it will not last much longer nor occur again." Several days later she wrote, "and I hope for a letter from mama now answering in the affirmative about coming home this summer as I have written 'write immediately "<u>Yes</u>"? or NO?'"

As it turns out, Mrs. Dr. Keck had fallen behind on writing to her daughter Cora because a warrant had been issued for her arrest in Champaign County, Illinois.[2] The secretary of the Illinois State Board of Health, Dr. John H. Rauch, had finally managed to arouse enough professional indignation among a group of regular doctors in the Champaign County Medical Society to persuade them to shoulder the expense and time commitment needed to drag "the quack practitioner" into court. The charge of practicing medicine without a license had first been made a year earlier in 1884, but Mrs. Dr. Keck had immediately posted bail of $500 and continued to meet with her regular patients as usual.

After a year's delay, on March 3, 1885, the Champaign County sheriff's deputy L. L. Johnson set off on horseback to issue subpoenas to twenty-two witnesses, commanding them to appear on April 1 before the circuit court to testify against the defendant in the case of *The People vs. Rebecca Keck*. It took him twenty-five days and 140 miles to accomplish this, for which he charged the court $12. Meanwhile, Mrs. Dr. Keck was on the road embroiled in a whirlwind of professional obligations, meeting with her regular patients in Quincy, Illinois, for four days from March 24 to 27 and then with her lawyer, Winfield S. Coy, to work out the final details of her strategy for preserving her lucrative practice in central Illinois. During the past month, she had been entirely consumed with preparing for her upcoming trial in Urbana on April 1.

Cora's mother never took on a fight that she couldn't finish. Her strategy was simple: she had enough financial resources to draw out the legal battle as long as it took to grind down the resolve of the local regular physicians, who were not wealthy and who generally preferred to spend their time treating their patients rather than pursuing quacks through the local courts. She had determined that the time and expense they would have to expend on her case would last as long as was necessary to exhaust their efforts to squelch her business.

SOMETIME DURING THAT LONG WINTER, as Cora opened a letter in her college parlor, a very nasty newspaper clipping fell out with "Cora" written across it in bold blue pencil. Because it was cut out of a Washington, D.C., newspaper, I believe that Cora's oldest sister, Belle Alexander, sent the clipping to her. Belle was the only member of Cora's family who ever visited Washington (in connection with her husband's employment there), and no adult outside of her immediate family would have addressed her by her first name; her teachers always addressed her as Miss Keck.

The Girl of the Period

The girl of to-day is raised up in the parlor to be an ornament and nothing more. She knows nothing of the kitchen; the place is a death-trap to her. . . . Her education consists of a few lessons in grammar, Latin, music and drawing. She completes nothing. A year after she graduates, she remembers nothing but her school flirtations.

As a musician, she is a nuisance. She studies music not as an art, but as an accomplishment. The result is that she not only succeeds in murdering music, but the poor victims who are often compelled to listen to her are made sufferers, too.

If you can afford to build a fine house, furnish it with rich and costly furniture, keep horses and carriages, and a groom to keep them in order, by all means marry the girl of to-day. She can spend your money as the girl of no other country can. She can play the queen to perfection and will not only master your household affairs, but will master you.

But if you are poor, keep away from her. You cannot help falling in love with her, but study well the expense you will be forced into in case you make her your wife. If you see you can't well make both ends meet, can't keep her and the hired girl too, then take our advice and marry the hired girl.

—reprinted from the *Cincinnati Enquirer*

This devastating screed, laced with sarcasm and contempt, was an excerpt from an article originally written by the antifeminist British journalist Mrs. Eliza Lynn Linton in 1868 for the *Saturday Review* in London and later reissued in book form along with a selection of Mrs. Linton's other "lurid denunciations" of female weakness and shortcomings. Short squibs from this smugly awful publication reverberated around in U.S. newspapers for decades afterward; it had such a huge impact on public opinion in the English language press on both sides

Antifeminist journalist Mrs. Eliza Lynn Linton.

of the Atlantic that it had been reprinted in Cincinnati, subsequently in Washington, and then mailed to Cora *seventeen years* after its original publication.

"As a musician, she is a nuisance." Was that what Cora's family thought of her piano abilities? It certainly tells us something about what Belle Alexander thought of her little sister. No wonder Cora never wrote her any letters. This fierce message issued by a top lieutenant in the Keck family was clearly intended to shake Cora up. The clipping cut painfully close to the bone at college. First Cora glued it into her scrapbook. Maybe she thought she deserved the tongue-lashing. Then she "braved up" and angrily cut it out of the page it had been glued to. Why didn't she throw it away? It's clear that she was perturbed and deeply offended by it.

For all her willfulness and wild expeditions off the radar at Vassar, Cora showed surprisingly little independence from her family, and she was vulnerable to their criticism. Her mother and her two older sisters, Belle and Lotta, called all the shots in her life. They saw a lot of room for improvement in her behavior, and as dominant, older females, they felt free to judge and reshape the way Cora chose to live her life. Belle, who was eight years older, was so busy with her business affairs that she was more like a parent than a sibling, and she was very capable of treating her younger sister with condescension and patronizing contempt. Cora's musical abilities were not profitable by the standards of a practical business world, and Belle measured herself and other people exactly and only by how much money they could make. But I think that there was more to it. Although Belle was beautiful, intelligent, and ambitious, Cora was the one who got sent to Vassar; Belle had not had that socially prestigious opportunity. She may have been jealous of her younger sister.

Ironically, Cora's advantages in life were all against her. In the eyes of the world and of her family, her achievements were always going to be seen as small when compared with the magnificence of what her mother had done. She arrived at Vassar poised to live her entire life in passive mediocrity. Her powerful mother took care of her material needs but did not have time to pay serious attention to her emotional life. Preoccupied with their own affairs, no one in her family took much of an interest in her musical talent. They expected to simply marry her off to a suitable husband, but Cora's spirit and talent deserved much more than that. Luckily for Cora, a few people in Davenport quietly admired her, most importantly her piano teacher Professor Braunlich, who believed in her talent and potential; the expectations he had for her brought up her level of playing enough to attract Miss Chapin's ambitious attentions.

On the surface, Mrs. Linton appeared to agree with many Vassar faculty members, including Jessie Chapin, that girls like Cora, who weren't serious, needed a scolding. However, Mrs. Linton's ideas about the proper goals for a British girl were fundamentally different from Vassar's uniquely American approach. Vassar expected its graduates to be independent, professionally productive, and self-reliant to the best of their potential. Cooking was not part of Vassar's curriculum. Jessie Chapin didn't think Cora was an ornamental nuisance who should squander her artistic gifts by becoming a housewife; she hoped that Cora could become a real musician.

Mrs. Linton's hypocrisy, her eagerness to slander her own gender in order to ingratiate herself with the rough, male-dominated world of journalism in nineteenth-century London and thereby advance her own position, is breathtaking. In contrast to what she instructed other women to do, she herself made a lot of money and built up a lucrative independent career by writing thousands of "antifeminist" items just like Cora's offensive clipping, talking down to young British women and praising the "sensible" ones who married as soon as possible and served their husbands by bearing large numbers of children and running their households with invisible efficiency. She warned that girls should not attempt to earn a lot of money or build independent careers, lest they become "tainted with masculinity and strong-mindedness." Meanwhile, she used the pen name E. Lynn Linton in order to sound more masculine while building up an independent career expressing her strong-minded opinions. She managed to hang on to her own husband, Mr. Linton, for only a few years. At the time, divorce in Britain was legally impossible without a public act of Parliament, so he fled to the United States, taking refuge on a pleasant farm in Hamden, Connecticut, and putting three thousand miles of ocean between himself and his childless "ex-wife."

THE BLACKOUT OF LETTERS from home finally ended later in the week: "Received 3 letters 2 from home (how happy I was) and one from Ed Corbett. Dear Ed. How I wish he would come up to Vassar. But he wrote that he would later + I will wait for the coming time . . . They think of having me come home." Poor Cora. Her family still hadn't decided what she was to do for the summer—they were *considering* having her come home over the summer, but this did not mean it was certain.

Throughout the spring, not only was she homesick, Cora's confidence was also clearly sinking rapidly. She wrote to her first piano teacher in Davenport for reassurance: "Received one letter this A.M. from Mrs. Smith she sympathizes with me in my music." She wavered in her commitment to Vassar and wrote anxiously about whether she would be able to return in the fall to complete her music studies, most acutely on the night before her final German exam in June. She was probably afraid that Vassar was sending negative reports about her work habits back to Davenport. She was perhaps also afraid of the challenges she faced at college and half hoping there was some way to escape them by quitting. As the April vacation approached, Cora became even more anxious, and themes of homesickness and longing for her family crop up more and more in her diary. She did not abandon her ironic sense of humor during her gloomy period, however: "Attended Doctor Hull's lecture at the 8 period, subject 'plumbing and draining' extremely interesting."

Luckily, Cora was now part of an institution that would not easily let a student slip through the cracks. Even in its darkest hour, when it was swamped with paying customers who weren't really up to the mark (I hate to include my own great-grandmother in this category, but I'm afraid it was true during her first year), Vassar continued to expect the best from the very people who were dragging it down and used the carrot and the stick with equal energy to animate them. Miss Chapin favored the stick, but not everyone at college was so stern. The place was filled with energy; the flow of absorbing and agreeable activities that filled the calendar was perfectly designed to motivate the students, as well as to give them pleasure. So, in the natural course of its regular activities, Vassar College stepped in to rescue Cora when she needed it most.

In late March, she attended the student recital that was held each spring to feature the leading talents in the music department. This experience transformed Cora's apathy into action and self-awareness; it was a miracle of inspiration: "The grand Concert by the Students of Vassar with the Artists of New York City. I long to think of next year, that I will be able to play so grandly. The girls certainly did grand and I only hope by the Lord's help I will do so well. I will be so happy if I do. I enjoyed Miss Capron's Sonata, by Beethoven, the best. She played her runs beautifully with no mistakes."

Cora noted in pencil on her program that Miss Capron's *Andante cantabile* was "very difficult." Their listings in concert programs that Cora kept show that Miss Capron and Miss Hayman were the best students of the music department in the spring of 1885. Georgina Hayman had just been featured as a vocal soloist at the March 11 concert at the Collingwood, and two weeks later she was equally well prepared to perform in a piano quartet, in Vassar's chapel in front of an audience of students and faculty, accompanied by three professionals: a violinist, a violist, and a cellist from the New York Philharmonic Society. The piece, Beethoven's Piano Quartet in E Flat, op. 16, was the concert's grand finale. Georgina Hayman played the first two movements, the *Grave* and *Allegro ma non troppo*, and Harriet Capron played the concluding movements, the *Andante cantabile* and the *Rondo*.

Cora leaned forward on the edge of the hard chapel bench, lost in admiration for how Miss Capron's hands and fingers executed thousands of firm and skillful movements so perfectly. She saw herself onstage seated in front of that piano and began to imagine being appreciated as a performer and earning the respect of everyone who heard her. Beethoven's musical themes filled her mind, the intervals and modulations so clear that they seemed to glow in curving rows of brilliant textures. She could see the music as she listened to it. She connected with a new part of her mind that was ambitious, confident, and focused. It dawned on her that she could be as good as Miss Capron. She could play at the same level as the artists of New York City, who were men at the top of their profession. Cora was a natural competitor, and she finally understood her game.

On March 26 she wrote: "I have more time to devote to my interesting Music and so practiced 6½ periods, being much inspired with the Concert of Wednesday evening. It was too grand for utterance." Each practice period was forty minutes long, so she put in four hours that day. Through the rest of the spring, Cora recorded in her diary a startling burst of energy and discipline in her piano practice schedule.

SATURDAY MARCH 28, 1885

Finished my Music Lesson with Professor Chapin. Had my piece much better, no solidity yet. Came home from Music Halle and found one letter from Mama and Lotta. They have decided (or are about to decide) to have me study German all summer in a German family: I don't know where. The news made me very joyful at first, but some joy wore off when I thought of not going home.

Practiced five periods then walked to town and met Marian at Dr. Millers. Made a call on Mrs Johnson and after going to "Smiths" returned home. Saw a good many "a la dudes" they were homely critters.

It was Marian's Birthday, hense a spread of the finest. We congregated in my parlor at 8 P.M. to enjoy the delicacies. We girls gave a spread for her consisting of Smiths ice cream and angel food cake. We had flowers from the Vassar florist culture for our favors & enjoyed ourselves immensely.

SUNDAY, MARCH 29, 1885

I never felt so badly after a spread as I did last night before retiring. It's certainly astonishing—how could I refuse ice cream from Smiths or Angle food either? I finally managed to get away with what I had and as to the other girls I leave them to tell for them-selves.

Two hours earlier, Cora had polished off a meal at the Vassar dining hall of turkey and rice pudding, among other offerings. All of this while wearing a tightly laced corset.

On Monday she practiced for nine periods (six hours), "more than I ever did in my life." Then the next day,

> I "heard of" an excellent compliment that Miss Chapin said about me but I could not get Marian to reveal it—if she merely referred to it, I was most crazy to know and we had such a time at the Dinner table.
>
> She finally concluded that a year from now at the very hour down to the minute she would reveal the delicious news to me.

Cora made a memorandum to herself about this "philopena" obligation on the inside back cover of her diary: "A year from this day on Mar 31, 1886, Marian Austin of Honolulu H.I. is to relate to me a compliment on ? at dinner—I wonder if I will be in glorious 'Vassar'?"

CHAPTER FOURTEEN

The No. 2000 Horse

At the beginning of April, Cora found herself spending a major vacation marooned at college for the third time that year. She put a brave face on her situation, including herself in her friends' happiness without complaining about her own dismal vacation plans as they packed their bags, organized their tickets, and departed. "The last morning of study before our week's vacation," she wrote on the first day of the month. "The College is closing at noon—we are all so happy over it. The girls are busy at noon bidding their friends farewell only to see them on the following Wednesday."

That same day, Cora's mother went on trial in Illinois. Cora's sister Lotta Dorn was with her mother at the courthouse in Urbana, a witness for the defense. The Keck family was tense, nervous, on the defensive; if they lost the case, it could be the beginning of the end for Mrs. Dr. Keck's medical business in all of Illinois. It would be a professional and financial catastrophe. Strangely, Cora makes no mention of the trial in her diary. At first, I scolded her in my mind her for self-centered superficiality. Then I realized that her family probably hid the crisis from her. She would have been extremely worried about her mother if she had known what was going on.

Stereoscope image of New York's Sixth Avenue shopping district at Eighteenth Street, ca. 1885. Courtesy of the Library of Congress.

Cora had very little to do during the week stretching ahead. The long, wide corridors of the Main Building were dull and unwelcoming in the bad weather of early spring; heavy rain beat constantly on the windows for days in a row, and Cora's mood was already less than buoyant. Her roommate, Laura Harris, was staying in the dorm too, so at least they had each other for company while everyone else was gone.

The college dining hall tried to lighten everyone's mood by serving comfort food: ice cream, charlotte russe, fruit, and other dessert treats. The rules were loosened, and the students were allowed to stay up as late as they wished at night. No matter—Cora was depressed anyway. The mail from home didn't cheer her up. In fact, it made her homesick, because her mother and older sisters still had not made up their minds about what she should do over her summer vacation. They were apparently too busy with the trial to get back to her about it. At least she knew one thing—they would have to make *some* plans, since the college closed in June and would turn Cora out onto the sidewalk. She took refuge in the music building and practiced hard.

Oh. I want to go home but it's doubtful what I will do. I long for D. [Davenport] so much but I will be there sometime or other.

I practiced 6 periods and received at noon a paper and a letter from Homer W. Dear Homer. How I used to like him, but aught do I care for him now. He is such a giddy youth, much suited to Lill Reid I dare say and I am quite contented to know that they some day will be matched if they are not engaged yet. Hattie is writing Lill now, so Homer wrote.

Back in Bloomington, Hattie Wakefield's younger brother, Homer, was trying to prod Cora into paying attention to him. Despite the engraved invitation he had sent her in December to a Christmas dance, attached to a cigarette with a silk ribbon, she wasn't being very responsive. Cora scanned his latest letter with bland indifference. The information that Homer's sister Hattie had begun to exchange letters with Cora's Davenport friend Lill Reid didn't make her jealous in the slightest. Compared to the gentlemen she had met in New York City at Kitty's parties, Homer Wakefield was a bumpkin. In her autograph book he drew stick-figure soldiers aiming clumsy artillery pieces, like a little boy. She was relieved to hear that he was interested in someone else.

On April 2 Cora noted that she had received two letters: "one from Florence 'I'm so sorry I offended her' and one from Lotta. Maggie thinks I better come home in June—I long to, too. Practiced only three periods in Music." Lotta's letter clearly did not mention the trial—another indication that the family hid the crisis from Cora. Cora heaved a long sigh of frustration as she read Flora's sharply worded message. Her relationship with her slightly older sister was often hard work.

It seems so lonely for us here during vacation + so many of the girls absent. I only wish I could go someplace. I long to go to Philadelphia to see Dear Warren but he has gone back on me—I feel too badly for any use, but I go home in June, and he must go too. I long to behold his winning eyes.

FRIDAY, APRIL 3, 1885

Laura had a Friend from New York and at noon we went up to the Observatory to see Professor Mitchell, who wrote a note in reply to Laura's:
  "come when we want and go where u like M.M."
I enjoyed this very much. In one room we saw the printed picture of M. Summerville, a girl astronomer who would insist upon looking at the stars when only 6 years old.

Cora and her friends could not have looked through the famous telescope on this visit because they went during the daytime, and the weather was cloudy. Instead, they would have talked with Professor Mitchell while she served them tea. How generous this brilliant teacher was. She responded to a simple note from two lonely girls from the ignoble preparatory section and School of Music and showed as much willingness to share her time with these lowly Vassar students as she did with the famous M. Carey Thomas of Bryn Mawr. Cora never forgot her visit. She clipped and saved two obituaries for Maria Mitchell when she died four years later.

On April 4 it was "a very rainy day such is April showers." Cora "received three letters one from Mama re: Sister. I was so happy to receive them. they have fully decided upon my coming home in Summer I am oh! so delighted." The falling out with Flora was serious enough that Mrs. Dr. Keck got involved with it in the middle of her trial. The second letter "was from Cousin Warren who had neglected me so shamefully horrid hardened wretch for such he is + then to find his letter was not in the least appolegetic." The third was an Easter card "from Mae Corbutt from Phila." Noting again that "it rained very hard all day," Cora nonetheless "managed to Practice three hours all the same."

On Easter Sunday, Vassar's chapel was closed, "so no long sermon from President Caldwell." Instead, Cora, her roommate Laura, and Eva Wilkinson took the 10:12 horse car to Poughkeepsie to attend a service at the Baptist church. They saw nineteen people baptized and listened as the minister repeated nineteen times: "'I now baptize u at the head of the great Church, in the name of the Father of the Son and of the Holy Ghost' Eva being a communicant we sat from 10½ A.M. to 1:20 P.M. more than if we had listened to a two hours sermon by Rev. Caldwell. it certainly was monotonous as we stayed for communion too." I can almost see the girls rolling their eyes and counting out loud from one to nineteen in droning voices to each other in the horse car on the way back to the college. The extended ritual took so long that they almost missed dinner.

Back at college after church, Cora did not write one letter. "Quite a difference from my usual way of spending Sunday and I was so sick—I had a severe head ache all after noon, so read & slept." She was rescued from this deadly routine by an invitation from Kitty's sister, Mame, to come down to New York that afternoon on the five o'clock train. "I hesitated a long time before deciding" (probably more than five minutes at least!), and then Cora launched herself into another "romance" in the city, firing off two telegrams to Kitty's sister and Ed Corbett to tell them she would be arriving in Harlem at five o'clock.

At the Lawrence mansion in Manhattanville, she joined Kitty's sister Mame, her mother, and her little sister, Sarah (nicknamed Dolly) for dinner at 8 P.M. but missed Kitty herself, who had already left to go to the theater with her father. Ed Corbett showed up at 8:30, and they chatted for three and a half hours, staying up until midnight. "Dear Ed," Cora remarked. Someone sent a note about Cora's visit with the Rogerses to the newspaper in Davenport, because the following notice soon appeared in the *Davenport Gazette*: "Miss Corize Keck, a student at Vassar, is spending the Easter vacation with her choice friends in New York City." This item probably made Flora mad with jealousy. Did Cora send the note?

TUESDAY APRIL 7, 1885

Arose at 8 A.M. and at 11 Mame and I went down 5th Avenue to see my Doctor Bulkley. He examined me and pronounced me perfectly so far and wants me to come again before I leave in June for the West.

Went home, had lunch and at 2:40 the children's party took place. so many little ones and all so cute too we waited on them and I enjoyed it immencely.

Kitty and Mame had three little sisters and a brother who would have been at the party: Dolly, age thirteen, William, age ten, Annie Estelle, age seven, and Blossom, age five.

In the evening, "Mr. C. E. Vedder and F. O'Neil called. they were very sociable. we spent the evening very much to our satisfaction. we had a collation at 12. and commenced the play—philopena. I succeeded in winning two but lost three. I said I would give the deed of my house a lot." Three different Vedders graduated from Columbia as doctors in Cora's time. C. E.'s brother, A. M. Vedder, invited Cora to write to him and scrawled his address on the back of a bowling invitation he had received from the Arlington Bowling Club and the Misses Cary of 2132 Sixth Avenue; he lived at 138th Street and the North [Hudson] River, on the bluff a couple of blocks north of Kitty's house. Frank O'Neil lived directly across the Grand Boulevard from the Rogers and was a great friend of Ed Corbett's.

Wednesday, April 8, was supposed to be Cora's last day in New York, but she missed her train and concluded "I was destined for another day in the City much to my delight as I had such a grand time by remaining over a day longer as I enjoyed Nick's company so much. He is so entertaining with his jestures. Went riding at two P.M. with Nick behind his No. 2000 horse." The two girls were probably sitting in the front parlor, talking with Kitty's mother, when Nick arrived and unexpectedly offered to take Cora riding in Central Park. His fast bay trotter stood outside, harnessed to a gig gleaming with dark green paint and polished brass fittings. I imagine him to have been a man of few words as he helped Cora up onto the high bench seat. They sat side by side, and she no doubt admired his profile as he picked up the reins in his gloved fingers, and chirruped to his bay stallion.

Turning out of the front gate onto the downhill straightaway of the Grand Boulevard, the horse knew it was time to show his stuff. He bent his neck to the side and looked back at Cora as his black mane and tail arced gracefully against his copper-colored coat. A fast trotter is the essence of civilized self-control, the opposite of a galloping thoroughbred; all his legs move in perfect synchronization in quiet pulses beneath his taut, muscled body, and the only noise he makes are delicate snorts of effort with each step. Nineteenth-century trotting races epitomized the restrained democratic values of Americans who worked their farm horses during the week in the fields and raced them on the weekends in town against their neighbors.

Cora and Nick went south on the Grand Boulevard, joining a crowd of many other elegant conveyances just as polished and perfectly appointed. Once Nick got settled into the drive, his conversation probably warmed up a little. He was a horseman's horseman. He told Cora that his horse, Santa Claus, had been timed at less than two minutes and twenty-seven seconds for a mile run on the Harlem Road when he was just a three-year-old. Because of that, he earned a listing as the two-thousandth standard-bred stallion registered with *Wallace's American Trotting Register*. Hence the No. 2000 horse.[1] Getting listed in the trotting register was merit-based, and any horse that could meet the standards was eligible. This policy was unlike that of the registers for aristocratic thoroughbreds, which were exclusively based on breeding. Cora mentioned that two doctors and a judge in Davenport had bred fast trotters that had been registered with *Wallace's*, but she couldn't remember their names, only that she had seen them run at the fairgrounds the previous summer.

*Santa Claus, the No. 2000 horse. Courtesy of the Harness Racing Museum and
Hall of Fame, Goshen, New York.*

Nick was accustomed to joining pickup races every afternoon (except
on Sundays), sometimes on St. Nicholas Avenue and sometimes up past
John Barry's hotel at Macomb's Dam Bridge, but seeing as he was riding
with a lady today, he said they would go to Central Park instead. Entering the park at Seventy-second Street, they passed a pair of mounted
policemen standing ready to enforce the park's strict speed limit of six
miles per hour, making the driving much safer and more appropriate
for a social occasion.

Cora wrote that they "went to Central Park, saw the great 'Oblisk.'
The park certainly is grand. It commenced raining so we had to take
shelter in a café. I had an attack of suspicion that I would miss my car
for Vassar but I enjoyed the treat 'tete a tete.' champaign." While they
drank champagne together under the cover of a decorated pavilion,
Cora taught Nick Vassar's salute song:

Here's to Vassar College
Drink her down
Here's to Vassar College
She's the fountainhead of knowledge

Drink her down
Here's to good old Vassar
For in fun can none surpass her
Here's to Vassar College
Drink her down

At this point, Nick began to talk much more freely about his horses, about himself, and about his feed business. It's not hard to believe that his grain company in Manhattanville supplied corn and oats to the stables at the Harlem mansion of ex-Senator Harry Genet, and maybe even to Jay Gould himself. (Remember that ex-Senator Genet's Harlem mansion had been built in 1871 out of lumber purchased by the City of New York but delivered to his private building site by crooked draymen working for Nick's older brother James.) Genet and Gould owned the two fastest horses in New York City. Both named their stallions after themselves, identifying publicly and personally with their horses' virile ability to produce numerous race-winning offspring. After downing the next toast, Nick wondered aloud how horse No. 2307 in *Wallace's* could be a stallion, since he was named Oscar Wilde and was owned by a New

Driving in New York's Central Park, ca. 1895.

York dandy whose name had been replaced in the directory with a long dotted line.

Cora had missed seeing Mr. Wilde on his U.S. speaking tour back in 1882, when he had made such a hit with the coal miners out in Colorado, and this remark went right over her head, but she snorted delicately into her champagne with giggles as Nick went on to amuse her by impersonating a certain horse dealer he knew, an artful swindler, a real three-story liar in fact, who colored the legs and face of a well-known horse gone lame with paint to hide its identity and resold it to a credulous gentleman farmer up in Greenwich, telling him that "this is a green trotter without a record who has just been taken from a milk wagon in New Jersey."

Cora noted that she "came home too late. Telegraphed Miss G. went with Nick to Barnums but got left as Kitty made her train." Another night in the city—and she was in trouble. Of course Matthew Vassar was a brewer, and that was how he'd made his fortune, and German families in Iowa would have been tolerant if she chose to enjoy a few brews with her family at a beer garden. But Cora's mother was a teetotaler who had launched her entire business with the help of her powerful friends in the temperance movement in Davenport, including Mr. E. W. Brady. Mrs. Dr. Keck would have been furious to discover what Cora had been up to with Nick. It also would have been bad for Cora if Kitty's family had found out. In New York in 1885, a single girl who wanted to protect her reputation did not go out drinking alone with a man, especially champagne, even in the daytime. Cora doesn't indicate what she told Mrs. Rogers about why she missed her train, nor does she suggest that the Rogerses were in any way judgmental about her behavior. It must still have been embarrassing to be at Kitty's house spending the night alone when she was supposed to be back at school.

As usual, however, Cora remained unruffled and recorded this about Thursday, April 9: "Arose at 6:30 had breakfast + waited for Nick but he did not come so I bad farewell to New York. Only arrived at Poky at 10:40, too late to prepair my German lesson but after making my nice little impromptu speech to Frouilein I was excused on the plea of not being prepaired."

Nick certainly enjoyed his afternoon driving around the park with a tipsy young college girl, but he might also have lost some respect for her. He had his couple of hours' fun with his niece's friend but made no more plans to spend time with her. I think it was callous that he did not return to take Cora to the station the next morning after causing her to miss her train the day before, but then, what would you expect? Nick did not take advantage of his situation in any physical way, but to Cora's chagrin, it appears that he lost interest in her as a result of this outing.

Kitty's parents were also unfazed by Cora's Central Park adventure. Mrs. Rogers continued to make kind inquiries about Cora's welfare, Kitty and her sisters Mame and Dolly continued to be Cora's friends, and Cora gives no indication in her diary that she suffered any fallout, although her unauthorized outings with Kitty to New York came to a halt for the rest of the year. Here's how I interpret the situation: Nick might have been slightly afraid of Kitty's mother, who seemed to have had a fierce glint in her eye, and preferred not to alert his older brother and sister-in-law to the fact that he had taken their young and naive houseguest out drinking, so Cora's social misstep remained a secret.

FRIDAY, APRIL 10, 1885

I have thought so much of yesterday, how I spent the day + how I got left. It certainly is most delightful. I thought considerable of my ride with "Nick" + how we had to stop + take shelter at the café—"This to Vassar College, drink her down drink her down, This to Vassar College, drink her down drink her down, This etc." and we did a bit.

In the evening Marian A., Mae + I had a picnic in the corridor + was squelched by Miss Goodsell.

SATURDAY, APRIL 11, 1885

Practiced piano 3 periods. Had permission from Miss G to go to town this A.M. . . . A lovely day went over to the dressmakers to get my black dress. went to "Mr Smiths" & bought a basket of fruit for Kitty R. poor girl who is up in the infirmary.

Kitty's health was not strong, and at the end of April, she had to leave college to recover from this illness at home.

Went up + saw Kitty read an hour or so and practiced an hour and 20 minutes. came home at 8½ + am now fixing up my accounts + writing in my diary. By gum, it's hard. How I long for June to come.

The days now seemed to stretch out in a tedious procession in front of Cora until the end of school. The Sunday after Easter was even worse. Roommate trouble erupted over issues that Cora didn't specify, although tension over her trips to New York and related fallout from Miss Goodsell probably played a role.

SUNDAY, APRIL 12, 1885

As it rained on Easter Sun. so it had to rain again today. We exercised anyway Laura + Mae C. with our bumber shoots [umbrellas]. I had to make up for last week, so I wrote 7 letters, yes 8. That was more than ever before for a Sunday's rest.

In the evening I had a dreadful time as usual the girls about worried the life out of me. Laura was meaner, she was so angry ꜔ I got real mad too, so that I did not attend the lecture but went up to the infirmary and sat and read for Kitty poor girl I feel for her being up there.

The next day Cora wrote: "Really I am tired of College at this time. Some times I think I will nare come back again but then when I am inspired I rejoice and think I would if I could but Papa + Mama have committed and I am to return whether or no." Later she added three words of encouragement to herself at the bottom of the page: "With Love Co." She really needed the encouragement; it was looking to be a bad week.

On Tuesday she wrote: "in German made several blunders; I had a horrible Music lesson: it is disgusting at times + then I think I never shall return to Vassar as I could do better at home in the way of advancing." On Wednesday, things were no better: "today everything went horridly both German & Music as well as Harmony. I am disgusted with every one + they with me. I do feel so horrid & never anticipated such a vile time." On Thursday, she felt very little like studying:

my Music proved aught. The girls are as mean as ever + I can't understand it. I hope tomorrow will bring forth some sunshine into my
benighted feelings, into my solitary being. I am miserable.

FRIDAY, APRIL 17, 1885

The last day + night that Laura + I will room together. I am so sorry
that she had to depart to the regions above, but "such is life at Vassar"
U can't stay in one place very long at a time.

The next day, Cora summed up her time as Laura's roommate in a
positive way: "The first day alone after my many months of pleasure
with Laura, as we had such a nice time." After all her suffering and all
the meanness and conflict during the previous week, Cora brightened
instantly when Laura resolved the problems they had by moving to a
different room. Then, amazingly, they stayed friends. Neither girl felt
any bitterness—they covered the glass transom over the door with a
thick jacket and, after lights out at 10 P.M., held an unauthorized "slum-
ber party" in their parlor as a farewell to Laura, with all the junk food
they could eat: "Marian and I made popcorn in our room. 4 of us slept
together in my parlor + we ate + ate till we could eat no longer. Did the
girls have permission to stay all night? Then we slept resolving to arise
at 6½ the next A.M."

CHAPTER FIFTEEN

Alas—So Vilely Played and So Carelessly Practiced

A s soon as the lawn in the athletic circle was dry, Cora and her friends started their spring tennis season on the third Saturday in April. The foursome took over one of the grass courts in the oval north of the Main Building before 7:30 in the morning. "Had a lovely set," Cora wrote, "we won as usual when Marian is on my side, two vantages in love 40 duce. Went to town at 10, then played tennis at 3 P.M. with Belle Townsend and Eva Woodmansee. Practiced etc. + after dinner, Belle, Eva, Marian + I had another lovely game in which we won. —had 8 games to 3 in my favor. It stood 15 love 30 love 30 all, 40 all duce, vantage in, vantage out duce vantage in, vantage in game."

This group of friends had already played together for months during the fall and they seem to have gotten good at the game quickly. Cora usually sided with Marian Austin against several pairs of familiar

The tennis oval at Vassar, ca. 1885. Courtesy of Vassar College Archives.

opponents. These included two of Cora's former roommates, Eveline Woodmansee and Laura Harris, and May Carbutt. In this game, Eveline partnered Belle Townsend, a wealthy beauty from Silver Cliff, Colorado, who dressed like a queen but was not embarrassed to wear her eyeglasses in the magnificent, large-size cabinet she gave Cora as a memento of their friendship.

Ignoring the limitations of their tight clothing, stiff skirts, bustles, and high-heeled leather boots, the young athletes sized up their competition and went for the jugular immediately. Marian had great respect for Cora's athletic ability and even more for her relentless drive to win, which Cora no doubt inherited from her mother. The respect was mutual, as Marian was not shy about crushing her opponents, and Cora preferred Marian as her tennis partner to all others.

Cora continued to goof off academically, despite the effort that Miss Hinkel put into encouraging her to study. "My giddy Sunday," Cora wrote on April 19, adding, with a quip, "we cut only a few times," as the girls spent the entire day in studied evasion of their religious and dormitory obligations.

> Nothing like a Sunday at Vassar without cutting Chapel etc. At three, four of us girls thought we would go astray so we walked over the wilds of "Vassar." we were quite brave + thought we could brave any tramp. We went over fences etc. and soon discovered that we could not get back in time for Services at 4. So concluded we would cut.
>
> Arrived home Eva, Miss Wilkinson, Marian + I in time for Dinner + after we thought we would take another walk and such we did, but it was late when we entered College, so we "cut" for the second time. Of course we will give in perfect at corridor meeting Monday evening.

The next day she added, "All broken up over the performance of yesterday + I feel a little wicked at what I did too. Cutting twice on a Sunday. I tell u I'm getting there fine." Serious students in the four-year academic program would have noticed what Cora was up to, and many of them would have disapproved of her carefree attitude. For Cora, youthful rebellion was personal, not political. It was about evading authority of all types to get what she wanted, which at the moment mainly involved adventure, freedom, consuming food, and chasing boys. Any rules that might get in the way were fair game. Cora's main moral dilemma was: "Will I get caught?"

CORA'S ENTRY FOR MONDAY, April 20, notes: "Slept with Marian but did not have permission. We had a giddy time talking of the past and near future." The meaning of this idiom has changed dramatically since 1885. Today, "sleep with" has an exclusively sexual connotation, but during most of the nineteenth century, it meant only that two people slept overnight on the same piece of furniture. The material abundance of the United States in the twentieth and twenty-first centuries has changed access to privacy so profoundly that it is easy to fall into anachronistic misjudgments about past customs. Victorian people lived crowded together in small houses; furniture was scarce and relatively expensive (and all the bedding had to be washed by hand), so bed-sharing was quite common among siblings, relations, and even same-sex acquaintances. Male travelers who lodged at country inns were often expected to double or even triple up with strangers, trading fleas and bedbugs and enduring miscellaneous snoring.

The 1866 *Vassar College Catalog* noted in the dry, completely unromantic tone of an efficient student housing office, "Some of the chambers contain single and others double beds, to suit the different tastes and circumstances of the students."[1] In 1890, the year Miss Goodsell had to retire from her job in the middle of the year because of poor health, her successor Frances Wood wrote, "The assignment of students' rooms is the most troublesome part of the work of the Lady Principal." She added a plea that was repeated over and over, with little apparent effect, through ten years of reports submitted to two college presidents by three different Lady Principals: "There is great need of more single rooms, and if this want could be met, much of the disagreeable friction would be prevented."[2] Sorting out the endless conflicts and emotional dramas caused by crowded sleeping arrangements gave Miss Goodsell and her colleagues more trouble than any other single issue at the college.

By Cora's day, Vassar still permitted friends to share beds overnight, but she was supposed to ask permission from her corridor teacher first. This was because the school needed to know that an empty bed did not mean that a student had gone missing. The United States was now a wealthier country, and girls were starting to expect and prefer to sleep alone in their own beds.

CORA'S ENTRY FOR TUESDAY, April 21, 1885, is short and tight-lipped: "Went over to the Music Halle." At this point in the semester, Jessie Chapin was really losing patience, and Cora's piano lessons were getting worse and worse. Less than a month before the recital on May 20, Miss Chapin stopped trying to fix what she saw as fatal problems with Cora's interpretation of the Beethoven sonata, and she suddenly took her student back to square one, assigning her a new piece by Joachim Raff, Étude Mélodique, op. 130. Miss Chapin wanted to remake Cora's musicianship, Cora's technique, and Cora's attitude from the ground up, and she put her back on training wheels to do it. Written for an intermediate student, Cora's copy of the Raff piece is marked up with vigorously drawn penciled fingerings for almost every note of its simple structure. I detect the angry input of Miss Chapin on this. Cora was so humiliated that she couldn't even write about it in the diary.

CORA WAS VERY NERVOUS about measuring up and making a good impression on the college community at the formal social events planned for Founder's Day, which was the most important celebration on the college calendar besides graduation. She wanted her musical performance to be perfect. She wanted everything about her appearance and public debut in front of the whole student body to be perfect. As the deadline approached, she became angry with her dressmaker, who sent her the following note: "Miss Keck, Please do not come to be fitted until Saturday [April 25] morning. I will be ready for you by 10 o'clock. I will have your dress ready for you to wear Friday [May 1] certain.

Respectfully, C. A. Lewis." Cora noted in her diary: "Mrs. Lewis is sick + wanted me to come in later to have my dress fitted—how angry I was. But I was consoled somewhat when she said it will be ready for the Reception."

Having a dress made in 1885 entailed a tremendous time commitment, because the tight-fitting bodices—the top "jacket" half of the garment, including collar, sleeves, and waist—required so many fittings. Sometimes larger establishments went to the trouble of creating individual dress forms for their regular clients to reduce the need for these long and tiresome repeated sessions. Butterick's sewing guide had this to say about the process:

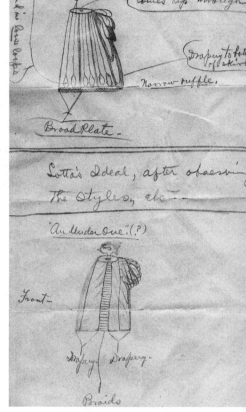

A dress design for Cora, drawn by her sister Charlotte Dorn, from Cora's scrapbook.

> if extreme care be observed all through the work and sufficient perseverance exercised, one can be reasonably sure of a good effect . . . the lining must be fitted, pressed open, and boned . . . the seams of the outer material must be slashed at the proper points . . . the boning must be the correct height for the figure that is being fitted and the "spring" of the bones must be just right . . . on all such small items depends the effect of the finished waist, and small mistakes account for the home-made look so often deplored.[3]

Students were expected to wear the school's colors of rose and gray on public occasions, so Cora's dress was being made of pink satin. Ellen

Swallow (Vassar class of 1870), who went on to study at MIT and later became a prominent environmental chemist, wrote home in 1868 that these two colors symbolized the college's unique founding mission: "The rose of sunlight breaking through the gray of women's intellectual life."[4]

THURSDAY, APRIL 23, 1885

On returning I found Kitty had returned from new York. I was very happy to see her + she looks much better. She brought me good news from New York as regards "Nick" etc. Received two letters: one from Ed. Corbett and secondly from Warren just for a change. "Variety is the spice of life." Spice in letters is just the same.

　　Oh! joy! Ed. coming for Founders. I will be so happy. but my . . . what if Nick accepted too.

After her most recent illness, Kitty was back. Cora was hoping that Nick would come up to Poughkeepsie for the cotillion dance on Founder's Day, on May 1. Cora enjoyed playing a risky game by scheduling overlapping visits of her male friends—but really, in her heart of hearts, she must have known that Nick was never going to show up to be her escort for the Founder's Day celebration, and that Warren Kleckner would probably never come either.

At 9:30 I received an invitation from Minnie Keiter for a spread in her room Friday evening. I went to Minnie Keiters spread where we enjoyed our selves immensely "we ate and we ate till we could eat no longer" She had a lovely collation and the cutest little menu. "Sandwiches, Saratoga chips, Gherkins, Olives, Charlotte Russe, Preserved Strawberries, Ice cream cake; Candy, sweets, Fruit."

Minnie was one of Cora's "projects." Cora liked to take a shy, smart, and homely girl under her wing and build her up socially, and she did this several times at Vassar, becoming extremely close to her protégée in each instance. Minnie had graduated as class valedictorian from Pottsville and St. Clair High School, in Pennsylvania, at the age of fifteen. Already a Vassar sophomore in 1885, she was still only seventeen years old.

Minnie's face shows the glowing innocence of a young person who has grown up in a very sheltered environment. She was self-disciplined and aware of her intellectual gifts but still full of spirit and affection for those around her. An only child, she had been raised carefully by three adults—her parents, George and Sallie, and her doting maiden aunt, in a small mining town in Pennsylvania where her father was a storekeeper. She and Cora had their Pennsylvania Dutch backgrounds in common, and Cora's nurturing filled in for the trio of hovering adults Minnie so missed when she left home to go to college.

Minnie was the walking incarnation of a "calico girl," a term used by the founder of Wellesley College to describe his intelligent, hardworking students of modest means, "each one of whom was worth two velvet girls."[5] Minnie was far as it was possible to be from an urban sophisticate. She was short and dressed in a style one could only call "country plain." For her class portrait, she tied a shapeless lace collar over her sensible

Minnie Keiter, Vassar class of '87. Courtesy of Vassar College Archives.

cotton dress with a ribbon, and in a small gesture in the direction of current fashion, she frizzled the thin fringe of bangs across her forehead. Cora loved to be desperately important in someone else's life, and she loved to be looked up to, especially by intelligent, academically gifted girls. She began to exercise a strong influence over Minnie.

○○

FRIDAY, APRIL 24, 1885

Another horrible day at my music lesson Miss Chapin thoroughly disgusted again with my horrible scales & the new piece she gave me for the Concert I was going on so hard (crying) and then she said I gave u this piece in hope that u would have it for the May concert, + alas + so vilely played—so carelessly practiced.

Cora hated that new piece. She was offended by it. Worse, Miss Chapin had disregarded the many hours of disciplined effort she was putting in to improve her Beethoven sonata and chose to punish her student by throwing a new piece that she didn't like at her to learn less than a month before her final recital for the year. The move seems to have been calculated to shake Cora's self-confidence and humiliate her. Miss Chapin may have been an accomplished musician, but her flaws as a teacher hint at sourness in her soul; she clearly wished she were doing something else with her life.

Took my exercise but "cut" my German resitation as I was feeling too bad to do my German after having such a time.
No letters from home.

Saturday, April 25, 1885
Went over to the Hall + practiced 3½ periods on my delightful piece for the Concert.

This remark must be taken as deeply sarcastic.

CHAPTER SIXTEEN

A Great Shock

Elizabeth Griggs knew everything about the Kecks and their scandals back in Davenport. What secrets might she have been whispering to her friends about Cora's family during the late-night spreads she was hosting in *her* parlor? Cora became consumed with worry, not only about how she might look in her new pink satin dress at the first formal cotillion ball of her life, but also with preparing herself for her debut recital on May 20, when the first-year students in Vassar's School of Music were to perform in the chapel in front of the entire student body and assembled faculty. It was her only opportunity to present herself to the Vassar community as a serious musician and put to rest any rumors that might be circulating about her and her family—that she was a mediocre parlor ornament from a shady family of disreputable patent medicine peddlers.

MONDAY APRIL 27, 1885

Practiced two periods, prepared my Harmony lesson + read 40 min or so—then practiced all evening. Practiced 8 periods today, a good beginning for the week but I am too anxious to accomplish a thing I see: like playing in the concert in May.

TUESDAY APRIL 28, 1885

Practiced eight periods had a good Music lesson. Then Miss Chapin jocundly informed me that I was to play in Thikla, much to my surprise + humiliation.

Cora probably annoyed Miss Chapin by declaring that she would be ready to play the ambitious Beethoven sonata for the big recital on May

20 instead of the simple little Raff piece, and Miss Chapin might have fired back something along the lines of, "Well, if you think you are ready with your sonata, you can try it at the Thekla workshop tomorrow." Cora "braved up," "practiced well," and by 9 P.M. "had it 'pat' + without a mistake."

Later in the afternoon, Cora took refuge from her problems outdoors with Marian, "hunting the bloodroot flowers + the little Vassar favorites." The sun beat down on their heads, threw long shadows through the leafless woods, and filled the air with a mysterious sweetness, a combination of all the scents from numberless shoots pushing up from the ground and new growth in the treetops. Rafts of spring beauties

The author Mark Twain (Samuel Clemens), in a caricature drawn by Joseph Keppler for Puck magazine in 1885. Courtesy of the Library of Congress.

carpeted the ground like light snowfall. As a little girl, Cora had spent a lot of time along the creeks and on the roadsides around Fairfield helping her mother search for the plants that were needed to brew Mrs. Dr. Keck's "catarrhochesis" remedy, but she had never learned these eastern plants. Bloodroot has a beautiful white flower that blooms for only a few days in the spring in deep woods. Its dark red roots are filled with a caustic sap that oozes like a broken vein when picked. Perhaps it reminded her of regular doctors opening veins to bleed their patients.

Returning to campus, they resorted to another time-honored anti-anxiety therapy—overeating. "Later we ate and ate till we could eat no longer + was thinking of the future + she would have Bennie + I Eddie."

Wednesday, April 29, was Cora's "fatal day when I had to make my debut, as the girls call it." She entered the Thekla recital room with her sheet music under her arm for the *Scherzo* from Beethoven's Piano Sonata No. 3 in C major, op. 2. Miss Chapin's merciless eye was trained on her. Miss Hayman and Miss Capron probably sat together in the front row, watching as Cora sat down at the piano, their bland smiles willing her to flounder, their low whispers daring her to tremble, falter, rush, forget, or otherwise mess up her piece. There is not a music conservatory program anywhere in the world that is not shot through with competitive angst. Students listen in on each other at the practice room door, gossip, measure, and compare the inept and inadequate players and form a consensus about everyone's rank in the group. Good musicians must have boldness and courage to stand up to this scrutiny.

> I was third on the Programme but had it down pat & played my Sonata satisfactorily. But three weeks from tonight on the 20th I will make my debut in Chapel at the "May Concert" Oh. I just know I will be distracted by the time it comes my turn to play.

Cora did not record whether Miss Chapin softened enough after the program to compliment the effort. It was obviously very hard to earn her praise. Miss Chapin's pedagogical approach can be contrasted with that of Cora's German instructor, Miss Hinkel, who had recently given Cora tea and spent an evening singing and playing the piano together with her worst student.

On Thursday, April 30, Cora was "still longing for an answer to my Invitation for Founders. I expected an answer by Telegram from Warren but none so far." Who was she fooling? Just how many men did she need for Founder's Day? Warren obviously wasn't interested in coming. Cora enlisted a friend from the Prep III class, Clara Crossley, to go with her to the telegraph office for moral support as she made a desperate, last minute appeal to him only two days before this event. He easily could have given Cora an answer to her invitation within half a day, had he not been so obviously dragging his feet. All he had to do was to ask the telegraph boy in Philadelphia who delivered Cora's message to wait five minutes while he wrote a short answer, which could be wired to Vassar as soon as the boy bicycled back to his telegraph office. While the process wasn't instantaneous, as would be the case with Twitter or instant messaging, it is nonetheless still true that in the twenty-first century many hosts planning social events suffer from notorious delays of days and even weeks before their guests bother to answer their e-vites, not unlike Warren's evasive behavior. Cora would have had to do something drastic to head Corbett off if Nick had answered, too. Poor Ed. Cora had known for a week that he would be coming, but she still wanted others to bring the party energy up to a satisfactory level.

In the meantime, Cora wrote, "I am so anxious about going home in June." Apparently, the plan made earlier in April for a home stay with a German-speaking family had been shelved, and now Cora's time with Flora and the family was to be made productive by a slightly punitive-sounding focus on piano study and horseback riding: "They intend fixing the house over [renovating it] so I am not to have any company but devote myself to Music and riding." Vassar also continued to exert pressure on Cora, who looked for escape from its control in the privacy of her friends' rooms. Authorities with high standards were always pacing the hallways. "Miss Davis made her appearance and frightened us dreadfully," she joked one evening after making lemonade with Kitty after lights out, but Cora's self-discipline and desire for hard work increased steadily in this structured atmosphere. In contrast to her spirited resistance to Vassar's rules, Cora seemed to accept all commands and restrictions from her family with startling passiveness. She took the tack of ignoring controlling pronouncements, because there was usually no follow-up and her bosses frequently forgot to check up on what happened later. Subconsciously, she understood that when summer came, she would most likely be able to pursue her own activities as usual.

THAT SAME WEEK, President Caldwell must have retired to the privacy of his office, hidden from his wife and family while he sat alone at his desk pondering God and his college, weighed down by a relentless sense of foreboding. During the six years of his presidency, he had seen Vassar's enrollment level sink at an accelerating rate, even in the academically inferior preparatory department. In the previous year alone, total enrollment had shrunk by twenty-five students, representing nearly 10 percent of the college population.[1]

Now a cold chill crept up his back as he stared at a new sheet of information that had just been handed to him by Mr. Stephen Buckingham, the elderly secretary of the executive committee of the college board of trustees. As June approached, the latest figures showed that the school was in the red by $13,795, almost double what it had been the year before.[2]

A reporter from *The Poughkeepsie Courier* had quoted a hidden enemy inside the college administration who declared Caldwell to be "a dead failure as President of Vassar."[3] In his response to this attack, Caldwell blamed the "impertinent" group of activist alumnae who he supposed were the source of most of the news leaks about the dire situation, women whom he considered to be nothing but "interfering outsiders, with no connection with or work in the college." But deep in his heart, he knew why things were going bad. The economics of the college had been flawed from the beginning. Mr. Vassar's initial donation had been sufficient to get the buildings built and operational and to staff them, but nothing was left to create an endowment for future needs. From its founding in 1861, the college had had to accept many inferior applicants to fill all the beds in the Main Building, since all running costs had to be covered by tuition payments. When the first group of 353 young women enrolled in the fall of 1865, many were underqualified. This problem had never gone away. Without a large cushion of funding, it was difficult to make any changes at the college to respond to the pressures of change.

Down in Philadelphia, Bryn Mawr College was set to open its doors for business in September, and an unnervingly ambitious and canny woman of substantial presence from that institution named M. Carey Thomas had just passed through Vassar's campus earlier in the spring to try to recruit Professor Mitchell and, who knows, maybe several other disgruntled teaching talents.

But Caldwell simply couldn't bend his pride to start asking rich people for money. "That is not my business here," he said out loud, repeating the words he'd given to the newspaper reporter. "I couldn't well do it without abandoning part of my duties as president. Such

work was never done by my predeces-
sors. The president is not supposed
to be a beggar. The trustees attend to
finances." Admittedly, they weren't getting very far with this task. Caldwell
had pointed out these external trends
to the trustees four years ago, but they
had done nothing for three and a half
years. Finally, they formed a committee in January to "look into" building
up the endowment. Bitterly, he recalled
how the Alumnae Association had
secretly formed its own committee to
look into the situation and then turned
the blame on him personally, pointing
the finger squarely at his "want of the

Rev. Samuel L. Caldwell, the controversial president of Vassar from 1878 to 1885. Courtesy of Vassar College Archives.

necessary executive and administrative ability" to run Vassar College.

Caldwell could not shake off his cloying sense of paralysis. The year
before, he had tried to retire into the shadows to escape his overwhelming responsibilities, but the trustees had not accepted his letter of resignation. He could see certain doom rushing up at him at the end of the
school year in June; either the college would shortly go out of business,
or he was about to be thrown out of his job, publicly, humiliatingly, and
forcefully. Grimly, he decided to hold on to whatever shreds of dignity
were left to his position with the help of several elderly clergymen who
were his allies on the board of trustees, including Matthew Vassar's old
friend and colleague Mr. Buckingham.

FOUNDER'S DAY WAS CELEBRATED Friday, May 1, and Cora noted
that it was "<u>Rainy</u> . . . our College duties were suspended. Owing to
the inclemency of the weather, very few came but I received a telegram from E. Corbett stating that he would come. We girls had a giddy
time all day + enjoyed it immensely." Cora "wore a pale pink satin with
Egyptian lace and diamond ornaments with Jack roses." She put her

hair up in a fashionably simple hairstyle, in a loose coil on top of her head with the bangs "montagued" over her temples. Then someone had to help her assemble the elaborate layers of her ball dress, starting with a tightly laced whale-boned corset, which required the help of a second person to put on because the laces were threaded through two rows of grommets up the back. Cora's dress was trimmed with diamond-shaped embroidery and fresh flowers. Jack roses had large, bright red blooms with a lovely scent and were popular ingredients with Victorian perfumers. Cora might have worn them as a corsage at her neck or tucked into her waist above the draped Egyptian lace that covered the front of her gown. Making a final adjustment to her hair at the mirror, she took a deep breath of anticipation, and after some banter with her roommates, they swept out of the room together to meet their escorts. Ed Corbett and Frank O'Neill arrived in Poughkeepsie on the 6:30 train. At the college, each received a tiny handmade program outlining the evening's events in a rose-colored silk cover bound with a gray silk cord. The following sentiment was handwritten in ink on the front:

Cora Keck's Founder's Day program, May 1885.

"Woman has the same right as man to intellectual culture and development."

—M. Vassar

"Corbett came at 8½," Cora wrote. "I heard Mark Twain read + had two dances with C. met several other guests." Mark Twain and his daughter Susy both recorded their memories of this exact evening.[4] "How charitably she treats that ghastly experience," he wrote. Oh, really? Having arrived late in the afternoon in the pouring rain after a long, exhausting trip, the distinguished author and his thirteen-year-old daughter were shown upstairs in their wet clothes into a cold parlor with no fire in the grate and made to wait by themselves, shivering, for several hours. President Caldwell was apparently preoccupied with other matters relating to his tenuous job security. Twain continued: "He did not put in an appearance until it was time for me to step upon the platform in front of that great garden of young and lovely blossoms. . . . Of course my resentment did not extend to the students, and so I had an unforgettable good time talking to them. And I think they had a good time too, for they responded 'as one man,' to use Susy's unimprovable phrase."

Twain read "A Trying Situation" and "The Golden Arm," a Caribbean ghost story with a terrific, jolting ending that he first heard when he was growing up in Hannibal, Missouri. A story very much like "The Golden Arm" was a regular feature at teenage sleepovers I went to as a girl, and we all used it to scare screams out of each other at 2 A.M. "Give me back my golden arm . . ." I had never recognized its literary pedigree before.

"I do not remember that President's name," Twain wrote, "and I am sorry . . . a sour old saint who has probably been gathered to his

Mark Twain. Courtesy of the Library of Congress.

fathers long ago, and I hope they enjoy him; I hope they value his society. I think I can get along without it, in either end of the next world." Poor, foolish President Samuel Caldwell; on the verge of being fired, he then had the misfortune (or bad judgment) to offend a great author, as a result of which he has been immortalized and will be remembered forever after by the general public and by all readers of Mark Twain's autobiography as a detestable, "sour old saint."

Cora was about to turn twenty on Sunday, which added to her buoyant excitement during Founder's Day weekend. Birthday boxes and cards rained in from all directions, sent by various relatives and friends. Cora's mother was nothing if not sensible—she sent her daughter underwear for her birthday, a corset, and two dozen cabinets. These were duplicates of Cora's own portrait that she would then be able to give out to her friends as mementos before the end of the school year. Her friends reciprocated, and that's how she got many of the pictures for her photo albums. A card came from her brother Willie decorated with an orange ribbon: "Compliments of your Bro. for May 3rd and many happy returns." Her sister Belle sent her an oxidized silver necklace, and Lotta and Gay Dorn a birthday card and candy box from John Kranz Fine Confectionery, in Chicago. Cora noted in her scrapbook that the candy was "Too quite too far more than most perfectly delicious."

On Saturday morning, May 2, "O'Neil, Corbett, Mamie, Kitty + I with L. Yates, Wix + Holz with their gents went over to the Lyceum. There we locked the door + waltzed." The music students took turns at the piano to provide the music. Vassar's music instructors frowned on dance music, particularly waltzes, and music students had to practice these pieces on the sly, during vacations, purchasing the sheet music themselves—popular music was not available from Vassar's highbrow music library.

Later they "went down to the lake + took the gents out rowing—then went out to the Tennis Ground + I won with Corbett two games." That evening punctually at eight, Corbett returned to the college, climbed the steep entry staircase, and presented his card with "New York via Vassar" written on it, and Cora advanced down the tower staircase to the public parlor on the main floor to meet him. Corbett had just settled down in a chair with his bowler hat on his knee and started a conversation when Nettie, the messenger girl, appeared with a note from downstairs: "Miss Austin, Miss Clark + Miss Harris request the pleasure of Miss Keck's company in Room 10½ immediately. We're real sorry about this but the [ice] cream was ready before we knew u had come. Do as you think best."

Men were not allowed to go downstairs to the basement corridor where parlor 10½ was located. Cora flung a brief farewell to Corbett over her shoulder and rushed off to the all-girl spread put on for her birthday celebration before the ice cream melted. He listened to her footsteps rapidly fading away down the stairwell, with his mouth hanging open in consternation. Several of the other young people sitting in the public reception rooms turned to look at him. He stood up, straightened his linen collar without looking at anyone, and departed from the college, embarrassed, annoyed, and alone.

The girls' celebration involved a competition for a brass curtain ring, which Cora won and fastened to one page of the scrapbook, labeled: "One ahead May 2, 1885."

SUNDAY, MAY 3, 1885

Expected Corbett out at 11:15 A.M. but some how he failed to make his appearance and I just heard this A.M. that he did not go home last night either. I guess I was scarcely cordial enough.

Arose at my usual time but was very tired from my yesterdays exertion. Played tennis most all day. won /6 games on my side—Went to Bible class and after Dinner Marian + I went up on "sun set" hill to read.

Cora returned to the same spot on Monday, carrying one of the books on her reading list, *Three Vassar Girls Abroad*, by Lizzie W. Champney. Published in 1883, it was the first volume in the best-selling Three Vassar Girls series. After several pages, Cora put the book down, tilted her head back against the tree trunk behind her, and inhaled deeply. What a privilege to be sitting on this hill at Vassar, living this life. She was aware that for most of the book's readers, her daily routine was an unattainable dream. In modern terms, you could say that she was basking in the glow of owning a luxury brand experience.

She did not spend all day reading under a tree, however: "Practiced 5½ periods. read in our weekly Quartette—with Miss Hayman, Wix + Chapin. C. + I on the first piano. I think I am improving in reading as well as in time greatly." Harsh as she was in her lack of sympathy for Cora, Miss Chapin also knew her business and was extremely competent at improving Cora's piano technique and building her knowledge of the repertoire. She had two pianos in her studio. Sitting side by side with Cora on one bench, while Lotta Wix and Georgina Hayman sat together on the other, the teacher and her three students played two pianos at once (which Cora referred to as playing in the "quartette"). This forced all three players to keep a steady pace with their teacher as they read unfamiliar pieces, running smoothly through hard sections as well as easy ones to build confident playing at a steady tempo. Building a wide repertory by sight-reading many different pieces during one's youth is a fundamental tool for any serious pianist hoping to pursue a musical career. The next day Cora commented that "My piece seems to be getting on beautifully. I sincerely hope I will have it perfectly by May 20 for the May Festival."

On Wednesday, Cora was suddenly "interrupted by the messenger girl, saying that Miss Goodsell called me up immediately. my heart was in my throat + I 'most fainted. I could not account for my misdeed. I then thought of my German resitations." It was an Inquiry. Fed up with Cora's careless work habits and poor attitude, Miss Hinkel appears to have made a report to Miss Goodsell detailing her student's many absences, evasions, tardy entrances, and bungled recitations in German class over the past month. The Vassar Students' Manual was clear on this point: "Students are expected to be punctual in observance of all College appointments. Rolls are kept, and all delinquencies are placed on record for inquiry." "This has become a serious matter," the Lady Principal told Cora. "The tendency in this direction has been increasing for some time." Cora used her best "apologetic style" to try to defend her behavior. Her excuses and apologies may not have been precisely the response that was desired.

The miscreant then asked if that was all? "Yes, that is all."

Chastened, Cora hurried away down the bare hallway to her room, her steps echoing loudly in her ears. She wrote nothing more in her diary for the evening about this session with the Lady Principal, and at 8 P.M. she was back to attending a spread with "an elegant Menu," noting that "Marian partook of the olives from sense of duty only."

But the next morning, she was called up again. "A Messenger was coming + telling me that Miss Goodsell wanted to see me + lo when I entered she told me in a most quiet way that I could not play at the next concert." Cora stared at her in shock. "The reason was that I had been deficient in my German. How I do feel it's a shame." Miss Goodsell told her, "The matter grieves me deeply," and might have counseled the young woman: "Learn self-control and how to direct it."

> Any way, I know I have had a dreadful time all this year + I feel oh! so bad. To think that if I keep on in this way, I cannot graduate next year. I sincerely hope I will commence + do better.
> Woe is unto Corize Keck.

CHAPTER SEVENTEEN

The Animated Stump

O n Friday, May 8, although Cora "practiced my usual amt. of periods," she was "hardly recovered from my great shock of the preceding night. I am so angry." Her anger alternated with dread that she
might flunk out of college completely. Later that day, she tried to forget
her troubles with a burst of giddy, wild partygoing: "Received an invitation from Marian for her spread tonight. I went and had a glorious time.
The most fun was with the Soda Water—I would insist upon opening
my Bottle in the midst of the crowd. We ate and we ate till we could eat
no longer. I only wish I had something to write about—it is so stupid
writing in a Diary."

Back in her room after lights out, she tossed her faithful diary into a
drawer and banged it shut. How horrible it was that she still had to be
polite to Miss Goodsell in order to carry on with her weekend plans.

SATURDAY, MAY 9, 1885

Received permission from Miss (horrid) G to go to town. She wants
me to hurry up my Dressmaking. I wonder if she is going to limit me
to nothing in the way of going down town

Cora arrived at Mrs. Lewis's establishment at two in the afternoon
only to find that her dressmaker had too much work on hand and could
not complete some suits Cora wanted for her trip back home to Iowa.
Slamming the door with "a wooden Damn" so hard that the entry bell
jangled for two minutes afterward, Cora went across the street to Mrs.
Castle's shop and hired her to make one traveling suit for $12 before the
first week of June. She then retraced her steps to Mrs. Lewis's, where
they "had quite a dissention on the subject." On top of everything, her
brother-in-law Gay had sent her the wrong trimmings for the suit.

Cora (in drag, wearing a false moustache and holding a cigar) posing at the Pough-keepsie tintype shop with fellow music student Lotta Wix (right) on May 1, 1885.

"I wonder if I'll be at Vassar next year?" Cora wondered on May 11. "I want to in one sense of the word and not to in another. Received from St Louis Mo. an application for a position. I think I will apply." The application was from the Central School Agency, which placed young women in teaching jobs. One of Cora's friends in the School of Music may have suggested to Cora that she apply for a job as a music teacher. However, this goal was unrealistic in Cora's case. Good schools usually hired Vassar graduates from the academic program who had solid credentials in Latin, higher mathematics, and other subjects that Cora had not studied, in addition to their musical skills. The pristine, blank application form still folded into the brochure tells me that Cora never followed through with the idea.

For the tiny fraction of Vassar's music students who were really serious about advanced musical training, it was necessary to do "post-graduate" study elsewhere. Augusta Harvey left Vassar in June 1885 to continue her studies at the Boston Conservatory of Music, and Jessie Chapin traveled to Germany in order to reach a level of skill where she could be hired by her alma mater as a piano instructor. Regardless of how much training and study talented nineteenth-century Vassar musicians pursued, the historical record shows that none of Cora's classmates succeeded in building a prominent career as a concert performer.[1] Miss Hayman certainly didn't. She stayed in Poughkeepsie all her life, married a physician, and raised several children. The common wisdom from our modern perspective has always been to belittle the School of Music for turning out dilettantes and parlor ornaments. Perhaps that harsh judgment should be reframed to take into account the total lack of professional opportunity these young women had in the outside world of professional music.

It was actually possible, although extremely rare, for a girl of Cora's age and background to overcome gender discrimination and make a career onstage. Cora's younger sister Maggie had a classmate, Esther Mae Plumb, who became a well-known contralto and enjoyed a significant national career as an opera singer, including a tour in Europe. Esther graduated from Davenport High School in 1891 and majored in music at Drake University. She sang the Wagnerian aria "Dich, teure halle" at the debut concert of Davenport's symphony orchestra in May 1916 at the Burtis Opera House, part of a sophisticated program including pieces by Schubert, Saint-Saëns, and Tchaikovsky.[2] Miss Plumb never married, settled in Chicago, and became a voice teacher. However, she was an exception, not a trend. And she was a vocalist, not a pianist. Women vocalists had a much easier time than women instrumentalists.

Unless a young woman was born into a family already connected with the professional world of music or theater, going onstage simply was not socially possible, no matter what level of talent she had. Conversely, families in the theatrical world were not sending their daughters to Vassar; socially, they were even farther beyond the pale than families in the patent medicine business.

MR. STEPHEN M. BUCKINGHAM, Esq., of Poughkeepsie, who was one of the longest-serving members on the board of trustees of Vassar College and who was the secretary for the board's executive committee, was feeling wrung out by the open political attacks and behind-the-scenes turmoil roiling the college. The New York Alumnae Association's hostile letter about President Caldwell that had been leaked to the press in January careened across the tossing deck of the Vassar crisis like a loose, ten-ton cannon. A newspaper clipping in Cora's scrapbook shows that a reporter for the *New York Herald* had recently sneered in print at the petty squabbles among the aged trustees.

Mr. Buckingham felt personally attacked by the harsh words from the alumnae in New York and Boston about the management of the college. Like the other trustees, he was enraged that the women had presumed to "thrust" their "interfering opinions" onto the trustees, causing all kinds of complications and "impeding" the board's efforts to guide the college.[3]

A seventy-seven-year-old retired merchant and widower, he liked to escape from his preoccupations and avoid visitors by inspecting his greenhouse, where with the aid of two equally elderly gardeners, he produced glorious fruit and flowers out of season. His much younger wife, Catherine, had died three years earlier at the age of forty-nine in 1881. He lightened his loneliness by conducting several polite courtships with a series of attractive young Vassar girls—he had a particular taste for girls from the South, who were less inclined toward excessive modernity in their approach to life. The girls treated him with a fond respect that he found delightful. Right after his wife's death, he made friends with a girl from Tennessee named Grace Richmond, and after she died in 1882, he turned his attentions to Mary Poppenheim of Charleston.[4]

Everything I know about Mr. Buckingham's relationship with Miss Poppenheim comes from letters that Mary and her younger sister Louisa wrote home to their mother. It was all above board and extremely respectable. Nevertheless, his intentions were obvious to both the girls and their mother, who were clearly flattered. His visits always involved gifts of fruit and flowers to the young ladies. These snippets of sweet biology gave off the delicate but unmistakable scent of romance.

Mr. Buckingham began by sending Mary a note at college asking her to call on one of his cousins, Miss Alice Brewster of Hudson, Ohio, who was an advanced student in the School of Music. Mary confided to her mother that she found that she did not enjoy Miss Brewster's company much. When Miss Brewster returned the call as etiquette required, Mary steeled herself for the task of being polite. Miss Brewster lingered for an hour and a half, driving Mary's sister Loulie out of the room, and remained oblivious that her hostess was restless even after a pair of Mary's friends popped in twice to ask her to finish up and come have fun with them downstairs. She hid her boredom effectively enough so that when Mary came back to college as a sophomore in the fall of 1885, Mr. Buckingham remembered her kindness to his cousin and called on her again. There should be more to this story, except that Mr. Buckingham was so old that he died before he could pop the question to Miss Poppenheim, and no marriage resulted.

Victorians had no trouble accepting the idea of wealthy old men marrying beautiful young women, as long as they were not obviously dumping an existing wife in order to do so. The most famous example was Cora's contemporary Frances Folsom, age twenty-one, who would marry the bachelor President Grover Cleveland, age forty-nine, at the White House the next year on June 2, 1886. So even though seventy-seven-year-old Mr. Buckingham was pushing the envelope by courting college girls, he was in no way out of bounds with his fantasies.

TUESDAY, MAY 12, 1885

At 6 Minnie Keiter + I went out walking on College Avenue met two of our acquaintances out riding. they spoke oh. so nice. Came home and on the way, I imagined I saw Nick Rogers, when a gent whistled and I turned around, but I could not make out exactly the kid. I did not "dare stair"—nothing like making a half pun u know. We thought we would cut chapel so we did + was not caught either

Cora and Minnie's acquaintances were townies on horseback from Poughkeepsie, busily circumventing the college rules that were supposed to prevent the students from socializing with strange men. Everyone seems to have met several times before. These young men regularly rode their horses on roads and streets near Vassar precisely in order to meet young ladies under these circumstances. Minnie's parents undoubtedly would have been horrified if they had ever known that Cora was taking their daughter out cruising for guys on the sidewalks of Poughkeepsie. It was logical, though: they had few other ways to meet young men, so Cora of course took advantage of what opportunities she had.

"Oh! how I wish for the 4 of June I will take the very first train for the west." Cora's thoughts were turning toward home more intensely, and she was trying to line up people to travel with her on the train to go back to Iowa. She and Miss Drake made tentative plans to travel together as far as Chicago via the Lake Erie route, and Cora wrote to Warren and his mother, Aunt Kate, to ask whether he would travel with her too. "Expected letter from Warren but none as yet." For the rest of the week, Cora wrote over and over about homesickness, while the student recital from which she had been dropped loomed over her. She would not be playing. The sudden emptiness had knocked her sideways; her new ambitions had been nipped in the bud.

On Wednesday evening, May 20, Cora swallowed her pride and went to the concert at 8 P.M. Waiting until everyone had gone in to sit down, she and Kitty Rogers slipped in to the back row of the chapel, taking two empty spots that happened to be near Miss Hinkel. Cora was doubly glad of the darkness; she was deeply ashamed, because most people in the audience knew she had been dropped from the program, and on top of that, she was upset about having wasted hundreds of hours practicing to prepare for nothing. Publicly stigmatized, reduced by the judgment and contempt of yet another clique of powerful women to a mere "musical nuisance," her dream to "play like the grand musicians of New York City" had come to nothing. "The day that I longed for so when I would make my debut. But you know I got left—I was dreadfully disappointed."

Once the music started, Cora stopped dwelling on her own problems and began to analyze everyone else's playing. "The Concert was grand. 23 pieces but I think Miss Drury led off with all her maneuvers." Miss Drury's attempt at an *Andante* and *Presto*, also played by Miss Harker (from Beethoven's Sonata in F, op. 2), she felt was "a little too much." She liked the pieces played by Misses Burtis, Goldstine, and Harker but marked Miss Cooley's rendition of a Chopin nocturne as "vile."

"Kitty and I went so late to the Concert that the Programmes were all out so Fraulein Hinkel gave me her programme." The friendly relationship between Cora and her German teacher was perplexing to me; Miss Hinkel was the one who had reported on Cora's poor performance in her class and caused her to be dropped from the program, yet Cora felt no resentment toward her. Later that week, Cora wrote, "at Dinner time Fraulein is as good as ever I like it so much in the German Halle," referring to the table where they dined together at every meal. Cora seems to have taken full responsibility for her own failure in German, and didn't blame her teacher for her own shortcomings.

IN LATE MAY, a photographer started hanging around at Vassar Lake by the willow trees, offering to take tintypes of the girls as they rowed past his camera setup. Cora and a friend "went out rowing & had our tintypes taken too in a nice little boat & he was enamoured and wanted us to sit for a sample picture u know." The rowing was as vigorous as corsets, long skirts, and bustles permitted. Cora and Miss Drake regularly raced each other the full length of the lake, up and back.

The photographer always asked a girl to stand up in the middle of the boat in every picture that Cora had, presumably to improve the composition of his picture. Unfortunately, it's a fundamental rule in small boats not to stand up unless you plan on tipping over and taking a short swim. Despite their agility, on one of these occasions, Cora and Kitty flipped their boat. The photographer

Rowing on Vassar Lake: Kitty Rogers in the bow, Cora at the oars, Lotta Wix standing, and another friend posing as the "animated stump" in the cox seat.

flirted wickedly with the girls to get them to pose. One day, Cora wrote, "the fellow called me an animated stump."

Why is the stump so animated??
Don't u know. It lives."
Poor fellow. somewhat enamored with the stump.
and its somewhat animated? Just like the photographer.

On June 3, he added, "u bet yr bussel," in a saucy reference to their elaborate undergarments.

BY LATE MAY, Ed Corbett was back on the scene. Two weeks after Cora had deserted him in the front parlor on Founder's Day weekend, Ed decided to overlook the incident, which he might have decided to blame on Cora's "careless scheduling" rather than taking it as an overt snub. On the surface it looked very bad that she had taken his birthday visit for granted, but maybe he chose to see the situation in terms of her vivacious energy and popularity, which put his continued attentions in a more flattering light. Cora wrote that she "found a telegram from Corbett saying he'd be up tonight & he did come with a friend, Mr. Munger. They came in time for Chapel & afterward we went in the Parlors and Kitty + I brought our Memorybils & albums up to entertain the Youths."

This time she made more of an effort to be welcoming and civil. The four friends took over a corner in the main-floor parlors and spread out several heavy leather albums. Cora had three items to share: her informal memoryabil, filled with tintypes and saucy written comments; her first scrapbook, with the owls on the cover; and her formal photograph album. They were less than half full as yet. She showed Ed and Mr. Munger pictures of her parents, her sisters, brother and brothers-in-law, and cousins. No names were ever written down to identify the photographs because they weren't needed—these albums were meant for sharing in person, and it is only accidentally, by virtue of time's passage, that they have come to preserve family information for posterity. She showed around pictures of several actors and actresses that she admired and her sister Belle Alexander's black-coated Newfoundland dog, Jumbo, who was named after P. T. Barnum's $10,000 circus elephant. Opening up her memoryabil, she showed around snapshots of flirts from Poughkeepsie and funny poses that she and her Iowa friends had set up with costumes and props.

It's tempting to compare this activity of social networking in the parlor with its modern online equivalents such as Facebook, Instagram, and whatever new Internet sharing sites people are jumping to now. Universal electronic access from a distance may be new, but the idea of creating visual icons of your identity in a presentation format and using them to socialize with your friends and relatives was already common practice in the late nineteenth century. Then, as now, the immediate process was everything—it was face-to-face sharing, with physical books instead of electronic files, conversation about the scrapbooks instead of walls, and trading of cabinet portrait photos, visiting cards, and tintypes instead of tagging digital snapshots. Posterity was nothing but an afterthought, in every sense of the word. That's why it was so hard for me to figure out what the material meant after the people who had created the albums had died. The traces they left behind of their vanished time and place are extraordinarily incomplete.

BACK IN APRIL, Cora wrote in her diary that her parents were already committed to sending her back to Vassar in the fall of 1885. By late May, she was still grappling with uncertainty about returning for her second year. This came from her own insecurity about her ability to meet the mark that college set for her. She worried that Jessie Chapin didn't want her as a student anymore. She worried about her poor academic performance. Maybe someone would squeal about her wild off-campus escapades. Perhaps she imagined she might find love and get engaged over the summer and that marriage would cancel her college career.

On Tuesday, May 26, Cora "felt very lonely + homesick & long to be home + I still feel as if I never wanted to come back to V. next year, but I will if my Parents are willing. The Thikla was called in room D. + I was one of the candidates for Vice President of Thikla; Miss Thompson being against me." She was very confused. The vice presidency of Thekla would require her to return to Vassar after summer vacation, but she also writes that she never wants to come back to college. These contradictions were probably linked to her anxiety about her final exams in German, which started the next day. Naturally, she was dreading the inevitable outcome.

WEDNESDAY, MAY 27, 1885

I had an examination in German @ the 5- period on Adj. nouns + pronouns –in the Grammar + it was horrid too awfully hard.

THURSDAY, MAY 28, 1885

had another examination but failed on the preceeding one which made me oh. so angry but tried hard at this + it was on verbs— + I managed to get through.

After this ordeal, Cora's academic responsibilities were done for the year. She felt so relieved that she decided that she would definitely return to Vassar. On June 3 she wrote, "but I want to come back very much + think of it often as I want to see how much I can improve in another year."

ALL THROUGH THE FOLLOWING WEEK, Cora and her friends were involved in a hectic round of celebrations. They gathered in their rooms every night to eat together, wolfing down the contents of the many boxes of delicacies sent to them by friends and family. Cora even shared some of the bounty with her corridor teacher. The eating marathon was outrageous.

FRIDAY, MAY 29, 1885

Received a box of delicious Fruits from E. Corbett. perfectly lovely and I took them around + gave them to Miss Davis, the corridor teacher + Fraulein Henkel. Nothing like having a mash. I made myself nearly sick trying to digest the viands but to no avail, they would stick. + @ night I was so restless that I had to eat more to get settled down. Woe be unto to Corbett if he supplies me with such delicacies in the future.

SUNDAY, MAY 31, 1885

Had callers all morning a perfect picnic. Marian, Lotta Wix, Belle T., Eva. W., Minnie K. Kittie + I in my room had a farewell Sunday affair + carried on high. These sturdy Vassarians ate + ate till they could eat no longer + then suffered + at noon I commenced packing my Saratoga trunk. Finished before tea. Where will I be a week from now?

MONDAY, JUNE I, 1885

Received two letters, one from Mama containing a check for $30.00 to come home with. I was not well last night so did not sleep hence did not hear the rising bell and had a fly time [had to hurry] getting our checks and tickets for the west.

WEDNESDAY, JUNE 3, 1885

At 6:48, Kitty came in & woke me up + insisted upon my getting up + packing my trunk + my boxes. we put every thing together u know. Our trunk had to be ready at noon. I practiced two periods in the evening + I went up with Miss Chapin to hear the rehearsal for the commencement concert on June 8. I went around giving every one goodbye + enjoyed it very much in fact I enjoyed my last week at Vassar immensely

I think that Miss Chapin was suddenly afraid that Cora would not come back, and she gave her wavering student an extra conscientious send-off: "My last day at Vassar + probably my last for ever. who knows how things will change in three months? After breakfast I went over to take my final Music lesson from Chapin. she kept me two periods on the horrid scales—the trial of my life. Oh! ye shades!" Miss Chapin also made time to invite Cora to watch Miss Capron and Miss Hayman rehearse for their commencement recital.

Cora's future seemed to hang in the balance as she left for Iowa: "Lunched @ 11 & was excused from German. Lillie Yates + Lotta Wix went to the lodge with me with Kitty too. On the train, I went with Miss Morphey, Miss Marcellas and Miss Starka as far as Albany. I changed at Rochester & went with a Sleeper & retired at 10 P.M."

CHAPTER EIGHTEEN

Dear Davenport Dear Home

O n the day Cora boarded her train for Iowa, a swelling crowd of excited friends and siblings, proud parents, angry alumnae, and doddering old trustees began to gather for Vassar's twenty-first commencement, filling the hotels and boardinghouses of Poughkeepsie to overflowing. Several different agendas were under way simultaneously. From all across the country, families and friends were arriving to celebrate the young women graduates' academic achievement. The besieged trustees were convening for their annual meeting determined to beat off outside interlopers and maintain exclusive control. The alumnae were answering the call to arms for *their* annual meeting, determined to push the trustees into action and rescue their beloved college from degeneracy and imminent collapse.

The Rock Island Line's LaSalle Street Station in Chicago, where connections could be made directly to the lines serving Poughkeepsie and New York City during the 1880s.

A delegation of prominent women from the Boston chapter of Vassar's Alumnae Association emerged from the Poughkeepsie station smoldering from the snubbing they had received the previous fall. Their letter to the trustees had never been answered. More representatives from the large and well-financed New York chapter of the Alumnae Association, wearing steely expressions, arrived on their heels. Their January letter had been ignored just as coldly, even after it had been leaked to the press. After six months of delay, three of the "old fogies" finally sent an anemic response to the New York chapter a day or two before the meetings began. Instead of addressing the specific, critical problems the alumnae were calling their attention to, it was filled with passive, shoulder-shrugging excuses, ranging from hard economic times to Vassar's high cost and entrance standards. In closing, the trustees dismissed the alumnae's concerns with preposterous condescension: "The best interests of the college would be looked out for," they declared.[1] Don't you worry your pretty little heads about it, they said in effect, trading one insult for another.

More outraged alumnae from Pittsburgh, Chicago, and St. Louis joined the crowd, ready to do battle. The women had been publicly calling for President Caldwell's resignation since the previous April, and now, more than a year later, it was time to force the issue onto the unwilling trustees. He was a dead failure. It was time for Caldwell to go.

THE END-OF-THE-YEAR CEREMONIES began on Sunday, June 7, when the Reverend Caldwell stepped up to the podium in the chapel to preach the baccalaureate sermon on the topic of "Friendship—Its Virtues." Straying from his usual safe and dull style, Caldwell took as his text Prov 27:17: "Iron sharpeneth iron; so a man sharpeneth the countenance of his friend."[2] What a strange topic to choose for young lady graduates! However, it was a fitting one for Caldwell, who seized this chance to speak out publicly on the subject of his own wounded feelings.

The members of the Alumnae Association understood the power of smart public relations and kicked off their visit to Vassar by releasing a report about their recent activities to journalists who were swarming the campus from the major New York papers hoping to scoop a story about the Vassar management crisis. The alumnae made no reference whatsoever to President Caldwell. They announced that during the past year, they had raised $9,000 to support the new physical training program at the college, $1,500 for scholarships, and nearly $18,000 for endowments. This was the equivalent of about $3 million in today's money. Everyone knew that the trustees had not been able to raise much of anything. The money said it all.

Confident in their obvious effectiveness, the alumnae then sent over their demand to the trustees that President Caldwell must resign immediately. The money was on the table. Mr. Buckingham was overruled; the trustees had no choice but to accept the ultimatum. After the board voted to fire Caldwell, three board members tendered their resignations. Three other trustees had refused to attend in the first place, so it appears that the confrontation opened up quite a few slots for new blood, ideally for younger men of business who would be able to help pull the college out of its financial tailspin.

This was progress, but it wasn't good enough. The women were determined to attain their next goal: for the first time, one or more female graduates of the college must join the board of trustees. It was high time for Vassar to recognize that its graduates were qualified to participate in the management of their own college. The crisis ironically provided Vassar's alumnae with their first great opportunity to assert themselves in running their institution. They saw their opportunity, and they took it.

The headlines in all the papers

> **ne 11, 1885.**
>
> ## THE TROUBLES AT VASSAR
>
> *THE RESIGNATION OF THE PRESI-*
> *DENT CAUSES REJOICING.*
>
> WHAT THE ALUMNÆ COMPLAINED OF AND
> WHAT THEY SUGGEST—THE COMMENCE-
> MENT EXERCISES.
>
> POUGHKEEPSIE, N. Y., June 10.—The resignation of President Caldwell, of Vassar College, yesterday, while it was not expected by the Alumnæ, is hailed with rejoicing by many of them, who believe that his administration has been of great injury to Vassar. The opposition to President Caldwell and the composition of the Board of Trustees has been growing in strength for the last two years, and during that period has twice found expression in communications to the board. At the meeting of the Alumnæ last year the question of the causes for the decadence of Vassar was thoroughly discussed, and it was agreed that President Caldwell's lack of execu-

Newspaper clipping from Cora's scrapbook dated June 11, 1885.

the next day on June 11 were spectacular: "The Troubles at Vassar"; "The Resignation of the President Causes Rejoicing"; "What the Alumnae

Complained of and What they suggest." But the newly resigned ex-president still had to lead the commencement-day procession into the chapel for the graduation ceremonies, with all the trustees following behind, and then sit on the dais and look out across a sea of indifferent and hostile faces. That certainly took some courage. Ten or twelve presentations of papers, debates, and musical performances followed; then an usher brought in a silver platter heaped with the parchments for the graduating class, each roll fastened around the center with a ribbon, to be handed out by the president. Among those receiving certificates from the School of Music were one of Cora's friends, Ida Leila Yates, and Cora's idol, the brilliant pianist Harriet Capron.

BY THIS TIME, Cora was already far away from Poughkeepsie, traveling west toward Chicago on the Lake Shore Railway's Night Express, following the endless southern shore of Lake Erie as the farms and forests of western New York, Pennsylvania, and Ohio slipped past, then faded away into the gloom. Unfortunately, she was traveling alone again. Her cousin Warren was so evasive it drove her crazy. "Warren says he can't go west. I am very angry u know." She gave up trying to sleep early the next morning because the departing passengers made "a great clatter " getting off the train at the many stops in Ohio between Sandusky and Toledo. In those days, all trains were locals and stopped at every town along the route. A porter passed by and folded Cora's Pullman berth up against the ceiling, while glimpses of water and shoreline flashed by and she ate her breakfast out of a basket at her seat. She longed to be home with every fiber of her body. At 10 A.M. she was "in Toledo where I met Uncle Tom and Aunt Hattie. Wanted to stop off very much but could not. Made numerous acquaintances on the train, Denslow of St. Paul being ever so nice." No doubt Denslow was a good-looking dude; Cora never missed any opportunities in that department.

Cora arrived in Chicago at 8 P.M., and her sister and brother-in-law, "Lotta + Doctor," greeted her with dinner at the flashiest hotel in the city, the Palmer House, where the floor of the barbershop was actually tiled with real silver dollars.[3] Visitors with refined sensibilities from the East Coast and Europe, including Rudyard Kipling, complained that the loud and crass conversation about money clouded the air of the establishment worse than the cigar smoke. Cora saved several different postcards and menus from the place.

Lotta was the only other Keck daughter living away from home in 1885. She had striking black eyes and long dark hair that she wore braided into a strand that circled her head behind her ears, with a row of curly black bangs carefully arranged across her forehead. Lotta was a good listener. She cared about the personal things that Cora shared

Cora's sister, Charlotte (Lotta) Keck Dorn, in a portrait taken in Chicago.

with her about her friends, music, dress designs, and other unbusiness-like topics and put that information into action in a useful way.

Cora asked Lotta and Gay about their move to Chicago from Peoria the previous July. Dr. Dorn's first efforts to establish a medical practice in Peoria had stumbled badly. Illinois was one of the first states to start bringing its professional licensing requirements up to modern standards and had passed a Medical Practices Act in 1877 that was one of the nation's toughest.[4] He had received his state medical license without incident, but his mother-in-law, Mrs. Dr. Keck, was locked in a bitter battle with the Illinois State Board of Health over her lack of official credentials to practice medicine. Regular doctors in Peoria believed that Dr. Dorn's tainted association with her "irregular" practice on 515 Fulton Street and in Champaign County and Decatur amounted to "unprofessional conduct."[5] Worse than that, Dr. Dorn was Mrs. Dr. Keck's son-in-law. The Peoria Medical Society coldly refused to admit him. The vindictive atmosphere was so bad that it forced him to move to Chicago. Ironically, Lotta's strategy to reinforce her mother's medical standing in Peoria had backfired, and she realized that she would have to abandon her position at Mrs. Dr. Keck's office on Fulton Street if she wanted to stay with her husband.

In Chicago, no one was prosecuting Mrs. Dr. Keck because she stopped advertising there in 1878. Gay's father, William Dorn, had a good name in the city as a successful merchant; he was a partner along with several of his brothers in a substantial business, Dorn Brothers Company. This was crucial, because social reputation was a fundamental prerequisite to establishing a new medical practice in the nineteenth century. His Chicago family connections allowed Gay to become the medical assistant to a well-respected homeopathic doctor and surgeon at Cook County Hospital named Dr.

Cora's brother-in-law, Dr. Gay Dorn, M.D., shortly after his graduation from Chicago Medical College in 1883.

Bayard Holmes. The Dorn family was even listed in Chicago's *Blue Book*, a roster of social respectability published from 1890 to 1916 that modeled itself on New York's *Social Register*.

Lotta and Gay had been married only for a year and a half, and they were still in love. In fact, they never lost their affection for each other. Like his father-in-law, John Keck, Gay respected and admired his feisty wife and her excellent business skills, addressing her as "Darling Lotta" in letters throughout their long marriage. Her support helped him through his professional difficulties. Dr. Dorn no longer agonized about his embarrassing downstate medical debut because, quite frankly, the profession did not get much respect in big-city social circles. Being a country doctor involved a lot of hard work with bad hours—and was not very well paid. In Chicago, Lotta was getting her husband involved with buying land and property to supplement his medical income. She was working with her sister Belle to scope out real-estate

Chicago's famous Palmer House hotel at State and Monroe streets. The Parisian Suit Co., the finest dressmakers in the Midwest, occupied space on the corner.

The main dining room of the old Palmer House where Cora dined with Lotta and Gay Dorn in 1885.

investment opportunities for Mrs. Dr. Keck's profits out of a rented office on Chicago's South Side that Lotta managed with great energy and efficiency.

At college, Cora had missed her sister keenly. Gay was also fond of his sister-in-law, even if she was inclined to be giddy and talk too much. Cora's cheerful energy single-handedly transformed any meal into a party. The Keck style matched the style of the Palmer House—unashamedly proud of its new wealth. After the delightful and expensive meal and much animated conversation, Dr. Dorn summoned a hackney cab for the ride back to the well-appointed boardinghouse where they were living on the South Side of Chicago, down Cottage Grove Lane, as it was then called, which passed through the upper-middle-class community of Englewood, the hometown of Cora's friend from college Miss Drake. (This avenue later became a major north–south route by the University of Chicago and the whole area sank into economic desolation.)

Cora and Lotta stayed up late that night talking about marriage, love, and family. Lotta and Gay loved children, and Lotta hoped that they would have a big family, as their mother had. She planned to work, too; having acted as her mother's business manager for so long, she was confident that she knew more about practical money matters than her husband did, although she didn't think it courteous to mention the fact when all three were dining together. In Cora's eyes, her big sister Lotta seemed like she could do anything; in her energy and courageous response to challenging situations, she took after their mother.

SATURDAY, JUNE 6, 1885

Lotta, Doctor, and I took our Breakfast at the Restaurant + at 10—
we went down town to the New Board of Trade + at 2:10 I was on
the train waiting for my arrival at D. thinking strongly of who would
be in wait for me. At Ottawa [Illinois] Belle came on board + so we
approached D. nearing it every ½ minute.

I was very much interested in a sick Lady on the train, Her husband
+ we talked so much, in fact he was so very interested, that I really
think he for-sook his Dear sick wife to hear about Vassar College. he
was a Graduate from Harvard College class of 81. Arrived home at 6:58

CHAPTER NINETEEN

The Black List

———

The tracks rose gently above the flatlands of Rock Island and crossed the Mississippi on the Government Bridge; a blur of steel girders flashed past the train windows. The familiar deep, loud sounds alerted Cora and her sisters to wind down their conversation and get ready to disembark. The poor sick wife no doubt heaved a sigh of relief that the annoying young woman making a mash on her husband was finally getting off. The Kecks rose from their seats in a rush, squeezing their bustles down the aisle while juggling handfuls of bags and hatboxes, and stepped down off the train onto the street-level platform at the depot on Perry Street in their beloved hometown, accompanied by Dr. Dorn. The local paper recorded the event in its typically error-ridden style: "Miss Peck, daughter of Dr. Peck, of this city, arrived on Saturday evening from Vassar College, accompanied by Dr. and Mrs. Doarn, of Chicago. Miss Peck will return to Vassar in September."

After spending ten months in Poughkeepsie imagining a glamorous future for herself as a New York socialite, Cora was brusquely reminded of her real station in life by the sight of five homely Midwesterners waving to her from the platform as she arrived. "Mama, Mr. Hoover, Willie, Maggie, + Bert Brockett met me at the depot—they had changed considerable + Mama looked very tired but Maggie + Willie were so horribly ugly Maggie looked as if she was on stilts Willie doubled that."

Mrs. Dr. Rebecca Keck, whose indomitable will and ambition powered the family's material existence, makes her first personal appearance in Cora's diary in a cloud of negativity—in fact, these lines are the most negative assessments of her family that Cora ever made in any of the material I have. Stressed by her ongoing legal problems in Champaign, Rebecca Keck looked careworn, too busy for fashion or for careful coiffure, with slightly greasy hair and a hint of dandruff dusting the dark silk shoulders of her out-of-date dress, and she had gained

The front hallway at 611 Brady Street, Davenport.

weight. Maggie's little pointy hat was ill chosen and drew attention to her peaked face, narrow shoulders, and pencil-thin arms with elbows sticking out in both directions like railroad spikes. Her gawky brother Willie had had a growth spurt and didn't seem to know what to do with the extra inches that had just appeared at the end of each of his limbs. Cora said nothing at all about her old beau, Bert Brockett. He was studying at the Davenport Business College and Telegraph Institute to prepare himself for a job as a telegraph operator, which was something Cora did not care to contemplate in connection with her own future.

View of Davenport's riverfront and Government Bridge in 1885. Courtesy of the Richardson-Sloane Special Collections Center, Davenport Public Library.

The family made the short walk from the station up to the Keck Infirmary in the low, warm light of the late afternoon. Her luggage, including the huge Saratoga trunk, was coming up later on a dray. They had to wait to cross Fifth Street to let their panting train crawl through town bound for Nebraska, belching black smoke and cinders down onto everyone's clothes and filling the air with a dense particulate haze.

The Brady Street horse car passed the large group without stopping, and Cora began to recover her sense of humor. She retold her story about the "Ah! There, Stay! There" expenditure with Kitty and Mame in New York City. "It's just like at Kitty's house," Cora laughed. "You can never get a horse car to take you up the steep hill!" As they passed the brick business block housing the small offices of Dr. Edward L. Hazen, M.D., eye and ear specialist (the ousted, former tenant of 611 Brady Street), Cora caught a glimpse of Dr. Hazen's daughter Auzella glaring down at her through the window of her upstairs art studio. Cora's spirits rose even more. She did not feel sorry for Auzella, who could not afford to study art at Vassar, since her father had had to close his eye and ear infirmary.

Triumphant in her return from Vassar, Cora swept up the steep front steps into the Keck mansion surrounded by a mob of adoring relatives. Home for the first time in almost a year, she tilted her head to take in the sixteen-foot corniced ceilings in the spacious rooms on the first floor, which were filled with dark, medieval-styled furniture, oil paintings of popular subjects in gilt frames, and thick Brussels carpets. She was reassured to find that the familiar interior was unchanged. Woven draperies hung from carved wooden rods in the tall archways between each room, and three ornate gas chandeliers floated in endless reflections between two huge mirrors that faced each other across the entire back of the house between the parlor and the music room. She ran her hand down the keys of her piano to say hello and hurried up the circular stairway with her sisters to the second floor to change her clothes and wash the dirt from the trip off her face and hands.

The Brady Street hill looking up from Fifth Street in Davenport. Mrs. Dr. Keck's infirmary is behind the trees on the far right. Courtesy of the Richardson-Sloane Special Collections Center, Davenport Public Library.

A supper was served immediately for the hungry travelers, and once again, the Kecks assembled in their palatial dining room. Having compared her home with several more traditional interiors she had seen in the East, Cora took great pride in the delicate, "modern" Viennese-style chairs with cane seats that surrounded the table and the Oriental rugs that crisscrossed the floor. The avant-garde, European-inspired decor was accented by a pair of Texas longhorns hung over the small dumbwaiter in the corner, and a coyote pelt with nose and paws lurked on the floor next to the upright piano in the hallway. The Kecks had clearly rejected the steamboat Gothic look as out of fashion and out of date.

As darkness fell, the gas chandelier cast a soft warm glow onto the faces of Cora's "beloved ones." She commanded a rapt audience of eleven people (William R. H. Alexander was missing, having finally gone off to Washington without his wife to his job in the Pension Department) as she described the highlights of her year away at college—her friends Kitty and Marian, Lotta Wix and Minnie, the tennis gang, her two official visits to New York City (but not the secret ones), the concerts she had attended at the Collingwood Opera House in Poughkeepsie, the cotillion at Founder's Day with Mr. Corbett, the ghost stories read by Mr. Clemens (whom everyone called Mark Twain), sleighing in the winter, and seeing President Garfield's sons when they came to visit Vassar. Cora might have finished by stating that she thought she had more friends than Elizabeth Griggs. Pleased with everything that she heard, Mrs. Dr. Keck must have smiled and taken another bite of boiled beef, chewing it with firm satisfaction.

Cora lost the spotlight when the topic shifted to arranging her life for the next two months. Each of the ruling females had firm, independent ideas about what she should be doing during the summer that were different from what the others thought.[1] A loud discussion ensued, and various factors that blocked other factors were aired and repeated: the renovations planned for the house, Cora's piano studies with Professor Braunlich, Cora's need for outdoor exercise, Willie's work at the laboratory preparing Mrs. Dr. Keck's remedies (he was now a "chemist"), Cora's language study with the German family, the problem of Cora's unmarried condition, Cora's need for more time at the Methodist church (would she ever put in the effort to become a full communicant?), Belle's travel schedule, Lotta's travel schedule, Mama's travel schedule, and so on. By the end of the meal, nothing had been decided.

∞

MONDAY, JUNE 8, 1885

Sunday morning Maggie, Grandmama and I went to Church. saw a few that I knew Addie Seele, Lillie W. May B. and I also saw Alle Krugh. Last Sunday I was in Vassar College perambulating around.

Expected to go riding in the evening but there was a terrific storm so of course remained at home.

The sudden, severe windstorm that kept Cora at home that day lasted only thirteen minutes. People who were caught outside without shelter ran for their lives to escape falling tree limbs and flying lumber, which caused considerable property damage and caught one young woman under her skirts and blew her completely across a street from one sidewalk to the other, setting her down on her feet. A horse, struck by lightning, fell dead instantly in the traces of the carriage it was pulling. It was the last exciting thing that would happen for weeks. Cora immediately sank into the routines of her pre-Vassar life.

Cora's first Monday home was "a lovely day but extremely warm." Flora and Cora were once again getting along well, and the two sisters went out riding together in the morning. "We put up the tennis court in the afternoon," Cora wrote; "Played tennis all afternoon." Toward evening, Charlie Meier came by and he and Cora went out riding again to admire the new electric arc streetlights in Rock Island: "I was very much surprised to see Charlie. by gum its nothing like being in College."

Charlie Meier was bent on living well with a minimum of effort and was actively pursuing a number of wealthy young girls in town with the idea of marrying his money instead of going to all the trouble of earning it. Just to hammer in the point that she was now much more sophisticated and cosmopolitan than she used to be, Cora hurried him on his way when the evening was over with a short burst of pseudo-French farewells: "Came home at 10 very tired I bade Chas an au revoir as he moved away—an au revoir." She was always friendly with him but seems never to have entertained any idea of marriage to such an obvious pilot fish type. Like Ed Corbett, Charlie was always hovering on the periphery of Cora's life, but she never let either one of them in to become a full partner with her. She was looking for someone peerless, superlative, preeminent; these guys did not even come close to her ideal.

All of these leisure activities took place on a Monday, so it is evident that Cora was not expected to play any role in the daily operations of Mrs. Dr. Keck's Palatial Infirmary. Family businesses can be ruthlessly judgmental; the children are inevitably evaluated on their capacity for business sense from a young age, and a parent's unfavorable decision cannot be overruled. Years later, Cora's daughter (my grandmother) mentioned in a letter she wrote to her Aunt Belle that her mother had terrible business skills, and my grandfather, who also knew her well, reported that she "had little business sense." So it's not surprising that Cora was now left out of the management of Dr. Keck's medical mail order business completely. She was being "married off" instead. What else could they do with her? They had to get her off their hands somehow.

This insight made me think back to Cora's determined-sounding diary entry for March about her marriage plans, in which she swore to herself that she would not end up as an old maid and added that the man of her ideal was "to be an Eastern fellow at that." What at first seemed to be a rebellious, headstrong point of view could be looked at quite differently in this context. Marriage looks more like a job option, or even a life raft for Cora, since she faced marginalization in the business world both from her own family and from Victorian society, which offered working women of average abilities few attractive options. Cora might even have received some hints or even instructions from her mother that I could summarize as: "Try for an Eastern guy."

Flora sometimes traveled and helped her mother with patients at the "branch offices," but she was not working either. She had been married to her railroad engineer, Mr. Hoover, since November, but if she was riding around in town and playing tennis with Cora on the front lawn, she was certainly not pregnant. Mr. Hoover was always on the road and could not spend much time with his wife. Flora still lived at home and had few friends, and Cora put in a lot of time entertaining her sister.

On Tuesday, June 9, Cora and Lotta "went out Driving had quite a nice time. at 10:30 Belle, Maggie + I went out to Belle's farm. It looked lovely. Remained there till 3 o'clock had our pictures taken in the Different views." Fertile farmland lined the Mississippi shore to the west of Davenport, in Rockingham, where Belle had just purchased her first piece of investment property at age twenty-six. Belle's farm was close enough to town that they could drive out to visit along Telegraph Road in a carriage and back in half a day—it was probably about four or five miles each way. Unfortunately, I have never found the photographs documenting Cora's visit to Belle's farm. However, I did discover a lawsuit in the Scott County Circuit Court records that describes in detail what the farm was like. Belle signed a lease that March with a tenant farmer named J. R. Wright who promised to work her land, for which he agreed to pay her $300 a year in rent. The farm had several acres of vineyards, an orchard, and a wood lot, which Mr. Wright had to work in the winter to cover a wood tax. Among other tasks, he agreed to plow, ditch, and manure the vines and to look after Belle's dog, Jumbo. In June, when Cora accompanied her two sisters to see the farm, things were going along nicely.

A married man who supported a family, Mr. Wright was also employed as a yardmaster for the Chicago, Milwaukee & St. Paul Railroad Company in Davenport. Working these two jobs must have been too much to handle, and he was later unable to make the balloon payment of $140 for rent that came due on October 31. The harvest was already in but was obviously inadequate to cover the balance that he owed, and he was in big trouble. By November, he owed Belle $205. For two years afterward, Belle relentlessly pursued the debt through the courts. She hired the most prestigious law firm in town, Davison and Lane (Mary Lane's father was one of the partners), moving to garnish Mr. Wright's wages from his employer in January of the following year. The records are incomplete, so the final outcome is unknown. However, given Belle's tenacious business instincts, she was unlikely to have yielded in this case, nor in any other she entered into, and the Wright family might well have ended up in the poorhouse.

Cora mentions her social time each evening in her diary, naming friends who came to call and the time she spent with various siblings, but she does not often mention either of her parents. Her social life was everything and her local friends the most interesting; her music seems to have fallen off the radar: "Maggie + I visited one of the Country Schools. Came home at 3 very tired. At 7:30 Papa, Maggie + I went down to the depot to meet Doctor. we came home and had a nice time. in the evening Grace Barlow + Lucy Dash called. retired at 10:30." Despite all the discussion about planning Cora's summer vacation, no concrete action appears to have been taken in any direction.

The newspaper in Bloomington, Illinois, where the Wakefields lived had taken note of Cora's arrival back home: "Miss Corize Keck, whose many friends in Bloomington will remember her visit last summer with pleasure, especially in musical circles, has returned from Vassar College, and will spend her vacation at her home in Davenport." Homer Wakefield showed up at Cora's house on Wednesday, pursuing her front and center on the tennis court in the yard on Brady Street. She was unimpressed and wrote, "Nothing new going on . . . in the afternoon we played tennis all afternoon with Doctor, Homer, Lotta, and I."

Undiscouraged by Cora's frosty response to his ardent letters to her back in April, Homer wanted to tell her about his big plans. Over the past several months, maybe using capital provided by his brother, Homer had set up a storefront business in Bloomington selling and installing incandescent electric lamps (and the batteries that were needed to run them), as well as magneto and electric bells, electrical medical equipment, annunciators, burglar alarms, and all kinds of electrical novelties and experimental apparatus. This was the "high-tech" field of his era. He was excited about new technology—it was like an Internet startup of the nineteenth century. Maybe he boasted that he was going to build up a fortune as large as his father's and his brother's. Cora probably rolled her eyes and served the next ball right at him.

Despite Cora's comment of "nothing new going on," thirty thousand visitors flocked to Davenport for the Seventeenth Annual Iowa Firemen's Tournament that week, which dominated the town until it ended on Friday, but Cora and her family paid it scant attention. At ten o'clock on a cloudless, perfect June day, a mile-long parade of two thousand firemen from one hundred fire companies from across the state of Iowa accompanied by twenty-five brass bands outfitted in a variety of magnificent, colorful uniforms marched by two blocks from the Kecks' house, but Cora and her sister Lotta decided to go riding instead: "every one crazy over the Firemen's Tournament Lotta + I were out riding."

Maybe Cora and her family preferred to forget about the dangers of fire because they had some bad memories. Cora's adolescence was dramatically interrupted in March 1882 when she was sixteen. According to a short news item published in the *Davenport Gazette*, she had been very ill as the result of a vaccination and woke up in the middle of the night in the darkness of her upstairs bedroom. As she got out of bed and struck a match to light her lamp, she overturned it. The flames spread instantly to the pool of oil spilled on the bedside table and onto the floor and then jumped across to light the droplets spilled on her nightgown. Cora screamed in pain and horror as the flames burned her skin and rose toward her arm and neck. Her father and mother were there in an instant, and their quick reactions smothered the flames, saving Cora's life and everything they owned.

Recovery from a severe burn like this is still dangerous, and infections are a constant danger. In the early 1880s, germ theory was not well understood, and there were no antibiotics. If an infection had set in, Cora would have died. Even in this dire situation, it is unlikely that Davenport's regular doctors would have consented to treat Cora. Three years before, in 1879, the Scott County Medical Society had opened its Black List "for the convenience of all members" to keep track of "individuals who were an imposition to the medical fraternity."[2] It was understood that these people were to be excluded from medical care. Given the unrelenting ferocity of the attacks that the medical society made on Mrs. Dr. Keck, it is certain that her name was on this list. If so, any doctor who went to the Kecks' house would have been thrown out of the Medical Society, whose stated code of ethics called for any member "accused of consulting with an irregular practitioner . . . to be expelled for associating with quacks and irregulars."[3] It's no wonder that Cora had lied to her parents about her visits to the dermatologist in New York.

As an eclectic physician, Mrs. Dr. Keck's mantra was: "Don't let medicine do all. Nature will do better."[4] Cora's mother thus might have chosen the simplest treatment and let nature do the rest, allowing her daughter's body to heal itself. That was the eclectic philosophy. Ironically, from a modern medical perspective, Cora was probably better off than if one of the regulars in the Scott County Medical Society had attended her. Mrs. Dr. Keck avoided the more elaborate "heroic" measures that were recommended by regular doctors at the time for burns, such as applying an ointment made of chalk powder, painting a burn with varnish, or spreading a layer of carded cotton dipped in lime water and linseed oil across it.[5] Simply covering a burn with a light, clean bandage to exclude air differs little from what is recommended today for first aid for first- and second-degree burns. In this instance, "knowing less" and doing less was probably a medical advantage. The burn took a long time to heal, and Cora had to stay in bed for weeks afterward. The *Davenport Gazette* was right when it noted that "Miss Keck, although suffering," was recovering "more luckily than she might reasonably have expected."

Cora's friends at Davenport High School did everything they could to cheer her up during her grueling convalescence. Edith Ross wrote her letters filled with all the latest high school gossip. Bert carried the messages to and fro. Less than a year after the accident with the lamp, Cora's recovery was complete.

How could Cora doubt her mother's medical skills after this? How could anyone? Mrs. Dr. Keck had defied the medical establishment and triumphed. She had rescued her family from disaster and successfully treated her daughter's severe burn. She was part of a "greatest generation" who handled emergencies with intensity and competence. She could go west into the wilderness alone and survive, prosper there and make a stand against the world. There was evidently no challenge that she couldn't handle. She could even do without doctors.

So why, Cora wondered, did the educated class of people in Davenport, the ones whom Cora longed to be friends with who sent their daughters to Vassar—the Griggses, the Lanes, the Cooks, the Pecks, and the LeClaires—continue to look down on her family? Why did they cross the street when they saw her coming, why did they relentlessly slander her mother and ignore certain undeniable facts, such as her recovery from the burn? The answer is fundamental: social prejudice operates outside of strictly logical thinking. A basic social climbing tool that every child encounters in schoolyards all over the globe is how to disregard inconvenient facts to gain advantage over others and move up through the ranks.

Mrs. Dr. Keck's indisputable wealth and the lifesaving medical treatments that she administered to members of her own family were inconvenient facts that Davenport's social establishment simply erased from their conversation. If Cora wanted to travel in those circles, even far from Davenport, she was going to have to confront this unreasonable perception. During the summer of 1885, Cora's faith in her mother's medical skills had already begun to waver after just one year away at college among the educated Easterners. The nuggets of biting sarcasm she had overheard from the attractive Columbia College medical students at the glittering parties in Manhattanville; the constant public ridicule of the irregular eclectics on top of quick, polite silences whenever Cora's mother's activities might come up during a conversation with her Vassar friends and teachers; the unspoken question hanging in the air afterwards, "Are you one of us or not?"—all of these realizations were forcing Cora to make a brutal choice.

CHAPTER TWENTY

My Year's Absence from D

T he *Davenport Daily Gazette* finally printed a correction about
Cora's arrival home from Vassar a week later in its "Davenport
Briefs" section: "It was Mr. Keck's daughter who returned from Vassar college Saturday evening, not Mr. Peck's." The glaring misprint that
mixed up Dr. Washington F. Peck's name with that of the most notorious
lady quack in the state of Iowa probably roused the famous surgeon into
an apoplectic fury. Recognized by his peers as "one of the six most successful surgeons in the United States" and chairman of the Surgical Section of the American Medical Association, Dr. Peck was famous for his
dominating personality and was "highly sensitive to injuries to his pride";
"his favorite exercise was the bringing of charges."[1] The correction carefully leaves out any mention of Mrs. Dr. Keck and once again features
a major copy editing error, accidentally demoting Dr. Peck to civilian
status by calling him "Mr. Peck." Was that an intentional dig of revenge,
slipped in by Mrs. Dr. Keck's friends in the editorial department?

THURSDAY, JUNE 11, 1885

They said Mr. Dorlan would arrive Thursday morning early + so I
was getting prepared for his coming + he did come early. Mr. Dorlan
arrived at 9 A.M. He seemed quite nice. No a la dude though. we went
out Tennising bright and early. Had Dinner at 1.

Mr. Dorlan and Cora had never met before, so Cora's mother and
one of her older sisters, whom she refers to as "they," must have arranged
the visit. In this case, Cora's first glimpse of Dorlan sounded fatal: "No a
la dude though." He lacked Eastern polish.

[234]

Cora and her visitor skipped the Firemen's Ball, held that evening in two locations, at the Turner Hall and Lahrmann's Hall. It may have been that those attending came from different socioeconomic strata from that of the Kecks. Many of the firemen visiting from dry towns in the state's interior "indulged to excess in spirituous liquors and were unduly boisterous in the streets" that night; at the Washington Beer Garden, the evening was livened up by a general fist fight that broke out after a tournament committeeman fired his revolver at a gatecrasher.[2] Such festivities were a little too rough even for Cora.

Boats tied up on the Mississippi shore across from Davenport in Rock Island, Illinois. Courtesy of the Richardson-Sloane Special Collections Center, Davenport Public Library.

FRIDAY, JUNE 12, 1885

W. Dorlan came up at 10. We talked, I telling all the jokes.

At 2:10 Lotta, Doctor and I went out Driving in Rock Island went over on the Island + over to Farnhamsburg [the town of Rock Island] u know and then to Frank Welches he made me a present of a very large bottle of olives. Went over to Black Hawk's Tower and had a lovely time. went to the train station with Dorlan in the carriage just in time for W. to make his train for Cedar Rapids. we had so much fun about Cham. [champagne] + Beer. came home.

au revoir Dorlan.

Bachelor number 2? Nope. "Next."

On another afternoon, Cora went with several friends in the Keck's carriage to the Fair Grounds. "I saw a few I knew, u know, among them was Flick. I came home in a Hack. So very warm could not stand it. I had some Lemonade without any Sugar u know." Later that evening, she "went down to the Kimball House—down to Taylors. There I met Cameron and Lill Reid. Came home + thought we could get some lemonade. stopped at several places and at last succeeded on Harrison St. by gum it's fun."

I first read about Cora's Davenport friend Lill Reid in April, when Cora was suffering so much from loneliness at the beginning of her spring vacation at Vassar. Homer wrote her that his sister, Hattie, had become close friends with Lill Reid, clearly dropping a big hint that Cora should be worried that he might be entertaining some competition. Six weeks later, in May, Cora was still annoyed about this connection between her out-of-town admirer, Homer, and Lill: "I think I will not take so much pains to have my visitors get very intimate with my Davenport friends as it soon lends trouble as Lill R. with the Wakefields." Now Lill surfaces again, in the company of a different gent named Cameron.

The four young people met up at the Kimball House, next to the Chicago, Rock Island & Pacific Railway elevated tracks facing Perry

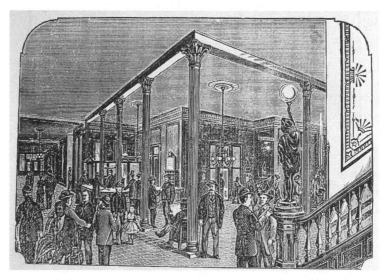

Lobby of the Kimball House hotel in Davenport. Courtesy of the Richardson-Sloane Special Collections Center, Davenport Public Library.

and Fourth streets. Built in 1873, Davenport's premier hotel boasted 150 rooms with running water, gas lighting, elevators, and telegraph service. It was evidently not a problem for Cora to spend the evening with her friends in the middle of Bucktown. Unaccompanied sporting men in need of a quick nip of restorative spirits could leave the hotel and cross Fourth Street to a small saloon next to the railway embankment, an establishment conveniently flanked by three brothels. Respectable people paid no notice.

On another evening later that week, Cora finally took advantage of Davenport's musical talent and heard a concert at the German community's Turner Hall: "In the evening we went out riding and at 8:10 we went out to the Grand Concert by Strasser's Band at the German Theater stayed till 11. came home. Had some Refreshements such as Beer ever so good u know." Although the churchgoing principles of temperance were central in Mrs. Dr. Keck's life, Cora made a point of drinking alcohol whenever she thought she could get away with it.

But Cora clearly also had some strict restrictions on her leisure activities that she obeyed. Next to the Kimball House was the Burtis Opera House, which seated fourteen hundred and hosted hundreds of world-famous performers throughout the second half of the nineteenth century, including Sarah Bernhardt, Maurice Barrymore, Otis Skinner, Henry M. Stanley (of "Dr. Livingstone, I presume" fame), and the actress Fanny Davenport, whom Cora had never seen until she went to the theater with Kitty in New York. Great artists of the era commonly toured throughout the Midwest because they could travel up and down the Mississippi on riverboats in luxurious accommodations. Davenport was one of the main stops along the river. Cora's mother must have disapproved of these theatrical events, because Cora did not save a single program from any performance at the Burtis. In New York, she sneaked out to the theater by lying to Miss Goodsell, but she did not dare defy her mother's edicts in her hometown.

ON SATURDAY, JUNE 13, "It rained considerable. at 5:10 Lotta & I went down town. came home in time for Dinner & at 7:40 Frank

Anderson and Will Mossman called. they looked ever so nice having improved in my years absence from D. I wonder if it was mutual.—oh. I know." Will and Frank lounged against the stoop. Cora enjoyed her old high school friends' regard. She could not resist boasting about visiting Kitty's family in New York City and her widening acquaintance with sophisticated people on the East Coast. She dropped the names of several New York City mayors into the conversation. Frank's mother ran a boardinghouse in Rock Island and was raising four children on her own. Will was learning to be a bricklayer. Will's father, Albert, had started as a laborer in a print shop and would rise up through the ranks to buy the company outright with a partner by the end of the 1880s. (Albert also served as the secretary and music librarian of the local Mendelssohn Society for a number of years. Working-class German immigrants formed the backbone of the classical music scene in Davenport; the town's most prominent musician, Jacob Strasser, supported his large family as an underpaid bookkeeper.)

Cora and her friends visited on the steps for an hour, "when who should come but Mrs. Whisler, Mrs. Myer and Rose Myer. I made three breaks. That about used me up viz. that of going up and down the steps three times to greet Mrs. Whisler—calling Mama & Willie + kissing Rose + Mrs. M. I was nearly dead afterward." Cora's "breaks" refer to the effort she made to run up the long, steep flight of steps from Brady Street to her front door to call her mother and then back down to greet an old family friend who was also one of Mrs. Dr. Keck's most important public supporters in Davenport. Mrs. Whisler's daughter May was a living testimonial to Mrs. Dr. Keck's effectiveness as a practicing physician, and she acted as a powerful public advocate for Mrs. Dr. Keck's medical legitimacy for many years, as did Rudolphus Hoffmann, the quarry worker once rumored to have died of tuberculosis despite Mrs. Dr. Keck's treatments.

☙

SUNDAY, JUNE 14, 1885

Rained very hard all day Mama, Maggie + I went to church in the rain Lounged around the rest of the day reading my German tales to

Maggie. In the evening Maggie, Willie, Bert B. and I enjoyed ourselves by talking.

MONDAY, JUNE 15, 1885

Played Tennis about all day. practiced piano and in the evening Florence and I went driving.

TUESDAY, JUNE 16, 1885

Miserable day for me. Played Tennis. May Whisler and her mother called.

These three short entries are it for the summer. Cora wrote nothing more until September. The first time I read the short section of the diary in which Cora described her life at home in Davenport, I was almost desperate for her to reveal more about her family and bitterly disappointed that her descriptions petered out so quickly. A large part of my drive to research this book came from that frustration. However, what Cora didn't write is eloquent in its way. If she didn't give me much description of her parents, maybe this is important. She was obviously not interacting with either her mother or her father in a way that struck her as important enough to record. Cora's parents do not seem to have taken much notice of her return from Vassar, nor do they seem to have realized how much she had been changed by her experiences there. By June 20, Cora's mother was already back to traveling on her circuit; a notice in the *Bloomington* (Illinois) *Daily Bulletin* announced that she had arrived in that city. Even though Cora had been gone from home for ten months, no one recognized the work she had begun to put in to develop herself into a real musician.

As summer in Davenport stretched out into the dog days of August, time slowed to a crawl. General Grant's funeral took place on August 8, but Cora showed little interest in the ceremonies that were held in Davenport. She wished that she could have seen the real funeral parade in New York down on lower Broadway. The Haymarket bombers' trial was grinding along in Chicago, but Cora was not interested in crime or labor politics. She felt cast adrift without Vassar's structured schedule. Every day, she got out of bed and got dressed, and every day, although she was entirely free to do anything she pleased, she found that she always ended up doing more or less exactly what she had done the day before.

In the heat and humidity of high summer in Iowa, her dress was soaked with perspiration by 9:30 in the morning, which encouraged lassitude. What was there to do? Ride around in the family carriage while trying to avoid that gold-digger Charlie Meier? Sit in the shade under the trees in the yard and then play a few rounds of tennis with her sister Flora? More roller-skating? A boat trip up the river? Was that *all* there was to do? Her gang of friends never seemed to do anything new. Her freedom at home in "good old D" was beginning to resemble monotony. Cora lived in substantial luxury and comfort, and she never had to struggle for anything, so what was the problem? Like many American adolescents in any era living in those presumably enviable conditions, she was overwhelmed with too many easy options and starved for hard goals.

As summer rolled on, her hunger for challenge began to overcome her self-doubt. Cora never felt that she was at loose ends at Vassar. There were far fewer freedoms or comfortable luxuries at college, but she felt a pang of longing for the closeness she had enjoyed with her school friends, who came from so many different backgrounds and who had ambition and specific plans for the future.

I have no clues to tell me how long Cora's wavering lasted during the summer of 1885. However, at some point, she resolved to return to college, Vassar proved willing to take her back, and her family decided to continue to support her musical education for a second year.

CHAPTER TWENTY-ONE

My Interesting Stranger Friend

ora wrote to Miss Goodsell to ask for permission to arrive on
campus a week early. The Lady Principal wrote back from her
seaside vacation in Marblehead Neck, Massachusetts: "Your pleasant
letter has just reached me. It was forwarded to this place from Vassar
College . . . I shall be glad to give you occupation in some little ways
if you would like to return a few days early." Miss Goodsell closed by
telling Cora that she hoped to see her soon "well and happy" and signed
her letter "With love, Your A. F. Goodsell." Cora kept this letter in her
scrapbook. The "horrid" Lady Principal had mellowed out, and both of
them seem to have forgotten all about the great shock and disappointment Cora had suffered in her office the previous May.

Postcard from Cora's scrapbook: "Gunther's Confectionery,
212 State Street, Chicago."

On August 20, Cora mailed a form to claim her room for the fall semester, which she had prereserved when she went home for summer vacation. She now had twice as much clothing to take with her, and she traveled east with two Saratoga trunks instead of one. The *Davenport Gazette* weighed in with an announcement of Cora's plans (and only one serious error, for a change): "Miss Lorrie Keck departs tomorrow morning for the east, meeting a number of Chicago girls at Chicago, enroute for Vassar College in Poughkeepsie, New York."

MONDAY SEPTEMBER 14, 1885

My last Monday in D. I was extremely busy getting ready as on the morrow I was to sail for fair Vassar—Packed trunks all day. Co Taylor was visiting me she helped me pack my two Saratogas. The night before leaving home for College—I felt as if something grand would be in store for me on my return to College

at 8 P.M. Co Taylor in company with J. Thackery called for me I won't forget my last eve home. Good bye Dear Davenport Dear home.

The next morning, Cora woke at 7:10, dressed quickly, and, carrying her lunch bag, started for the depot an hour later, surrounded by a crowd of family members. Someone must have ridden with her as far as Chicago, where she was "deserted" at 3 P.M. "Had to wait for my train till 7:31 Went downtown with a lady, to Gunthers bought a box [of candy] came back late & made a mash on the lovely ticket agent. Miss Anderson [who was starting her junior year at Vassar] from Salt Lake made her appearance and introduced herself. I was surprised to see her but happy, we had such a jolly time. She was also going to Vassar."

Pullman sleeping berth "section."

Then, Cora noticed a new student she didn't recognize enter the car they were in; the girl passed down the aisle looking very nervous about being alone and sat down several seats in front of her. "On the train I met my Stranger Friend Miss Weeks from Chicago going East to Vassar. I was delighted, I took a step first + made the acquaintance." Helen, whose nickname was Ned, was an only child from Evanston, Illinois. Shy and academically gifted, she had already earned a bachelor's degree from Northwestern University.[1] She was skipping her freshman year and would enter Vassar as a sophomore, with a double major in the School of Music. Cora declared herself "so happy" to make a new friend and wrote that "we got very well acquainted as we journeyed on. She wanted me to sleep with her. This I would not do. The porter and conductor were extremely kind and thus gave me a section [a sleeping berth]. At 10:00 before retiring on Tuesday Evening retired at 10:30 au revoir."

WEDNESDAY, SEPTEMBER 16, 1885

Second day on train. Awoke at 7:10 by the racket of people that awoke early. I wanted so to sleep longer. I slept with $300 near me too so I kept kinda an eye open such as I did.

My Friend soon awoke and thus we renewed our conversation. I found my Friend extremely interesting. She had a grand Basket of delicacies and & we thus enjoyed ourselves & so I enjoyed my self immensely too. we ordered our coffee by porter at the different stations and later on we concluded to get off and prominade up and down. We wrote a few letters as we journeyed on. I wrote one to Mama. retired at 10 I skipped across the isle [aisle].

During the fall, Cora revisited her intensely felt memory of this moment two different ways in empty sections of the diary, using pages from July that she had left blank during the boring weeks she had spent at home in Davenport. Each time, she added more details.

Miss Weeks was lovely and at 10 I crawled dressed only in my drawers and sacque across the isle and slept with her—

On Wednesday evening at 10 I found I had to give up a part of my section to a miserable fat man overhead, so with a little persuasion from my Friend "Ned" I crawled across the isle, she holding the curtains together at top and I at the bottom. I had nothing on save my Drawers & a dressing sacque of white muslin. I was so frightened, as it was my first experience sleeping two together but had a rich time.

I found a portrait of Miss Weeks in Vassar's Special Collections; her features were gentle, almost fragile in appearance.[2] Her clothes were girlish and modest, not the slightest bit elegant. She looked vulnerable. Leaving home for the first time, she reached out to Cora on the train like a weak swimmer grabbing for a life raft. Cora had incredible emotional antennae and a constitutional preference for taking charge and nurturing younger, emotionally needy women. She was returning to Vassar fired up to do well with her music, filled with hope and ambitions. She projected energy that Ned fed on; people who are obviously excited about their goals are very attractive to others. The dynamic was just like Cora's friendship with Minnie Keiter, only this time, Cora and her new acquaintance instantly felt a powerful physical chemistry.

Helen "Ned" Weeks, Vassar class of '88. Courtesy of Vassar College Archives.

Although Cora herself never used the word in her diary or scrapbooks, it was a classic Victorian college "smash," or intense crush.

THURSDAY, SEPTEMBER 17, 1885

At 4 o'clock A.M. a horrible hour we were awaked by the porter to dress as we were nearing Poughkeepsie. Miss Weeks' Father had telegraphed on for a hack and escort. We were met by a policeman and he conducted us to our hack. I can't bear to think of it. Arrived at Vassar 4:45 A.M. Saw dear Miss Goodsell.

Cora was not at all embarrassed that the porter knew that the two young women were sharing a bed; it was obviously not an unusual situation in 1885. However, she was mortified by the presence of the policeman who escorted them to their hired carriage. Ned's overprotective parents were so concerned about her arrival alone in the middle of the night in Poughkeepsie that they had made advance arrangements with the Poughkeepsie police department. Cora was much more self-sufficient. Either she had been planning to arrange for a hack by herself at 4 A.M. without help from her parents, or knowing that a large group of students would be arriving in the early morning, the college might have sent the horse car to meet the train.

Behold, dear Miss G. put Ned right by me. We awoke in time for Breakfast + at 7:35 went to the dining room + Ned + I seemed so devoted to each other, and Mlle. Goodsell having given her a fine impression of me in the way of stating the fact that I was a devoted student etc. she at last said, "You may take the room next to Miss Keck, number 8½."

A devoted student? Cora? This was something new. Miss Goodsell was not the kind of person who would waste her time with empty flattery, but if she publicly set high expectations for Cora, it might inspire the young woman to rise to meet them during the coming year. During the summer Miss Goodsell must have worried she had pushed Cora out of college for good after their confrontation over Cora's bad German grades and the canceled recital. No wonder she was so delighted that Miss Keck had decided to return to face Vassar's challenges. "Little did I think of being here again, last year. I did come back," Cora wrote later in September.

The Vassar students entering or returning to school that fall were arriving at a college whose leadership was still unstable. For the moment, it was under the interim control of the Reverend J. Ryland Kendrick, a member of the board of trustees, who would serve as president only until the board could find a permanent replacement for the Reverend Caldwell, who had been so ignominiously forced into retirement in June. Like his predecessor, Kendrick was a Baptist minister.

Cora's Davenport neighbor Elizabeth Griggs had passed her entrance exams in June and was being admitted to the freshman class for September 1885. Her success vindicated the high quality of the education offered at the Davenport High School. According to the *Davenport Gazette*, "Because of the creditable examination passed and the excellent standing maintained by recent graduates of Davenport High School at Vassar College, undergraduates will hereafter be admitted to that institution without examination or condition. Principal Stratton received a letter to that effect this morning from the president of the college." Cora's bad grades presumably had no effect on Davenport High School's new status. She was, after all, just a music student. Marian Austin did Elizabeth Griggs one better; she not only passed her entrance exams, she skipped a year and advanced directly to the sophomore class. Both Elizabeth and Marian moved upstairs out of the basement corridors to room with their classes upstairs, Marian joining the class of '88 and Elizabeth joining the class of '89.

For the second year in a row, Cora was assigned to rooms many girls thought were the least desirable in the entire college, on first corridor North, on the ground floor, facing the Athletic Circle. In 1890, the Lady Principal Frances Wood wrote, "There is great objection to the first corridors, and every pain should be taken to make these doubly attractive in arrangement and furnishing."[3] Cora never objected, however.

Cora showed her new friend "Miss W" around, and "at 3:10 P.M Cousin Warren appeared. I was so happy to see him. He having waited in New York since Monday for my coming on to college. He only stayed

Cora Keck's dormitory room in 1886, "Parlor 9,"
on the north corridor of the basement level.

40 minutes + so I suffered." It sounds to me as if he were more or less bamboozled into paying Cora a visit by his mother or some other authority figure in his family and that he showed up from a sense of duty only. Once again, Cora felt emotionally short-changed by Warren. He had his own life goals beyond Cora's awareness, and he played his cards extremely close to the vest. She couldn't have known this at the time, but based on additional evidence from my grandfather's recollections, I am certain that Warren was gay all his life.

"We were very tired from our Journey," Cora wrote. But Ned suffered more from the exhaustion and "fainted" during her first evening on campus; her health was apparently quite fragile. Cora "called for help—a 'man'—he went for Doctor Mosher + made us come up to the Infirmary

+ we both went up to the Infirmary at 8:40 as she was so ill. Thus we slept all night there. At about 11 P.M. I awoke + concluded that I was getting damp + Ned really was wet by the explosion of a hot water Bottle."

So what did Cora get out of this relationship? Ned's neediness would have driven a lot of people crazy. However, she gave Cora a sense of emotional purpose, made her feel important and useful, and helped settle her into a disciplined and productive routine. Cora was subconsciously imitating her mother, taking on the role of a nurturing healer. Ned's constant health emergencies not only added drama to Cora's life, they kept Cora close to campus and made her less wild. Also, Ned's admiration built up Cora's confidence as a musician. Ned the brilliant scholar was only a beginner on the violin, and Cora could show her the way forward.

> Expected to go to town but "Ned" was under the weather had fearful cramps etc. so I stayed at home @ 4 P.M.
>
> Today I waited drearily around for my practicing periods to be assigned me as I am so anxious to begin. . . . A week ago today I was departing from D. . . . I kinda dreaded to go. Still at the same time I knew + really wanted to go + so after a week's time I find myself stationed here for a year. my practicing periods given out and I will thus be very busy, as I mean to do well in it, and thus finish in credit both to my Parents and my College Friends. I'm crazy after my music.

THURSDAY, SEPTEMBER 24, 1885

> At 8:30 P.M. who should knock and then fly? no one. Kitty R. made her appearance in a kind of misterious manner. I found her afterward at "Mrs. Johns" hiding in the W. C. [the bathroom, with a pun on the name of the woman who ran the college storeroom] Then Ned crawled in the back window. She did not want Kitty to see her as her hair was all up in gum strips.

FRIDAY, SEPTEMBER 25, 1885

> I was extremely happy over Kittie's arrival and my chum [Ned] was very smitten with her much to my delight. We had a lovely time

Friday, with 4 of us Girls together + Ned affiliated beautifully. Our affections seemed to improve day by day. Ned going "hanging on" as she terms it. Jackson Balls, gum and cigarettes for a change.

Cora and Ned had fallen head over heels in love with each other; it was a classic Vassar "smash." On the day of their arrival together at college on the 17th Cora wrote, "at night Ned + I slept for the first time in my room and together too." Over the weekend of September 26 and 27, Ned and Cora joked that they had officially become a couple: "we have professed our love and declared our engagement and thus will be married she after my wealth I for her degree . . . Second Sunday in Pokeepsie for a change. Ned and I wanted to go to town to Church but concluded to go the following Sun. being Communion Sunday—we are engaged and soon to be wed she sleeps with me nightly and I think I will like her."

Ten years earlier, a Yale student wrote the following cheerful and nonjudgmental explanation of what he and his friends understood a smash to mean in 1873:

> This term is in general use at Vassar . . . when a Vassar girl (usually older) takes a shine to another (usually younger) she straightaway enters upon a regular course of bouquet sendings, interspersed with tinted notes, mysterious packages of "Ridley's Mixed Candies," locks of hair perhaps, and many other tender tokens until at last the object of her attention is captured, the two become inseparable, and the aggressor is considered by her circle of acquaintances as—"smashed." The mortality, so to speak, resulting from these smashups, is frightful to contemplate. One young lady, the "irrepressible," rejoices in more than thirty. She keeps a list of them, in illuminated text, framed and hung up in her room like a Society poster . . . Vassar numbers her smashes by the score.[4]

This Yalie sounds envious of his competition. He was hoping he could pick up some tips from these unusual suitors on to how to make more conquests of his own the next time he came up to Poughkeepsie to loiter at the tintype shop.

The iconic American writer Henry Wadsworth Longfellow approved of passionate romantic friendships between young women, seeing them as "a rehearsal in girlhood for the great drama of woman's life" (that is, marriage)."[5] This was the man who gave us "The Midnight Ride of Paul Revere" and "The Courtship of Miles Standish." As an internationally famous celebrity poet, Longfellow was criticized during his lifetime for being a popular sell-out who catered to mass taste. He was not a rebel. Like many Americans, he probably still believed that women were physically incapable of independent desire. As a matter of fact, Miss Goodsell might have felt the same way about girls' relationships. She saw nothing wrong with assigning the two friends to room together upon their arrival at college, and I believe it would be difficult to find a person from any era in U.S. history with a stricter vision of correct moral behavior than Miss Goodsell.

In Europe, where society was more advanced and sophisticated, influential thinkers such as Sigmund Freud were just beginning to analyze human psychology in terms of its sexual nature in the 1880s, and the idea that women had their own sexuality independent of male desire was starting to gain acceptance there. In England, powerful, independent women were already much more aware of the singular nature of strong physical attraction between members of their own sex. Eliza Lynn Linton, whose judgmental rant about girls who presumed to study music had upset Cora so badly the previous March, wrote a book in 1880 called *The Rebel of the Family* about the British women's rights movement. According to modern scholars, it includes one of the first literary portraits of the late-Victorian lesbian community in London, in the form of two supporting characters named Bell Blount and her "little wife," Connie. Mrs. Linton disapproved of and portrayed the relationship in unpleasant tones.

The phrase "little wife" shows up in Cora's scrapbook and in her memoryabil at least five times as a joking description for herself, Lotta Wix, Minnie Keiter, and several other friends posing next to her in her tintypes; so the term, if not a full understanding of its sexual connotation, had already jumped the Atlantic to Vassar by 1884, four years after Mrs. Linton used it.

⚭

MISS CHAPIN SEEMS TO HAVE RELAXED her guard during her summer vacation too; in early October Cora wrote she was "somewhat encouraged by Chapin." The polite mask that tightened on her face whenever Cora entered her studio for lessons began to soften. Her most frustrating student might not be completely hopeless. Cora regretted how she had let her practicing slide in Davenport. She resolved to use her piano talent to get her mother to pay more attention to her. She woke up every morning feeling nervous about the challenges facing her in Miss Chapin's piano studio but was glad to have them.

The dreadful German recitations still haunted her; she had done almost nothing over the summer to try to catch up: "Freshman German is fearfully hard and hurts me awfully so much so what I don't think I will continue it much longer as I want some time to myself this year." No one in the family had focused on her failing grades in this subject, and no arrangements had been made to have her live with or visit a German-speaking family to build up her language skills, even though at least three-quarters of the inhabitants of Davenport were immigrants or children of immigrants who spoke German fluently. In three months at home, she could have made huge strides, but that opportunity had been overlooked.

Meanwhile, a theatrical agent named George Wallace Williams wrote to Cora in Davenport, and the letter was forwarded to her at Vassar in early October.

> Miss Corize Mae Keck:
> I mailed you a copy of <u>The Day Star</u> in which there was a notice of the Vassar Girl's Vocal Quartette. I desire a few more voices and may conclude to make a double quartette. The composition will be such as to insure social recognition in all the large cities. If you or any of your friends are interested, kindly write.
> Truly Yours, Geo. Wallace Williams, manager.
> 25 Union Sq. New York City

How did this man get Cora's name and address? Not through the right channels, apparently. I would love to know who was in that quartette, and whether the singers had really been students at Vassar's School of Music and under what circumstances. Cora wrote in ink on the outside of the envelope: "Impudence personified." Then she cut out the concert announcement he sent and pasted it into the scrapbook, along with the impudent letter. In this case, she not only had reservations about going onstage as a performer consistent with the social restrictions of her era, she also hated the idea that an inquisitive stranger had found out who she was and where she lived.

∽

CORA SPENT SO MUCH TIME practicing that fall that her eyes began to bother her from squinting at her music in the dingy practice rooms. Her mother sent her a telegram about the situation. "Leave eyes alone, await my letter, just rest," prescribed Mrs. Dr. Keck. Next to that message, Cora pasted a card from Van Keuren Bros. Opticians about weak eyes and vision problems corrected by prescribed "lenses." Throughout her life, Cora seldom appears with glasses in any of her portraits. She was evidently vain about the way they looked, because she wore glasses regularly.

Here is a typical joke she clipped from the *New York Graphic* sneering at the dismal dating skills of a clueless, overeducated girl wearing glasses, with "Boston" crossed out by hand:

What Broke the Charm?

"Have you seen that pretty ~~Boston~~ Vassar girl recently?"
"I took her out walking the other evening. I put my arm around her and kissed her."
"What did she do?"
"She looked over her glasses and said, 'Let me remove the binocular protection from the sclerotic covering of my organ of vision.'"
"Well, when does the happy event come off?"
"Eh?"

Roller skate polo on the cover of Harper's Weekly, September 8, 1883.

"When will you be married?"

"We won't be."

Throughout the fall, Cora's relationship with Ned was all consuming. She spent every night with her in the dormitory and took daily walks with her and visited her in the infirmary when she was sick. Ned's mother appreciated Cora's influence with her daughter and wrote to thank her for helping her daughter adjust to life away from home at college.

As the fall semester wore on, Cora wrote less and less each day in her diary—the newness of Vassar was wearing off, her energies were more and more focused on her music, and she no longer felt the drive to record the details of her daily activities as she had when it was all an exciting novelty. Right before she stopped writing in it for good, she met "Miss Day from town." Lydia Stark Day was a new student in the School of Music.

"A lovely Day but I felt so mean," she wrote in her last entry, on October 18. Was that a pun on Lydia's name?

Even though the diary ends, this is not the end of the story by any means. Cora continued to fill her scrapbooks with informative items. The next big thing would be the boys from Poughkeepsie.

CHAPTER TWENTY-TWO

The Sentimental Satellites

During the week of November 8 to 13, Cora missed her corridor meeting, neglected her outdoor exercise, was unprepared for German on the 10th, missed her Harmony class on the 11th, was late on another day, and skipped chapel on the 11th, 13th, and 14th. She proudly displayed this dismal attendance slip in her scrapbook—maybe it was a new low for her? Was she wavering in her resolve to become a serious Vassar student?

Not everything was going badly. Two weeks earlier, Cora had finally been asked to be on the Thekla committee along with another newcomer, Miss Jennie Warren, of Bay City, Michigan. As two Midwesterners, Miss Warren and Miss Keck were flattered at being asked to take charge. All that they were expected to do was to copy out the programs by hand (in an era before photocopiers) and organize the refreshments to be served after each small student workshop performance, but they were making inroads into the territory formerly controlled by the socially prominent "nice" girls who had dominated Thekla's leadership the year before. Cora was also asked to perform in front of her Vassar classmates for only the second time after her nerve-racking debut with the Beethoven sonata at the workshop the previous spring.

She presented the simple arpeggios and linked chords of Raff's Mélodique to her fellow students, feeling Miss Chapin's eyes drilling into her back the whole time. She must have proved to her teacher that she could listen to the music and create her own phrasing and expression, instead of pumping out streams of unanalyzed notes at top speed, because after this performance, Cora was allowed to resume playing advanced pieces. Miss Chapin assigned her pupil two Chopin impromptus, op. 29 and 36, which she marked with the following notes: "Wilber Derthrick method" and "'Sphengali' Triplits."

Sphengali? Sounds like more glamour than you would require from a routine piano drill. And what was the Wilber Derthrick method? In her scrapbook, Cora saved a piano technique exercise that Miss Chapin wrote out for her on staff paper: "chin quiet—mouth open—piano smooth—Tha-la-da Tha-la-da—Na-ma-na chin quiet, [again]." Was the Derthrick method one of those "good for you" teaching exercises like race-walking that looks extremely silly to onlookers? I'll probably never know.

On Thursday the 12th, Ned hosted her first spread in parlor 8. Cora was glad to see that her young protégée was finally launched at college on a solid footing with a social life of her own; she tried to fade into the background (which was very hard for her to do) and let Ned shine as a hostess. Miss Warren's roommate, Lydia Day, came too. It was said around the college that Miss Day was as wild as a western mustang; "the girls called me a wild girl," she wrote about herself later in the year.

While Ned's guests spread jam on pieces of cake, dropped olives into their mouths, and spooned up the last of the melting ice cream from Smiths, they discussed the latest rumors about the college's administration; some of them had heard that the interim president, Kendrick, would not be returning after the Christmas break.[1] Throughout the fall, bitter struggles among different factions backing different presidential candidates intermittently emerged into public view in the newspapers, and the students were all too familiar with how precarious their college leadership was. Maybe the trustees had found a new president or Kendrick was in trouble in some way. They all felt a mixture of hope and anxiety. What if the infighting blocked a rescue? What if the college couldn't solve its financial problems? No one said out loud what was really on their minds: What if Vassar had to close its doors?

That same day, Cora received an urgent telegram from her mother with a strongly worded command: "Go to Philadelphia immediately & rest for two weeks." Was she wearing herself out and getting sick with stress and overwork? Cora ignored her mother's instruction. Instead, Kitty Rogers invited her to go down to New York City that Saturday to see a comedy by Henry Arthur Jones, appropriately titled *Saints and Sinners*, at the Madison Square Theater. Cora was soon on the train not to Philadelphia, but to Manhattanville.

AS WINTER APPROACHED, the emotional intensity of Cora's smash with Ned began to fade. Their sizzling beginning felt dramatic at the time—they were alone together, on a train, headed for the unknown. However, in the big picture, they were just two young women on their way to college, and once everyone settled down into the school year's routines, Ned's personality was too small and mild to hold Cora's attention and they drifted apart.

Going to the theater with Kitty in New York made Cora stop and think. Where was her old gang of friends? Marian Austin had spent the fall tennising without her, while Jane Edwards, who was from a "nice" Brooklyn family, the Joralemons, started to spend her time with Mary Poppenheim's clique. As the energetic and musically talented Midwesterners took on a larger role in organizing Thekla workshops, the Eastern socialites, the Poppenheims and McKinlays, moved on, left music behind, and began to dominate the tennis club, while Cora faded off the courts. Cora's ex-roommate Laura Harris had become completely absorbed with acting in plays for Exoteric, the preparatory students' drama club. Cora missed her old circle of friends. It seemed like her entire fall semester had slipped by in a dream.

Cora was not in love any more, but she wanted to be. It felt natural to build up some new momentum in her romantic life with young men. Back in Davenport, Grace Barlow was getting married. Cora remembered that she was supposed to be finding a fiancé. The clock was ticking and she would soon be done with her course of study in June, but she didn't have any definite relationship to count on. She had had a lively flirtation with Ned's Chicago friend Hugh Jones when he came through town on that business trip earlier in the fall. As the son of W. H. Jones, president and director of the Plano Manufacturing Co. (makers of the Plano Harvester & Twine Binder & New Warrior Mower), he certainly had good prospects in life. But Hugh Jones lived a thousand miles away. Cora had to sigh. Vassar was in truth very isolated and presented her with more obstacles than social opportunities.

Frustratingly, the administration expected the students to study while on campus. A New York City newspaper article that Cora clipped written by a classmate described the social atmosphere on campus in 1885 in sober terms: "Probably a majority of the students are mature young women qualifying themselves for a life work as teachers and endeavoring to get the most and best out of the school. These give the tone to the place. Its aspect for the most part is studious, almost severe. The frivolous and flighty ones are in a minority and they often reform." Maybe the article's author, Mary F. X. (Sheldon, Vassar class of 1888), was thinking specifically about Cora and Cora's set of friends when she wrote that last sentence. How notorious were they on campus? Might not the daughter of an unperturbed "notorious woman" in Davenport fall naturally into the role of an unperturbed "notorious girl" at Vassar?

Marrying the wrong man was one option for attaining notoriety. The mysterious source interviewed for the "Vassar Virgins' Vagaries" article that Cora had put in her scrapbook the year before focused on the popular topic of rebelling against one's parents by eloping from college.

> Whenever a marriageable male strays inside the high cedar hedge which divides the Vassar grounds from the rest of the world, he is regarded with suspicion by twenty pairs of [faculty] eyes until he has satisfactorily accounted for his presence there. The girls, as a natural consequence, form no acquaintances worth mentioning among the opposite sex. Naturally, then, they have to amuse themselves as best they can.
>
> There are generally several girls in Vassar who have been sent there by stern parents because they have contracted undying passions which are not approved of at home.
>
> These young persons with broken hearts in my day always had a sentimental following of other girls who were not in love, but who were dying to be. The sentimental satellites were always ready to assist in any romantic adventure that had a young man in it . . .
>
> Let me confess that I assisted in one runaway marriage . . . a back window in the basement of the college through which I and another girl poked the would-be bride into the would-be bridegroom's arms, and a night ride over the hills to Peekskill and a minister defeated the

old folks . . . the bride came back to school by herself in a rickety old stage coach and the bridegroom took a train for Boston. It was some months before the parents found out, and when they did there was a storm.

Cora often fantasized about eloping. But a young man from outside of the college had to already know you before you could duck under the fence into his outstretched arms and race away with him into the wide world of wedded bliss. At the college itself there were no young men. Cora was from out of town and was having trouble settling her affections on a person who felt the same way about her. She was not so stupid as to run off with someone she didn't actually love just for the thrill of it, but she chafed every day at the restrictions that blocked her goal, and she began to lose some clarity of thinking.

The college's restrictions, designed to protect the students from romantic entanglements so they could launch themselves into independent lives as single, working women with good careers, ironically served to magnify the perception that opting for romance and marriage was an independent, rebellious action. It transformed the routine business of swearing to undertake decades of obedience, housekeeping, monogamy, and child-raising into a sparkling adventure. Hence the interest in eloping and defying the authorities; marrying without

Eloping couple from a stereoscope, ca. 1890. Courtesy of the Library of Congress.

out permission was the really decisive way to rebel against convention. In Victorian Vassar, it was perfectly acceptable to fall passionately in love with your roommate; the nightmare for the college staff would be if you ran off and married her brother.

By the time of my mother's generation, born in the 1920s and away at college before and during World War II, the change in young American women's attitudes was dramatic. By the middle of the twentieth century, a pervasive paranoia about "deviant" sexual relationships between women at college emerged into the open, along with awareness of the modern term "lesbian." The climactic ending to Mary McCarthy's popular and once controversial 1963 book *The Group* about Vassar students in the early 1930s turns on this exact point. The situation became polarized and politicized, and a great deal of the easy fluid intimacy characteristic of Victorian female friendships was lost as a result.

THE NEXT SATURDAY, after classes ended for the December vacation, Cora paid a visit to the tintype shop and flirted with an "Andover dude" and a "Fresha@Yale." Maybe one of Will Marmon's friends came looking for her and dragged a buddy from Yale along for the ride. In the picture, the young Yalie is wearing an overcoat of checked wool with a cape attached, in the British style favored by Sherlock Holmes. His perfectly gloved hands are holding a fancy cane with an ivory knob, which would have been monogrammed with his initials. He had probably come back recently from a Grand Tour of Europe, a traditional educational ritual for children of wealthy, elite families on the East Coast who aped the customs of the British aristocracy; the coat might have been a souvenir purchased from a fancy London tailor. His friend from Andover is dressed more conservatively, in a dark, well-cut coat and suit, but he has cocked his bowler hat back on his head in an effort to look blasé and rakish for the camera, a pose that shows up frequently among Cora's less polished male friends out in Davenport.

As was typically Cora's experience in these situations, she made a good mash on the spot, but she could never get the ball rolling in any permanent way with these desirable dudes. Once they disappeared back to their remote and prestigious lairs in New Haven, Cambridge, and other parts of New England, there was no serious follow-up. They seem to have hovered in the remote middle distance, slightly out of her reach, and no doubt they preferred it that way. Cora's clothes were a little too plain, too ill-fitting, her demeanor a little too provocative and undis-criminating—she was a fun girl, but not a marriageable one.

ON THE LAST DAY OF THE SEMESTER, Kitty Rogers wrote "Good-bye and Merry Christmas" on the little notepad on the outside of Cora's door and left for New York City. Mrs. Dr. Keck carefully organized her daughter's vacation plans, making up for the year before when she had been so preoccupied with work that she left Cora stranded in the empty college building over Christmas break. She sent money and permission for Cora to visit Pennsylvania for two weeks, and Cora took the train to Allentown on December 19.

At the Strausses' house by the old mill, the postman delivered two letters to Cora forwarded from Vassar. She tore open the envelopes with excitement. One was from Ned's friend in Chicago, Hugh Jones. He addressed Cora as Miss Keck and wrote in a style that incorporated lots of deliberate misspellings ("know" for *no*; "slaying" for *sleighing*). He said that he was busy and that he might be taking someone else sleigh-ing with him, and that he hoped to see her sooner than later. He was a catch. His father was a farm machinery inventor with keen business skills who had hit the big time, and his family firm later became part of International Harvester. But as far as I can tell, Cora never heard from him again. One of Cora's Ilginfritz cousins from Ohio, Lieuten-ant Elmore Taggart, also sent her a Christmas card from Salt Lake City decorated with frogs carrying umbrellas in a rainstorm. Elmore was a cocky, ambitious young army officer with an off-color sense of humor, and he was completely irreverent about anything religious or romantic. Two years out of West Point (class of '83), he now lived on a rough army base in the middle of the Mormon desert in Utah, where he was earning a reputation as a crack sharpshooter. One would not expect to receive any cute Santa Clauses or lacy biblical sentiments from Lieutenant Tag-gart for the holidays.

Two days after Christmas, Cora and Kitty Strauss posed together at a tintype shop in Allentown in their beaver coats to "memorialize" their friendship. Cora then left Allentown to visit her Vassar friend Minnie

Keiter in St. Clair, about fifty miles to the west. This village, where Minnie grew up, has not changed much in the intervening years. It is still a
small mining community with a single main street lined with two-story
brick business blocks, newly constructed in the 1880s and still housing
stores and offices 125 years later. It lies near Pottsville in a narrow river
valley choked with great mounds of slag heaps and mining tailings in
the heart of the now-exhausted coalfields of Schuylkill County. Coal
mining in the Mahanoy and Shamokin valleys once fueled steel fur-
naces all over eastern Pennsylvania.

As one of the youngest graduates in the history of Pottsville High
School at age fifteen (class of '84), Minnie was widely admired and
knew a lot of young people in the area. She was barely seventeen years
old but was already a college sophomore, and her intellectual gifts easily put her on a par with her twenty-year-old college friend. During
Cora's visit, Minnie introduced Cora to a number of young men she
knew, including Elmer Marshall, Charles Carr, William Bauer Jr., and
Harry Seligman. Cora was particularly interested in Harry Short, with
whom she shared some champagne. Harry was twenty-four, attractive
and popular. A friend of his who wrote for the small local newspaper
Splinters described him as "a splendid specimen of physical manhood,
being tall and well-proportioned, with a pleasing countenance and
affable manners, and a favorite socially in Pottsville and in the region."
Raised along with two sisters and three brothers by his widowed, invalid
mother, Harry had been given only a "common school and common
sense" education, but he took over the management of his mother's shoe
store at a young age and was building it up into a substantial enterprise.

In rough-hewn communities outside the exclusive sphere of America's sophisticated eastern city society, "common school and common
sense" were widely seen as sufficient for a man. It was typical for a
Victorian wife to be better educated than her husband; women "carried civilization," taught school, and insisted that their families attend
church, while the menfolk swung their axes and cleared the wilderness
or battled each other for supremacy in the rough world of industry,
commerce, and agriculture. In the approving words of one news item
that Cora read and clipped in 1885, "a majority of the educated people
of the country are women." Out West, a self-made man thought of his

cultivated mate as prestigious; she brought up the level of his family socially.

Cora clipped scores of articles from newspapers she read in New York, Washington, Pennsylvania, Illinois, and Iowa on the topics of educated women, Vassar, and marriage between 1884 and about 1895. Journalists of the day, who were almost all men, wrote frequently about their observations of the behavior and marriageability of young women, using a personal, opinionated voice that occasionally drew on the wisdom of experts and professional pundits. Here's more from Cora's 1885 clipping noted above:

> *Educated Girls*
> *Are men shy of them?*
> *Vassar Girls as Old Maids*
> Is the man of the period shy of the educated girl of the period?—that is the question. . . . It is stated, on what looks like authority, that out of 596 graduates of VC, only 188 have married since that climax of their career. Of course, in the case of some, only a year or two has elapsed; but most of them graduated years ago, and some of them are old maids of the deepest dye.

What is this? Less than a third of Vassar's Victorian-era graduates chose to marry following their graduation? Clearly, the first couple of generations of Vassar graduates were a cussedly independent group. Despite the misleading headline, the man who wrote this article did not see these feisty women as having had loneliness forced upon them; he saw them as individuals who cheerily rejected marriage, "unwisely scorning a suitor who spelled 'separate' with three 'e's . . . [a basic spelling error] but who might yet be a tender-hearted, sagacious and even mentally profound man, worthy of all acceptation." In other words, he took these young ladies' choice to stay single personally. He was annoyed by their difficult and excessive choosiness, which worked to the disadvantage of potential suitors such as himself.

> What is the matter? It cannot be that they are so unattractive as to have had no offers. Every Jill has her Jack—sometimes a whole platoon

of them, and every girl can get married if she will. Does intellectual training make girls fastidious, finical, perhaps, difficult to please, unwilling to accept the honest hands of and sincere hearts of youths less brilliantly veneered?

In a word, yes. In fact, his complaint sounds kind of whiny. The Victorian Vassar women really did develop a high opinion of themselves. Contrast that pride with today's "common wisdom" on the subject of working women with advanced educations. Popular magazine articles and television pundits speaking about educated, heterosexual women now often take a defensive tone, as if they had to beat back a commonly held assumption that successful singletons usually feel unwanted and unhappy. This seems to imply that the pendulum has swung the other way and it is now thought that less-educated men are actually avoiding marriage with more-educated women. I mention this only because Elena Kagan, a twenty-first-century nominee to the Supreme Court, who happens to be a brilliant, unmarried middle-aged woman, suffered exactly this kind of unnecessary and intrusive analysis of her personal life as she went through the public approval process. Why is this kind of inquiry still happening?

AS NEW YEAR'S EVE APPROACHED, Cora left St. Clair to visit her cousin Warren at 1812 North Twenty-first Street in Philadelphia. Once she had passed Vassar's gatehouse, she did not need anyone's permission to arrange her vacation activities, and she apparently traveled by herself, at will, for two weeks. Together they went to the special New Year's Day matinee performance of Gilbert and Sullivan's *The Mikado* at McCaull's Opera Comique on Chestnut Street; the next day, she received a telegram from Ed Corbett from New York City: "Did you receive my letter & what time will you meet me? make it near one: 'mat.' O.K. answer." Cora rushed to New York in time to meet Ed at the theater for the Wednesday matinee at Daly's Theater, catching a comedy called *A Night Off, or A Page From Balzac* and then returned to Vassar on the evening train. Cora never tired of going to the theater; it was forbidden fruit at home in Davenport and therefore tasted twice as nice in Philadelphia and New York.

On January 12, 1886, a fierce cold snap swept across the country. Temperatures plunged to twenty-two below zero in Poughkeepsie in a matter of hours, closing most factories and causing terrible hardships for the laid-off workers, who lived hand to mouth. Tree limbs and wooden awning posts snapped in the sudden frost, sounding like gunshots. Skaters and ice boaters raced across unbroken ice that stretched for thirty-two miles down the Hudson River from Newburgh across Haverstraw Bay and the Tappan Zee all the way to Nyack. Equipped with its own gas and steam-heating plants, Vassar's Main Building kept all the students so warm that Mary Poppenheim wrote to her mother that her room was still comfortable with the window open a foot from the top.

In New York City, Vassar's interim president, J. Ryland Kendrick, braved the frigid temperatures to meet with the New York chapter of Vassar's Alumnae Association. Rumors of his resignation were premature. Kendrick made the trip to New York, hat in hand, reporting to his audience of formidable, intelligent women that "the college has recently passed through 'agitation' but morale is good and enrollment is steady."[2] He even made a tentative offer to put some alumnae on the board of trustees in the near future.

During the winter of 1886, the alumnae continued to demonstrate to the trustees that they could not only present their point of view effectively in the media, but also deliver substantial amounts of money to the financially beleaguered institution. Under the leadership of their president, Mrs. Bissell, they were in the middle of a fund-raising campaign to raise $20,000 for a new gymnasium and department of physical culture and an additional $10,000 to endow Vassar's astronomy department. Mary Thaw Thompson, class of '77 (a much older half-sister of the infamous Harry Thaw, who shot the architect Stanford White), had kicked off the effort by offering $5,000 as a challenge grant, to be given only if the alumnae could raise the other $15,000.[3] The trustees were not producing money at all. From now on, they had to reckon with the alumnae, openly and with respect. President Kendrick could no longer ignore their input if he expected them to deliver this substantial and badly needed funding to the college.

Cora clipped this article and threw it into a box where she was saving things to paste into another scrapbook. The first scrapbook—the one with the owls on the cover from her first year at college—was now full, and she was too busy to organize starting a second.

CO

KITTY ROGERS HAD RETURNED to college for her spring semester, but in late January she became seriously ill with a lung ailment. Cora saw her off at the Lodge gatehouse. Kitty left all her clothes and personal belongings in her dorm room, but Cora was worried. Kitty had missed many weeks of school the year before because of a string of different illnesses, from the mumps to *la grippe*. She seemed to fall prey to every illness that came through the campus.

That same day, Lydia Day left a note for Cora. Bundled up in her brown beaver fur coat with its matching hat, Cora made the trek to the music building to meet her. Lydia was from a scenic village called Tunckhannock on the Susquehanna River in northern Pennsylvania's Wyoming County, near Scranton. Lydia was not a serious Vassar student, and she left no traces of herself at the college after her year there except a single listing of her name in the 1885–1886 Vassar catalog. According to the 1880 census, her parents were wealthy; her father was a gentleman farmer whose health had been ruined by the chronic pain of neuralgia. She had two older brothers, and that's about all I know about Lydia Day from historical sources. We can guess the rest from what Cora saved in her scrapbook. Lydia had a master plan in mind.

Later that week, discreet letters and messages were sent back and forth between the college and some young men in Poughkeepsie, who, for the benefit of Miss Goodsell and other authorities, claimed to be brothers, cousins, and all-around responsible adults related to the interested parties. Glad that the weather had warmed up from the severe freeze, Cora, Minnie, and Lydia walked briskly toward town on College Avenue, cut across on Cherry Street, and then slowed to a stroll along the sidewalk on Hooker Avenue. All the young gents who rode or drove good horses came this way, on the main avenue that led out to the edge of town toward the Hudson River Driving Park where the Grand Circuit races were held.

It was also the right spot to go to meet Vassar girls. The girls who were courageous enough to flout the college rules and stroll the sidewalks of Hooker Avenue (the name is inadvertently severe; they weren't actually hookers) had their pick of willing escorts and could be as aloof and choosy as they wished. One of Cora's friends, probably Lydia Day, wrote Cora about one dude who passed "to and fro on the Highway near Mill Cove Lake at Vassar College." She called this distant object of her affection "divine" three times, "too far more than most awfully grand, swell etc." "No one ever looked so grand in the eyes of a college girl . . . is it not a wonder that I might be infatuated."

Desire + Obstacles = Excitement. This equation should be at the top of the page in the first lesson of Chemistry 101 at the Academy of Romeo and Juliet. Without the obstacles part, it's really much harder to get the young men interested; they're slaves to excitement, a useful operating principle that is fundamentally understood by all successful computer game designers and military recruiters around the world.

At 10:30, the girls paused in front of the Cottage Grove School, and sure enough, within five minutes, two familiar horses trotted into view from South Street. It was Mr. Wendell Booth and Mr. Isaac Sutton. They pulled to a halt next to the young ladies and dismounted. With alternate bursts of whispering and loud laughter, they organized their logistics while the impatient horses tossed their heads, rattling their bits and snorting loud clouds of steam into the winter air.

The next Thursday, on February 18, Cora, Min, and Lydia made their excuses in a bland and neutral tone to Miss Goodsell, without betraying the slightest hint of their suppressed, explosive excitement. Mr. Booth and Mr. Sutton joined them at the Poughkeepsie train station, and they boarded an afternoon train to New York City. At 8 P.M., they stood in front of Wallack's Theater at the northeast corner of Broadway and Thirtieth Street in Manhattan. Elegant carriages jammed the street in front as Cora and her friends crossed the sidewalk toward the box office while ticket scalpers yelled at them from all sides. They had tickets waiting for them for the evening performance of a play called *Valerie*.

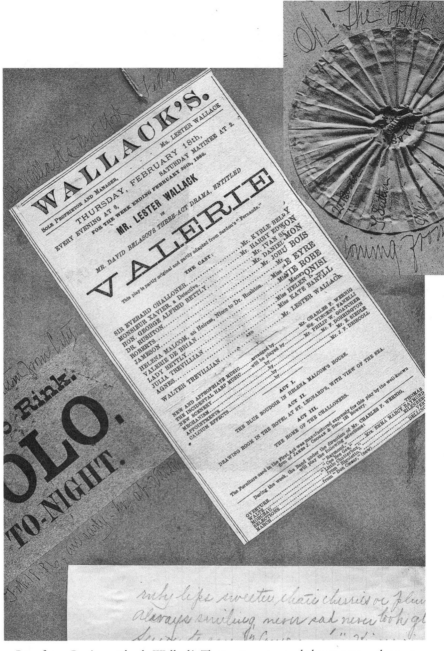

Page from Cora's scrapbook: Wallack's Theater program and champagne cork cover;
"Oh! the bottle coming from the city . . ."

Mr. Lester Wallack had just moved uptown from Thirteenth Street four years before. His new venue was only two stories high but had a large brick billboard on the roof that screamed WALLACK'S in white block letters, while a vaguely Grecian-looking portico supported by fancy columns covered the front of the building and framed the main entrance doors. The play was partly original and partly adapted by Mr. Wallack from a play by the French dramatist Victorien Sardou, *Fernande*. A master comedian even in the later years of his long career, Lester Wallack gave performances that were described by the critic William Winter as "clear, crisp, and glittering—sharp in outline, delicate in spirit and emphatic in effect."[4]

On the train back to Poughkeepsie, the five young people drank a bottle of champagne manufactured by E. F. Haas. "Oh! the bottle, coming from New York," Cora wrote next to the lead foil she had peeled off the cork and attached to a page in her scrapbook. A public telephone had recently been installed at Wallack's, allowing Lydia to order their tickets from Vassar's telegraph office right under the noses of the faculty. "Because the phone was in a private booth, we could get away with it," she boasted. They collapsed in helpless laughter—Wendell's last name was Booth, and the theater had one too, for tickets. Even the famous actor Edwin Booth was a booth. The whole group was absolutely plastered.

They clattered through the Poughkeepsie station in near darkness, trying to sound quiet, and instead of returning to college, they went to the Casino Rink, where they did some roller-skating and the young men joined a "polo" match. "On our return from City, Feb 18, at an early hour at Vassar," Cora wrote with sarcastic understatement next to the polo card in the scrapbook. It had to have been about three in the morning when she slipped back onto campus through the darkness with her two friends. They climbed inside through a ground-floor window one after another. Someone, maybe Ned, was in on the plan and waited at a prearranged spot to help them get in without being caught. It was the most daring thing that Cora ever did while she was away at college; the trio risked instant expulsion had they been caught.

CHAPTER TWENTY-THREE

The Vassar Trio

D espite her illicit extracurricular activities off campus, Cora's music lessons were going extremely well for the first time since she had entered Vassar a year and a half before. On January 15, Miss Chapin assigned her two transcriptions by Liszt of popular passages from two Wagner operas, "Einzug der Gäste auf der Wartburg," from *Tannhäuser*, and "Elsas Brautzug zum Münster," from *Lohengrin*. Cora had finally earned the privilege of being allowed to resume playing at the level of difficulty she thought she deserved. These pieces were already thirty years old when Cora worked on them; they became so well known that the operatic originals have now been reduced to clichés. They suited popular taste in Victorian America and at the same time were spectacular showpieces for virtuoso piano technique. Audiences who would never have the chance to hear the famous operas sung onstage in their full glory could at least hear the musical ideas of one musical genius as condensed for home listening by another.

The biggest honor was still to come. Later in the month, Miss Chapin announced that Cora would play the last two movements of Weber's Quartet in B flat at the Soirée Musicale recital in April with three professionals from the New York Philharmonic, along with Georgina Hayman, Dr. Ritter's favorite. Cora's star had indeed risen high. She would be filling the spot that had been vacated by Harriet Capron, who had inspired her so profoundly the year before. Miss Chapin could finally present a major success story to her department director and the entire college.

Even though Miss Chapin had influenced Cora in the direction of musical self-control, Cora continued to push the tempo of the rest of her life faster and faster in pursuit of her two main goals: first, to perform at her final recitals to the best of her abilities, and, second, to get engaged to an Eastern dude before the first week of June. She typically

Ice cutters on Vassar Lake. Courtesy of Vassar College Archives.

practiced seven or eight periods a day, between four and five hours. Minnie Keiter and Lydia Day dropped by her room on a regular basis, alone or together, with plans to draw her into various entertainments with their group of Poughkeepsie friends, and Cora managed to work these tempting invitations into her schedule frequently in order to work on goal number two. Cora did not mention any problems with passing German this second year—she had dropped back to the easier curriculum in the preparatory-level class, and I am guessing that Minnie did her homework for her and pulled her through academically. "Crazy after my music," she wrote. "I mean to do well in it, and thus finish in credit both to my Parents and my College Friends." She did not have much time left.

Minnie, Lydia, and Cora, who now called themselves "the trio," met often with their gang of young men friends from Poughkeepsie as spring approached. They strolled together on Hooker Avenue on the road to the fairgrounds, stopping at Willie's or at "the cottage"; they met at Vail Brothers, the photographer's studio; and they roller-skated in a large, competitive mob at the Casino Rink on polo nights. On Sundays, they met up at church in Poughkeepsie. Another Vassar friend, Florence

Plass, a Prep Level III student from Harlem (on the east side of Manhattan, near Fifth Avenue), joined them from time to time. They paired up and split up, frequently and amiably, feeling around for the right personality combinations that might spark true love.

Wendell Booth seemed to be playing Cora and Minnie off against each other when he sent this note addressed to Miss Keck:

> Your message was delivered to Mr. Hasbrouck yesterday. He requested me to say that he had previously accepted an invitation from another friend (Miss Newkirk) [Dolores Newkirk, Prep Level I, of Bay City, Michigan] and would have to decline with many thanks. My <u>friend</u> Miss Keiter was at the rink Saturday and would not speak to me— must have some suspicion of Friday evening—<u>Sorry.</u> Thanking you for a very pleasantly spent evening, I am as ever,
> Your Friend W. P. Booth.

Wendell Booth, who always wrote to Cora with neat handwriting in black ink and in a formal, proper tone, worked as a clerk in his father's tea and coffee imports store. He was also obsessed with the Grand Circuit trotting races. He knew all the winners' statistics and which officials could judge a race well, and why. When he wasn't out at the fairgrounds watching the horses, he spent the rest of his free time studying the angles of purchasing and training a fast, young horse. It was a complicated, challenging process loaded with hidden pitfalls that he found totally absorbing. Today, a guy like Wendell would probably be equally focused on cars or motorcycles. He paid much less attention than he should have to his father's tea and coffee business.

Cora's group of attentive young men were all from respectable families and were certainly potential marriage material, probably better educated and more focused on their material futures than most of her beaus were back in Davenport. Willie Caire was a salesman at his father's large pipe and pottery factory and lived in a boardinghouse on Hooker Avenue. Isaac Sutton's family had a prosperous farm in Dutchess County. Cora and her friends also spent a lot of time with Harry Reynolds, a Poughkeepsie resident studying at Yale's Sheffield

Scientific School (usually abbreviated as SSS), who came home for spring vacation for a week in late April, and Louis Hasbrouck, a doctor's son with an entry-level job as a bookkeeper at the First National Bank in Poughkeepsie.

Cora's closest pal of the moment, Minnie Keiter, was very interested in Charles Eastmeade, a clerk in his family's wholesale tobacco business. Charlie's father had just died, so he was pushing himself to assume control of his father's half of the business with the help of his mother and his father's partner. He felt intense pressure to grow up quickly to keep the family's livelihood from slipping out of his grasp, but he seemed to wear it lightly. He acted very sure of himself. Charlie was a charmer. He spoke with an alluring Scottish burr (both his parents were immigrants from Britain), and he used so many puns in his letters that he sounds silly to modern ears; modern fashion has decisively deleted puns from the category of "wit" and reassigned them to the "dumb jokes" column.

Harry Reynolds often brought friends home from New Haven to visit him in Poughkeepsie, and another Yale student named Schuyler Carleton may have been one of them, as Cora mentions someone named Mr. Carleton several times in conjunction with the others during the week in April when Yale was on vacation.

On Saturday, March 13, Cora returned to New York City for a follow-up appointment with Dr. Bulkley at his office on East Thirty-seventh Street to consult about her eczema and squeezed in a short visit with Kitty Rogers. The next day, back at Vassar, she recovered from her outing by sending in an order for a sick tray (which consisted of an omelet, milk toast, fruit, and chocolate) to be brought to parlor 9 and lounged in bed, flipping through the pages of a copy of the *Harvard Lampoon* that some dude had given her recently. (One of the editors of the issue Cora was reading was George Santayana, who was about to graduate Phi Beta Kappa with a B.A. from Harvard in June. The son of a Spanish father and an American mother, Santayana coined many famous aphorisms still well known today, including his most famous: "those who cannot remember the past are condemned to repeat it.") She saved a cigarette from the New York outing that made "a deep impression" and

a Chinese napkin from her springtime spread later in the week, conducted in secret with the lights turned as low as they could go.

"Spread Parlor 9—@ 11 o'clock sharp—P.M.
gas low tide; olives and ham, brown bread and jam"

EVERYONE WAS LEAVING COLLEGE for spring vacation at the
beginning of the last week in March. Kitty Rogers had been away from
Vassar since January and wanted to see Cora in the worst way.

W. 134th St. & Grand Boulevard
Dear Corize,
    I saw by this morning's paper that you have a Lenten vacation.
couldn't you make arrangements to come down on the half past four
o'clock train which stops at Harlem If you can telegraph & some of us
will meet you. I think I will be back to work by the first of April. Every
Monday for the last three weeks I have planned to go up to see about
my things but either Mama or some one has been ill. we have had an
awful winter we are all better now.
    I hope to see you tomorrow afternoon I have so many things to ask
you. come for Mama wishes you to. Remember me to Miss Goodsell.
Your friend
K. B. Rogers

Cora immediately made arrangements to go down on the train. Illness had caused Kitty to give up on her education, but death had been
held at bay. The fear of an early death from disease was real and ever
present for everyone Cora knew. Kitty was now trying to restore her
own health enough so she could go back to work. I have no clue about
what kind of work she was doing, unfortunately.
    Nick's name never came up, but Miss Goodsell's did. No matter how
strict she was in performing her job, Cora, Kitty, and most of the other
students seemed to feel warmly about the Lady Principal once they were
gone from school. And we can see that Kitty's mother adored Cora.

"Bring back your friend," she told Kitty. "I want to see her too." These Victorian women knit together warm relationships across the generations as easily as they did with their peers.

Cora saved programs from a play called *The Rajah* at the Madison Square Theater and another from a "Grand Floral Exhibition" presented at the Metropolitan Opera House on Saturday afternoon. It was a light "pops" classical concert conducted by the Met's young conductor, Walter Damrosch, combined with a flower show. This strange programming concept was designed to lure in a hesitant female audience, known to be skittish about the heavy, intellectual German opera repertoire that had been introduced the year before by Walter's father, Leopold. "That memorable day in New York at the Metropolitan it rained," Cora wrote next to the program in her scrapbook. The Damrosch orchestra played selections from Bizet, Gounod, and Wagner (all melodies we now know as musical clichés, including *Lohengrin*'s Procession of the Ladies, the Ride of the Valkyries, and the Prize Song from *Die Meistersinger*). The programming was aimed at Americans like Loulu Poppenheim, who reported to her mother in one of her letters that the music she heard at one Vassar concert was "a little too classic" but the "singing was very pretty."[1] Many of the well-bred and social girls were very, very tentative about classical music.

The Poppenheims were in New York City too; they had been invited to spend their vacation visiting Addie McKinlay at her house on Riverside Drive at Seventy-second Street (now an on-ramp for the West Side Highway). Addie was a velvet girl, a shorthand term for girls from plutocratic families that today would be described as the "upper .001 percent." May wrote to her mother in an awestruck tone that the McKinlays had forty-seven rooms in their house. "Can it be possible . . . ?" her mother answered. "That sounds here like they take boarders, or rent rooms. I can understand the three Pianos better."[2] The McKinlays' gilded New York lifestyle was on so grand a scale that it made the sisters' home life as upper-middle-class socialites back in Charleston look humble. Even Kitty Rogers's colonial-era wooden mansion on the bluff above Manhattanville, enlarged with two huge temple-shaped porches, Doric columns, pediments, pilasters, and other Greek Revival architectural details, would have looked shabby and outdated by comparison.

IN THE DINING HALL ON MARCH 31, a Wednesday, Cora glanced up from her meal and noticed Marian Austin sitting with her back to her on the other side of the room at the sophomore table. A thought suddenly struck her. This was the day of the philopena, the secret compliment about Cora that Miss Chapin had made to Marian exactly one year before, which Marian had heard and had teased Cora about so mercilessly without telling her what it was. At the time, Cora had written a reminder to herself that Marian would reveal the compliment a year later, "no matter where we are but I must manage to be at Dinner with her as that is when it is to happen."

Cora waited by the doorway and caught Marian by the arm on the way out. What was that compliment about me you heard from Miss Chapin last year?, she wanted to know. What did she tell you? Marian looked blankly at her for two beats, then started to laugh. Cora really wanted to know. Miss Chapin's opinion of her mattered much more now than it had the year before. "I can't believe you remembered to ask me," said Marian. She narrowed her eyes wickedly. "I'm still not going to tell you. You'll have to meet me here *next* year to find out."

Unlike many of Vassar's aspiring preparatory students, who dropped by the wayside in droves without even attempting to pass the freshman entrance exams, Marian had experienced spectacular success and emerged as a campus leader. She was not only beautiful, smart, and athletic, she was also talented onstage. She played the lead role in a performance of Dickens's *Dombey and Son* in February, and most prestigious of all, she sang the lead part in *The Mathematickado*, a funny satire that improbably combined songs from Gilbert and Sullivan's *Mikado* with themes from Olney's trigonometry textbook. The sophomores organized "trig ceremonies" each year for the freshmen; this one presented as a gift "from the class of '88 to the class of '89, 'A warning.'" Many Vassar students dreaded trigonometry, which was a required course, and the idea was to soften the impact for the newcomers with some light satire on the topic.

Marian and Cora stayed close friends during Cora's second year at college, although they no longer roomed together. As soon as the weather improved, Marian ("Miss Short") and Cora ("Miss Tall") enjoyed another risky off-campus adventure. Cora described the escapade in a poem dedicated "To Marion" and signed "the loving 'wife,'" in a small booklet made from cut sheets of paper that she sewed together with thread and folded into an envelope marked "private." The address side is half ruined by glue. What shows is an address in Philadelphia for "Mr ____" of the Central National Bank. Cora was obviously recycling an old envelope from Warren.

One spring evening in late April after supper, they set out on a long walk on the College Road away from campus toward Jordan Lake. Cora complained that she had to get up at five o'clock the next morning, but Marian shouted, "Carpe diem!," and off they went. They planned to be gone for only an hour, expecting to return to Vassar by 8 P.M., but somehow the time got away from them in the long spring twilight. They soon heard the sound of wheels by their side, and a voice they recognized immediately said softly, "Would you like a ride?"

Of course they would. It was Harry Reynolds, whose father owned a successful flour wholesale business in Poughkeepsie. Harry was described by his classmates at Yale's engineering school as "short, fat and saucy, and having a great deal of self-possession, and popular."

Away they sped in Harry's surrey, pulled swiftly by "Harry's neat little trotting horse, past houses and fields, past churches and tempting little streams," while the sun went down across the river and a full moon came up. Then in a panic she looked at her watch and realized it was almost nine o'clock. The doors to the Main Building would be locked in a few minutes and they could not climb in through her parlor window because it was screened against mosquitoes. The only thing they could do was sneak through the tall grass behind the barn into the music building and then emerge from it as if they had been in there practicing piano all along, since that activity was permitted later at night. Once the six strokes of the final evening bell rang at 9:35 P.M., it would be too late even for that. Every student had to be in her room by the end of the last stroke of the bell.

"Just look. The barn isn't far at all," said Harry in an anxious, guilty tone.

"Now, Harry, give me my hat and pin, and I hope we are safe," said Miss Tall grimly, as she poised herself to jump out of the buckboard the instant it came to a stop.

"Was this a very big sin?" wondered Miss Short. Good question. In the big picture, probably not. But from Miss Goodsell's point of view, it was assuredly "a great evil," especially if they lied about it. Marian and Cora plodded as quickly as they could through grass three feet tall, quaking with fear at every sound and peeping around thick pines and bushes. They quietly entered the music hall door. What if they made a noise and were caught? They faced expulsion—"when each girl with blanched and pallid face must pack her trunk and leave Vassar." But once inside the music building, they were safe; and turning on their heels in the dark hallway, they walked right back out, shutting the door noisily behind them, and immediately assumed the demeanor of diligent music students.

> They are so tired. How their fingers do pain
> They think that Music's a perfect bore.
> They will never practice so long again.

Their roommates were waiting anxiously for their return, watching the minute hand inching toward the moment of doom, and welcomed them to safety with open arms. They felt the darts of a guilty conscience all night and tossed and turned with worry in case a squealer had seen them and might turn them in the next day. But as I delicately pushed the little booklet back into its envelope glued to the brittle page, I wondered, how did Cora get her poem back from Marian to save in the scrapbook? Or did she never send it to her?

IN THE FIRST WEEK of April, the *New York Times* reported that the Reverend James Taylor had been elected the new president of Vassar College. According to a short biography of Mr. Taylor that Cora also clipped, he was a "scholarly, refined and a manly man, with a marked taste for historical research." His wife was a Vassar alumna. He had graduated from the Rochester Theological Seminary and rose to his new position of prominence as a college president from his previous position of minister at the Fourth Baptist Church of Providence, Rhode Island. He came from a distinguished family; his father was a leading Baptist minister in Brooklyn, and his sister, Mrs. Dr. Mary T. Bissell, M.D., was not only a Vassar graduate, but also a medical doctor and, not coincidentally, the president of the Vassar Alumnae Association.

Page from Cora's scrapbook: Engraving of Vassar's new president, James Taylor.

Cora cut out the engraving of his portrait that the newspaper included. The students were as relieved and happy to hear this news as the alumnae and trustees. Everyone hoped for some kind of miracle to get the college back on its feet.

CHAPTER TWENTY-FOUR

U Played Just Like a Wild Girl

A small calendar pasted into Cora's scrapbook refers to April as "Dear Month," and April 16 is underlined. That was the date of the Soirée Musicale at 8 P.M. in the chapel, when Cora would make her debut, performing an advanced chamber-music piece in front of the entire college, accompanied by professionals from the New York Philharmonic Society. Cora would share the glory of playing the final number, Weber's Piano Quartet in B flat. After Miss Hayman played the first two movements, Cora would take the stage and conclude with the *Allegro* and difficult *Presto* as the evening's finale. Miss Hinkel canceled her German classes that day. She was always on Cora's side; she knew that Cora's musical talent was more important to her life than her flailing efforts to memorize irregular German verbs.

During the rehearsal, Cora was introduced to the three string players from the New York Philharmonic. She had seen them come up to Vassar the year before to accompany Miss Capron and Miss Hayman at the grand concert that had inspired her so profoundly last March. Concealing her nervousness, she shook hands firmly with each one of them: Mr. Herrmmann, violin; Mr. Schwarz, viola; and Mr. Bergner, violoncello. Cora was now about to attempt to fill Miss Capron's extremely talented shoes. She and Miss Hayman briefly discussed with Professor Ritter where they would sit before they played and how they would make their entrance onstage. Then Cora took her place at the piano for her run-through. She felt confident, but her fingers were sweaty and she could not keep her mind from darting around and getting stuck on irrelevant thoughts. Miss Hayman was watching her. They were rivals for the top spot in the music department.

To her horror, Cora's run-through began poorly, and she stumbled on her entrance in the *Allegro* and had to restart twice, even though it was an easy thing to come in on a downbeat at the beginning of the

Members of the New York Philharmonic Club, part of the larger Philharmonic Society, ca. 1885. Friedhold Herrmmann (second from right), played violin with Cora in the April 16 concert. Courtesy of New York Philharmonic Archives.

Vassar College chapel, site of all Cora's concerts and piano recitals. Courtesy of Vassar College Archives.

main theme. After that bungle, the ensemble feeling in the *Presto*, a delicate dialogue between strings and piano, never materialized. Cold prickles broke out on her back, and she was ashamed to look at the Philharmonic players when she left the hall to go prepare for dinner. They smiled smoothly; their professional courtesy was impeccable. Maybe they did not expect much from a college girl. That made it worse.

The rest of the day crawled by. She could never forget the public shame of missing her first big recital last May, when Miss Goodsell had pulled her from the program because of the problem with her German grades. She could not bear the thought that this concert might be another moment of humiliation in front of the entire college.

At a quarter to eight, the students and faculty already filled the chapel pews and the balcony above to overflowing. Lydia sat next to Cora in the audience. As the first performers took their places on the stage and tuned up, Cora's nervousness increased, and she started writing a note to Lydia in the program: "at last the concert don't mention my nervousness mistakes." On the inside page, the following "texted" dialogue continued between the two friends, in real time, in pencil:

"are u nervous?"
"tell me something funny before I go"
L: I see Mr. Carlton—
Oh. do u? where is he?
L: 3rd row—next to the Japanese
co: no that is not he. u can't come that on me
L: Mr. Booth
no puns please
yr time is up, do u realize it
go it [go play it]

Cora arrived at the foot of the stage like an automaton, with a blank look on her face, suddenly overwhelmed with stage fright. All the noise and light in the hall seemed to shrink down to a single bright spot, far in the distance. Miss Hayman was already launching into her second movement. The repeated eighth notes of the minuet's main phrase sounded like clanging gongs summoning her underground to the infernal regions, and Cora couldn't think or even breathe. Miss Chapin was

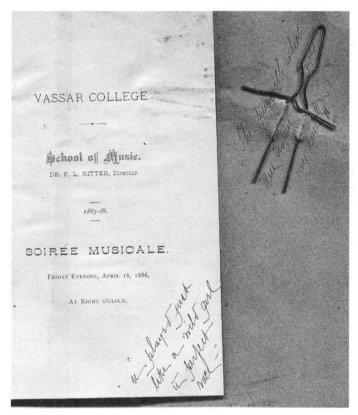

*Page from Cora's scrapbook: "The pin with which
Miss Chapin fixed my hair."*

waiting for her below the stage. Seeing Cora's panic, she took her gently
by the shoulder. Pulling a pin out of her own hair, she reached up to
fix a loose strand hanging down across Cora's forehead and smoothed it
back against her temple. From that single, unexpectedly intimate gesture, Cora realized that her teacher truly believed in her ability and
knew that she would succeed. Compared with the agony she had suffered through to earn Miss Chapin's respect, anything else, even playing this concert, would be easy. In that instant, the room sprang back
into its normal shape, Miss Hayman's playing sounded like music again,
and the minuet ended. Cora sprang up the steps with vigor and moved
gracefully across the stage to the piano, acknowledging Miss Hayman
with a curt nod as they traded places.

[L:] u played just like a wild girl. A perfect race
[C:] My debut oh! Joy

The concert was a triumph.

ON PALM SUNDAY, Cora, Lydia Day, and Minnie Keiter walked into Poughkeepsie to attend services at St. Paul's Methodist Church while enjoying the excellent weather. Cora recalled how the year before she had moped alone at college watching the rain run down the windowpanes. Or at least she had for part of the time, until Mame had invited her to New York and she had gone riding with Nick Rogers in Central Park.

As they strolled along Hooker Avenue, swinging their palm frond fans trimmed with pink ribbons, the flirting was intense—"The trio," she wrote next to the fan fragment; "Our walk in and out Hooker Avenue Our cut etc." On the fan fragment she wrote, "Lydia, Min, Coz, Booth and Eastmeade, pass Willie's at 7½ no supper—lunch from infirmary." She also wrote, "Palm Sunday—another from Flo. P—Apr. 18, '86." Two days later, Isaac Sutton's mother held a birthday party for Minnie at the Cottage. The same group of six young people who had flirted at St. Paul's the Sunday before met there again for Easter services, and afterwards, the college served an Easter dinner of turkey with oysters, cranberry sauce, peaches and jelly, chocolate, ice cream, and cake.

THIS YEAR, CORA HAD NO WORRIES about scraping together an entourage of young men to serve as her escorts for the dancing on Founder's Day, even though Ed Corbett telegraphed her, "It will be impossible for me to be with you this evening. E.C." She did not bother to telegraph Warren Kleckner in Philadelphia. Nick was off her radar. She was going with two guys from Yale, Harry Reynolds and Harry's friend Cyrus Field Judson. Mr. Judson's grandfather, Cyrus W. Field, was a famous man— he laid the first trans-Atlantic telegraph cable and earned a fortune from it. Did she have a new dress made for the occasion?

The tone of this Founder's Day celebration was certainly much more uplifting than it had been the year before, but probably a lot less entertaining. The wisecracking cynic Mark Twain, who lectured mainly for income and relied on his quick wit to amuse his audience, had been quite touchy during his rain-soaked visit to Vassar. This year, the late spring weather was cooperative. Acting President Kendrick knew his business and did not leave his distinguished celebrity visitor, the Reverend Edward Everett Hale, to languish alone for hours in wet clothes after his arrival. Hale assumed the podium in the chapel and launched into his address. He was an idealist who believed in a utopian vision that individuals could and should take responsibility for doing the right thing for their fellows, by means of "practical kindness and courage." He inspired his listeners to think outside of themselves and to consider the needs of others. "I am only one; but still I am one," he declared. "I cannot do everything; but still I can do something; and because I cannot do everything, I will not refuse to do the something that I can do."[1] Such secular, modern, altruistic institutions as community organizing, international nongovernmental organizations, and philanthropic efforts in support of civil and human rights are direct descendants of the popular, volunteer-based social service organizations started by the Reverend Hale and his like-minded contemporaries.

Sitting next to Minnie and Lydia, Cora thought hard about what she was supposed to do in practical terms, as the Reverend Hale had advised, to improve the lot of her fellow citizens. What could a musician do for society at large? Music meant so much to her; she thought about how to share her enthusiasm. Other young people with untapped talent must be given the chance to study somewhere. That was "the something that she could do."

As I imagined Cora's thoughts while she was listening to Hale's lecture, I caught myself thinking how shallow and "female" her sentiment sounds, except . . . except, it isn't. America's disapproving Puritan forebears had no time or respect for performance or music or story-telling or interior ornamentation of any kind; the United States in Victorian times continued to be practical minded, centered on business and the getting of wealth; business was literally the business of men, and many of these men openly disdained culture as a secondary and largely female pursuit. Generally, it was the wives of the titans of nineteenth-century industry—not the titans themselves—who supported the great art museums and then went on in the early twentieth century to start the magnificent urban symphony orchestras in Cleveland, Chicago, Philadelphia, Los Angeles, and elsewhere. What if nobody bothered to study music or support performances? Can we really say that a talented college girl's interest in music is categorically unimportant? In times of economic austerity, Americans have always been careless and quick to cut funding for music, literature, and the arts. But what kind of civilization has no cultural expression of itself?

The food and dancing offered by the college (only four dances: a lanciers, a quadrille, another lanciers, and a Virginia reel) left Cora's energetic gang of friends unsatisfied, so when the official events concluded, they organized a private after-party. Mr. Reynolds brought his college friend, Mr. Judson, to meet the ladies in the college Lyceum in "Room J." Hairpins went flying and Cora's hair was "waltzed down" as the couples swirled around the floor to the intoxicating rhythms of one piece after another. "Spoon. Spooner. Spoonery.—On the pound—" Cora's ironic re-quotes were like re-tweets of the evening's flirtatious words and banter; the words were written across her scrapbook's page next to the actual hairpin, retrieved from the floor of Room J and glued to the paper. The visiting Yale friend was invited to come back the next evening on Saturday for Cora's birthday. Late that night, after the young men had gone, Cora went to a spread consisting of blackberry jam, wafers, olives, fruit, and lemonade. The Smiths delivery tag was sarcastically addressed to "Mrs. Idles" for "Miss Wellman, 5 P.M.," and included a cake. The hostess scratched out her menu on a rough piece of paper cut from a grocery bag. This fast-paced informality was quite a switch from Cora's first-year spreads, which she and her friends had planned so carefully, with menus and formal invitations written in neat handwriting on fancy paper. They had become so confident and experienced that they didn't take time for that kind of fussy social detail anymore.

When she finally extinguished the gas and climbed into her narrow bed late Friday night, Cora did not sleep. Harry was bringing Cyrus Judson, a young man from a famous family, of Yale College and of Gramercy Park in New York City, to call on her—Cora Keck of Davenport, Iowa.

CHAPTER TWENTY-FIVE

Poor Boys Who Have Become Rich

T he next morning, Cora lay in bed late, sleeping off the combined effects of her late-night wakefulness and the previous evening's debauch of eating and dancing. A music student named Irene Hinnes woke her with several sharp raps on the door and handed her a tartly worded note from Miss Chapin. Cora was being summoned to the music room "at once." A sour feeling in the pit of her stomach reminded her of the many withering lectures she had endured from her piano instructor over the past year and a half. She added in pencil on the back of the note: "The fiend awfully unwell, Miss Hims, too much last night."

Cora threw on some barely buttoned clothes and made her appearance in the music building. Cracking open the door of Miss Chapin's teaching studio as cautiously as she could, she was astonished to find her instructor in a mild mood. There was to be no chewing out after all. In fact, it was the opposite. Miss Chapin quietly told her that Professor Ritter had been so impressed by her virtuoso performance at the Soirée Musicale two weeks before that he had just agreed to choose Cora to perform her Liszt piece

Cyrus Judson's grandfather, Cyrus W. Field (at right, with long hair), wields a sword labeled "Elevated railroad grabber" on the June 1884 cover of America's most popular humor magazine. Courtesy of the Library of Congress.

as the final number at the graduation recital. The final number was an honor reserved for the best student in the School of Music.

Cora's jaw must have hit the floor when she heard this news. She thought back to the dark days of late April the year before, when Miss Chapin had been so "thoroughly disgusted" with her horrible scales and the new piece for the concert that Cora had broken down in tears in her lesson. Me? The Careless Practicer? The Vile Player? I'm playing *after* Georgina Hayman? She grew even more amazed as Miss Chapin praised her courage for handling her stage fright. Not only had Cora played her piece with no mistakes, she had played with a relaxed body, with great beauty of expression, and entirely free from the stiffness and keyboard mannerisms that had plagued her playing in the past.[1] In short, her performance of the *Allegro* and *Presto* in the Weber piano quartet had been both professional and artistically mature—it was superb.

Cora left Miss Chapin's music studio in a rush to share this news with Minnie and Lydia, her joy charged with a frightening shot of adrenaline as she thought about the moment when she would have to step out onstage again in front of all those faces. Her parents would be there. The audience would include students, faculty, trustees, parents, and the general public—and a reporter for the *New York Times*.

Later in the morning, Cora inked an update to herself on the back of the summons, "9:15 A.M. all peace oh! joy." All her hard work finally meant something—she would now be known at college for being a wonderful musician, not for being notorious.

THAT EVENING, Cora welcomed her birthday guests to the public parlors of Vassar's Main Building. Five young men were announced and shown upstairs: W. P. Caire, C. M. Eastmeade, Wendell Booth, Harry Reynolds, and Cyrus F. Judson. Two of the regular gang, Mr. Sutton and Mr. Hasbrouck, were not invited; Cora and her friends could not expect to have seven men come to college, as they were supposed to have only one visitor each. They were already one over the limit as it was.

Harry, a junior in Yale's class of '87, and Cyrus, a year behind him in the class of '88, were playing hooky from school—they had no vacation at this time.[2] They decided to blow off several days of classes fewer than three weeks before their final exams to travel several hours from New Haven by train. Cora was flattered and delighted. Unlike Harry, who was short and stout, Cyrus Field Judson was almost six feet tall and extremely thin. He had bright red hair and lived in his grandfather's mansion at 123 East Twenty-first Street in New York on Gramercy Park with his widowed mother. He dressed better than any man Cora had ever met. His grandfather had $300,000 a year in income.

Everyone knew about Mr. Judson's grandfather; Cyrus W. Field was the rags-to-riches millionaire who had laid the first trans-Atlantic telegraph cable between the United States and England several years before Cora was born. She had recently read a colorful version of the details of his biography in *The Life of Cyrus W. Field*, a booklet published as a cigarette card from a pack of Duke's Cigarettes. The series title was *Poor Boys Who Have Become Rich, And Other Famous People*. No matter that he had a pronounced overbite, a receding hairline, and a prominent, razor-thin nose that sprang out from his face like a toucan's beak—Mr. Cyrus W. Field was a pop-culture icon right up there with the American actress Mary Anderson and the rakish British socialite and actress Lily Langtry (also known as the Jersey Lily). Cora felt slightly dizzy as she reached out to shake the grandson's hand, but carried it off with sangfroid, showing the same vigorous determination at the tea table that she had demonstrated to the whole college on the chapel stage at the piano two weeks before.

Florence, Min, Lydia, and Cora had prepared an elegant collation for their guests consisting of cake and ice cream from Smiths. Small plates were served and handed around. Cora's friends loyally tried to control their impulses to hover around Mr. Judson; *she* was the hostess, it was her birthday, and they all knew about her urgent marital engagement deadline coming up in June. But they were also all dying with curiosity to know what someone like Cyrus Field's grandson would have to say for himself. The young men gave Cora birthday cards (all four have been lost—only the envelopes remain glued into the scrapbook along with the visitors' calling cards) and some simple birthday presents, mostly mementos of life at Yale.

Cora, who was so obviously sociable with the young men of Poughkeepsie, wanted to know whether Mr. Judson had made friends with many girls in New Haven. He replied rather formally that some of his acquaintances entered New Haven society, and that while most described it as "cultivated and refined," in practice, they also found it to be "stiff and cold" and "rather cliquish." He may have been being too polite; his Yale yearbook also contained this admonition: "Do anything to keep out of New Haven society." Although thirty of his classmates claimed to find it pleasing, two thought it poor, and one called it "a regular farce."[3] As to the looks of the local girls, only two responded that they were beautiful.

A rush of conversation ensued. Cora's friends filled Mr. Judson in on how much fun they had on a regular basis in Poughkeepsie at the roller rink and during their secret jaunts to Wallack's Theater in New York City. They boasted about how they made their own social arrangements and chose their own pleasures. Mr. Judson admitted that he envied their freedom. The girls he knew in New York and elsewhere had no liberty for that and did very little besides get dressed in silk every day and talk to their mothers about plans for society balls and tea engagements, as far as he could tell.

During the brief break in the conversation that followed that comment, Cora thought she heard the squeak of a footfall on the parquet floor in the hallway beyond the parlor's sliding wooden doors. Was someone listening? Far too much incriminating information was being aired. She quickly steered the conversation in a new direction—dancing at Founder's Day and other formal parties. Mr. Judson said that he escorted young ladies of his social set to a great many balls in New York. In an offhand remark, he noted that he never set foot in Germania Hall and that the New York Armory was a dancing resort "where the 'chippies' nest," using the polite slang for cheap young prostitutes.

Taken aback, Cora frowned but said nothing. Back in February, she had gone with Kitty Rogers, Ed Corbett, and Corbett's friend Mr. O'Neill to a concert at the Park Avenue Armory put on by the band of the seventh regiment of the National Guard in honor of Mr. C. A. Cappa, the band's long-time conductor. Although the weather had been cold and stormy, they had enjoyed themselves very much. They went there all the time. Kitty later mailed Cora another Armory program for the third annual charity ball in aid of the City Hospital later in the spring. Kitty Rogers was not a chippie and neither was she. She thought to herself, how dare he say that?

Harry began kidding Cyrus about his cousin, John E. Judson, who was a year older and Harry's classmate in SSS '87—"He says he's planning to be a missionary to Patagonia when he finishes his engineering degree." Cyrus responded that of the "37 and a half" relatives he had who had attended Yale, John Edwin was the most fatuous, but as he was a free thinker who dressed well, he was certainly the most fun to spend time with. Who was the half? A half-cousin, of course. Harry and Cyrus kept trading jokes about young men none of the rest of them knew and launching into descriptions of deadly cane-rushes, blood-curdling initiation ceremonies, entertaining midnight group expeditions off campus, occasional expulsions, costly rowing races, and disastrous football games. When they got into the ins and outs of mechanical engineering and the complex virtues of the "Otto Gas Engine," they reduced even the glib Charlie Eastmeade to listener status.

Cyrus suddenly turned fierce when the conversation touched on the breaking headline news from Chicago about labor violence and the Haymarket bombing. He made a contemptuous remark about the dirty foreigners from Germany and applauded the prompt police round-up

Contemporary etching of a bomb blast in Chicago, blamed on German anarchists, that provoked the famous Haymarket Riot of May 4, 1886, and set off a wave of fear about domestic terrorism. Courtesy of the Library of Congress.

of all the shaggy-haired barbarian socialists, wild-eyed anarchists, and bomb-throwing nihilists who were stirring up trouble for Cyrus McCormick at his factory and who in his opinion had deliberately provoked the recent riot. The serious nature of the topic brought the conversation to a jolting halt. Harry smoothed things over with a joke about how much worse the freshman rioters on the Old Campus were when they found out that they had failed their examinations, and the wobble in the conversation passed.

The guests had such a grand time that they didn't call for their carriage until a few minutes before 10 P.M., when the college closed for the evening. Harry Reynolds rose reluctantly from his place on the old horsehair sofa in the corner. Cora, who was almost six inches taller, leaned down slightly to thank him for coming. She liked Harry. Humorous and confident, Harry promised he would stay in touch and write to her. She nodded politely to Mr. Judson and thanked him for his card. Her opinion of Cyrus Judson had shifted; his painful, bigoted comment about dirty German foreigners particularly stuck in her mind. Back in Davenport, her intelligent and kindly piano teacher, Professor Braunlich, was nothing if not a German socialist; the price of his youthful idealism during the Dresden uprising back in 1848 had been to cause his entire family to be sent into exile to America.

They shook hands all around and said goodbye. As she returned downstairs to her room on the north corridor, Cora reflected soberly that the subject of her recitals and her recent triumph on April 16 with the musicians of New York City had not come up in the conversation once.

CORA'S REAL BIRTHDAY had happened the previous Monday. A huge box filled with presents picked out for her by her sister Lotta and brother-in-law Gay Dorn arrived from Chicago. Late in the day, a messenger girl appeared at Cora's parlor door with a note for her to go immediately to the telegraph office. The clerk handed her a telegram from her mother. Expecting birthday congratulations, she tore off the end of the envelope and unfolded the message, but was shocked to read the following news: "Lottie been very sick. Better now. Goods sent.

Happy Birthday. Mama." The situation had been grave, as I discovered from this clipping from the *Davenport Gazette* that her family sent Cora later in the week: "Mrs. Dorn, the amiable daughter of Dr. Mrs. Keck, who acts as private secretary for her mother, met with quite a severe accident at Cedar Rapids last Saturday, by falling down stairs at the Grand Hotel in that city. The shock was quite severe, but aside from a few painful bruises, she escaped without receiving serious injury. Her husband is now with her at the Willson Hotel in that city and she will soon be herself again, under the tender care of her mother."

Lotta might simply have fallen down a steep flight of stairs at her hotel in Cedar Rapids, as reported. In an era before safety concerns led to strict building codes, Victorian staircases could be much steeper and longer than we are accustomed to seeing today, and often they had no railings. Women's dresses reached to the floor, and women sometimes stepped on a hem and pitched headlong on the way down.

But it is also possible that something else was going on that could not be spoken about openly in the paper. Fifteen years later, in 1900, Lotta told the census taker that she had given birth to four children in her lifetime, but family records show no trace of them. I presume that she must have delivered four infants who were born dead or died soon after birth. It's not that difficult to read the phrase "fell down the stairs" as a euphemism for a spontaneous late-term miscarriage, and Lotta could have become seriously ill from a hemorrhage or infection afterward. Staircase accidents and miscarriages were intertwined in writings of the time; nineteenth-century women who wanted to self-abort unwanted pregnancies sometimes deliberately threw themselves down a flight of stairs. Being childless was a tragic disappointment for Cora's favorite sister. If she really did fall down some stairs, maybe this accident caused Lotta internal injury that prevented her from delivering a healthy baby for the rest of her life.

ON TUESDAY, Wendell and Harry tried to come back to college to visit Cora in the evening, but Miss Goodsell would not let them up to see her. On Thursday, Wendell sent Cora a letter, addressed to "Miss

Keck," to apologize for not coming to visit and telling her that Harry had left for New Haven on Wednesday, taking a pin of hers with him, which he promised to mail back to her. Unusually for him, Wendell's crisp, formal language was actually shaded with emotions—embarrassment and regret. "I am very sorry that anything of the kind should have happened, and what her [Miss Goodsell's] reason is for the course she has taken I cannot imagine. If she has told you, please to tell me what it is," he begged. Cora remembered the squeaky footstep she had heard during her birthday party and wondered who the spy had been who had been listening to their conversation behind the parlor doors, and who had carried tales of their wicked activities to Miss Goodsell. What a horrible and underhanded thing to do.

More discouraging things: the mailman delivered two invitations to far-away events that she couldn't attend. She received a wedding invitation from Hattie Wakefield, who was about to get married to Albert Brady on Saturday, May 10, at the First Unitarian Church in Bloomington, Illinois. Everyone who was important to her in Davenport would be going to that party. Albert's father, Edwin W. Brady, had stepped up to the plate after Cora's humiliation on Brady Street the previous June, with a public endorsement of her mother's integrity in the *Davenport Gazette*. Albert's older brother, Oscar, was someone Cora considered an interesting candidate for romance—he was a fiercely ambitious newspaperman, and he loved music and played the cornet well. She wished she could play something wonderful on the piano for Hattie's ceremony or at the reception afterward and attract his attention with her own musical gifts. But it took two days of travel each way to get to Bloomington, and there was no time to go and come back in a single weekend.

Then Cora was invited to a May Party at Walker's Hall, St. Clair, Pennsylvania, featuring music by Weston's Orchestra, organized by Minnie Keiter's friends in her hometown. On the committee of eight young men who had organized this party was Harry P. Short, the handsome shoe-store owner with whom Cora had drunk champagne last year right after her Christmas in Allentown. A regretful RSVP of "no" went out for that one, too.

In mid-May, Harry Reynolds sent her the May 8 issue of the *Yale Record*, signed on the cover "H. Reynolds, 43 College St.," along with the hatpin. Here was the most interesting of all of her beaus, but located too far away for her to spend time with. By the time Harry finished his exams at the end of June and returned to his family home in Poughkeepsie, she would be long gone.

Not all of her classmates felt as left out and cut off from the world outside Vassar as Cora did. The "nice girls" in the Poppenheim's social set were invited to socially prominent Ivy League events through family social connections that she did not have. Cora had freedom, but the nice girls had access. In the hierarchical social order of the nineteenth century, you had to choose one or the other. Louisa Poppenheim wrote to her mother that her older sister May and their friend Addie McKinlay would be wearing new sleeveless gowns to the West Point cadet ball that spring, and they had been planning since February for the Columbia ball in '88, two years in the future.[4] Mary knew J. P. Morgan's wife's niece at college. She hobnobbed with college trustees and chatted with the Rockefellers. Her ability to network socially was immense and supported by a thick web of social connections. Cora, on the other hand, was trying to advance completely on her own. Her mother was a social outcast, traveling from hotel to hotel a thousand miles away on the other side of the Mississippi River. Cora was not going to the West Point cadet ball and never would—she was limited to strolling the sidewalks of Poughkeepsie to meet dudes.

A fat catalog arrived from Woodward & Lothrop, the "Boston" Dry Goods House in Washington, D.C., wrapped in a brown-paper sleeve and filled with interesting general articles to read, a short story, beautiful etchings, and even poetry, in addition to lists of items offered for sale. Cora pored over the pages of costly offerings for an entire afternoon. She wanted so many of the items shown in its pages. It was intoxicating—they could be summoned up almost instantly by sending in an order form and a check. Her mother had been rebuking her again for spending so much money, but she wanted to go onstage to play her graduation recital in style. It was so hard to resist material temptations. Was she really as bad as they said—just a "spend schrift"?

What about that huge diamond pin that Belle had ordered for herself under her mother's name from the Davenport jeweler T. Kircher while Mrs. Dr. Keck was out of town visiting patients back in 1882?

Two months later, the jeweler had publicly confronted Belle on the front steps of her mother's infirmary with a summons for a court appearance in an attempt to shame her into paying the bill, which was more than $700, as much as the cost of Cora's entire year at Vassar.[5] Everyone in Davenport knew about that incident. I wonder whether Elizabeth Griggs had spread that story among Cora's college friends. If so, it would have made Cora's face burn red when a sympathetic party advised her about the humiliating information leak. Unlike her older sister, Cora always paid her bills. Belle had a lifelong habit of paying her bills only when she had to and not a minute sooner; her pen often hesitated over half-written checks, and she always paid less than she was legally obligated to whenever she judged that she could get away with it. Nevertheless, it was understood among the members of the Keck family that Belle was so good at making money that it was also hers to spend, neither of which was the case for Cora. The whole situation was very unfair.

SUMMER YAWNED AHEAD of Cora with a fierce edge to it; instead of offering relief from Vassar's intensity, it leered at her. Commencement was literally the beginning of the next phase of her life, and she still didn't know what that phase would consist of. Miss Chapin had surely brought up the topic of Cora's future. Study in Europe, particularly in Germany, was the best route to take if you wanted to progress to the next level as a pianist, Miss Chapin said. That was what she had done herself. She recommended that Cora read Amy Fay's book on the topic, *Music Study in Germany*, because girls were freely admitted to the study of piano in that country, and she pointed out that all American musicians of note had gone there to make their careers.[6] Cora's generation was still fundamentally limited by America's moral prejudice against respectable women "going on the stage," as Miss Chapin herself had been limited fifteen years before, but she hoped that her own crushed dreams of musical glory could be redeemed in some way if she could persuade her immensely talented student to continue her studies. Miss Chapin was, in truth, nothing but an underpaid music instructor with no pension plan. She and Cora both deserved far more than that. They might even have discussed the careers of several women pianists who had recently become internationally successful on the concert circuit. It was not realistic for anyone Cora's age to contemplate an international career (according to the famous piano teacher Nadia Boulanger, if a child wasn't already well along as a performing prodigy by age seven, "it was already too late"[7]), but perhaps Cora began to fantasize anyway.

In the 1870s, audiences all over the United States from New York to Cincinnati to California had flocked to hear the young Venezuelan prodigy Teresa Carreño, nicknamed "the Valkyrie of the piano," who made her debut as an eight-year-old prodigy and later introduced Grieg's piano concerto to wild acclaim across the country under the baton of Leopold Damrosch and the New York Philharmonic in 1883.[8] She also composed prolifically. After her German debut with the Berlin Philharmonic in 1889, even the misogynistic conducting genius Hans von Bülow put aside his prejudice to declare that she was the most interesting player of his day. By the mid-1880s, two other major female talents at the American keyboard had emerged: Julia Rivé-King, known as an intellectual and classicist, who crossed the country on tour every year during the 1880s, including twice with Theodore Thomas and his orchestra; and Miss Fannie Bloomfield, who had just made her American debut in Chicago two years before in 1883. Mrs. Rivé-King and Miss Carreño were both born into musical/theatrical families already involved with show business, and each had a musically informed parent or close relative who actively managed her training and career from a young age and traveled with her. Cora, of course, had no such relative available.

CHAPTER TWENTY-SIX

The Gem of the Evening

A s June approached, the romantic intrigues among the Vassar Trio (Cora, Minnie, and Lydia) reached a climax. Minnie Keiter became secretly engaged to Charlie Eastmeade. Minnie's roommate in parlor 157, 5 corridor (who I assume was Lydia) wrote a note on rainbow trim paper on Tuesday, May 18, addressed to "Caress" (who I assume was Cora) about how Miss Goodsell is "on the alert and thinks I know a few too many [dudes]." The writer wasn't Cora (different handwriting) or Minnie (mentioned in the third person in the letter), so it had to be Lydia. Lydia said that she and Min had been called up by "Miss G" in the morning for being out with Charlie on the lake the day before and as a result were grounded—they couldn't receive visitors. She continued with the most important dish: "I freed Min by giving it away by exposing the Engagement & she did not mind it at all. Would that I were engaged now. Then u 2 fair ones could come + demand the 2 VC heroines from the hands of the fiendish Lady G. + if she refused what fun a double elopement would be— for fear something has been forgotten u + Chas. can consult each other—I say 10-derly yours and do answer—." The writer signed with the same name she had used to address her intended recipient: "Caress." The identities of both the sender and the addressee remain secretive and mysterious. Then someone balled up the letter as if to throw it out, changed her mind, smoothed it out, and put it back in the envelope.

This relationship situation was complicated, as they say on Facebook, and because I am missing a lot of information, I am not quite sure what was going on. On the same scrapbook page, Cora saved a note that Charlie wrote to her in an extremely intimate tone, dated "Mott Cottage, 4:30 P.M. 5/19/86" addressed to "My sweet Coz," in response to a letter Cora had just sent him. It is enclosed in an envelope addressed by

Cora Keck holding her certificate of graduation from Vassar College.

someone else, marked "private" to "Miss 'Karess' M. Ceck, Cassar Vollege, KoPeepsie, Y.N.":

> Why can't you come and "Caress" me and try and cheer my drooping spirits . . . I am sorrowful nigh unto the "gravy" and my poor head is still the same "aching void" that it has always been . . . I am <u>certainly</u> just as sorry as you are, that Minnie did not tell Miss G—that we are engaged, and that we became so when the flowers began to "bloom in the spring." Hoping to hear from you before your marriage which I hope <u>will</u> take place less than a 100 years from now, <u>eye</u> (put-on-my) clothes [i.e., I close the letter] with much love—You're a-door-ing but broken ♥ed
> Coughing,
> Charlie.

Charlie was not totally sure of his commitment, *apparently*. Cora was playing a double game, *apparently*. It looks as if Charlie agrees with Minnie that he is engaged to her. But it doesn't sound as if he can be particularly enraptured with that commitment if he is confiding about some kind of painful sorrow to Cora, and hadn't Lydia already spilled the information about the engagement to Miss Goodsell? So with all the irony, torrents of horrible puns, reverse humor, and double entendres, it's impossible to tell what Charlie actually feels either for Cora or for Minnie. Maybe it was hard for them to tell what he was feeling, too. He sounds like one of those good-looking, wiseguy types who would rather die than express a sincere, meaningful sentiment to a female. He liked to keep them guessing about his intentions—a strong position to take in any strategic operation.

Cora liked to keep them guessing, too—she had recently gone dancing with a new guy, Richard Brown (who was not a member of their group), just to shake things up with the other dudes. Then she came down with a bug, probably the stomach flu, something fierce and short in duration, and had to go into the infirmary. Maybe she caught it from "coughing" Charlie. Minnie sent her a note offering to write to Cora's mother and her cousin Warren Kleckner to advise them that she was sick, and also to write to Will Caire to cancel some plans Will and Cora had made for the afternoon. Then she revealed an even more confusing and unexpected turn of events:

> I am so broken-hearted about Charlie and he promised to write me just one more letter—the last—and I am worried because it does not come. So I shall write to Will and casually remark about Charlie and ask Will if he has seen him. I suppose Charlie will tell Will all about it. Your loving Min
> Get well very soon, my dear for I am so lonesome without you especially after parting with Charlie.

Either Miss Goodsell informed Min and Charlie's parents about the secret engagement and the young lovers were forced to break it off, or, more likely, Charlie dumped Min on his own. Either way, the break happened without his even saying goodbye to her. These events seemed to have rushed by within a few weeks, or even days. Why am I not surprised? Smart women, foolish choices . . . some things never change. Charlie Eastmeade was a fast customer and a commitment-phobe, and it looks as if Minnie Keiter, who was young for her age and as innocent as she was intelligent, got skunked.

Will Caire was different from Charlie. He was generous, for one thing. He had recently sent Cora a "mash" package using an address label from his father's company (Adam Caire, Vitrified Stone & Pressed Drain Pipe), and he gave her a signed cabinet portrait, which none of the other guys bothered to do. He sounds a little sweeter than the rest, willing to help Charlie's unhappy ex-fiancée by easing some communication blockages, and probably less flashy than the heartless, double-dealing Charlie Eastmeade. Nor was he as dry, stiff, and narrowly focused as Wendell Booth,

Cora's signed cabinet photograph of Will Caire, of Poughkeepsie.

who knew how to train horses and judge trotting races, but not much about anything else. What about Richard A. Brown? The only trace he left in Cora's story is a visiting card he gave to her on Thursday reminding her, "Don't forget our next waltz." Mysterious but unimportant, I'm afraid.

HATTIE WAKEFIELD (now Mrs. Albert Brady) and her new husband surprised Cora by coming through Poughkeepsie on their honeymoon. On Monday the 17th, Cora received a telegram sent from the Hudson Depot in New York City: "Will be on 7.11 Pull train—Meet us. —Albert Brady." The newlyweds stayed the night, and during the rush of conversation, Cora got an avalanche of news about two families who were her family's closest friends, the Bradys in Davenport and the Wakefields in Bloomington, now linked by ties of marriage.

Hattie's husband Albert was slim, with dark eyes and a thoughtful expression. His strong and forceful personality pointed toward a future filled with worldly success. During breaks while he was an undergraduate at Knox College in Galesburg, Illinois, Albert used to hop a freight car with his friend S. S. McClure and the two pals would peddle suitcases full of small items all over the Midwest to earn extra pocket money, even though Albert's wealthy father paid for him to live in a comfortable boardinghouse. He did it for sport, for the challenge, and for the lure of new experience. He enjoyed solving difficult math problems and once impressed McClure by working eighteen hours straight to solve a particularly tough one.[1]

Hattie's brother Homer had asked after Cora; however, Cora was interested in Albert's brother, not Hattie's brother. Oscar and Albert had recently transformed a small temperance publication owned by their father, the *Northwestern News*, into a mainstream newspaper called the *Davenport Times* that was now competing with the *Davenport Gazette*. Albert and his brother wanted to move to New York City; his college friend McClure had just founded a news distribution service called the McClure Syndicate that was handling cutting-edge journalism and fiction by internationally known authors, including Robert Louis Stevenson, Sir Arthur Conan Doyle, and Rudyard Kipling. After less than a year, it was a huge success. S. S. McClure would go on to found

Oscar Brady (left, standing) and his younger brother Albert with two women, probably their wives, Etta (Peck) and Harriet (Wakefield).

McClure's magazine and become one of the most important journalists and publishers in the United States, introducing the country to muckraking journalism with Ida Tarbell's 1902 exposé of the abuses of John D. Rockefeller's oil monopoly. Albert Brady became the magazine's business manager.

Hattie gave Cora an invitation to the marriage reception they were planning for June 1 at the Brady home at 1101 East Front Street in Davenport, but of course Cora had to refuse because her graduation was on June 7.

∞

AS DECORATION (MEMORIAL) DAY approached, the ticket agents
set up shop in the lower office, and immediately after dinner Cora went
downstairs to see about getting her rail passage to Davenport. As she
laid down her $16 on the desk and the agent passed her the ticket, she
realized that she was actually dreading the thought of returning to Davenport. Would she have to live in the mansion with her family until she
died an old maid? It was a common fate for wealthy educated women
of her generation.

Anyone who wasn't planning to attend the graduation ceremonies
was leaving as soon as classes ended. None of the graduating seniors was
close to Cora. They had all been juniors when she entered in the fall of
'84, and her friendships were with younger students who were still in the
midst of their educational careers. She was headed out into the world
beyond Vassar's walls pretty much on her own. Of the seven other music
students slated to receive certificates in 1886—Brewster, Goldstine, Hayman, Hines, Orton, Pompilly, and Rabe—none was close to her.

The majority of Cora's friends would be returning to college in the
fall, aiming toward graduation from the four-year academic program.
Marian Austin, her first roommate, would graduate in 1888, along with
Jane Edwards, her erstwhile tennis pal, and Ned Weeks, her biggest
smash. Elizabeth Griggs certainly didn't fall into the category of one of
Cora's friends, but I should mention that according to her yearbook,
she graduated Phi Beta Kappa in 1889. Cora's first-year "college quartet"
of lonesome newcomers were also headed for full academic diplomas.
Laura Harris and Fannie Clark were slower than the rest but persistent,
and both finally graduated in 1890, along with Cora Louise Scofield,
while the precociously brilliant Minnie Keiter, who had been admitted
to Vassar as a sophomore straight out of high school, was due to receive
her diploma at the age of nineteen the next year, in 1887. She and Verlista Shaul would be rivals for the honor of valedictorian. There had been
a lot of inventory shrinkage among Cora's less academic friends, including her "third wife" Lotta Wix, who had not returned to the School of
Music in the fall of 1885, and Kitty Rogers, who never completed her
second year in the School of Art.

As she walked down corridors disordered and crowded with busy young women packing their trunks, the sight of empty parlors where she had spent so many delightful hours caused her anxiety. She would not be back to see them filled again with new students and redecorated with their interesting belongings. Cora agonized that these young women to whom she had become so attached were rapidly slipping through her fingers. She knew in her heart that in all likelihood, she would never again be in a place that made her as alive and emotionally fulfilled as Vassar, surrounded by close female friends and constantly inspired by other people's energy and high expectations. She couldn't believe that just the year before, overwhelmed by pressure, she had considered not returning. Now she wished that she never had to leave; she had found the courage and met the test Vassar put to her.

What had she made of herself after two years at college? Rising above the scorn of Davenport's social elite, she had become a popular girl with a large circle of gifted and talented friends, despite anything Elizabeth Griggs might have said or done behind her back. As a musician, she had earned the respect and admiration of her demanding teacher and recognition from the music school's distinguished director, Professor Ritter. Her newfound self-discipline at the keyboard gave her pride and confidence; she was no longer tortured with self-doubt. She had become a young woman with independent goals.

But she was not engaged to be married. She had not found her "Eastern fellow." She wondered whether she could stand up to her mother on this issue.

ON FRIDAY THE 4TH, enough students remained on campus to hold the first annual tournament of the Vassar College Tennis Club. Cora saved the tournament schedule. There were eight contestants in the singles (Burge, M. L. McKinlay, Butler, A. M. McKinlay, Acer [to replace Copeland, who dropped out], Skinner, Platt, and Pompilly) and five pairs in the doubles (M. L. McKinlay and Blackwell; Leach and Butler; Burtis and Bush; Skinner and A. M. McKinlay; and Platt and J. J. Edwards). Many of these names show up in the Poppenheim sisters' letters as part of their "set" of nice girls.

Why didn't Cora enter the competition as a team with Marian Austin? Maybe Marian had already left for Buffalo, where she planned to spend the summer with relatives. However, because Cora never once wrote about "tennising" during her second year at Vassar, I am afraid that the McKinlay sisters and their socially exclusive friends may have made her feel unwelcome in the tennis club to a point where she had dropped the sport.

Play began at 8:30 in the morning. Addie not only organized the tournament, she played thirteen sets and was the overall winner in both the singles and the doubles. Her doubles partner, Miss Skinner, was so exhausted by the last set that she sat on her racquet in a back corner of the court, except when she had to receive a serve, while Addie single-handedly demolished their competition. (Belle Skinner's brother William would later donate an entire Gothic building to house Vassar's music department in 1928 in her memory after her untimely death from pneumonia.) The weather must have been problematic because the tournament was halted temporarily but resumed at three o'clock. Cora failed to fill in any information on her tournament card about who won. Addie McKinlay was awarded a "gold medal of dainty design" at 6 P.M.[2]

MEANWHILE, ALL THE PEOPLE who were planning to attend the graduation ceremonies for Vassar's class of 1886 were on their way to Poughkeepsie. Over the weekend, the out-of-town trustees and alumnae thronged the city's hotels, which were also filled to the back corner rooms with proud parents, friends, and siblings of the candidates for graduation. Among them, as a Davenport newspaper reported, were two people whom Cora wanted to see most of all: "Mrs. Dr. Keck and husband took the train east yesterday to attend the graduation exercises at Vassar college of their daughter, Miss Corize. From there, they will take a two month's vacation with friends and relatives in New York and the New England states."

The Kecks probably left Iowa on Saturday, because they missed the Sunday baccalaureate ceremonies. While they were on their way east, Belle sent a night message (at a cheaper rate) via Western Union

Telegraph Co. to Cora: "Heifer calf—ask Pa what I shall do with it. Mrs. Alexander." Unlike other areas of her life, where she was controlling and fiercely independent, at the farm Belle was forced to depend on her father's practical experience now that she had driven off her tenant with the lawsuit about the unpaid rental contract.

Following breakfast on Sunday, June 6, Vassar's acting president, the Reverend J. R. Kendrick, delivered the baccalaureate sermon and address in the chapel to the graduating class at 11 A.M. All the windows were propped wide open to provide some small drafts of ventilation for the overwarm, crowded space inside, while the audience members discreetly fanned themselves with the paper programs. The piano had been pushed to the side of the stage, which remained undecorated for this college religious service.

The Reverend Kendrick based his sermon on this text from Rom 14:7: "For none of us liveth unto himself," an altruistic starting point that in his hands rapidly assumed a strange quality as he revealed himself to be a member of the antediluvian faction of the board of trustees. He was exactly the kind of trustee who was running the college into the ground, one of the group whom the New York Alumnae Association had described as old fogeys and superannuated clergymen in their public letter to the *New York Times* the previous winter. Kendrick emphasized his ideal of "character" as a passive female virtue. "What we are rather than what we do is a matter of supreme consequence," he said. This was especially important for women, he declared, because a woman's elevated character was the only way to influence others in the domestic and social spheres, which was their main role in life. He spoke of the young ladies leaving a "half-cloistered life" at college and going out into the world with an ultimate goal of "refined strength, genuine culture, and capacity for useful service . . . the duty of unselfish devotion to others."

Instead of encouraging the many brilliant and ambitious young women in his audience to persist in their goals despite adversity, he gave them a condescending pat on their collective little heads in closing: "Do not suffer yourselves to be disappointed and soured if you shall fail to achieve any sort of distinction or find what is called a 'career'; if the trivial round and common lot are reserved for you, never mind. They furnish plenty of room for noble service and they are more fully associated with the best joys than are enviable stations and wider spheres."

This sermon epitomizes the stale, reactionary thinking on female education that Matthew Vassar was explicitly trying to overcome by starting Vassar College in 1861. He was probably turning over in his grave during the sermon, and I can only imagine stalwarts in the faculty such as astronomy professor Maria Mitchell (awarded international fame and recognition and a friend of Agassiz and Humboldt) and Professor Priscilla Braislin (a noted mathematician) sitting in the audience quietly struggling not to look disgusted with what they were hearing. I am glad that Kendrick had limited direct influence over Vassar's future, although his wife served as Lady Principal for twenty-two years starting in 1891 when Miss Goodsell retired. I liked Caldwell's sermon from the year before—about eating salt with faithful friends during times of great stress and adversity—much better. He spoke from the heart, although it must have been difficult for his audience to bear the public exposure of his personal suffering and humiliation, which amounted to theater of cruelty, or an awful episode of reality television.

Around noontime on Monday, Mr. and Mrs. Dr. Keck sent a telegram from Yonkers telling Cora to meet them at two o'clock at the station in Poughkeepsie. Cora rushed to the Lodge to catch a car into town. She was there on the platform fifteen minutes early, wearing a new hat and waiting to greet her parents when they disembarked from their coach. They looked so small compared with how she remembered them. Her father was starting to stoop with age and arthritis, and her mother had taken to pulling her hair back so tightly against the sides of her head that it made her look slightly shrunken and emphasized the fact that she had lost some of her side molars to age. Oh, and that dandruff on those strong, rounded, black silk–covered shoulders . . . Cora looked away carefully so as not to notice the little white flecks as she hugged her mother tightly to her heart. They were still the "beloved ones" she cared most about, the people whose presence at her graduation made her almost perfectly happy.

They rode in a hack cab together out to Vassar. Cora heard that another Davenport girl would be enrolling in Vassar's School of Art next fall; her name was Belle, and she was the daughter of E. S. Ballord, the banker and druggist. Cora barely knew or remembered her, except that she was a close friend of Elizabeth Griggs—but what a crowd of Davenport girls had descended on the college all of a sudden! And all of them expected to reflect social glory to their families back home, Cora mused, with penetrating recognition of her own mission to elevate the Keck name. Her parents asked about her New York friends. Cora told them that a gentleman friend from New York City, Ed Corbett, would be coming up to Vassar on Wednesday for commencement exercises on the 9th. He had better come, she added to herself.

Because the students who were not attending graduation had left college, empty rooms in the Main Building were made available to out-of-town guests. Cora installed her parents in their room, made sure they were comfortable, and hurried away to prepare for her evening's performance.

AT A QUARTER TO FIVE on the evening of Cora's last Soirée Musicale, Miss Chapin met with her student in the chapel before the concert to assess her state of mind. Cora was better prepared for the wave of stage fright than she had been at her recital in April. She had conquered her fears once before, and she could do it again. She had played with the professionals, the New York Philharmonic musicians. She knew her piece. She would approach the stage like a professional. Miss Chapin gave Cora one of her rare smiles.

A large and brilliant audience attended the annual musical exhibition at Vassar College that evening. Every seat in the college chapel was filled, all the way to the ends of the balconies. In the opinion of the reporter from the *New York Times* who covered Vassar's graduation, Cora's performance stood out among all the others: "The gem of the evening was the Wagner Liszt march from Tannhauser by Miss Corizze Mae Keck, of Davenport, Iowa, and next to it was the rendition by Miss Georgine Hamilton Peck Hayman of Poughkeepsie, of Moszkowski's Tarantelle."

Cora's eyes were shining when she stood up from the piano bench to take her bow. The applause swelled around her like a sudden storm of rain pounding through a dry forest, and she felt triumph—finally recognized and admired not only by hostile young socialites like Elizabeth Griggs and the McKinlays, but by the ones whose opinion she most cared about, two elderly people from Iowa who had never seen her showered with public glory before. When it was all over, Cora went from room to room through the parlors searching for her parents. As the paper reported, "The college corridors were thronged with ladies and gentlemen . . . and the drawing rooms, parlors and reception rooms were brilliant with groups of parents, relatives and friends of the pupils, among them being the General Manager of the Toledo and Ohio Central Railroad and a party of ladies, who came here on a special car . . . to witness the graduation of Miss Ferris."

Cora's triumphant sensation hadn't faded yet. Where were they? Had they heard the music, heard the feeling and the hundreds of hours of effort she had put into creating the beautiful technique that allowed her to share a corner of her soul?

I think that she found them, one tall and thin, one short and worn-looking, standing alone together by the old Matthew Vassar sofa in a corner of one of the college parlors. Neither parent had gotten past elementary school, and Vassar's atmosphere would have overwhelmed both of them—even Mrs. Dr. Keck, who ordinarily exhibited unflappable self-confidence during her showdowns with the county sheriffs at her public courtroom appearances. This playing field filled with sophisticated intellectuals and artists, socialites, political luminaries, and nationally known business leaders had a different set of rules from those the good doctor was used to out in Iowa and Illinois.

Miss Chapin appeared suddenly from the throng, so tiny that she had been hidden by the crush of taller bodies. Cora introduced her parents to her music teacher. Jessie Chapin might have smiled again. I am sure that her courtesy was genuine. She did not appear to notice Mrs. Dr. Keck's dandruff. After praising their daughter's diligence and musical abilities, she must certainly have mentioned to the Kecks that she hoped Cora would continue serious study of the piano, perhaps traveling abroad to do it? They leaned in to listen more closely. She has great potential as a musician, Miss Chapin added, with emphasis.

The graduation weekend was so hectic that Cora did not save any of the small notes and scraps from her activities that had previously given

Tintype of Cora Keck with her parents, John and Rebecca Keck,
ca. 1892.

me so much insight into her life and inner thoughts. I have to confess that I have no direct evidence that Miss Chapin actually told Cora's parents that her best student had the potential to become a professional musician. Nevertheless, I believe that she felt that way. It fits with everything that has gone before, for which I have abundant evidence, so I have taken the bold step of inventing Miss Chapin's glowing optimism about Cora's musical future. In fact, if she didn't say it, she should have. So then I can imagine that Cora examined her parents' faces, trying to read what they were thinking. They must have been startled . . . but what were their expressions? Amazement? Bafflement? Pride tinged with a touch of horror? This outcome was completely different from what they had intended in sending their daughter away to Vassar. All they wanted was for Cora to outclass Mary Lane's social clique back in Davenport and find a blue chip Eastern husband. Now they had an independent-minded girl with a possible professional future on their hands.

Cora felt immensely proud of herself. For at least one day more, she was part of a social world that she longed for and that she could reach out toward with the power of her musical talent. She had great potential as a musician and as a performer. What might she be able to do if she tried? The idea rang in Cora's ears for hours afterward.

∞

CLASS DAY CEREMONIES did not begin until three o'clock in the afternoon on Tuesday. During the morning hours, Mr. and Mrs. Dr. Keck strolled with Cora on the shaded pathways, admiring the two parallel rows of young white pines that led from the Lodge across the college quadrangle to the Main Building, which was covered with a green mass of Virginia creeper vines. Rose and gray decorations hung from some of the small trees.

In the music building, the Kecks admired the twenty-five college pianos in the practice rooms and went upstairs to the Art Gallery to view the paintings in the student art exhibition. Cora pointed out one or two canvases hanging in the exhibit that Kitty had completed before leaving college during the winter. I am sad to report that all record of what her artistic subjects were and what her technique looked like have been lost. At Cora's suggestion, they crossed the little creek behind Main, passed through the wooden gate on the dirt lane beyond, and walked to the top of Sunset Hill where a park bench offered them a chance to sit and admire the farm fields spreading in the milky June haze north and west all the way to the Catskill Mountains.

To visitors, the college looked serene, an unruffled pond on a calm day, a water garden decorated with courteous greetings, hat-doffings, and hand clasps. However, the placid surface of commencement weekend activities concealed dramatic power struggles going on underneath. The annual meeting of the board of trustees was scheduled for that morning, along with the fifteenth annual meeting of the Vassar College Alumnae Association. Predators and prey darted in and out of the shadows to take their lunges at control and survival. The pond itself was in danger of drying up completely. In conversations throughout the corridors and across the tables in the dining hall, rumors flew about certain decisions and business transactions that might be taken that would have an important bearing on the future government of Vassar. Cora clipped an article from the Poughkeepsie newspaper:

> For nearly a year there had been rumors that the Trustees were in favor of retiring Maria Mitchell from the Astronomy Department and having Astronomy taught by the professor of Mathematics [Priscilla H. Braislin]. Also there has been talk of abolishing the position of Lady Principal. In the school of Music, it has been suggested that a Professor of Vocal Music be appointed and in the Language Department a Professor of Modern Languages. Should such changes be made the departure will be quite radical.

The biggest news of the morning occurred while the Kecks were strolling up Sunset Hill. The trustees filed into a large hall in the Main Building. The doors were shut, and Vassar's new president, the Reverend Dr. James M. Taylor, took charge of his new college. At the same hour, a large group of Vassar alumnae assembled in a separate room. They had thrown a great deal of money into the pot to address emergency financial problems facing the college. Those in attendance were mobilized for the moment when they would make themselves heard, exert their leverage, and start telling the trustees how to run Vassar.

The president of the Alumnae Association, Dr. Mary Taylor Bissell, M.D., made her appearance at the all-male trustees meeting down the hallway. Standing next to the new president, she announced to the assembly of elderly and conservative gentlemen that the association had raised $11,500 to endow the astronomy department ($10,000 for a permanent fund, the rest to pay for immediate repairs and needs in the observatory), and then, as had been done the year before, laid a check for this sum on the table in front of the trustees. The startled men were forced into a quick reversal of their plans to fire Professor Mitchell, and they decided not to abolish the astronomy department. A reporter noted the next day that the money had been raised "for Professor Mitchell who, by the way, has been reinstated with honor." The alumnae were also halfway toward their goal of raising $20,000 for a new gymnasium for the new department of physical culture, being built to match similar facilities already available at Smith and Wellesley.

Taylor (brother) and Taylor Bissell (sister) shook hands. That solved that matter. "Next item," President Taylor announced. Mrs. Bissell graciously accepted the reluctant gratitude of the trustees assembled in front of her as if it had been offered with enthusiasm and returned to her alumnae meeting at the other end of the building.

The trustees then pulled out the dismaying accountants' reports. The great success of the young and vigorous alumnae in their fund-raising contrasted sharply with the mostly elderly trustees' failure to grapple with Vassar's dire financial situation. They could not help noticing the fact that the ladies were clearly good for a lot of money. The men could no longer pretend to offer seats to these capable women on the all-male board of trustees in the indefinite future; if they wanted to get their hands on more of this money, they would have to swallow their pride, set a date, and actually do it.

For the rest of the day, the ladies of the Alumnae Association discussed other topics—should the position of Lady Principal be retained? (Yes, for the time being.) Should the alumnae be given a vote in the college? (Of course. Some should be put on the board of trustees as soon as possible.) Should Vassar continue to offer preparatory classes, since they bring needed revenue? (Get rid of the preps immediately—there are far too many dropouts and dimwits going around boasting about their time at Vassar who don't deserve to make that claim.) What about maintaining the highest academic standards? (Yes—see previous agenda item; also hire more professors and recruit better students.) There was also the matter of the great need for scholarships in the East and West. (See previous agenda item.)

Finally, they took some time to relax with a little sentimental ceremony. A Class Cup was awarded for the birth of the first baby from a member of the class of 1882. The cup was sent out to Japan to Princess Stematz Yamakawa, now the wife of Prince Iwao Oyama, Japan's minister of war, who had been one of the most popular and active students of her year.

Mrs. Bissell's forceful presentation to the old trustees marked a watershed moment for the history of the college and of women's education in the United States. A year after these events, in 1887, three alumnae were appointed to join Vassar's board of trustees for the first time: Helen Backus, class of 1873; Florence Cushing, valedictorian of the class of 1874; and Elizabeth Poppleton, class of 1876. The despised and embarrassing preparatory division would be dismantled immediately afterward in 1888. The alumnae had finally linked their voice to the administration, trading grateful dependence on benevolent benefactors for the modern goal for which they had been educated: articulate autonomy and active control over their own college.

COMMENCEMENT EXERCISES took place at 10:30 A.M. on Wednesday. Ed Corbett telegraphed a second time to say that business once again prevented him from coming up to be at the ceremony. The Kecks, minus Mr. Corbett, joined the other guests of the graduating class in Room J, and at 10 A.M. they were conducted to reserved seats in the chapel. The procession to chapel moved out promptly at 10:30 A.M., with the trustees and president leading the way and the graduating class bringing up the rear. Miss A. M. Ely was the class marshal. Nearly every young lady was profusely decked with flowers, some carrying bouquets in their hands, while others wore them as corsages, while still others were content with a simple rosebud half hidden in their hair. Cora clipped the article that ran in the *New York Times*:

> Poughkeepsie, June 9—Vassar College was crowded this morning
> with the parents, relatives and friends of the pupils to participate in
> the Commencement exercises which occurred in the chapel at 10:30
> o'clock. The acting President, the Rev. Mr. Kendrick; the board of
> trustees, and the Faculty occupied seats upon the platform, which was
> ornamented with ferns, palm leaves and hothouse plants. . . . The top
> students presented short speeches on topics ranging from "Conversa-
> tion as a Fine Art" by Carrie Lindly Borden [a second cousin of the
> not-yet notorious, ax-wielding Lizzie Borden], Emma Louise Nelson

on "Fair Treatment of the Negro a Necessity" and a critical piece on The Knights of Labor by Esther Witkowsky of Chicago, who spoke against the union, calling it the "Pirates of Labor." Helen Reed spoke about "Careers for Women," and two students debated the topic pro and con "Should Religious Instruction be Given in the Public Schools?" Then Kendrick and two speakers representing alumnae and students all welcomed President Taylor, who responded at length, saying that he aimed to respond to the changes then agitating the college world, and that Vassar must not rest content merely with high standards but must act so that there are none higher. The address was well received.

Concern about racial inequality, hostility toward organized labor, the dilemmas of working women, and the proper role of religion in public education? These young women boldly addressed fundamental public controversies that continue to dominate U.S. politics 125 years later—still unresolved, and still fueling bitter partisan rancor. Another indication that Gilded Age America was a template for our own times.

The management of the college was now in the hands of leadership that believed in the professional potential of the young women of Vassar, but the new graduates and their classmates faced a difficult road ahead. A reporter from a Poughkeepsie paper closed out his coverage of the day's events with casually devastating condescension: "At night most of the fair ones had flitted to their homes." Even if Vassar could create an environment of excellence for women at school, building a solid, independent future outside of Vassar's supportive walls would not be easy for any of the graduates—not the least for those hoping to make a career in music. However, no one could prevent Vassar from fueling their dreams.

CHAPTER TWENTY-SEVEN

Life Underground and Its Dangers

C ora's two years at Vassar were over. Having entered through its famous gatehouse for the first time in September 1884 as a nobody from Squeedunk, joking to everyone that she displayed "less taste than was wanted," a potential piano-playing parlor ornament and a social-climbing husband-hunter, Cora subsequently made her departure from the School of Music as the finest performer in the music department and a beloved companion to dozens of intelligent and talented female friends. She was showered with praise and admiration for her courage and talent by her peers, her parents, the *New York Times*, and, most unexpectedly of all, her stern, unmovable piano instructor, Jessie Chapin.

Her triumphant departure was bittersweet. Miss Chapin's thoughts as she watched Cora climb into the carriage waiting in front of Vassar's Main Building for the last time must have been seasoned with equal measures of hope and futility. Did she drill her soon-to-be ex-student up until the last minute before her departure on scales and more scales, as if she could somehow give her an extra shove in the direction of continued serious study on the piano? Did Cora again exclaim, "Oh! Ye shades!" about the ordeal? Did they look at each other this time and laugh? Was Cora amazed to hear her teacher laugh? Rarity can make a minor thing such as that seem extraordinarily precious. As her talented protégée disappeared out of her life forever, I can easily imagine that Miss Chapin felt as if her own dreams were fading slightly too. She might have been thinking that no matter how perfectly she did her job, her students departed into a world that did not offer them real artistic opportunities. Her own career did not offer an encouraging template for Cora; her safe-looking life was permanently set to a temperature of medium-low. She would never be more than a piano instructor at a ladies' college, albeit the most famous of all ladies' colleges.

Frontispiece from the 1873 best seller Life Underground, *by Thomas Knox.*

SO WHAT HAPPENED to these young women, so beautifully prepared for their careers but with no place in the nineteenth century to go do it for real? In Cora's case, immediately after her graduation, she literally went underground. Victorian tourists were evidently extremely curious about dangerous subterranean locations and activities, and Cora shared this interest. Cora was supposed to spend several weeks vacationing with her parents, but she quickly parked her old folks with the Strauss cousins at their flour mill in Allentown and raced off to visit Minnie Keiter in St. Clair for the second time. According to a report about her visit that ran in the local newspaper, *Splinters*, Cora, like everyone else who came to the area, wanted to see the interior of a coal mine. The prosperity that coal brought magically transformed the ugly machinery erected above the pits into alluring engines of wealth. Even the slag heaps that advanced up and down the narrow valley along the edge of the river added drama to the scene. The entrance to the mine they would visit was a mile or so away from Pottsville, about a hundred yards from the county line, and was topped by a tall, soot-blackened slanting structure about three stories high called a breaker. A *Splinters* reporter noted, "Such visits to the mines are of frequent occurrence, many of the ladies of town having been down various mines frequently with their guests, and Minnie herself was no exception to the class of courageous explorers of the deep, dark workshops of our brave coal miners."[1]

Stereoscope image of a coal mine, ca. 1890. Courtesy of the Library of Congress.

The Chamberlain Colliery, owned by the two Thompson brothers who lived next door to Minnie's family, had all the latest equipment, including large fans used to blow fresh air in and push out "firedamp," or methane, the odorless, explosive, and lighter-than-air gas that collects in mining tunnels

at head height—the same level as the burning headlamps everyone in the mine had to wear to see where they were going.

At four o'clock in the afternoon, Cora, Minnie Keiter, and Harry Short entered the mine. When the car reached the turnout for the Little Tracy vein at the bottom of the main slope, the three young people were left with the car, in the dark, while an engineer named Mr. Harrison hurried off through the West Gangway to find their escorts. The dense darkness instantly closed in around them with a physical force that made their ears ring slightly. All traces of light vanished. Far in the distance, they could hear faint sounds of workers wielding their picks against the rock face and the ventilating fans' steady rhythm pushing fresh air into the grid of tunnels from far above. Even so, the close atmosphere was hardly breathable, tainted with the smell of iron, dynamite, coal dust, human sewage, and lubricating oils, and the pungent odors drilled into Cora's nostrils. The sharp, wet rocks of the ceiling were so close she could not straighten her arm above her head. She touched the clammy ridges delicately and rubbed her dampened fingers together.

One of the co-owners of the mine approached with lights for the visitors, and the young people started trading jokes and making fun of each other's nervousness. Everyone was given a regular miner's lamp, which gave off a much brighter light than the dim safety lamps, and they set out for the rock face of the Big Tracy vein. The heat was overwhelming. They bent their heads to avoid painful impacts with low-hanging knobs of rock and stumbled along the rough floor of the tunnel between the rails for the coal cars. Cora recoiled from the massiveness of the earth surrounding her, pressing in on all sides so strongly that the oak beams straining to support the ceiling sagged downwards in weak-looking arcs, and she hurried to keep up with the small, bobbing lights of the others with real desperation, suddenly terrified that she would get left behind in the darkness and become lost in the confusing labyrinth of dead ends and dangerous vertical shafts.

At the rock face, they gazed at a box of squibs, tiny sticks of explosives wrapped in paper with long, slow-burning fuses, which the miners used to break apart the rock to extend the tunnel and loosen the coal. Mr. Thompson explained that these squibs were so small that they were quite safe. He was proud of the fact that he ran a modern mine and had begun to use a new product called dynamite for blasting, which was a big improvement over the dangers of using liquid nitroglycerin and was much more powerful than the old method of using black powder.

They turned to leave. Cora bruised her forehead for the third or fourth time on a protruding shard of rock. They retraced their steps down several long galleries and around a number of corners to reach the intersection at the bottom of the exit shaft. The air began to improve as the noise of the elevator machinery got louder, and Cora's relief when the car carrying them upwards rose into the light at the surface made her gasp for breath. Standing on the rough boards at the mine's opening, Cora and Minnie stared at each other. Their clothes and faces were black with coal dust. Minnie leveled a challenge at Cora. "You weren't scared, were you?" she asked. Cora didn't know what to say. Being underground in that mine was the worst experience she had ever had. They had gone through so much together: risking expulsion from Vassar, Minnie rescuing Cora from flunking German, Cora comforting Minnie during her illicit romance and heartbreak—and then sharing Minnie's happy reconciliation with Charlie Eastmeade, who had finally consented to becoming officially engaged. But now Minnie, the little mouse, the humble calico girl who had risen to become an academic leader of the class of '87, had boldly shown Cora what visceral fear felt like. Cora looked at the sunlight in the treetops and felt the fresh breeze against her face. She did not say it, but she hoped Minnie would never make that trip underground again.

AS WAS USUAL with the Davenport *Gazette's* social notes, the information about Cora's family trip following her graduation was socially exaggerated—I know that she did not spend two months touring the fashionable resorts of the East Coast with her parents because according to Mrs. Dr. Keck's advertisements, she was back at work in Iowa by mid-July. During the long trip back to Davenport, Cora pressed her face against the glass of the Pullman car windows and gazed at the rolling farmland, lost in contemplation of the landscape outside. The wind braided the tops of the grasses in silver patterns, and the land was incandescent with powerful late afternoon sunlight. Gray clouds banked up high above them, casting dark shadows across the steel rails stretching behind them. The weather was huge, watchful, powerful, and unpredictable. Then, as the sun slipped below the western horizon, all the glory blinked out and disappeared. When her parents had gone west in the 1830s as pioneers, this landscape had been an open vista of freedom and opportunity. Now Cora was returning to their small, raw-edged Midwestern city oppressed with the feeling that she needed to escape. Even after two years at Vassar, she still did not have an exit strategy.

Swaying back and forth on the red plush seats, rubbing occasional cinders out of her eyes, Cora had her parents' full attention to herself. What did they say to each other, and what did they leave unsaid? Miss Chapin believed in her. Professor Braunlich believed in her. Did her parents care as much about her talent as these two magnificent teachers did? What might a strict Methodist like Mrs. Dr. Keck think of letting her daughter travel to Germany to live among strangers in order to take her talent to the next level? Who ever said she should have a career outside of the family business? Who would go with her? Cora certainly could not do it on her own, and she wouldn't have wanted to; she still couldn't speak more than a few sentences in German, despite all the tutoring that Minnie Keiter had given her, and she could hardly do enough arithmetic to keep track of her monthly allowance at school. Someone would have to manage the business side of things and provide her with companionship.

Would Belle drop her real-estate investments and her mother's medical business to work with Cora? Of course not. She wouldn't even do that for her own husband's career. Lotta was equally embroiled with running the Kecks' Chicago real-estate investments and trying to start a family of her own, and she had a husband building up his fledgling medical practice in Chicago. Florence? That was a silly question. And what might a fond, old-fashioned Mennonite papa think of his little girl leaving home to possibly perform onstage in front of strangers in a foreign country?

Cora's parents would have believed they had her best interests in mind when they delivered their crushing decision: Cora would not travel to Germany to pursue her future as a musician. No one would disagree that building a career as a professional musician in the nineteenth century extracted severe sacrifices from women, who had to put aside every pleasure and safeguard of a regular life in their quest for professional credibility and maybe, just maybe, if they were extremely lucky, for fame. Cora's passionately sociable nature, her emotional vulnerability, and her energetic longing for marriage might not have been a good fit for this kind of sacrifice, either then or in any era. "It's a rough life being a musician, whether you are a man or a woman. Period," observed Doriot Dwyer, a professional flautist who was also the great-great-niece of Susan B. Anthony.[2]

But Cora's resentment and frustration began to build.

CORA KEPT HER VASSAR DIARY close that summer and revisited her time in college page by page in the hot humid rooms of the Wilson Hotel, where she stayed with her mother in Webster City, Iowa, for about a week in July. Miles of hot, flat cornfields and wheat fields, oats, potatoes and sorghum, timothy and grasses stretched to the horizon in every direction from the tiny downtown baking in the sun; trains came and left at the small station several times a day, bringing in patients from far-flung farms and taking them home again, and Cora must have wished that she could climb the steps and get on the train back East many times. She probably felt as if she had transferred from Vassar to another planet.

Her older sisters, Belle and Lotta, were usually the efficient and businesslike ones who helped Mrs. Dr. Keck at her branch offices. According to the Cedar Rapids newspaper, Charlotte Dorn had recovered from the bad fall she took down the hotel stairs back in May ("All will be pleased to learn that her daughter Mrs. Dorn, who is business manager for her mother, has entirely recovered from the accident and illness through which she passed while in our city last spring"), but perhaps Lotta was in Chicago with her husband and trying to get pregnant and Cora was filling in for her in Webster City.

Maybe Cora wanted to experience her mother's relationship with the patients and with her healing practices at first hand, to try to regain confidence in the integrity of her family's business after hearing so many disparaging remarks about patent medicine hucksters from her sophisticated acquaintances in New York. I have no doubt that she was concerned about this, because she saved an editorial endorsement of her mother's business tucked into an envelope in the back of her diary:

Dr. Mrs. Keck, the well known lady physician finishes to-day another, and a very successful, visit to Webster City, and leaves this afternoon for Davenport. Hamilton County contains many men and women who may well bless the name of Mrs. Keck. She has been instrumental in performing cures in cases where hope of relief had almost fled. Many such cases might be cited. But Mrs. Keck's reputation as a skilled healer of disease is not confined to our surroundings. It is widespread. It has been earned by hard honest work, and by the same will be sustained and added to. The lady has The Tribune's best wishes for success wherever she may be.

Cora's mother, who was no fool, would have invited her wildest daughter along on the business trip in order to keep close tabs on her. Cora's dreams of traveling to Europe for further piano study had just been dashed to the ground—who knows what kind of trouble she might have dreamed up to fill the hole left by that disappointment? She had nothing else to occupy her over the summer.

How much did Cora accept her mother's control without open complaint? No direct evidence survives, except for one subtle thing I discovered in her second, largest scrapbook. At some point after Cora returned home, she came across the loose "Girl of the Period" clipping in a box of college mementos, and she went to a lot of trouble to replace it in her second

Tintype of Cora Keck (center) playing banjo with two friends.

scrapbook, taping it back into the same gaping hole in the page where she had angrily cut it out while she was still at Vassar. Right next to it, she pasted the glowing *New York Times* review of her final recital, in which her performance was described as "The Gem of the Evening." "So there!" she must have said under her breath; "here is direct proof that I am not a useless parlor ornament." She glued in a second copy of the "gem" review at the beginning of the scrapbook, just to be sure people would see it.

MUSIC AT VASSAR COLLEGE.

THE ANNUAL SOIRÉE ATTRACTS A LARGE NUMBER OF THE PUPILS' FRIENDS.

POUGHKEEPSIE, June 7. — The annual soirée musicale at Vassar College this evening was under the directorship of Dr. F. L. Ritter of the School of Music. The college corridors previous to the doors of the chapel being opened, were thronged with ladies and gentlemen, and the drawing rooms, parlors, and reception rooms were brilliant with groups of parents, relatives, and friends of the pupils, among them being J. M. Ferris, General Manager of the Toledo and Ohio Central Railroad, and a party of ladies. They came here on a special car and will remain three days to witness the graduation of Miss E. A. Ferris. The musical programme this evening consisted of 11 pieces, opening with Schumann's Blumenstück by Miss Irene Co-rate Hunter Hines, of Kittrell, N. C. The gem of the evening was the Wagner Lisset. march from Tannhäuser by Miss Corizze Mae Keck, of Davenport, Iowa, and next to it was the rendition by Miss Georgine Hamilton Peck Hayman, of Poughkeepsie, of Moszkowski's Tarantelle, Susie Robinson Orton, of Poughkeepsie, daughter of Prof. Orton, formerly of the college, gave Leschetizky's nocturne very correctly and with true sentiment, and was heartily applauded. Caroline Augusta Rabe, daughter of ex-Senator Rabe, of New-Jersey, played Chopin's Bolero op. 18 with great aplomb. Rosa Gwendoline Goldstine performed Chopin's nocturne opus 15 and étude G flat very sweetly and with full understanding. Miss Harriet Taylor Thurston, daughter of Prof. Thurston, of Cornell University, sang two pieces with organ accompaniment with very fine effect. Annie Grace Proctor, of Ogdensburg, and ——— of New-York, the former a splendid alto and the latter a clear soprano, delighted all present with "The Angel" from Rubinstein, and "Non So Spugar," from Jotti, and were applauded to the echo. Alice Amy Brewster, of Hudson, Ohio, rendered Mendelssohn's capriccio opus 33, No. 1 very clearly and very correctly. It was evident from the generous applause from the audience that the listeners considered every piece on the programme a gem in its way.

After the concert there was more chatting and promenading for a brief period, which closed the evening's enjoyments. To-morrow is Class Day. All the hotels are filled with people who have come to participate in the various annual exercises. The annual meeting of the Board of Trustees will also occur to-morrow, and there may be some business transacted which will have an important bearing on the future government of the college. For nearly a year there have been rumors that the Trustees are in favor of retiring Maria Mitchell from the Astronomy Department and having astronomy taught by the Professor of Mathematics. Also, there has been talk of abolishing the position of Lady Principal. In the School of Music it has been suggested that a Professor of Vocal Music be appointed, and in the Language Department a Professor of Modern Languages. Should such changes be made the departure will be quite radical.

The Girl of the Period.

From the Cincinnati Enquirer.

The girl of to-day is raised up in the parlor to be an ornament and nothing more. She knows nothing of the kitchen; the place is a death-trap to her. She knows nothing of the art of cookery, and never proposes to learn the art, except circumstances force her to it; as, for instance, she marries some young blood who turns out to be poorer than a church mouse, and therefore she has to do without a cook. Then she goes into the kitchen, and, with a good deal of grunting and finger-burning, manages to scare up a meal barely fit for a dog. The girl of to-day belongs to the parlor. You can always find her there when she is not lying abed or shooting through the principal streets—shopping. Her education consists of a few lessons in grammar, Latin, music, and drawing. She completes nothing. A year after she graduates she remember nothing but her school flirtations. As a musician she is a nuisance. She studies music not as an art, but as an accomplishment. The result is that she not only succeeds in murdering music, but the poor victims who are often compelled to listen to her are made sufferers, too. She can dance, she can flirt, she can make love as no other girl in this wide world can, but when we have said that we have said all that can possibly be said in her favor. She is beautiful, charming, and almost interesting, but she is a mere ornament and nothing more. If you can afford to build a fine house, furnish it with rich and costly furniture, keep horses and carriages, and a groom to keep them in order, by all means marry the girl of to-day. She can spend your money as the girl of no other country can. She can play the queen to perfection, and will not only master your household affairs, but will master you. But if you are poor, keep away from her. You cannot help falling in love with her, but study well the expense you will be forced into in case you make her your wife. If you see you can't well make both ends meet, can't keep her and the hired girl, too, then take our advice and marry the hired girl.

Page from Cora's scrapbook: the 1886 New York Times review praising Cora's graduation recital as the "gem of the evening" (at left) pasted next to the "Girl of the Period" rant by Mrs. Linton that Belle sent Cora in March 1885 (at right).

I don't believe that giving up her piano performances was Cora's choice. She had been practicing between four and five hours a day for the better part of two years and had risen to a dominant position in a competitive conservatory program. I don't believe that she was happy to revert to her youthful pattern of indolent practice routines and endless rounds of partying with her blue-collar friends and small-town strivers. Vassar had changed her. She was once again drifting, but this time, having once tasted the freedom of a fully lived life, she was aware that she was sinking back underground. Society, in cahoots with Cora's family, appeared eager to stick her into a mouse hole for forty years or so with nothing to do. In his great nineteenth-century social critique of modern mediocrity, *Notes from Underground*, the Russian author Fyodor Dostoyevsky realized that the worst temptation facing all "underground dwellers" in Western Civilization, male and female alike, is to surrender to the power of conscious inertia.

I PAGED THROUGH Cora's scrapbooks over and over, searching for traces of her piano playing after she left Vassar. But among the hundreds of souvenirs she saved relating to her activities in Davenport between her graduation in 1886 and her marriage in 1889, I found only three programs that listed Cora performing in front of other people. I was astounded. There was something very sad, almost desperate, about the many duplicate copies of each program she saved from the tiny list of unimpressive appearances she made. She gave one private musical performance at her home in the summer of 1886 for her friends immediately after she returned from Vassar, and then did nothing more until she played a short number in a charitable fund-raising concert in November 1887. Then in the fall of 1888 she played a few simple banjo pieces at a church fund-raiser. She also played a brief wedding processional at her friend Ida Heinley's marriage to George Purdy in Muscatine. What happened to the courageous performer of conspicuously difficult Liszt showpieces who could play "as well as the musicians of New York City"?

Davenport was a musical city, and public performances by young classical musicians were happening all over town during these years. She could have had plenty of invitations to play in recitals that her teacher Professor Braunlich organized on a regular basis for his friends and students, female as well as male, at the Masonic Hall, the German Turner Hall, and other major venues in Davenport that were announced and reviewed in the *Davenport Gazette*. Cora's friend Bert Brockett's mother had a beautiful alto voice and sang operatic songs at the Turner Hall with Jacob Strasser's musicians in concerts organized by Charlie Meier's father. Multiple musical societies that welcomed both men and women met weekly all over town; many society hosts entertained their friends with home musicales that were also reported in the paper. A Davenport Music Students' Club was organized in the winter of 1884, but Cora does not seem to have been a part of this musical world in a way that meant enough for her to save a memento from it.

This sparse list of performances between 1886 and 1889 supports my guess that Cora's mama forbade her to play in public. The social stigma of Mrs. Dr. Keck's medical business undoubtedly also played a part in excluding Cora from Davenport's active musical scene, since amateur musical events were as much social gatherings as they were performances. Professor Braunlich's oldest son Henry received his M.D. from New York's Bellevue Medical College and opened a medical and surgical practice in Davenport in 1883; he quickly became an influential member of the Scott County Medical Society, and this affiliation between the Braunlich family and Mrs. Dr. Keck's professional enemies might have chilled Cora's ability to participate in her teacher's student recitals. She could not move ahead with her music in public—not in Europe, not in the United States, not even in her own hometown. Only inside her house, under her family's strict supervision.

Forward momentum from college carried Cora along for a while during her first months at home. After returning from Webster City, she organized her private musicale at the Keck mansion with Hattie, who was living in Davenport with her new husband Albert. At last, Cora was finally going to be able to impress Albert's brother Oscar with her musical skills. Hattie invited a violinist from Springfield, Missouri, named Etta Peck. (She was not related to Dr. Washington F. Peck, the nationally known surgeon and next-door neighbor on Brady Street whose name was always being mixed up with Mrs. Dr. Keck's name in the social notes of the Davenport *Gazette*). The Davenport zither club was present and "produced some very fine music," and the audience enthusiastically demanded that Miss Etta Peck "repeat some of her selections," while Miss Keck performed "several beautiful and very difficult pieces on the piano." Albert's older brother Oscar played a cornet solo that was "one of the features of the evening."

Unfortunately, Oscar fell for Etta Peck's violin encores, not Cora's piano fireworks, and he married Etta a year later in a ceremony to which Cora was not invited. It was a disastrous disappointment for Cora. The two brothers, Oscar and Albert Brady, soon moved their families to New York, and both began working for *McClure's*, taking up precisely the kind of sophisticated big-city life Cora would have liked for herself, on the Upper West Side of Manhattan, near Kitty Rogers and her family, while Cora was left behind in Iowa.

AFTER THAT SETBACK, Cora pursued a round of social events where she played only a supporting role, attending a musicale given by Hattie's sister Gussy Eddy at the Unitarian church in Bloomington, Illinois (where Cora did not perform), and the Thanksgiving marriage of Ida's sister Laura Heinley and Mr. W. G. Jones in Muscatine, Iowa, in which Cora's cousin-by-marriage Kitty Strauss from Allentown was maid of honor and Cora was "second maid of honor." On October 17, she sent her sister Belle a telegram from Bloomington: "send for Tuesday pink satin [gown] key is in lower bureau drawer." It was the dress she had worn for the Founder's Day cotillion at Vassar when she had heard Mark Twain. She traveled again with her mother to help with patients, spending a few days at the Tremont House in Quincy, Illinois, where the paid announcements about Mrs. Dr. Keck's visit that Cora clipped from the local papers included two completely false facts about her time at Vassar. She was supposedly "appointed to the high honor of marshal of her class" and "a friend of Miss Nettie Osborn, of this city, who is still at the school." Did Cora's mother supply the newspaper with this blarney? Did Cora? Court documents from Urbana, Illinois, reveal that Cora's mother then appeared in court to plead not guilty immediately after her regular Quincy visit, and Cora might have traveled with her mother to attend this trial, which would be drawn out by legal maneuvers orchestrated by Mrs. Dr. Keck's lawyer, Mr. Coy, for three years.

CORA CONTINUED TO FOLLOW events at Vassar from a distance, but the most dramatic Vassar-related news broke closer to home. In January 1887, one of Cora's classmates, Nina Van Zandt, electrified the nation by marrying August Spies, one of the condemned Haymarket bombers, by proxy in a prison wedding in Chicago. News of the pending nuptials broke unexpectedly on January 15th, and the *Daily Inter Ocean* wrote that Nina had "achieved fame in the short space of twenty-four hours in consequence of the announcement." She was the privileged only daughter of a soap manufacturer and chemist whose respectable Dutch ancestors had arrived on Long Island in the 1600s, and just to make the story even more tabloid-friendly, she stood to inherit almost half a million dollars from an elderly aunt on her mother's side. Why was this well-bred college girl marrying a barbarian, a foreigner, an anarchist, and a murderer?

Spies had been arrested in early May 1886 during the citywide round-up of prominent anarchists that followed Chicago's tragic Haymarket bombing and riot of May 4, an event of sensational national news that I am presuming Cora had discussed with her friends during her birthday collation with Cyrus Field Judson and the other Yalies "of the capitalist class" at Vassar. Along with six others, Spies was tried for murder and conspiracy during fifty-four days in July and August; despite a lack of evidence tying them to the actual bomb, five of the defendants were condemned to death in October. The Haymarket trial, described as "a show trial" in which "visceral feelings of fear and anger . . . ruled out anything but the pretense of justice right from the outset," was the news sensation of the decade and drew attention to Chicago's violent labor troubles from around the world; even Karl Marx's daughter and son-in-law arrived from England to visit the prisoners.[3]

Nina had started at Vassar a year before Cora as a Prep Level I but dropped out after her freshman year in June 1885. During the long, hot summer of 1886, she apparently had very little to occupy her time besides caring for her nine dogs. Along with several other young society women who were drawn into the courtroom drama, Nina first visited the trial escorted by one of her mother's friends from the Fourth Presbyterian Church, both attending as guests of Judge Gary.[4] Expecting the bombers to be "a rare collection of stupid, vicious, and criminal-looking men," as they had been portrayed in the mainstream press, Nina was startled to discover that in the flesh, they "had intelligent, kindly and good faces . . . I became interested."[5] As she listened to the legal theatrics, she became convinced that the accused were innocent of the charges made against them, and "desirous of discovering how I could serve those rendered helpless," she began to visit the men in jail. One thing led to another. Spies was handsome, charismatic, well-educated, unmarried, and in mortal danger. "My sympathy . . . gradually developed into a strong affection," Nina wrote in her preface to *Spies' Autobiography* that she helped him to write and then had privately printed around the time of their proxy marriage in January 1887.

Courtesy of the Chicago History Museum.

Nina's family was sympathetic to her involvement with the prisoners. As Nina's connection to August deepened, Mrs. Van Zandt grew closer to Spies's family, particularly his mother, Christine, and his sister, Gretchen, who often accompanied Nina on her jailhouse visits. The detailed press coverage gave readers in Davenport and across the nation many personal details of the affair. A *Tribune* reporter leafing through the Van Zandt's family photo albums in their front parlor spotted cabinet portraits of Christine and Gretchen, as well as a large medallion of Spies's profile hanging in a prominent spot over the mantelpiece. So it is less amazing to learn that Mr. and Mrs. Van Zandt publicly supported their daughter's decision to marry the condemned man. Working among the poor was "a sort of religion with all of us," Mrs. Van Zandt explained to a reporter.[6]

On January 16, Nina and August both still believed that the press "has been very just and kind" in describing their plans to marry. But public opinion quickly turned against them, and reporters began to horsewhip the entire family. News editorials in the Chicago *Daily Tribune* and the *Inter Ocean* thundered that the engagement was "a farce," that Spies was an unscrupulous libertine who was using Nina to gain sympathy, and that she was a deluded, superficial, "blue-blooded pest" and publicity-seeker. The mayor of Chicago called Nina "a fool," her parents were vilified, headlines crowed the news that she had been "disowned and disinherited" by her rich aunt, she received death threats, and a mob attacked the Van Zandt's elegant home on Huron Street near Lake Shore Drive, shouting obscenities and throwing rocks to break the windows while Nina and her mother cowered inside.[7] Speaking of her daughter's love for Spies, Mrs. Van Zandt admitted to a reporter, "The process was so gradual, we didn't see the conscquences clearly."[8]

Nina Stuart Van Zandt Spies. August Spies kept a copy of this portrait in his prison cell. Courtesy of the Chicago History Museum.

Vassar reacted promptly and firmly to the exploding public relations disaster. A reporter in Poughkeepsie interviewed "one of the authorities at Vassar College" on January 19, no doubt at the invitation of the college. Because the source had worked at Wilson College in Pennsylvania in 1880, it is certain that the spokeswoman was Miss Goodsell, who had been Lady Principal at Wilson before coming to Vassar. Who better than Miss Goodsell to handle a mess like this? President Taylor did not wish to dignify the situation by speaking about it himself. Coldly and politely, Miss Goodsell pushed the young lady as far beyond the college's perimeter as possible, stating that she knew Nina to be "ill-balanced and eccentric" and that after she dropped out after her freshman year, "we all felt that we had been relieved of a great responsibility." Then twisting the knife, she added, "her mother was a sweet little woman, but when mother and daughter were together, the daughter held the controlling power." Willful and unpredictable, Nina simply couldn't make the grade at Vassar, according to Miss Goodsell. Except for the widespread misstatement that Nina was a Vassar graduate, nothing more appeared in the press about her college connections. With one paragraph, Miss Goodsell curbed all further lurid inquiries about the girl, clear evidence of her executive skill and loyalty to the college's good reputation.

Cora clipped an item regarding the dramatic romance that had the headline "Save the Crazy Creature": "Something ought to be done to prevent that poor deluded Vassar College girl from marrying Spies, the Anarchist. The best place for her would probably be a home for weak-minded women. May be there is no such institution. Then a common lunatic asylum would answer the purpose well." I don't know what Cora thought about Nina's radical politics or about the reporter's negative commentary on female independence. Unfortunately, she didn't write a comment next to the clipping. The cruelly mocking tone of the journalist's prose echoes the sneers in the many antifeminist Vassar jokes that Cora clipped from newspapers. For Victorian girls, marrying the wrong person was by far the most effective way to rile up the authorities, no matter what the context, and the penalties for this were severe. "Had I married an old invalid debauché with great riches," Nina wrote in her preface, "these moral gentlemen [of the press]" would have "called me a very sensible girl" and "*so* sweet." As a single girl, back in October, no one had paid any attention to a heartfelt article Nina wrote about Spies and her belief in his innocence that she tried to place in the *Philadelphia Inquirer*, but after her proxy marriage, she made the headlines in Philadelphia week after week. Nina had taken action against what she perceived to be a gross injustice, but to her dismay, the reporters ignored her ideas and whipped up public shame to drive her back into Dostoyevsky's obedient underground of "conscious inertia."

I find the clipping notable because Nina's dilemma of what to do with herself after leaving Vassar highlights Cora's own dilemma: Vassar was supposed to give her firm opinions—was she going to waste her Vassar education as well as her life? She could practice piano as much as she wanted inside her mother's mansion, but without standing up against the forces that wanted to contain her within its walls and without risking her safe and secure existence in some way, she would never have a life of her own. But any independent action she might use to break away could bring real danger. Nina had shown her idealism, strong will, and tenacity using the only way open to her, through marriage to Spies, but look at how she was being publicly punished!

BY APRIL 1887, Minnie Keiter was nearly done with her senior year and expecting to graduate in June. Cora made plans to go to Poughkeepsie for the occasion, and Minnie planned to visit Cora in Davenport during the summer. During spring break, Minnie invited her academic rival, Verlista Shaul, to St. Clair. Once again, Minnie's friend Harry Short arranged an excursion to the Chamberlain Colliery, the same one that Cora had visited with Harry and Minnie the previous June. An unnamed young reporter who knew Harry Short and Minnie Keiter stepped in to write up the subsequent events for *Splinters*:

Accident in mine at the Chamberlain Colliery occurred

MONDAY, APRIL 11, 1887.

Dead: Verlista Shaul (of Sharon Springs, New York, & Valedictorian of class of '87), Harry Short, and Minnie Keiter (of St. Clair, Pennsylvania, a senior in Vassar's class of '87).

The Wind of Death

. . . The visit was to be made to the big vein where they were all confident there was no gas, but . . . an escaping "tail" of fire-damp or gas came from the door ahead of them and hovered over their heads, and one of the naked lamps was raised sufficiently high to reach this "tailing." Quick as lightning's flash the flame reached the body of gas at the face of the gangway, one hundred and fifty yards away; back came the dread "blow" with all the force and velocity of cannon balls which all miners fear even more than they do the roasting fire. In this case, the fire did but little damage, but the blow made sad havoc.

Edwin saw for only the sixtieth part of a second a ball of fire like a quickly falling meteor and then all was blank to him. He had been hurled from his feet by the terrible cyclone of gas and dashed to the ground where he lay unconscious. Meanwhile, Daniel Thompson, his brother Albert, in one part of the mine, and George Frantz in another, felt the wind of the explosion and realized at once that something serious had occurred. They soon came upon Minnie Keiter, a bruised and bleeding mass, begging to be taken home as she was dying . . . they immediately set to work to get the suffering victims out, fully cognizant of the fact that they must make all possible haste to escape the poisonous after-damp.

Teams were procured and the poor victims were hauled home. . . . On the way, Miss Shaul laid perfectly quiet, bearing her agony with remarkable courage, but Miss Keiter's injuries were beyond all endurance and her excruciating pain made her scream so that she could be heard a square away. Those terrible screams from the dying girl carried horror to all who heard them and brought back from the hearts of all the most earnest sympathy. . . .

Dr. Carr examined three of the victims and found that Miss Keiter had sustained a compound comminuted fracture of the left thigh, with one of the bones protruding fully six inches; a completely crushed ankle with the left foot hanging by but a few shreds of flesh; several serious burns on the face and hands, several ugly scalp wounds and a very bad fracture of the skull. He gave no hope whatever for her recovery. . . .

Cora felt the shock from the terrible news like a blow to her own body. She couldn't shake the image from her head of her friend, broken into pieces, being loaded into a mining wagon and carted through the center of town in public agony. She herself easily could have shared the same fate as Minnie and Harry (Verlista eventually recovered from her injuries, despite the newspaper declaring her dead); she remembered the bright flame in the miner's lamp she had worn the year before and was chilled by the thought that she might have passed only inches beneath some other tail of firedamp. She was probably racked by unnecessary remorse about her relationship with Minnie. How much of Minnie's college education had she sidetracked with their off-campus social activities? How much of Minnie's superior intelligence had been wasted on superficial schemes that now seemed uselessly small and childish? Minnie should have been the candidate for class valedictorian, not Verlista Shaul. Lying to college authorities was nothing close to a fatal day; being blown to pieces underground set everything into perspective. Life underground had literally destroyed Minnie.

Cora clipped local news items that she saved along with ones friends in St. Clair had mailed to her out in Davenport:

Page from Cora's scrapbook: "Minnie Keiter, killed in a mine at St. Clair, Pennsylvania."

The unfortunate Miss Keiter, who was killed in the mine explosion in Pottsville Pennsylvania last Monday was the bosom friend of Miss Corize Keck, who is a daughter of Dr. Keck of Davenport, and is stricken with grief.

Miss Keiter, who was killed in the mine explosion in Pennsylvania, mentioned in yesterday's [Davenport] Times was the Vassar "chum" of Miss Corize Keck of this city, who was graduated that institution last year. Miss Keck last year descended the same mines without accident, and deeply mourns the death of her friend who had arranged to visit her this coming summer.

Shortly after the disaster, a friend wrote this haunting sentence in Cora's autograph album: "Cora, She died, she died. Max"

The news of the explosion also reverberated through the halls of Vassar's Main Building. Louisa Poppenheim wrote about the accident to her mother on April 14, recapping many of the technical details that were reported in the press and describing with startling coldness how she and her classmates reacted to the tragedy: "The senior class immediately sent a great many roses and white lilies to the family. Everybody feels terribly about it especially as Miss Keiter had so few friends. I think I may say that she had but one friend in College."[9] That's quite a statement. After the Vassar Trio broke up and Cora and Lydia Day left college in June 1886, Minnie may have had fewer friends on campus, but it is hard for me to believe that she had none besides Verlista Shaul, who was presumably the one friend Loulu was referring to. Or was she thinking specifically of Cora Keck? It's likely that Loulu didn't condescend to mix with the academically gifted calico girls who would have been Minnie's friends, but she seemed to know exactly whom she meant to indicate with her pointed remark. The college administration did not award Minnie a posthumous diploma but crossed out her name in black on the commencement programs, which had already been printed.

After this blow, two more years of home life in Davenport rolled by. Cora sank farther and farther into comfortable mediocrity, slipping underground into a half-lived life while all the pride she had developed at Vassar gradually evaporated in the glare of the Midwestern sun. Increasingly rigid and confining patterns of emotional life that would characterize the twentieth century were already emerging in towns like Davenport in the 1880s. Fast-paced and practical; focused on money, social hierarchies, and raw politics—the new order, to many perceptive writers and observers who lived through these changes, seemed to choke off spontaneous and intuitive human feelings. Everyone from Sinclair Lewis to Sherwood Anderson to Upton Sinclair to D. H. Lawrence thought civilization was going to hell in a hand basket in the brave new world that Cora was set to enter as a young woman. Many of these men got famous in part by suggesting that sexual desire was the only escape route left.

Cora took up the banjo, spent time with her old flame Bert Brockett the telegraph boy, and briefly dated a dentist and a railroad express agent. "The piano may do for love-sick girls who lace themselves to skeletons, and lunch on chalk, pickles and slate pencils, but give me the banjo," remarked Mark Twain enthusiastically about the grand new fad for plinking that was sweeping the country.[10] I have to disagree with Mr. Twain; like Ko-Ko, the Lord High Executioner in *The Mikado*, who had banjo players high on his list for head chopping, I can do without them.

In the winter of 1889, a new family scandal erupted into the public eye for the amusement of the multitude of Davenport residents who disliked the Kecks. The grain dealers Dixon, Reed & Co. took Cora's brother-in-law William R. H. Alexander to court to force him to repay the ninety-day promissory note for $200 he had signed to six years before; now he owed Dixon $335 plus 10 percent interest. William argued that he should not have to pay because Dixon "well knew that all parties were engaged in illegal and gambling transactions for the fictitious value of grain . . . and prays to be dismissed with his costs."[11] Beyond this tantalizing fragment of legal equivocation, the file does not reveal the outcome of the case. Belle was so disgusted by her husband's messy legal problems that she refused to accompany him to Washington, D.C., two months later in March, where he had been sent to cover the inauguration of President Benjamin Harrison for one of the Davenport papers. Then, in August, the Scott County Medical Society hastily convened a special meeting to protest a move by the Iowa State Board of Medical Examiners to issue certificates to two women physicians practicing in Davenport, Mrs. Dr. Keck and Mrs. Dr. Stella Nichols, as they were "incompetent and unqualified to practice the art of medicine."[12] Mrs. Dr. Nichols disappeared from the city business directories, but not the immovably stubborn Mrs. Dr. Keck, who was still determined to establish her legitimacy as a practicing physician and would not give up her claim.

Cora yearned for contact with her college friends. Kitty mailed Cora a newspaper clipping from the *New York Daily Graphic* about a massive fund-raiser her mother had organized for the Manhattan Hospital, now proudly installed at 131st Street and Tenth Avenue in the new building that had been paid for by Rogers family fund-raising. Kitty and her sisters Dolly and Mame wore gypsy costumes and helped to auction off the famous $1,000 life-size portrait of the British singing sensation, the actress Lily Langtry, done in point-crayon by the artist Charles Frederick Naegele. Cora took this society clipping with her everywhere; she pinned and unpinned it from walls at least eight times. In November, she received more bad news by mail that I learned about only later from the parish ledgers of St. Mary's Church in West Harlem. Kitty must have written to Cora in the fall that her uncle Nick Rogers was ill with tuberculosis. Five days before Christmas, Cora's biggest college crush, the dashing sporting man, grain dealer, bachelor about town, and owner of the No. 2000 trotting horse, died of consumption at the age of thirty-four and was buried in St. Mary's churchyard.[13]

Meanwhile, Mrs. Dr. Keck kept her boisterous daughter close by her side during the fall, and they spent almost a month together in Chicago in October. Did her mother realize how much Cora doubted her competence in medical matters? Nothing musical or romantic happened, since Cora did not save any souvenirs from this trip, and she would have if she had collected anything worth saving in her own personal estimation. I wonder whether Mrs. Dr. Keck was trying again to interest Cora in working in the family business in a more serious way. She desperately needed a competent assistant and devoted disciple to carry on her medical theories after she retired. (Belle was not stepping into the role of doctor's protégée being offered to her and listed herself as a physician for only a single year in the *Davenport Business Directory*, in 1889.) If so, it was a futile effort; Cora was not only a doubter of her mother's expertise, she was a musician, not a doctor or a business manager, and she could not forget her dreams of a glamorous life in a big city far from Davenport and away from her mother's overbearing presence.

CHAPTER TWENTY-EIGHT

Cora's Heart's Desire

S o it happened that three years after graduating from Vassar, Cora found herself standing on the dark platform of Chicago's La Salle Street Station with the icy wind off Lake Michigan whipping around her ankles on a raw December evening, waiting for her exit strategy to show up. No one knew where she was except that one man. The wrinkled telegram balled up inside her glove said that the train coming in from Elkhart, Indiana, on the Lake Shore & Michigan Southern Line would bring him into the same station five minutes before her. Now it was twenty minutes to eight and too late for her to catch another train back to Davenport before the next day.

Cora suddenly thought about her family and felt a stab of panic. She pictured her mother's face as she discovered the note in her empty bedroom. "Oh! u wretch!" she fretted, thinking of all the things she had ever done to wrong her mother. What about her secret visits to Dr. Bulkley, in New York City? She had never come clean on that one. Now she was lying to everyone who loved her and openly defying her mother by risking a public scandal worse than any of the worst things any of her siblings had ever done, something that could seriously damage her mother's reputation if it went wrong. Mrs. Dr. Keck had developed a formidable reputation as a person of consequence specifically by quashing her own scandals by sheer force of personality to contradict widespread accusations that she was an uneducated charlatan. No one defied her without taking the consequences. But Cora was doing exactly that. Her whole future hung in the balance.

The thinning crowd of travelers revealed an empty platform covered with paper scraps and cigarette butts frozen into thousands of splatters of chewing tobacco "expectorations." Cora pulled the hem of her dress away from a half-eaten piece of pork pie squashed by a boot print. The dismal scene increased her anxiety. The problem with John Cook was that he was a man with a reputation. During his married life, he had been a handsome wanderer with a taste for taking long, profitable business trips to cities from New York to San Francisco that lasted for months or even years, while his first wife, Martha, entered a sour-looking middle age alone at home. After she died in 1881, John Cook took off on a new series of adventures, taking in the sights of Europe twice on the Grand Tour and visiting Havana in the summer of 1886 for several weeks with four male friends, an outing they commemorated with a cheap tintype taken in an open-air vendor's shed. A merry widower, Mr. Cook undoubtedly enjoyed plenty of delightful female companionship wherever he went without having to marry for it.

John Cook at about age forty in San Francisco, ca. 1865, the year of Cora's birth.

Cora thought about her available options if Mr. Cook broke his promise and her plans to elope fell apart; she would be in trouble immediately because she knew that her sister Lotta was out of town in Peoria. If she dropped in on her brother-in-law Gay, she would have to explain what she was doing in Chicago by herself and "once found, she would be lost." As a young, unmarried woman traveling alone in the nineteenth century, Cora could not safely check into a hotel, even if she had brought enough money to do so. To rub in the sordid aspects of her situation, an insolent masher with his bowler hat cocked back on his head was circling her; he whistled loudly and slowed down to examine Cora's bodice and the curves of her whale-boned waist. Cora braved up immediately. She wasn't bothered by mashers—in fact she liked to push them around and leave them confused. It was one of her favorite games. She gave the lout a wilting glare of boredom and then a focused sneer; to her satisfaction, he hesitated, then slithered away, slightly cowed. She smiled to herself and lifted her chin. She would choose her own course in life from now on.

She recalled with pleasure the electric sensation she had felt in June when her gloved hand touched John Cook's arm for the first time as he helped her down after a morning horseback ride at the Crescent Hotel spa. That trip to Eureka Springs in the Ozarks in Arkansas was one of several projects she had arranged with her extremely

Tintype of John Cook (seated, right) in Havana, Cuba, with four friends in 1886.

plump and worldly friend Ida Purdy to get out of range of Mrs. Dr. Keck's overbearing supervision. Ida, who had gotten married a few months previously on Thanksgiving in 1888 to a prominent Republican in the Missouri legislature, played the role of chaperone. The hotel arranged daily horseback rides on rented nags for groups of guests. Tall guests were sometimes put onto short horses, and vice versa. Cora and the other ladies rode sidesaddle, and everyone posed for group photographs that the hotel sold to the guests. By arranging these images in a sequence, I could see Mr. Cook's horse getting closer and closer to Miss Keck's horse, until by the last one, he was staring right up at her in admiration.

At the end of one of these outings, the old gentleman standing by her stirrup must have offered Miss Keck a hand down from her horse. Then she would have noticed his deep-set, steel-colored eyes, relentless

Cora Keck (far right) and John Cook (next to her) at the Crescent Hotel in Eureka Springs, Arkansas, June 1889.

and hard, but framed with dangerous charm at the corners. He must have been in the audience at the hotel's Grand Concert the night before on June 29 and seen her play her Liszt piece from *Rigoletto*. She had dominated the show. He was another short man, but she could see that he evidently admired courage and daring in a woman. She knew he was a business associate of her mother's. And old—sixty-three!—and canny and powerful as he was, as soon as she slipped down from that tall bay saddle horse and touched his arm, she suddenly knew she could get him. She saw that he was a risk taker and that he wanted her.

Cora rubbed her numb, gloved hands together in the cold Chicago air. Her anxiety lifted, and she felt the strength of John Cook's passion as a physical presence in the high-ceilinged, smoky station, which now seemed filled with delectable energy. She couldn't believe it, but she had the upper hand. His age made him *grateful*. This was her pull over a powerful man, and the feeling was intoxicating. Cora glanced again at the clock at the end of the platform. The large hand ticked forward to 7:51.

The uncertainty was almost killing her, but she could feel his presence. It was like a supernatural connection. Then she saw him emerge from the smoky darkness at the end of the platform. They walked quickly toward each other, with their hearts on fire, blind to the world around them, blind to the future, and blind to the past. Intensely alive in the moment, they embraced their fate together.

It's tempting to imagine that they checked in for some spectacularly sinful hours in one of Chicago's fabulous luxury hotels such as the Palmer House, where Cora had often dined with her family on previous trips, but that would have been too public, too obvious, too risky. Both of them knew people in Chicago, and they could not be seen together under these circumstances. Even the desk clerks would know that they weren't married. The two lovers most likely slipped out of town in a horse-drawn hansom cab, crossing the Chicago River and traversing the Loop to the Union Depot to board another train for Milwaukee, where nobody knew who they were or cared. They were married in a Methodist Episcopal church there on Tuesday, December 10, with the minister's wife as a witness. That was clearly Cora's choice, because Cook was not a Methodist. "You're going to marry me, and this is where we will do it," she said.

CORA NEVER DESCRIBED her dramatic departure from the claustrophobic Keck household at 611 Brady Street in any of her diaries. Was she blocked by remorse or guilt? Or was she simply so deliriously happy about her passionate and sensual escape from personal atrophy that no record was needed? This empty page in the otherwise detailed documentation of her young adult years means that I have had to imagine the entire scenario.

Cora would have planned her getaway using railroad timetables. Thanks to their meticulous obsessions, modern train-watching railroad enthusiasts are only too happy to make imaginary ticket reservations for historical travelers on routes that stopped running 120 years ago, so I got Cora's travel plans by e-mail.[1] She didn't have that many options, so this scenario is probably pretty accurate.

On the morning of the day of her escape, she made some kind of excuse to stay at home, perhaps complaining to her mother of a severe headache, and sat down on the edge of her bed, listening from upstairs for the front door to close as everyone left for church. Ten eternal minutes passed while her mother and father and several older and younger siblings and in-laws rode the four blocks up the Brady Street hill to the Ninth Street Methodist Church in the family carriage. When she was sure that they were really gone, she hurried to make her own private departure from the household, her fingers shaking wildly as she fastened the silk frogs of her heavy overcoat. Snatching up her small valise, she slipped down the back stairs and out into the icy alley behind, turning downhill on Perry Street in the opposite direction, toward the bars and brothels of Bucktown. Cheerful irony was Cora's style, and she remarked to herself that while the rest of her family was going up to heaven, she was going downhill to hell. Ha-ha! She was actually headed to the railroad depot at Fourth and Perry streets, where she would catch her eleven o'clock train to Chicago.

As Cora settled into her seat and looked around nervously, her gaze might have fallen on a folded newspaper on the seat beside her; and there it was, right on the front page of the *Davenport Gazette*, brightly illuminated by a cold beam of Sunday-morning sunlight: the huge two-column advertisement for Mrs. Dr. Keck's Infirmary, illustrated with a large, flagrantly inaccurate engraving of her own house, located just a short walk from the Davenport depot at 611 Brady Street. Cora felt as if everyone on the train must be looking at her, and she shrank down into her seat cushions. If they only knew . . . maybe someone would recognize her. It was widely known in Davenport and elsewhere that Mrs. Dr. Keck had been trying for months to squelch the romance between her twenty-four-year-old daughter and an old-man banker in Indiana. Of course, the more Mrs. Dr. Keck tried to block them, the more the relationship gained momentum, while love's favorite ingredients, secrecy and danger, poured explosive fuel onto the flames.

SO WHO WAS THIS PERSON whom Cora had left her family behind for? My great-grandfather was born in Indiana in 1826, only ten years after it entered the union, when John Quincy Adams was president. This is a mind-bending thought for me to say out loud in 2012, almost two hundred years later. Mr. Cook was an original settler, the kind of person who in Davenport would not have socialized with the Keck family under any circumstances. Cora was marrying up, and no matter if she deceived her parents to do it, I know that they were certainly going to come around quickly once the deed was done. Her new husband was described in the wedding announcement published in Davenport as "a retired banker and possessed of his full proportion of the goods of this world." His Indiana obituaries described him as "one of Elkhart's foremost citizens" and "the very soul of honor." He had the plainest of names, John Cook. Although he was not related in any way to John P. Cook of Davenport, I'm sure that the coincidence that his name was the same as that of the socially exalted figure who built the Keck family mansion added to Cora's infatuation. Cora's Mr. Cook was a man widely respected by his colleagues in northern Indiana and Chicago for his business integrity and keen, self-educated intelligence. Unlike Cora's mother, he was not a notorious person; he was a well-known one. Although Cora thought she was leaving her mother behind, the old rule of thumb is that everyone, male and female alike, ends up marrying someone just like his or her mother, no matter how hard they try to avoid it. Unlike Mrs. Dr. Keck, John Cook was exceedingly respectable and socially prominent in his small city. But he was also, not surprisingly, someone who could naturally take over and start running Cora's life for her in a benevolent way.

Given his sixty-three years, Cora's new husband was a very old man for his era, which, according to the short newspaper notice in the *Davenport Gazette* about the elopement, was the main reason her parents opposed the match. Although not mentioned in the newspaper, his wandering habits during his first marriage must have been another, real concern.

John Cook's carefully staged wedding portrait taken a month after Cora's bolt from home makes him look extraordinarily well preserved: his clean shaven jaw still sharp, with a trim mustache, deep-set eyes, and abundant dark hair. I remember how as a little girl I was shown a copy framed on the wall in my father's office, and he struck me then as a youngish man with a pleasant face that was so sensitive it almost looked

Cora Keck's wedding portrait.

tender. Earlier likenesses taken when he was in his forties in New York and San Francisco when he was a commission merchant during the Civil War show the gaze of a powerful merchant and businessman, but his persona was evidently later softened by his May-December marriage.

Cora looks very solemn in her wedding picture. She holds a long white fan made of drooping ostrich feathers and wears an elegant silk dress clearly made for her by one of Chicago's finest dressmakers especially for the occasion—maybe the Parisian Suit Company that she mentioned to her sister Lotta in connection with a "standing bet" they made with each other a year later. Cora looks as if she is feeling the heat of her parents' anger at her for deceiving them and running away. Her gaze is level and courageous: "Co-determined," as her friend Fannie Clark had once written about her in the tintype book at Vassar. Some level of reconciliation with the Kecks had occurred, since she and Mr. C, as she

John Cook's wedding portrait.

usually called her husband, were visiting the Davenport area; they did not go to the family's regular photo studio, however, but to Rock Island, Illinois (just across the river from Davenport). Maybe they felt more comfortable staying in a hotel on the other side of the river, too. Well, the marital boat was launched. There was no going back now.

In February, Mr. Cook and his bride returned to the Crescent Hotel for several weeks during the mild Ozark winter. Another photograph of the newlyweds on horseback posed in front of the hotel porch shows them reliving the good times of their early courtship. Cora was always gathering up new friends, and she forged warm, close relationships with a group of young couples they met at the Crescent from St. Louis, Missouri, and Manistee, Michigan. In more nineteenth-century social media activity, they exchanged portraits of themselves and their young children and photographs of their magnificent tract mansions to put into each other's albums. Cora was the life of the party there too, as she had been at Vassar.

Cora probably became pregnant while she and her husband were at the Crescent, and so they returned home to Elkhart, Indiana, a place Cora hardly knew, to await the birth of their daughter.

My grandmother was born in Elkhart on November 9, 1890, and was immediately declared "the delight of the house" by Cora, who started keeping a diary again in honor of the occasion. Cora's baby journals proved tough for me to read—both parents were outrageously besotted by their love child: "She laid in her Papas arms so sweetly this morning in bed and we were quite happy as a little family." Every new baby is like every passionate love affair— at once supremely unique to the people involved, but mathematically only one of millions of similar events, which gives these precious activities a gloss of monotonous sentimentality to outside observers. That's a good

Cora holding her new baby.

thing for the baby, but a chore for anyone who has to read about cute baby nicknames, fractional weight gains, weekly "one-week" birthday celebrations, lists of baby presents, blow-by-blow reports on baby's first steps, and so on. What I liked best about these notations was discovering what a loving and competent mother Cora was. "I can hardly wait till she wakes up," she wrote about her child. That attitude is what every daughter might wish for from her mother.

Cora's family became completely reconciled to the new marriage quickly, no doubt because of the groom's "full proportion of the goods of this world," and her parents and siblings, with the exception of Flora, all traveled to Elkhart to visit the new granddaughter. Lotta came from Chicago when the baby was three days old and stayed for five weeks. Brother Willie showed up for a short visit and amused the baby by carrying her around and singing opera tunes to her in his basso voice while she played with his black beard and hair with her little fingers. Mrs.

Dr. Keck wrote a brief note in the diary to "My sweet Baby" on March 13, 1891, signing herself "Youre Loving Grandma." During her visit, she straightened out some problems that Cora was having with breast-feeding, suggesting that she wean and use Nestlé's Food, and Cora was grateful for her help: "Dear Mama has done wonders for us."

The argumentative Keck family dynamics assumed Freudian dimensions when it came time to name the baby: "I have released all claims in naming her," Cora wrote a month and a half after their child was born, "and given it over to her Papa (Mr. Cook) and Grand Ma (Mrs. Dr. Keck). It now lays between the two parties." John Cook wanted to name the baby after his wife Cora and her sister Charlotte, but John Keck wanted them to name the baby after his wife, Rebecca, "and so it goes as late as Dec. 28th nothing is decided." It took Cora's husband two years to prevail over his two in-laws. My grandmother continued as Baby Cook, oblivious to her identity limbo, throughout most of her toddlerhood. The first time her official name of Charlotte Mae appeared in Cora's diary was on the occasion of her second birthday in 1892. "She takes after her Papa, enjoying moving around all the time," Cora wrote of her baby, in wry reference to Mr. C's wanderings and travels before their marriage. She dreamed that her daughter would grow up to be a musician and put her onto the piano stool and helped her to hit the keys with her little fists while she was still learning to walk. "She is quite promising indeed & in fact we think she will be a second Mozart," Cora wrote hopefully.

Cora reveled in the social life now opened to her as Mrs. John Cook; it was exactly the kind of life that she had been so harshly excluded from in Davenport. She threw herself into a round of literary groups, musical meetings, lectures, and tea parties and attended church services, dances, and parties with her husband that both enjoyed thoroughly. He enjoyed surprising his bride with magnificent presents; for her birthday in May 1891 it was a driving horse, surrey, and harness for Cora to use to drive herself around Elkhart, and the following Christmas "Mr. C. surprised me greatly by presenting me with a silver 'tea service' the whole outfit— each article was nicely wrapped up he produced the little table & then unfolded each article separately surprising me at each enhancement with its completeness all pronounced it beautiful." She tore herself away from her little family for two and a half weeks in June 1891 to travel east with her parents to visit relatives in Allentown, Pennsylvania, and Kitty Rogers, now twenty-six and still unmarried, accompanied her back to Elkhart for an extended visit. Kitty "is wishing for the opportunity of stealing our little Darling and wants us to move to New York and live next door to her." Kitty stayed three and a half months, and on her departure, she wrote a little note to my grandmother in Cora's baby diary, "may you ever retain your crowning glory; the faculty of creating love in all who come within the influence of your bright eyes."

CHAPTER TWENTY-NINE

Oh! How Little They Know. Anybody!

A few weeks after Mrs. Dr. Keck had suggested a better way for Cora to feed her baby and departed, Cora decided that the new Nestlé's Food did not agree with her after all and called in the Cooks' regular family doctor, Dr. Fisher, who suggested a change to a different kind of imported formula, called Ridge's. Surprisingly, Cora's mother seemed to support Cora's relationship with the prominent society physician, even advising her little granddaughter Charlotte to trust him and follow his directions when it came time for her to give up her baby bottle. I was impressed to discover that despite her lifelong feud with the fraternity of regular physicians, Mrs. Dr. Keck handled this delicate situation with her daughter's chosen doctors extremely diplomatically—giving advice only when asked, and then without criticism.

As Charlotte approached the age of two and began to object to taking her daily naps, Cora noted in her diary that Dr. Fisher started giving her "medicine to quieten her." I shudder to think of what might have been in it. Most regular doctors in the 1890s carried patent medicines, which often contained high concentrations of alcohol, opium, and cocaine. A typical M.D. such as Dr. Fisher would mix up his own favorite remedies and roll them into pills for his patients and on house calls would make use of powerful, toxic purgatives and cathartics including castor oil (made from ricin), calomel (mercurous chloride), rhubarb, jalap, and nux vomica (an herbal form of strychnine).[1] Germ theory, a cutting-edge European import, was beginning to trickle down into standard medical practice in the United States, but most doctors still understood illness in terms of symptoms and systemic imbalances, rather than infection by a specific microbe.[2] As a result, a basic medical premise of the era was that flushing out the digestive tract from both ends was the first step toward fixing most health problems. Dr. Fisher had no good tool to reduce fever or handle convulsions; aspirin, a real

Cora with her mother, daughter, and husband in Florida, 1893.

miracle drug in this context, would not be commercially available to doctors and the public until 1899.

During January and February of 1893, Charlotte came down with a series of bad colds and flus, sometimes described as "bilious fever and sore mouth," and Cora wrote, "Dr. Fisher is doing all in his power for her." The *Little Giant Cyclopedia of Ready Reference*, a popular source of information and common wisdom published in 1893, recommended the following as standard remedies for bilious fever: bryonia (a poisonous herb), nux vomica for constipation, and mercurius (a form of calomel) for nausea.

A crisis erupted on February 6, the day the family was scheduled to leave for Lake Worth, Florida. Mr. Cook noticed that his daughter was not as well as usual and canceled the hack that was to take them to the station, while Cora raced to Dr. Fisher's office for advice and medicines. The doctor prescribed belladonna (a tincture made from the toxic plant) to quiet the child and bring down her fever and gave Cora instructions for administering the remedy. Cora spent the evening anxiously watching over her daughter and dosed her with the medicine four times, according to the directions she had been given. At 10 P.M., baby Charlotte turned her eyes up toward the ceiling and went into convulsions.

Cora recorded every detail of what happened next in her diary. Shouting to wake up her husband and the hired girl downstairs, she rushed to run hot water into the upstairs tub, believing that a warm bath was a standard remedy for this situation, but the tiny spout on the old-fashioned plumbing was so slow that she scooped the convulsing child into her arms and staggered down the back stairs into the kitchen where she thought she could get the hot water faster. The unheated kitchen was so cold that she retreated back upstairs where the tub was finally beginning to fill. Mr. Cook could hardly get his clothes on quickly enough and ran for the doctor without a vest or hat. Charlotte lay in her mother's arms frothing at the mouth. Cora thought she was dying. She put Charlotte's feet into the hot water in the tub, which had finally filled sufficiently, and in about ten minutes her daughter began to revive. A different doctor, named Dr. Niman, arrived and cooled off the bath water and the baby with ice. Charlotte had three more spasms, and Dr. Niman gave her more medicines until Dr. Fisher arrived. The latter was surprised to see Charlotte sick and checked on how much belladonna Cora had given her, then said that Cora had "done all right." He administered a strong laxative "to get this trouble out," and no sooner left the house than "Baby went into another convulsion." Dr. Niman returned and administered another huge enema to "work off the trouble" and finally gave his diagnosis for the cause of the entire two-week bout of serious illness: an undigested half raisin with two seeds in it. The little girl was then kept in bed for two days with no food at all, while both doctors visited three or four times each day. She was so hungry by the third day that she cried for the three tablespoons of thin gruel she was allowed every two hours. "We did not dare give more for fear of loading up her stomach," Cora wrote, obedient to the doctors' orders. The ordeal turned Cora into a wreck: "I was so used up, I looked like a fright so all said, as if I had gone through a spell of sickness myself . . . Oh. it seems I never could forgive Dr. Fisher."

The Cooks then departed to Florida in a hurry, hoping that the change in climate would help Charlotte recover her health. "The pleasure of going into the orange groves and picking all we wanted was something never to forget," she wrote of their visit to the Indian River near Lake Worth, where the Cooks joined Mrs. Dr. Keck and Cora's younger sister, Maggie. They went on to Palm Beach, to the Cocoanut Grove Hotel, where baby Charlotte played with shells on the beach and "Papa John" hauled a shark in from the surf assisted by three other men. Unfortunately, more illness dogged Charlotte in Florida, and out of the three months of February, March, and April, she was gravely ill for a total of eight weeks. Cora wrote, "We thought that she would die, My medicine case saved her." In retrospect, Cora's belief in the remedies prescribed by Dr. Niman and Dr. Fisher feels spooky; the medicines in that case may actually have been the cause of many of Charlotte's sufferings. Back in Elkhart in May, Dr. Fisher continued to treat the girl, and her convulsions continued, once so severely that she turned blue.

> It was about this time that we made Mama [Mrs. Dr. Keck] come
> down and see Baby. Grand Ma and Grand Pa came to see Baby . . . as
> soon as Mama saw her complexion, which was brown, she knew she

was not right and gave her a dose of "worm medicine" that night . . . it was senna tea we gave . . . for one month she passed worms . . . Oh. how thankful we were to dear Mother and to God for saving her. She was being eaten up by worms for the want of the proper medicine. Oh! How little they know. Anybody!

But the doctors would not let go of their little patient and her wealthy parents. Dr. Niman took over from Dr. Fisher, declaring that all Charlotte's troubles had come from constipation, and he started giving her medicines for that. Once again, Mrs. Dr. Keck did not contradict the regular doctor but advised him to also give the girl hearty food, something to nourish her and digest afterward. As a gesture of support to the physician chosen by her daughter and son-in-law, she urged her granddaughter to "take her medicines nicely and get well so she could go to the World's Fair." Charlotte's health improved enough that in September 1893, aged three, she could join a crowd of relatives, including her mother, grandparents, aunts and uncles, and cousin Warren Kleckner, to go to Chicago to see the World's Columbian Exposition, the famous "White City," and stay in one of the hotels owned and operated by Lotta and Dr. Dorn near the Jackson Park fairgrounds.

Installed in the Alfonzo Hotel in Chicago far from the fashionable Elkhart physicians, Mrs. Dr. Keck could finally take charge of her granddaughter's health. "Next day Grand Ma said now we will not give Baby any medicines. She gave her some fine ripe pears to eat and it done the work . . . in three days her tongue was cleaned off as it had not been for six weeks and how she would run and kick and sing so happy, so good." At the top of the page of her diary, Cora wrote in large letters, "Don't let medicine do all. Nature will do better."

Charlotte was too young to remember much of what she saw at the exposition but screamed with delight as the electric fountain changed colors and gazed with amazement at the painted faces of the Indians in Buffalo Bill's Wild West Show. She enjoyed the parades of gaily decorated horses so much that she cried with disappointment when it was all over. Another day Cora and her daughter rode a cable car to the top of "the skyscraper of Chicago," a Masonic Hall that was seventeen stories high. Although Cora did not visit the Chinese exhibit, it was one of the most interesting to visitors, as the country had only recently opened to Western trade. Partway through the fair, the pavilion burned to the ground, and Lotta and Gay Dorn welcomed as many members of the now-homeless Chinese delegation as could fit into their hotel for the duration and afterward. The Cooks and the Dorns received "a continual string of fine Chinese gifts" from their grateful new boarders as a result.

In late September after returning to Elkhart, Cora vented her rage about the previous year's troubles: "Oh. how I feel toward Dr. Fisher words fail me. I don't care to see him to speak to him or go past his house." Her attitude toward the "regulars" had evolved significantly; she was no longer begging them to hurry and help but was blaming them for misdiagnosing Charlotte's long nights of convulsions and intestinal agonies and for ignoring her suggestion that they try commonsense remedies such as a simple mixture of brandy, sugar, and hot water to relieve cramping and diarrhea (perhaps a tonic her mother had given her as a child). "The best Doctors I cannot forgive them," she wrote sarcastically and bestowed on her child a fighting motto from Shakespeare's *Antony and Cleopatra*: "All the gods go with you. Upon your sword Tis laurel victory. Smooth success Be strew'd before your feet."

In February 1894, still "doctoring on and on with Dr. Niman," Cora and her husband noticed that Charlotte had had a regular sick spell every month for the past nine months that coincided with each visit from the doctor. Mr. C. saw that she was losing ground and decided to telegraph to Mrs. Dr. Keck in Chicago. She came on the first train. "Mother asked Dr.

Mrs. Dr. Keck with her granddaughter, Charlotte Cook.

Niman what he was giving her and he amazed us by saying 'calomel' and 'blue mass'—well Mother said you don't need to give us any more of that." Calomel and blue mass were two forms of a popular nineteenth-century medical panacea made of mercurous chloride, now known to be a deadly poison.[3] Mrs. Dr. Keck immediately took over the treatment. She brought Cora and baby Charlotte back home with her to the infirmary on Brady Street in Davenport, and Charlotte "commenced to improve at once, as if by magic . . . what a delightful change, my night's rest soon came and the dear little thing had perfect rest. Mother gave simple medicines and allayed all inflammation, all so necessary."

Seven weeks later, Cora returned to Elkhart with her mother and rejuvenated daughter: "Everyone spoke of the change in her appearance—as she did not look like the same child. She was so well and hearty."

According to Cora's baby diaries, my great-great-grandmother, the alleged quack, pulled her granddaughter Charlotte back from the brink of death not once but *three times* with her commonsense, naturopathic approach to managing sickness. My grandmother Charlotte stayed healthy for the rest of her childhood and young adult life, and Cora wrote in July 1894, "It seems as if the Doctors here in E know very little about Babies for they had no idea of her case and Grand Ma Keck just saved her life."

Epilogue

———————

Suffering is inadmissible in light stage plays.
—FYODOR DOSTOYEVSKY, *Notes from Underground*

When I started to write this book, I naturally assumed that Mrs. Dr. Keck was a flat-out rascal and a medical pretender—as my grandfather had believed and as so many of her contemporaries had said she was, and as even her own daughter seemed to believe as a young adult at Vassar. I felt nothing but delighted anticipation as I prepared to amuse my readers by exposing the fraudulent schemes of my wily patent medicine millionaire ancestress. It's much easier to write about wicked people than good ones. Business dishonesty was supposed to be a major theme in this story. I was greatly surprised to discover that, except for the fictitious grain deal between Belle's husband and Mr. Dixon and Belle's failure to pay her jeweler, no "smoking guns" of flagrant business dishonesty have turned up after years of research. If Mrs. Dr. Keck had ever injured anyone with her treatments, her powerful adversaries would have seized immediately on the case and publicized the facts widely to discredit her further. Yet, none of Mrs. Dr. Keck's court cases involved malpractice or swindling. They were all focused on her right to call herself a physician. As the process wore on, I began to empathize with Mrs. Dr. Keck and her family. I saw how Cora must have suffered from her reputation as the quack's daughter, and how, as an adult, she unwittingly absorbed the social prejudice against her mother to the point that she began to believe it. She rediscovered her mother's integrity and medical skills only through the suffering of her own child and her mother's repeated dramatic medical rescues. As Cora's mistrust of her mother's medical expertise evaporated, so did mine.

Cora was only thirty-six years old in 1901 when her husband died at the age of seventy-four after a long illness (said by some sources to have

Cora Keck, ca. 1915, at the time of her daughter's marriage.

been liver cancer). She never remarried and was a devoted single mother to her daughter. I don't have many sources of information about her adult years, although one thing is clear—she was not a merry widow. I've shaped my story so far as a "light stage play" based on Cora's youthful joy—I always want to think of her as "the Vassar girl on a string," surrounded by admirers and reaching out for her shining future. No one enters middle age without becoming acquainted with grief, strife, and suffering, so perhaps those darker tales should be reserved for another book. However, there are a few important facts about Cora's married life in Elkhart that should be told before closing, as well as interesting follow-up about what happened to some of the people closest to her.

In 1894, Cora finally acted on the inspiring words of the Reverend Edward Everett Hale that she had heard during his speech at Vassar's Founder's Day in 1886, when she had wondered to herself, "What could a musician do for society at large?" Following the example of Professor Ritter (who supported the idea of founding St. Cecilia societies across the country), she organized a St. Cecilia Club together with two friends, Mrs. Robert Winslow and Mrs. Alfred Jones, to promote the performance and appreciation of classical music in Elkhart. At the same time, she became the vice president of the Indiana State Music Teachers Association. The St. Cecilia Club quickly became the largest women's organization in Elkhart, having at its height five hundred women musicians as members and organizing recitals that, according to a 1935 Elkhart County historian, "became known far and wide" and "exerted wide influence and created a demand for good music among the people of the city."[1] Similar St. Cecilia societies were started in other towns all over the United States throughout the nineteenth century, a musical version of the Chautauqua societies and lyceums that spread westward into the hinterlands to elevate the intellectual life of rural America. They were perhaps following the example set by the St. Cecilia Society of Charleston, South Carolina, that evolved into the oldest and most exclusive club in the city, so selective by the 1880s that the Poppenheim family had not been invited to join.

Four months after the first small meeting of the three founders, the eighty-nine members of the rapidly growing group took over an entire issue of the *Elkhart Daily Journal* for a dedicated St. Cecilia edition on Saturday evening of June 30, 1894. Four women edited and four managed all the advertising, including Cora, now vice president of the society, who solicited three huge double-column ads. Worried that "it has been said that the musical idea is masculine," the club's manifesto pointed out that women amateurs "are fast gaining prominence as promoters of the highest standard of literature and art." The St. Cecilia editors were not afraid to include a short, nasty reprint (worthy of Eliza Lynn Linton) from the *London Figaro* complaining that too many modern girls were wasting their time with musical studies when they should be devoting themselves to family duties, since "conductors persistently refuse to engage young ladies as paid members of professional orchestras." The problem was that all the young people studying violoncello at London's Royal College of Music were girls, and to remedy this desperate situation, the college officials had been forced to devote several scholarships to male pupils.

Life got much harder for Cora during the mid-1890s. All the Cooks' household help left for Chicago to work at the World's Fair and never came back, leaving Cora in charge of the kitchen and without child care at the same time that her husband's health began to decline. Furthermore, an agonizing family conflict broke out between John Cook and his grown son and daughter-in-law that scarred his last years. During a brief visit to the Elkhart County courthouse I discovered that John Cook, his brother, his daughter-in-law and/or his adult son were plaintiffs or defendants in more than twenty civil lawsuits during that decade; I picked twelve that looked interesting and ordered photocopies, but subsequently wished I hadn't. This load of dirty family laundry was uniformly harsh and grim. Cora had to give up all her club work and was more and more thrown on her own resources. She focused her energy and efforts on raising her daughter to the best of her abilities, calling on all the emotional wisdom and passionate devotion she had at her disposal, perhaps to block out the increasingly awful news that rained into her life. Having a live, healthy child was not a small accomplishment in those days, as I discovered from reading her baby diaries and investigating the genealogical records of her closest friends.

As she rediscovered the usefulness of her mother's medical consultations, Cora reciprocated by taking more responsibility for caring for her mother's needs. In the fall of 1894, Mrs. Dr. Keck was having difficulty keeping up with the punishing pace of her work commitments. On October 20, Cora wrote, "I had lots to worry about for at that time poor Mother was very sick and yet out at her offices doing her duty as she said." Cora and her baby daughter took the train to Champaign to help and stayed with Mrs. Dr. Keck at her regular rooms at the Doane House hotel. "Baby and I went and found her in a house gown and looking so badly and seeing all the sick who came. It was a shame." Cora spent three days working with her sister Florence to manage the patients for the ailing physician until she could leave and return home to recuperate. In November, Cora's mother was still sick but traveled to Elkhart for

Thanksgiving and took charge of a fever that Charlotte had. She "broke it in two hours." The holiday was overshadowed by unspecified business worries hanging over Mrs. Dr. Keck in "C," which could refer to either Champaign or Chicago; she faced powerful enemies in both cities who were working tirelessly to put her out of business. "Grand Ma is about sick over the noon arrival of statements from C. She insists her business must be settled up before going south." According to my grandfather, the trouble referred to problems that Gay and Charlotte Dorn were having with the Keck family's real-estate investments in Jackson Park; the expected boom after the World's Fair ended never materialized, and "the city was in bad shape." Cora became her mother's mainstay during these last difficult years of her career, and she took her to Florida three winters in a row to help her recuperate.

As her daughter Charlotte reached her teenage years, I was surprised to find that Cora, who had always been so close to her friends, became relatively socially isolated. What happened to her old Vassar pals? Marian Austin vanished from Cora's circle after she married a homeopathic physician, Dr. Homer Clark, in Buffalo, New York, in 1889, and they had a son named Hale in 1890. A year later, while giving birth to Homer Jr. and attended by her husband, Marian was taken with septicemia and died of "childbed fever" two weeks later. Her distraught husband signed onto a passing ship as a surgeon, departed for the Caribbean, and left his motherless sons to be raised by relatives.[2] Two years after that, Cora learned that Kitty Rogers was to be married to John Humphrey Pratt in June 1893 in a double wedding with her younger sister Dolly (Sarah), who was marrying a prominent New York physician, Dr. Joseph Darwin Nagel. Kitty died a year later at the age of twenty-nine in August 1894, probably also in childbirth.[3] Dolly named her first daughter Kitty Rogers Pratt Nagel in her memory. Hattie Wakefield Brady seems to have gone her own way once she moved to New York, and Cora lost touch with her, too.

Although Helen "Ned" Weeks was already thirty-four in 1901 when she married a personal injury lawyer named Carroll H. Jones (known for defending the South Side Elevated Railroad Co. in the original banana peel liability case that launched a thousand vaudeville jokes), she gave birth to three healthy sons and sent them all to Harvard.[4] Elizabeth Griggs was another late bloomer, living at home with her wealthy parents in Davenport and running a monthly literary society called the Tuesday Club (Davenport's two most well-known authors—Susan Glaspell and Alice French writing as Octave Thanet—were members), until she suddenly eloped at the age of thirty-seven with Davenport's popular, athletic, and handsome but underpaid Unitarian minister, Rev. Arthur Judy. They were married in Brookline, Massachusetts, in March 1902. In May 1903, their only child died at birth as the result of a difficult delivery, and the congregation sought to comfort the grieving couple by making one hundred thousand paper peach blossoms by hand to decorate forty bare trees set up to create a fairyland of exquisite beauty for the annual church fair at the end of the year.[5] Lydia Day, that wild mustang from the Vassar Trio, never married but settled down and had a long, successful career as a school principal in New York City.

Hattie's brother Homer Wakefield gave up on his dream of marrying Cora, went to New York City to become a doctor, and graduated from Bellevue Hospital Medical College with an M.D. degree. He returned to Bloomington, Illinois, and married a girl named Julia in 1890. In September 1891 he applied for membership in the McLean County Medical Society, under the sponsorship of a well-respected eye, ear, nose, and throat specialist, a Dr. Taylor, who was a graduate of the College of Physicians and Surgeons in New York City. The society's censors disregarded Homer's credentials and his sponsor but scrutinized his father's career as the manufacturer of patent medicines. Seizing as an excuse on some small advertisements that Homer had run in the local paper when starting up his practice, they not only denied him admission to the local medical society, they wrote to Bellevue in New York and persuaded the college to drop his name from the alumni catalog "because he was a quack," in effect revoking his diploma. He and Julia moved back to New York City to live in the same building as Hattie at Ninety-fourth Street and West End Avenue, where the two siblings raised their numerous children.[6] Ed Corbett also gave up on Cora and married someone else but later divorced and stayed in touch with her on and off throughout the rest of her life—as always, on the periphery.

In June 1892, Professor Ritter retired. Vassar immediately closed down its School of Music, and Miss Jessie Chapin was out of a job. She moved to Springfield, Massachusetts, to live with her brother Campbell, the manager of a paper company, and in 1898 embarked on a year-long tourist visit to Europe with her twenty-two-year-old niece Susan. On her passport application, she listed her occupation as "A Lady."[7] By 1920, her brother was dead and her savings were beginning to run out. She tried to eke out a living by giving music lessons, but the taxes and mortgage on the large house she had inherited from her brother were very high. She had no pension from Vassar because she had stopped working for the college before the pension fund was instituted in 1898. In 1921, she had to sell her piano to a former friend and Vassar colleague, Miss Annie Whitney. The 1929 Depression wiped out what was left of her meager resources, and in 1932, at the age of eighty-three, with all her other friends and relatives "in the cemetery," she swallowed her pride and wrote to Vassar for help because her house was about to be foreclosed on, there was no real-estate market in which to sell it, and she had been forced to sell all her furniture to pay for food. She did not even have a table or chairs left to sit on. Graceful and positive even in this moment of humiliating despair, she added, "I am still active and able to do my share of the daily housework. My eyes and ears are as good as ever—Nature has indeed been kind to me."[8]

A compassionate college official named Clara Reed organized a campaign to send out letters to former music students asking for contributions; many wrote back that they had been "besieged by heartbreaking stories and were unable to respond," but Ida Yates, Harriet Capron, Mary Louise Anderson, and Lotta Wix were among the fifty who contributed what they could to help Miss Chapin. Cora could do nothing for her former teacher—she had died eleven years before in 1921. The college paid Miss Chapin's property taxes for a year, but Vassar's president Henry Noble MacCracken declared that he could not provide a pension for her without doing the same thing for the large number of other unpensioned former employees. Miss Chapin's ultimate fate is not recorded in Vassar's files, but it could not have been a happy or dignified one. By 1934, her case had become a "bother" to the college, and President MacCracken decided to cut her off since the money in the fund for her was exhausted. He somewhat ingenuously suggested that since "times are better than they were," she might now sell her house or find other sources of relief. It was a pitiable thing to outlive one's savings in an era before Social Security was created.

∽

MY GRANDFATHER WROTE in his memoirs that he met Warren Kleckner for the first time at a lunch in New York City in the early spring of 1915. He and Cora's daughter Charlotte had just gotten en-

gaged; Charlotte had a ring, and they were preparing to announce the news. By then, Warren was fifty-two years old, "an explosive and eccentric old bachelor" living on Thirty-ninth Street just off of Fifth Avenue. Highly evolved from his California Gold Rush childhood, he was a regular in the "old timers' row" of gay gentlemen opera fans down near the front of the orchestra at the Metropolitan Opera House. Wearing a well-trimmed little mustache and carrying a small cane in the manner of a swagger stick, he took a seat with Charlotte and my grandfather on one of the dining verandas of the famous Sunken Palm Garden of the Park Avenue Hotel at Thirty-second Street. "Anyone who lives more than a mile

Warren Kleckner in a portrait in Los Angeles taken by his partner, Scholl, ca. 1899.

from Forty-second Street is only camping out," Warren blustered, evidently comparing the rest of Manhattan unfavorably with the mining camp in the Sierra Nevada where he had lived as a boy. Warren was always entertaining. While they waited for Cora to arrive, my grandfather learned that Warren's long-time close friend Albert Seabury, a reserved and dignified broker of about fifty, had recently made the news when he was adopted by a wealthy, childless widow who was one of his custom-ers. Warren went on to complain to my grandfather that a letter Cora had written him was so messy "it looked like she wrote it on the ceiling."

Cora was so glad to see Warren when she joined them at the table that they all had a hard time at first drawing her attention to the new ring on Charlotte's finger. Starchy and irritable as he was, Warren was a constant, loyal presence at this and at all the watershed events in Cora's life. He walked Cora's daughter down the aisle when she married my grandfather three months later in June. After the wedding was over, Warren decided that Cora was the one girl he knew whom he wanted to give his late mother's lace scarf to, writing to her, "You were so calm, so unperturbed, so serene, so splendidly poised through all of the commotion."

However, Cora's emotional balance and vitality depended on the lov-ing care and attention that she enjoyed lavishing on the people around her. She needed the reciprocal energy of love to survive. By 1921, all the emotional pillars of Cora's life had been taken away: her husband died in 1901, her mother in 1904, her father in 1910, and now her only child was gone too. It was too much. Four or five months after Charlotte's sudden passing, in the summer of 1921, my grandfather took my father to Chicago to visit his grandmother. On an outing, they drove south, out of town to a small park with a pond, a bit of lawn, and a spring. The last photos Grandfather took of Cora visiting with her only grandson are heartrending. Although just fifty-six years old, Cora looked twenty years older; her hair was limp and badly cut, and her smile was only a brave effort put on for the little boy of five sitting next to her. Her clothes were drab, dark, a decade out of date, and rumpled. She could only watch while her grandson swung around the porch post of a tour-ist cabin and explored a small millwheel turning in the stream nearby. She had clearly suffered a terrible breakdown in her mental and physical health and had lost the spark of vitality that once graced her youth.

I can see her later alone, back in her Chicago apartment listlessly star-ing at her bound book of music lying open on a table, perhaps before taking it to the piano to play. Two of her sisters, her niece, and a brother-in-law had all gone to ride on a carousel with her grandson, but she could not bear to go with them. The flyleaf of the book had a vigorously penciled inscription, written when she was twenty-one: "Cora M. Keck

Vassar College Po-Keepsie N.Y. Class of '86 June 7, 1886." Picking up a pen, she slowly and carefully inked over the faded words, then inspired by her memories, continued to write: "Pieces I studied from time of entering Vassar—Regalleto de Verdi by Wagner-Liszt—I played for commencement My father and Mother John & Rebecca Keck were present. Sweet Charlotte loved my pieces & I often played or practiced while she was going to sleep as a child—She loved the classics and rare melodies."

Music, the other great pillar of her life, would never die.

DURING THE TIME I spent writing this book, I sometimes had a reason to open up the file folder with Cora's obituary in it, and each time I felt an unexpected shock of loss. Each time, I seemed to forget

My grandmother, Charlotte Cook, in 1915 at the time of her marriage.

that she had died. Like all her long-ago classmates at Vassar, I have fallen under her spell, seduced by her gift for creating intimacy, her boundless creative energy, and her penchant for spreading gratuitous warmth. She always chose to overlook and turn away from ugliness and bitterness and endeavored to bring people together instead of driving them apart. Subjected to harsh public notoriety and social abuse throughout her teens, she emerged unscathed as a principled young adult who understood how to give her best. She seized the opportunities that came her way at Vassar and worked gracefully to use her musical training to leave a positive legacy in the community where she spent her adult life.

Throughout my research, I have felt a dreamlike sense that if I get it just right, somehow, someone from the story is going to materialize out of thin air and tap me on the shoulder and whisper in my ear, "Yes, you got it right!" Or, if I have made bad blunders, to say, "No, it wasn't that way at all—you've got the wrong idea completely." These were, after all, real people. But that can't happen. They are dead and have been missing in action for almost a century. Most have no living descendants. They'll never come back to help me with unanswered questions. Neither can they tell me whether they are glad I have written their stories, or offended at the personal intrusion, or simply amazed that others would be

My father, John Nettleton, during a visit with his great-aunt Belle Alexander in Chicago in 1919. The deer came from Mrs. Dr. Keck's yard in Davenport.

interested at all in reading it. Even as I have struggled to verify every "fact" of every detail in Cora's story, writing about history has been more like gazing into a glorious fictional mirror that is obedient to my deepest vanities and desires. Perhaps that is a secret truth for all historians. But this is a family story, not a story about famous strangers. While breathing life into the names, the friends, the faces, and the foibles of long dead people, while pulling them back from the brink of oblivion, I have found that time has been my greatest enemy and love my greatest ally. So it is with all our human connections.

ACKNOWLEDGMENTS

During the seven years I have spent working on this book, I have received enormous encouragement and help from a long list of friends, relations, colleagues, and interested experts. I owe a deep debt of gratitude to all of them.

I began both the book and my relationship with Vassar College thanks to Jean McKee (Vassar '51). Professor Emerita Elizabeth Daniels, the Vassar College historian, quickly stepped on board to support this project with the full power of her considerable expertise. Other members of the Vassar community I thank include Rebecca Edwards, professor of history on the Eloise Ellery Chair; Paul Kane, professor of English and co-associate chair; Elizabeth M. Clark (Vassar '41); Cristina Biaggi (Vassar '59); Sarah Canino, music librarian; and Dean Rogers, in the Vassar Library's Special Collections. If any inaccuracies about Vassar history have crept into the text over the years, these are all entirely mine. Peter Dimock; Helen Horowitz, professor of American studies and history emerita at Smith College; Sharon Wood, professor of history at the University of Nebraska; and Linda Kerber, professor in liberal arts and sciences at the University of Iowa, were also kind enough to listen and give me advice and encouragement during the early stages of my research.

The people who have helped me transform this project from idea to reality and who have been beyond generous with their time and professional skills include Robert Rushan, who created my author website and Marge Hetzel, who provided many hours of time on genealogical research. For the first edition, hats off to David Wolk, Tamara Glenny, Jorge Madrigal, Liz Barhydt, and Gregory Lalire. Also, Kathryn Shattuck Papay, Christopher Lukas, Jaclyn Vorenkamp, Jane Gross, Kathy Sykes, and Joan Konner provided essential critical feedback and encouragement throughout the writing process. For the second edition,

I particularly want to thank everyone I have worked with at the University of Iowa Press, including Jim McCoy, who decided to take a chance on an unknown author, and my copy editor Jessie Dolch, whose careful eye for detail has been invaluable. Additional information about Nina Van Zandt came from Timothy Messer-Kruse. For both editions, Kathleen Lynch provided the beautiful cover artwork.

In Davenport, Iowa, I am indebted to Judy and Henry P. Braunlich; Eunice Schlichting, former chief curator of the Putnam Museum; the entire well-informed staff of the Davenport Public Library's Richardson-Sloane Special Collections Center; the Upper Mississippi River Valley Digital Image Archive; Eleanor Mooney and Pastor Ron Carlson of St. John's United Methodist Church; Karen Anderson and Sue and Rex Grove of the Scott County Historical Preservation Society; the Davenport Community School System's historical library; Deborah Lynn Williams of the Oakdale Memorial Gardens; Jerry Wala of the Davenport Unitarian Universalist Church; and Janet Meyer of the Rock Island Historical Society. Also, many thanks to the Quad Cities Heritage League, including Allana Callender of the Palmer Foundation for Chiropractic History and Kelly Lao of the German American Heritage Center. In Fairfield, Iowa, I thank local historian Richard Thompson and the staff at the Fairfield Public Library. In Illinois, I particularly thank Bill Kemp, the librarian/archivist of the McLean County Museum of History in Bloomington, who has been combing their microfilmed newspaper files for information about Mrs. Dr. Keck on my behalf for years. Professor John S. Haller Jr. of Southern Illinois University and Professor Michael Flannery at the University of Alabama, Birmingham, provided essential help with the history of eclectic medical practitioners in the Midwest. I also thank Robert Baker at the Champaign County Circuit Court; Howard Grueneberg at the Champaign County Historical Archives; Heather Speckler at the Rush Medical University Library; Ron Sims at Northwestern University's Galter Health Sciences Library; L. J. Dean, a volunteer researcher at the National Railway Historical Society in Philadelphia; Linda Aylward at the Peoria Public Library; Karen Deller at Bradley University Special Collections; and Dr. Victoria Hineman Loberg. Jeanine Rhodes at the Elkhart, Indiana, Public Library; the staff at the Goshen, Indiana, Public Library; Lexie Sylvester and the staff at the Elkhart County Courthouse in Goshen, Indiana; and in Hawaii, Hanalei Abbott at the Hamilton Library at the University of Hawaii at Manoa also provided information and assistance.

In New York, the Reverend Earl Kooperkamp and Miss Gwen of St. Mary's Episcopal Church Harlem and Lauren Georger of the Manhattanville College Library gave me access to original information available nowhere else. I also thank Patricia Gallagher at the New York Academy of Medicine; the staff at the Harness Racing Museum in Goshen, New York; the staff in the local history department of the Poughkeepsie Library; and the staff at the Archives and Rare Book and Manuscript Libraries at Columbia and Yale universities.

Finally, I express my appreciation to all my friends and relations who have given generously of their advice, encouragement, and support, including Matt Zebiak, Annie Rasiel, Helena Peskova, Rajesh Dhawan, Steve Marsh, Gail Gilberg, Ruth Collins, and Bill Kenah. Annemarie Ziegler translated the old-style German sentences scattered throughout Cora's diary. My two sisters, Sally and Charlotte, did as much as they were able to help. My mother, Susanna S. Sutro, taught me all the basics about the right way to research and write history term papers early on and has been an invaluable source of ideas and expertise throughout my research for this book. My husband, Rex Lalire, and our two sons, Alexander and Luc, who comprise two-thirds of the total population of the quack's great-great-great-grandchildren, have supported my commitment to this project from the start, and whenever things seemed to be flagging, they urged me on toward the finish line by constantly asking, "When are you going to get that book finished?" So now it is . . .

GLOSSARY

March 29, 1885. Some Selections provided by the Anti-slang
Society in Parlor 9:
"Don't mention it" —M. Carbutt
"Catch on" —C. Keck
"Fork over" —L. M. Harris

—FROM CORA'S DIARY

The British journalist Mrs. Eliza Lynn Linton accused girls who used slang of "bold talk, general fastness . . . laziness, love of luxury and selfishness." Girls at Vassar described slangy talk as "reprehensible" but went right on speaking that way anyway. Even the billionaire's daughter Mary Thaw condescended to use a slang word, "fizzled," in one of her letters home from college, although she underlined it, put quotes around it, and wrote this disclaimer: "excuse the expression, which has the sanction of general usage." Today, many of the words dismissed as slang by Cora's contemporaries have become standard English idioms.

after-damp The suffocating mixture of carbon dioxide and nitrogen that forms following an explosion of methane in a coal-mining accident.

brave up To collect your courage to do something difficult.

bustle A wire cage worn under the skirt of a lady's dress, tied to the waist, to make it protrude backwards. "U bet yr bussel."

cabinet A formal portrait taken in a photography studio and mounted on a thin piece of cardboard.

called up Summoned to the Lady Principal's office for a reprimand or punishment.

cane rush Canes were thin whips used by schoolteachers to punish lazy students and by college students to haze their fraternity brothers during rush week.

chippy A cheap young prostitute.

chromos Before color photography, these were the first inexpensive, mass-produced color images, manufactured using the chromolithograph process on paper.

collation An elegant luncheon buffet for an event.

davenport A small wooden writing desk, and, later, a small couch.

drawers Underpants.

dude A wealthy, well-dressed young man with good expectations; a nineteenth-century version of today's Ivy League preppy.

firedamp Explosive methane gas in a coal mine.

flirting The meaning hasn't changed much; in contrast to mashing, nineteenth-century flirting between men and women was more of a skilled art, more vague about any future commitments, and therefore more innocent.

fly time A big rush to get something done.

getting left (on something) Running out of something, or being caught short of something, or being left behind by someone.

going back (on someone) To disappoint, betray, or fail to come through on something.

gone girl Several possible meanings, depending on the context. In order of severity, they ranged from merely having "gone away," to being deeply infatuated with someone, to being in a generally hopeless situation, or to being pregnant and therefore ruined.

hack A horse-drawn taxi cab.

lunch A small meal or snack, served anytime, even late at night.

make your toilet Elegant nineteenth-century term (from French) for getting dressed and putting up your hair.

mashing Bold, off-color remarks and behavior that could be interpreted as propositioning someone. A masher was a man who sexually harassed young women on the street or a pimp looking to recruit new girls.

meet your fate When a girl became engaged to be married.

memoryabil The name Cora used for her informal photo album of tintypes.

Mugwumps Republicans who refused to support the 1884 Republican presidential candidate, James Blaine, because he was badly tainted by political patronage scandals and who switched their votes to the Democratic candidate, Grover Cleveland. Famous Mugwumps included Mark Twain, Henry Adams, and Thomas Nast, the political cartoonist, as well as Charles W. Eliot, the president of Harvard University.

philopena A small gift given as a penalty in a social game in which friends had to remember to respond to a secret word or sign; a token of friendship.

romance A story of fabulous, wild adventures, such as one would discover in reading a novel or "romance." Not specifically a story about love.

sacque A dressing gown or elegant bathrobe that could also be worn like a sweater in chilly weather over a dress.

section A sleeping berth on a Pullman train car.

shinplasters Private IOUs issued by businesses that were used in the cash-short nineteenth century as a substitute for real money. Since shinplasters were often worth less than the paper they were printed on, their name suggested a general perception they could be better put to use lining boots for warmth in the wintertime.

smash A college love affair between two women.

spooney Silly, foolish, or unduly sentimental, or sentimentally in love without real passion.

squelcher A letter or message sent to break off a romantic relationship, usually sent by a woman to a man.

squib A very small explosive charge used in mines to set off a larger explosion at the rock face; also a very short paragraph in a newspaper or advertisement providing an interesting fact or a plug for a person or product.

steam car A railroad car; "steam road" was also sometimes used instead of "railroad."

tintype A cheap, informal photographic image printed on a thin iron plate.

type A dude or a guy, probably derived from a similar French slang
   word.

W.C. (water closet) Toilet or privy.

waist(e)s Shirtwaists were a type of plain, tailored blouse worn with a
   simple skirt.

NOTES

ABBREVIATIONS

DPLRS Davenport Public Library Richardson-Sloane Special Collections
   Center
MCLJC Manhattanville College Library Jennings Collection
VCASC Vassar College Archives and Special Collections

PROLOGUE

1. Mrs. Dr. Keck ran thousands of advertisements in hundreds of newspapers across the upper Mississippi River Valley between 1873 and 1900. Using the search string "Mrs. Dr. Keck," I was able to find and read more than a thousand of them, primarily on Newspaperarchive.com and the Quincy (Illinois) Historical Newspaper Archive. A four-page advertising flyer, "Dr. Mrs. Keck's Medical Infirmary," from 1894 came out of one of the family trunks. I also found her advertisements and newspaper articles mentioning her in the *Chicago Tribune*, the *Chicago Times*, and newspapers in Peoria and Bloomington, Illinois.

2. *Chicago Daily Tribune*, February 7, 1880, p. 15.

3. Peoria Medical Society Minutes, May 4, 1880, quoted by Dr. Victoria Hineman Loberg in "Peoria's Pioneer Female Physicians Part II," *Peoria Medicine*, March 1999, p. 38. Controversy surrounding her name was mentioned in the minutes and official annual reports published between 1879 and 1890 by the Illinois State Board of Health (Google Books), the annual reports for the Peoria Medical Society (Bradley University Cullom-Davis Library), and unpublished historical surveys written by retired physicians for the Scott County Medical Society (DPLRS) and the Jefferson County Medical Society, in the Fairfield, Iowa, library.

I. THE WICKEDEST CITY IN AMERICA

1. Iowa Writers' Program, *Scott County History*, p. 103.

2. Wood, *Freedom of the Streets*, p. 3 and Map 2, p. 83.

3. Ibid., Map 2, p. 83.

4. Online copies of the Iowa State Agricultural Society Annual Reports from 1866 through 1876 (Google Books) and the U.S. Industrial Census for 1870 (ancestry.com) provided information about Cora's childhood in Fairfield.

5. The *Davenport Gazette* ran two long articles about Mrs. Dr. Keck's purchase of the John P. Cook mansion on June 2, 1879, and November 13, 1880 (DPLRS).

6. Bloomington, Illinois, *Leader*, reprinted in Decatur, Illinois, August 1883.

7. January 14, 1883, page 4.

8. Illinois State Board of Health, *Sixth Annual Report,* p. 166.

9. Scott County Circuit Court records for 1889 (DPLRS).

10. Information on the move is from a clipping in Cora's third scrapbook.

2. THESE LEAP YEAR GIRLS ARE GETTING AWFULLY BOLD

1. Carvey-Stewart, "Watch Tower Park."

2. Rosen, "Superpower of Franz Liszt."

3. Iowa Writers' Program, *Scott County History,* p. 103.

4. The staff at the Davenport School Museum provided an overview of the history of Davenport High School.

5. I obtained various factual information about individuals from relevant U.S. census data but do not note each instance throughout the book.

3. VASSAR'S CRISIS AND CORA'S HUMILIATION

1. Vassar's economic crisis has received detailed behind-the-scenes scholarly attention in several books about the history of the college, particularly *An Administrative History of Vassar College, 1861–2003*, ed. Ronald D. Patkus and Elizabeth A. Daniels (Poughkeepsie, NY: Vassar College, 2004). I have focused on statistics from the official Vassar annual college catalogs from 1883 to 1889 and on contemporary newspaper accounts that Cora saved in her scrapbooks to give an outsider's sense of how the public perceived the unfolding events.

2. Vassar College Bulk Files Folder 1.4, Advertising (VCASC).

3. The story of college education for women in England is told in Bingham, *History of Royal Holloway College.*

4. Information about Cora's gossiping classmates comes from the 1880 U.S. federal census; their fathers' biographies in *History of Scott County*; cemetery records from the Oakdale Cemetery in Davenport; the *Vassar College Catalog* for 1883–1884; and photographs from the Upper Mississippi Valley Digital Image Archive (DPLRS).

5. Peoria Circuit Court records for April and May 1880.

6. *Davenport Democrat*, February 1, 1884 (DPLRS).

7. Cora wrote in her diary about her father's accordion, and photograph albums show his beard.

8. Decatur, Illinois, *Daily Republican*, April 16, 1880 (Newspaperarchive .com).

9. Matthew Vassar, "Communications to the Board of Trustees by Its Founder, I. February 26, 1861," Vassar Encyclopedia, http://vcencyclopedia. vassar.edu/trustees/communications-to-the-board-of-trustees/index.html.

10. Complaints about Vassar College's falling admission standards were an important topic in all the articles describing the financial crisis at the college.

11. Twentieth Annual Catalogue of the Officers and Students of Vassar College, 1884–1885, p. 28.

4. MEMORABLE DATE OF ENTRANCE

1. Clipping from Cora's scrapbooks. Other details of Cora's arrival are reconstructed from notes she made in her scrapbook and photographs of Vassar's buildings in VCASC.

2. Cora's copy of Lossing, *Vassar College and Its Founder*, provided extensive information about the layout of Main Building, particularly the locations of offices and student parlors.

3. My grandfather, Kenneth Nettleton, wrote up his own unpublished memoirs in 1955 and included several descriptions of Warren Kleckner, whom he liked and admired.

4. Harriet Wood, letter home, April 17, 1892, Vassar College Archives Bulk Files, 1860–1914 (VCASC). Family information about Cora's roommates and friends at Vassar is from 1870 and 1880 U. S. census records, ancestry.com, and Vassar College Admissions Records Microfilm Series 1 and 2 (VCASC).

5. All quotations and descriptions of Mary and Louisa Poppenheim come from Johnson, ed., *Southern Women at Vassar*.

6. *Biographical History and Portrait Gallery of Scott County, Iowa* (Chicago: American Biographical Publishing Co., 1895), p. 504.

5. GREEN GIRLS

1. Information about Vassar's Main Building comes from Horowitz, *Alma Mater*, pp. 32–68, and Lossing, *Vassar College and Its Founder*, pp. 116–142.

6. MUGWUMPS AND OYSTERS

1. Information about Vassar's School of Music comes from Vassar College annual catalogs (VCASC), Cora's bound book of sheet music, and the complete set of concert programs for 1884–1886 in Cora's three scrapbooks.

2. Johnson, ed., *Southern Women at Vassar*, p. 61.

3. The summary of Matthew Vassar's role in founding the college comes mostly from Elizabeth Daniels's online Vassar Encyclopedia about Vassar history and from Cora Keck's copy of Lossing, *Vassar College and Its Founder*.

4. Vassar College Archives Bulk Files, 1860–1914 (VCASC).

5. E-mail from L. J. Dean, a volunteer researcher at the National Railway Historical Society in Philadelphia.

6. Rock Island *Union Weekly*, December 17, 1887.

7. COLLEGE PIE WITH TOMATOES

1. Vassar College Admissions Records Microfilm Series 1 and 2 (VCASC).

2. Fiedler, *Molto Agitato*, p. 7.

3. McCarthy, *The Group*, p. 263.

4. Johnson, ed., *Southern Women at Vassar*, p. 61.

5. Horowitz, *Alma Mater*, p. 39.

6. Quotation from the Vassar Students' Manual glued into Cora's scrapbook.

7. Bruno and Daniels, *Vassar College*, p. 48.

8. Scofield, Diary.

9. Horowitz, *Alma Mater*, p. 289.

8. ABANDONED AT CHRISTMAS

1. Vassar College Admissions Records Microfilm Series 1 and 2 (VCASC).

2. U.S. census for 1870 and California Gold Rush Checks, 1874–1876, datelined La Porte, Cal., drawn on Bank of La Porte, signed by Amandes Kleckner, president, offered for sale online.

9. FIRST TIME OUT FROM COLLEGE

1. Binnewies, *Palisades*, chaps. 1 and 2.

2. Jennings, *Manhattanville*, and Washington, *Images of America*, p. 47.

3. Baptista, "D.F. Tiemann."

4. St. Mary's Episcopal Church Archives.

5. Salwen, *Upper West Side Story*, p. 66.

6. New York State, *Documents of the Senate of the State of New York*, 96th session, 1873, Vol. 2, nos. 25 to 37 inclusive.

7. Jennings, *Manhattanville*.

10. VASSAR GIRL ON A STRING

1. My story relies on (and quotations come from) the *New York Times*, January 8, 13, and 18, 1885; April 18, 1885; and July 29, 1890.

2. The description of this concert and the quotations are from Johnson, ed., *Southern Women at Vassar,* pp. 61–62.

3. Scofield, Diary.

11. OH! U WRETCH!

1. Auchincloss, *The Vanderbilt Era,* p. 8.

2. Quoted in Chesterton, *Annotated Innocence of Father Brown,* p. 36.

3. Vassar College Archives Bulk Files, 1860–1914, folders 3.83 and 3.84 (VCASC).

12. ONLY 17,000 MINUTES TILL OUR NEXT VACATION

1. Quoted in Horowitz, *Alma Mater,* p. 115.

13. THE GIRL OF THE PERIOD

1. Jessie Chapin Faculty Bio Folder (VCASC).

2. Champaign County Circuit Court records for April 1885.

14. THE NO. 2000 HORSE

1. Harness Racing Museum Research Library, Goshen, NY, and Wallace's *American Trotting Register,* Vols. 4 and 5.

15. ALAS—SO VILELY PLAYED AND SO CARELESSLY PRACTICED

1. VCASC and Horowitz, *Alma Mater,* p. 91.

2. Vassar College Archives Bulk Files, 1860–1914, folders 3.83 and 3.84 (VCASC).

3. Harris, ed., *Authentic Victorian Dressmaking Techniques* (a reprint of Butterick's *Dressmaking Up to Date* from 1905), p. 44.

4. Vassar Encyclopedia, "Ellen Swallow Richards," http://vcencyclopedia .vassar.edu/alumni/ellen-swallow-richards.html, and "Vassar Traditions" (quotation), http://vcencyclopedia.vassar.edu/traditions/.

5. Horowitz, *Alma Mater,* p. 53.

16. A GREAT SHOCK

1. Vassar College, nineteenth and twentieth *Annual Catalogue* (VCASC).

2. Vassar College Archives Bulk Files, 1860–1914, folders 5.25 and 5.27 (VCASC).

3. Newspaper article and other information in Vassar College Archives Bulk Files, 1860–1914, folders 1.58 and 1.59 (VCASC).

4. The story of Twain's visit to Vassar with his daughter and quotations are found in "Susy Reviews Her Father's Performance," at http://etext.virginia

.edu/railton/onstage/susyrev.html, and Samuel Clemens, *Autobiography of Mark Twain,* Vol. 2, ed. Benjamin Griffin and Harriet Elinor Smith (Berkeley: University of California Press, 2013), pp. 16 and 465.

17. THE ANIMATED STUMP

1. *Bulletin of Vassar College* (VCASC).
2. Told by Esther's niece at the Davenport High School Museum, July 2009.
3. Vassar College Archives Bulk Files, 1860–1914, folder 1.58 (VCASC).
4. Johnson, ed., *Southern Women at Vassar*, pp. 75, 117.

18. DEAR DAVENPORT DEAR HOME

1. Vassar College Archives Bulk Files, 1860–1914, folder 1.58 (VCASC).
2. Information about this day and the controversy comes from a June 10, 1885, newspaper clipping in Cora's second scrapbook headlined "The Troubles at Vassar."
3. Gilbert and Bryson, *Chicago and Its Makers,* p. 137.
4. Illinois State Board of Health, *First Annual Report for 1878.*
5. Decatur, Illinois, *Review and Republican,* September 6, 12, 13, and 15, 1883.

19. THE BLACK LIST

1. Kenneth Nettleton, unpublished memoir, 1955.
2. Morrissey, *It Was Salubrious,* p. 117.
3. Ibid., p. 11.
4. Cora Keck diary for September 10, 1893.
5. Armstrong, *Little Giant Cyclopedia,* p. 326.

20. MY YEAR'S ABSENCE FROM D

1. Morrissey, *It Was Salubrious,* p. 55, and *History of Scott Co., Iowa.*
2. *Davenport Gazette,* June 12, 1885.

21. MY INTERESTING STRANGER FRIEND

1. Vassar College Admissions Records Microfilm Series 1 and 2 (VCASC).
2. Vassar College Archives Photograph Files, ca. 1865–2008 (VCASC).
3. Vassar College Archives Bulk Files, 1860–1914, folders 3.83 and 3.84 (VCASC).
4. Horowitz, *Alma Mater,* p. 67.
5. Longfellow, *Kavanagh,* p. 39.

22. THE SENTIMENTAL SATELLITES

1. Johnson, ed., *Southern Women at Vassar*, p. 76.
2. Newspaper clipping in Cora's scrapbook dated January 31, 1886.
3. Ibid.
4. Matthews and Hutton, eds., *Actors and Actresses*, p. 290.

23. THE VASSAR TRIO

1.Johnson, ed., *Southern Women at Vassar*, pp. 104–105.
2. Ibid., p. 107.

24. U PLAYED JUST LIKE A WILD GIRL

1. Suzy Platt, ed., *Respectfully Quoted: A Dictionary of Quotations Requested from the Congressional Research Service* (Washington, DC: Library of Congress, 1989; New York: Bartleby.com, 2003), no. 899. http://www.bartleby.com/73/8 99.html.

25. POOR BOYS WHO HAVE BECOME RICH

1. Description taken from teaching advice given by the nineteenth-century Venezuelan concert virtuoso Teresa Carreño, quoted in Ammer, *Unsung*, p. 68.
2. Yale University Yearbooks, 1880 to 1885; information about Cyrus and his family comes from "Descendants of Cyrus West Field," by Diane Druin Gravlee, available at History of the Atlantic Cable & Undersea Communications, http://atlantic-cable.com/Field/FieldDescendants.htm.
3. Yale University Yearbooks, 1880 to 1885.
4. Johnson, ed. *Southern Women at Vassar*, p. 91.
5. Scott County Circuit Court records.
6. Ammer, *Unsung*, p. 78.
7. Rosen, *Piano Notes*, p. 92.
8. Ammer, *Unsung*, pp. 63–69.

26. THE GEM OF THE EVENING

1. McClure, *My Autobiography*, p. 126.
2. Vassar Encyclopedia, http://vcencyclopedia.vassar.edu/.

27. LIFE UNDERGROUND AND ITS DANGERS

1. *Splinters*, April 15, 1887.
2. Ammer, *Unsung*, p. 251.

3. "The Dramas of Haymarket: Act III, Toils of the Law," Chicago Museum, http://www.chicagohistory.org/dramas/act3/act3.htm.

4. Chicago *Daily Tribune*, January 15, 1887.

5. Van Zandt, *August Spies' Autobiography*, preface.

6. Chicago *Daily Tribune*, January 20, 1887, p. 2.

7. Averich, *Haymarket Tragedy*, p. 325.

8. Chicago *Daily Tribune*, January 20, 1887, p. 2.

9. Johnson, ed., *Southern Women at Vassar*, pp. 162–163.

10. Philip Gura and James F. Bollman, *America's Instrument: The Banjo in the Nineteenth Century* (Chapel Hill: University of North Carolina Press, 1999), frontispiece.

11. Scott County Circuit Court records.

12. Morrissey, *It Was Salubrious*.

13. St. Mary's Episcopal Church Archives.

28. CORA'S HEART'S DESIRE

1. *Travelers' Official Guide*.

29. OH! HOW LITTLE THEY KNOW. ANYBODY!

1. Dary, *Frontier Medicine*, p. 172.

2. Beier, *Matter of Life and Death*, p. 31.

3. Stage, *Female Complaints*, pp. 46, 49.

EPILOGUE

1. Bartholomew, *Stories and Sketches,* p. 147.

2. U.S. federal census 1900 and 1910; *Bulletin of Vassar College*; and records of Forest Lawn Cemetery, Buffalo, New York.

3. St. Mary's Episcopal Church Archives.

4. *Bulletin of Vassar College*.

5. Ibid.; records of Oakdale Cemetery, Davenport, Iowa; Betty Kopp Gorsche, "Unitarian Church, Davenport Iowa, 125 Years, A Place to Grow," unpublished manuscript, 1993.

6. Beier, *Matter of Life and Death*, p. 76.

7. Passport applications at ancestry.com.

8. Quotations from letters in the Vassar College Archives Faculty Bio Files.

BIBLIOGRAPHY

VASSAR COLLEGE ARCHIVES

Admissions Records Microfilm Series 1 and 2.

Bulk Files, 1860–1914.

Bulletin of Vassar College, Alumnae Biographical Register Issue, vol. 29, no. 2, Poughkeepsie, NY: 1939.

Cataloged records, 1861–1984.

Faculty Bio Files.

Nineteenth Annual Catalogue of the Officers and students of Vassar College, 1883–1884.

Photograph Files, ca. 1865–2008.

Twentieth Annual Catalogue of the Officers and students of Vassar College, 1884–1885.

Twenty-first Annual Catalogue of the Officers and students of Vassar College, 1885–1886.

Twenty-second Annual Catalogue of the Officers and students of Vassar College, 1886–1887.

Twenty-third Annual Catalogue of the Officers and students of Vassar College, 1887–1888.

Vassarion, Vassar College Yearbook for 1889.

SCOTT COUNTY, IOWA, ARCHIVES

Scott County District Court Calendar, 1880–1884.

Scott County, Iowa, *USGenWeb Project*: Cathy Joynt Labath, 1997–2007.

ST. MARY'S EPISCOPAL CHURCH, MANHATTANVILLE, NEW YORK

Church Archives. Vols. 2, 2a, and 3, 1829–1912.

COLUMBIA UNIVERSITY ARCHIVES

Columbia College Alumni Directory, 1754–1931.

Columbia College Handbook, 1884, 1885.

Columbia College Matriculation Book, 1882–1890.
Columbia College Yearbooks, *Columbiad*, 1884–1887.

YALE UNIVERSITY ARCHIVES
Yale University Catalogs, 1880–1885.
Yale University Yearbooks, 1880–1885.

NEWSPAPERS AND PERIODICALS

Bloomington Pantagraph
Bloomington Weekly Leader
Chicago Daily Inter Ocean
Chicago Daily Tribune
Davenport City Business Directories,
   1865–1890
Davenport Daily Gazette
Davenport Democrat
Decatur Review
Dubuque Herald
Fairfield Daily Ledger
Industries of Peoria
Lincoln (Illinois) *Herald*

New York Times
Peoria City Directories, 1880–1885
Peoria Journal
Peoria National Democrat
Peoria Transcript
Philadelphia Inquirer
Rock Island Argus
Rockford (Illinois) *Daily Gazette*
Quincy Journal
Quincy Whig
Washington (Iowa) *Farmer*
Woodford (Illinois) *Sentinel*

BOOKS, ARTICLES, AND WEBSITES

Ammer, Christine. *Unsung: A History of Women in American Music*. Portland,
   OR: Amadeus, 2001.
Andreas, A. T. *Illustrated Historical Atlas of the State of Iowa*. 1875. Rpt. Des
   Moines: State Historical Society of Iowa, 1975.
Appleton's Dictionary of New York and Its Vicinity: The Centennial 1889 Inaugu-
   ration Edition. New York: D. Appleton, 1889.
Armstrong, K. L. *Little Giant Cyclopedia of Ready Reference: 1,000,001 Figures*
   and Facts. Chicago: Francis J. Schulte, 1893.
Auchincloss, Louis. *The Vanderbilt Era: Profiles of a Gilded Age*. New York: Col-
   lier, 1989.
Avrich, Paul. *The Haymarket Tragedy*. Princeton, NJ: Princeton University
   Press, 1984.
Baptista, Robert J. "D.F. Tiemann & Co. Color Works, Manhattanville, New
   York City," July 7, 2009, at http://www.colorantshistory.org/TiemannCol-
   orWorks.html.
Bartholomew, Henry S. K. *Stories and Sketches of Elkhart County*. N.p.: 1936.

Beier, Lucinda McCray. *A Matter of Life and Death: Health, Illness and Medicine in McLean County, 1830–1995*. Bloomington, IL: McLean County Historical Society, 1996.

Ben-Zvi, Linda. *Susan Glaspell: Her Life and Times*. New York: Oxford University Press, 2005.

Bingham, Caroline. *The History of Royal Holloway College, 1886–1986*. London: Constable, 1987.

Binnewies, Robert O. *Palisades: 100,000 Acres in 100 Years*. Bronx, NY: Fordham University Press, 2000.

Biographical History of Scott County, Iowa. Chicago: American Biographical Publishing Co., 1895.

Brown, Helen Dawes. *Two College Girls*. Cambridge, MA: Houghton Mifflin, Riverside Press, 1886.

Bruno, Maryann, and Elizabeth A. Daniels. *Vassar College*. Charleston, SC: Arcadia, 2001.

Bush, Julia. *Women against the Vote: Female Anti-Suffragism in Britain*. Oxford: Oxford University Press, 2007.

Carvey-Stewart, Elizabeth. "Watch Tower Park," in *Rock Island: Yesterday, Today and Tomorrow*. Ed. B. J. Elsner. Rock Island, IL: Rock Island History Book Committee, 1988.

Champney, Lizzie W. *Three Vassar Girls Abroad: Rambles of Three College Girls on a Vacation Trip*. Boston: Estes and Lauriat, 1883.

Chesterton, G. K. *The Annotated Innocence of Father Brown*. Ed. Martin Gardner, Mineola, NY: Dover, 1998.

Clarke, James Frederic. "A History of Medicine in Jefferson County Iowa." *Journal of the Iowa State Medical Society*. December 1934 to December 1935 (published serially).

Clemens, Susy. Handwritten biography of her father [Mark Twain], 1885, unpublished. http://etext.virginia.edu/railton/onstage/susyrev.html.

Dary, David. *Frontier Medicine: From the Atlantic to the Pacific, 1492–1941*. New York: Vintage, 2008.

Dostoyevsky, Fyodor. *Notes from Underground*. New American Library. Trans. Andrew R. Macandrew. New York: Signet Classics, 1961.

Downer, Harry E. *History of Davenport and Scott County, Iowa*. Vol. I. Chicago: S. J. Clarke, 1910.

Fiedler, Johanna. *Molto Agitato: The Mayhem behind the Music at the Metropolitan Opera*. New York: Doubleday, 2001.

Gilbert, Paul, and Charles Lee Bryson. *Chicago and Its Makers: A Narrative of Events*. Chicago: Felix Mendelsohn, 1929.

Harris, Kristina, ed. *Authentic Victorian Dressmaking Techniques*. Mineola, NY: Dover, 1999.

Hawtrey, Charles. *The Private Secretary: A Farcical Comedy in Three Acts*. New York: Samuel French, 1907.

Hill, Thomas E. *Hill's Manual of Social and Business Forms: A Guide to Correct Writing*. Chicago: Hill Standard Book Company, 1883.

Hineman Loberg, Victoria. "Peoria's Pioneer Female Physicians Part II." *Peoria Medicine* 2.1 (March 1999): 38–39.

History of Scott County, Iowa. Chicago: Inter-State, 1882.

Horowitz, Helen Lefkowitz. *Alma Mater: Design and Experience in the Women's Colleges from Their Nineteenth-Century Beginnings to the 1930s*. Amherst: University of Massachusetts Press, 1993.

Huebinger, Adam. *Das erste album der stadt Davenport, Iowa*. Davenport, IA: Huebinger's Photographic Art Gallery, 1887.

Illinois State Board of Health. *First Annual Report of the Illinois State Board of Health*. Springfield, IL: Weber, Magie, 1879.

———. *Sixth Annual Report of the Illinois State Board of Health*. Springfield, IL: H. W. Rokker, 1884.

Iowa State Agricultural Society. *Annual Reports*, 1866–1876.

Iowa State Census, 1854.

Iowa State Gazetteer and Business Directory for 1880–81. Detroit: R. L. Polk., and A. C. Danser, 1881.

Iowa Writers' Program of the Work Projects Administration in the State of Iowa. *Scott County History*. Davenport, IA: 1942.

Jennings, E. Allen. *Manhattanville, an Architectural Retrospect*. N.p.: 1940. Unpublished collection of photographs and accounts of Manhattanville.

Johnson, Joan Marie, ed. *Southern Women at Vassar: The Poppenheim Family Letters, 1882–1916*. Columbia: University of South Carolina Press, 2002.

Knox, Thomas W. *Underground; or, Life below the Surface*. Hartford, CT: J. B. Burr and Hyde, 1873.

Library of the World's Best Literature: Ancient and Modern. Vol. XXX, Synopses of Noted Books. New York: R. S. Peale, 1896.

Linton, Eliza Lynn. *The Rebel of the Family*. Ed. Deborah Townsend Meem. 1880. Rpt. Orchard Park, NY: Broadview Press, 2002.

Longfellow, Henry Wadsworth. *Kavanagh: A Tale*. 9th ed. Boston: Ticknor and Fields, 1859.

Lossing, Benson J. *Vassar College and Its Founder*. New York: C. A. Alvord, Printer, 1867.

Lothrop, Charles H. *The Medical and Surgical Directory of the State of Iowa for 1880 and 1881.* Clinton, IA: Allen Steam Printing and Binding, 1880.

Matthews, Brander, and Laurence Hutton, eds. *Actors and Actresses of Great Britain and the United States.* Boston: L. C. Page, 1900.

McCarthy, Mary. *The Group.* New York: Harcourt, 1963.

McClure, S. S. *My Autobiography.* New York: Frederick A. Stokes Co. and the McClure Publications, 1914.

MacKay, Anne, ed. *Wolf Girls at Vassar: Lesbian and Gay Experiences, 1930–1990.* New York: St. Martin's, 1992.

Morrissey, George E. *It Was Salubrious: A Chronicle of Midwest Medical Practice, Progress and Opinion 1856–1892.* Davenport, IA: Scott County Medical Society, [1966?].

New York State. *Documents of the Senate of the State of New York, 96th Session, 1873.* Vol. 2, nos. 25–37 inclusive.

Noun, Louise. *Strong-Minded Women: The Emergence of the Woman-Suffrage Movement in Iowa.* Ames: Iowa State University Press, 1986.

Picturesque Tri-Cities: An Art Work, Containing Illustrations of Scenery and Portraits of the Prominent and Representative People of Moline, Illinois, Rock Island, Illinois, Davenport, Iowa, the Rock Island Arsenal and Vicinity. Davenport, IA: C. J. Martin, 1901.

Riley, Glenda. *Divorce: An American Tradition.* Lincoln: University of Nebraska Press, 1991.

Riordan, William L. *Plunkitt of Tammany Hall: A Series of Very Plain Talks on Very Practical Politics.* New York: E. P. Dutton, 1963.

Rosen, Charles. *Piano Notes: The World of the Pianist.* New York: Free Press, 2002.

———. "The Super Power of Franz Liszt," a review of *Liszt as Transcriber* by Jonathan Kregor. *New York Review of Books* (February 23, 2012).

Rowell, George Presbury. *Forty Years an Advertising Agent, 1865–1905.* New York: Printers' Ink, 1906.

Rudofsky, Bernard. *Are Clothes Modern? An Essay on Contemporary Apparel.* Chicago: Paul Theobold, 1947.

Salwen, Peter. *Upper West Side Story: A History and Guide.* New York: Abbeville, 1989.

Scofield, Cora Louise. Diary, 1881–1884. Unpublished manuscript. University of Iowa Libraries, Iowa Women's Archives, http://digital.lib.uiowa.edu/cdm/compoundobject/collection/iwai/id/30/rec/1.

Slobody, Evelyn, Lawrence Slobody, and Philip A. Pines. *Currier and Ives:*

Trotting, the National Pastime of Early America, a Pageant of Horse Prints from 1840–1895. Peekskill, NY: Benson, 1984.

Smith, Doug. *Davenport.* Postcard History Series. Charleston, SC: Arcadia, 2007.

Stage, Sarah. *Female Complaints: Lydia Pinkham and the Business of Women's Medicine.* New York: W. W. Norton, 1979.

Swidersky, Richard. *Calomel in America.* Boca Raton, FL: Brown Walker, 2008.

Travelers' Official Guide of the Railway and Steam Navigation Lines in the United States and Canada. New York: National Railway Publication, 1886.

United States Census Records for 1850, 1860, 1870, 1880, 1900, 1910, and 1920.

Van Zandt, Nina. *August Spies' Autobiography: His Speech in Court and General Notes.* Chicago: Self-published, January 27, 1887.

Vassar Encyclopedia. http://vcencyclopedia.vassar.edu/.

Vedder, Henry Clay. *American Writers of To-day.* Boston: Silver, Burdett, 1894.

Wallace's American Trotting Register, Vols. 4 and 5. New York: National Association of Trotting Horse Breeders, 1882 and 1885.

Washington, Eric K. *Images of America: Manhattanville, Old Heart of West Harlem.* Charleston, SC: Arcadia, 2002.

Webster, William G. *A High School Pronouncing Dictionary of the English Language—Abridged from the American Dictionary of Noah Webster.* New York: Mason Brothers, 1859.

Wilhelmi (Zechmeister), Alexander. *Einer muss heiraten.* Ed. William Addison Hervey. New York: Henry Holt, 1905.

Wilson, Jennie Lansley. *Legal Status of Women in Iowa.* Des Moines: Iowa Printing Co., 1894.

Wood, Sharon. *The Freedom of the Streets: Work, Citizenship and Sexuality in a Gilded Age City.* Chapel Hill: University of North Carolina Press, 2005.

Young, James Harvey. *The Toadstool Millionaires: A Social History of Patent Medicines in America before Federal Regulation.* Princeton, NJ: Princeton University Press, 1961.

Name Index

Because they appear on nearly every page, the Keck family names have been left out of this index.